# *Praise for* Teaching As Leadership

"I have spent twenty-seven years working in schools of poverty and am constantly searching for ways to improve my practice and meet the needs of underprivileged students. This book inspires those of us in the trenches with the possibility of making the difference we so desire."
—**Betsy Rogers**, 2003 National Teacher of the Year

"Teach For America has captured the hearts and imaginations of the best and brightest of our current generation of young people. *Teaching As Leadership* communicates the critical issues and solutions on how to become a highly effective teacher in urban and rural school settings. All new teachers should read this book. It offers a clear and inspiring road map for success in the teaching profession."
—**Shane P. Martin**, dean and professor, Loyola Marymount University School of Education

"One of the novel contributions of the *Teaching As Leadership* framework is the central understanding of race, socioeconomic status, and diversity as realities—and assets—in effective leadership. This book is a valuable resource for interns, teachers, administrators, and educators invested in ensuring that all children have access to a high-quality education irrespective of their social identity."
—**Richard J. Reddick**, Department of Education at University of Texas and faculty affiliate in the John L. Warfield Center for African and African American Studies, and co-editor of *Legacies of Brown: Multiracial equity in American education* (Teach For America corps member in Houston, 1995)

"Ever wonder what makes a teacher extraordinary? Teach For America's Steven Farr can tell you. Built from the work of some of Teach For America's most successful teachers, this book reveals the common "secrets" of their success. Pick it up and enjoy these remarkable teachers' stories—their hard work, setbacks and most importantly, their triumphs."
—**Joan Baratz Snowden**, former director, Educational Issues Department at the American Federation of Teachers, and vice president for Assessment at the National Board for Professional Teaching Standards

"Not only do I constantly use *Teaching As Leadership* as a guide in developing the curriculum and course work for our Master's classes, but I'm continually impressed by its ability to give language to the tough-to articulate actions teachers *must* take to drive student achievement. *Teaching As Leadership* simultaneously provides a powerful over-arching framework for closing the achievement gap *and* a set of explicit day-to-day actions that teachers must aspire to perfect."
—**Brent Maddin**, director of Teaching & Learning, Teacher U at Hunter College, M.Ed. and Doctoral Candidate at Harvard Graduate School of Education (Teach For America corps member in South Louisiana, 1999)

"Too many children in America attend schools where they are denied the opportunity to learn. *Teaching As Leadership* describes what Teach For America is learning from highly effective teachers about changing that disturbing reality. While more is needed to ensure that all children receive a quality education, these insights are critical to improve learning and begin to close the achievement gap."
—**Pedro Noguera**, professor at Steinhardt School of Culture, Education, and Human Development at NYU, and author of *The Trouble With Black Boys: And Other Reflections on Race, Equity, and the Future of Public Education*.

"We have long known *who* Teach For America teachers are. This important book tells us *what they do* to get the classroom results they get. Lots of lessons for teachers and trainers of teachers!"
—**Jane Hannaway**, director, Education Policy Center & CALDER, The Urban Institute

"Teach For America recruits have been raising the bar in our classrooms, and classrooms across the nation. This book offers a distillation of the strategies these remarkable teachers use to beat the odds and raise student achievement. Great teaching is the *only* path to increased achievement—and *Teaching As Leadership* shares the classroom approaches that have helped some of our most challenged students learn more, and learn faster."

—**Peter C. Gorman**, superintendent, Charlotte-Mecklenburg Schools, NC

*"Teaching As Leadership* makes a powerful case for the capability of students in under-resourced schools and provides concrete guidance for teachers committed to helping students achieve dramatic academic gains."

—**Deborah Loewenberg Ball**, dean, University of Michigan School of Education

"For twenty years, Teach For America has been working to understand what makes a teacher great. *Teaching As Leadership* captures what they have learned and is a true gift for anyone whose goal is to ensure that all kids have the educational opportunities they deserve."

—**Dave Levin**, co-founder of KIPP: Knowledge Is Power Program (Teach For America corps member in Houston, 1992)

"This framework reminds us how valuable and important teachers are."

—**Matilda Orozco**, principal, Houston ISD, TX

"Not only did the *Teaching As Leadership* framework provide me with the strategic actions that were essential to my success as a teacher, it has also served as a foundation for the training and support I offer novice and veteran teachers as a school leader."

—**Kristin Reidy**, Arizona Teacher of the Year, 2007 (Teach For America corps member in South Louisiana, 1999)

"Our students have benefited from working with some of the teachers who helped generate the insights and best practices in *Teaching As Leadership*. These teachers demonstrate not only sincere care for our students, but also a fanatical pursuit of student learning, every day, every class. These teachers are prepared, passionate, and constantly seek student improvement."

—**Jesus O. Guerra, Jr.**, superintendent, Roma ISD, TX

"In a knowledge economy, nothing is as important as education. Teach For America continues to drive its urgent agenda for change with this erudite, thoughtful, and important book. Every teacher educator in the country, as well as policy makers and business leaders, ought to read this book."

—**Douglas Lynch**, vice dean, Graduate School of Education, University of Pennsylvania, and author of "The role of educational tools in reform" in *The Demand Side of Education Reform*

"The amazing teachers who contributed to this book are showing us that we can close achievement gaps. To go from isolated examples of excellence to raising performance across the board, we need to replicate these teachers' 'whatever it takes' approach in the policies and systems we put in place. This book addresses the most pressing issue facing our country and contains important lessons for policymakers as well as practitioners."

—**Ross Wiener**, executive director, Education and Society Program, The Aspen Institute

*"Teaching As Leadership* is a research-based model that I see replicated in classrooms where students are most successful year after year. It captures the commitment to success, to the school, and to the community that I look for when I hire teachers."

—**Ed Koch**, Community Education Partners and veteran teacher and principal in Philadelphia public schools

"This book is like having more than one-hundred-and-fifty mentors helping you immediately close the achievement gap in your classroom. It is a tremendous resource."

—**Preston Smith**, chief achievement officer for Rocketship Education (Teach For America corps member in the Bay Area, 2001)

# TEACHING
## AS LEADERSHIP

# TEACHING
## AS LEADERSHIP

The Highly Effective Teacher's
Guide to Closing the Achievement Gap

**Steven Farr**
**Teach For America**

FOREWORD BY JASON KAMRAS, NATIONAL TEACHER OF THE YEAR, 2005
AFTERWORD BY WENDY KOPP, CEO AND FOUNDER OF TEACH FOR AMERICA

JOSSEY-BASS
A Wiley Imprint
www.josseybass.com

Published by Jossey-Bass
A Wiley Imprint
989 Market Street, San Francisco, CA 94103-1741—www.josseybass.com

Readers should be aware that Internet Web sites offered as citations and/or sources for further information may have changed or disappeared between the time this was written and when it is read.

Limit of Liability/Disclaimer of Warranty: While the publisher and author have used their best efforts in preparing this book, they make no representations or warranties with respect to the accuracy or completeness of the contents of this book and specifically disclaim any implied warranties of merchantability or fitness for a particular purpose. No warranty may be created or extended by sales representatives or written sales materials. The advice and strategies contained herein may not be suitable for your situation. You should consult with a professional where appropriate. Neither the publisher nor author shall be liable for any loss of profit or any other commercial damages, including but not limited to special, incidental, consequential, or other damages.

Jossey-Bass books and products are available through most bookstores. To contact Jossey-Bass directly call our Customer Care Department within the U.S. at 800-956-7739, outside the U.S. at 317-572-3986, or fax 317-572-4002.

Jossey-Bass also publishes its books in a variety of electronic formats. Some content that appears in print may not be available in electronic books.

Library of Congress Cataloging-in-Publication Data

Farr, Steven.
  Teaching as leadership : how highly effective teachers close the achievement gap / Steven Farr ; foreword by Jason Kamras; Afterword by Wendy Kopp. — 1st ed.
      p. cm.
  Includes bibliographical references and index.
  ISBN 978-0-470-43286-0 (pbk.)
  1. Effective teaching. 2. Academic achievement. 3. School improvement programs. 4. Educational leadership. I. Title.
  LB1025.3.F37 2010
  371.102—dc22

                                          2009041095

Printed in the United States of America
FIRST EDITION
*PB Printing*   10  9  8  7  6  5

# CONTENTS

# FOREWORD

**ON THE FIRST DAY OF SCHOOL IN 1950,** an eleven-year-old named Spottswood Bolling walked up to the doors of the brand-new John Philip Sousa Junior High School in southeast Washington, D.C. and made a simple request: he wanted to enter.

He was turned away because he was African American.

Mr. Bolling, along with ten of his peers, challenged school segregation in the District of Columbia by arguing that the policy was inherently unconstitutional. Ultimately the U.S. Supreme Court unanimously agreed with Mr. Bolling and overturned segregation in the nation's capital in *Bolling* v. *Sharpe*, a companion case to *Brown* v. *Board of Education*. Representing the Court in the 1954 decision, Chief Justice Earl Warren wrote that segregation was tantamount to a "deprivation of [the students'] liberty."

Forty-two years after *Bolling* v. *Sharpe*, I began my teaching career at Sousa (then Middle) School as a member of Teach For America. In the more than four decades that had passed since the landmark decision, many things had changed at Sousa. The school facility had gone from state-of-the-art to dilapidated. The neighborhood had gone from upper middle class to low income. And the student body had gone from all white to all African American.

One thing that hadn't changed, however, was that Sousa Middle School was, to a large extent, still depriving children of their liberty—not by exclusion, but by failing to provide many of the students in its classrooms with the education they deserved. A number of dedicated individuals were doing extraordinary work on behalf of the children there, but as a whole, the school was not adequately serving the majority of its students.

Over the past couple of years, Sousa has made significant strides in student achievement. So too has the District of Columbia Public Schools (DCPS) as a system. But we, like many other school districts serving low-income children across the nation, are still failing too many children. In doing so, we are politically, economically, and socially disenfranchising millions of young people. In Chief Justice Warren's words, we are depriving children of their liberty.

This inequity, which has given rise to the indefensible achievement gap, is the greatest injustice facing our nation today. It is at the very core of why I chose to become a teacher and why I joined Teach For America over thirteen years ago.

The reality of the achievement gap is staggering. According to the 2007 National Assessment of Educational Progress, the percentage of high-income fourth graders in America who are proficient in reading is more than three times greater than that of low-income fourth graders. And the data show us that only one in ten of those low-income fourth graders will graduate from college.

As I traveled the nation in 2005 as National Teacher of the Year, I met countless educators who are fighting to close the achievement gap every day in their classrooms. From Olive Branch, Mississippi, to Los Angeles, California, they're ensuring that every child who walks through their doors, regardless of background, excels.

But I also came to learn that some individuals in this country still believe that the achievement gap exists because children of certain backgrounds—namely, low-income or minority children—are inherently less capable than others. Nothing could be more false. My students were every bit as bright and every bit as capable as any other children I have ever met. They inspired me daily with their intelligence, creativity, resilience, and humanity.

Every day that we allow the injustice of the achievement gap to continue, we turn our backs on those who deserve our attention the most. In doing so, we weaken our democracy and jeopardize the very future of our great nation.

After all, the achievement gap is not just an education issue; it is also a civil rights issue. We have an obligation to make a simple but powerful commitment to our children. We must promise them that the opportunity to pursue their dreams will be constrained only by the limits of their imagination and their diligence—never by their skin color, family income, language status, country of origin, religion, gender, sexual orientation, or any other label.

And I believe deeply that as a nation, we can fulfill this obligation. I believe this because I have seen the achievement gap succumb to the greatness of my own students. Nearly all of them lived below the poverty line. But they did achieve. They made dramatic gains and, in doing so, fundamentally redefined others' perceptions and expectations of them. Bringing equality of opportunity to all children in this nation is not an insurmountable goal. We can do it.

As a teacher who has had some success in a high-poverty school, I am often asked what we as a nation can do to close the achievement gap once and for all. Over the past few years, I've wrestled with this question. I've considered my own classroom experience, the latest education research, and the many insightful conversations I've had with Americans from all corners of this country.

I have come to believe that it all comes down to people. Effective teachers—those who not only have the highest of expectations for their students, but also know how to help them reach those expectations—are the most important piece of the puzzle.

Of course, there are countless factors that influence student learning and achievement that are beyond the control of the teacher: joblessness, the lack of affordable health care and affordable housing, and the nefarious legacy of institutionalized discrimination. We must address these issues if we are to mount a holistic assault on the achievement gap. We cannot accept the fact that 9 million American children live without health care and that 1 million experience homelessness every year. And we cannot deny that these statistics have consequences for learning and achievement.

But excellent teachers can make a dramatic difference in children's lives. In fact, I believe that teachers are the locus of power in the fight to close the achievement gap.

As I've traveled the nation, I've found that what separates high-performing, high-poverty classrooms and schools from their low-performing counterparts is rarely the per pupil expenditure, the textbooks or curricula used, or even the state of the school facility. Rather, it's the effectiveness of the educators. This book captures what these high-performing teachers are doing in their classrooms. It makes concrete the ineffable and demystifies the magical. It helps us change the debate from *if* the achievement gap can be closed to *how* the achievement gap can be closed. As such, this book is indispensable reading for every educator in America.

*Teaching As Leadership* reveals that teachers who are successful at closing the achievement gap do exactly what all great leaders do when they face seemingly insurmountable odds: they set big goals, invest their organization (students) in working hard to achieve those goals, plan purposefully, execute effectively, continuously increase their effectiveness, and work relentlessly toward their objective of closing the achievement gap for their students. Teach For America developed these six pillars after spending thousands of hours observing and talking with their most effective teachers: first- and second-year educators who were moving their students two, three, and sometimes four grade levels in a single year. These teachers are some of America's greatest leaders.

One of the many things I find so inspiring about their work is that it's teachable: we can all learn to become even more effective by following their example. But I'm also inspired by their humility. Having had the great honor of meeting a number of the educators profiled in this book, I know they would all say that there is still much to learn about effective teaching in low-income communities. I humbly welcome you to this conversation.

As you make your way through this book, do not forget Spottswood Bolling. Over half a century ago, he fought to make our nation more just. Now it is up to us to complete his work. I've been thinking a lot about both the history and the future of our country, as I've recently become a father for the first time. We cannot rest until each of us would be satisfied with randomly assigning our own children to any public school in the nation. Only then will Mr. Bolling's efforts be complete. *Teaching As Leadership* will help bring us one dramatic step closer to that reality.

JASON KAMRAS
National Teacher of the Year, 2005

# INTRODUCTION

**IMAGINE YOU ARE JOINING US** as we visit a school where a number of Teach For America teachers work. While we walk up the steps of the red-brick elementary school next to public housing in Baltimore City, we note that almost all of its students are living in poverty and only about half of its fifth graders are performing at the state's minimal level of proficiency in reading and math.[1] Stepping into the poorly lit hallway, we think about the fact that across the nation, fourth graders growing up in low-income communities are already two to three grade levels behind their peers in high-income communities.[2]

Or perhaps, instead, we are visiting a middle school on the Texas-Mexico border that serves a large population of first-generation-American migrant children—children who, during the part of the year they are not working with their families in the fields, live in unincorporated *colonias* made up of half-built homes that sometimes lack water and electricity. Most of the students inside this school qualify for free and reduced-price lunch programs, and statistics suggest that only about half of those children will graduate from high school[3]—a number that reflects national trends for children of color living in low-income communities.[4] As we enter the school, we recall that in some wealthy (and usually almost exclusively white) communities, graduation rates are between 98 and 99 percent.[5]

Or maybe today we are navigating a maze of chain-link fence on the campus of a massive high school in the Watts district of South Los Angeles, a school where students worry about the threats of gang violence every day. As we walk past security guards and metal detectors, we consider that this high school's freshman class includes around a thousand students, and yet the graduating seniors number 240—only 30 of whom have the prerequisites on paper to even apply to college.[6] As we walk into the building, we think about the harsh reality that on average, the African American and Latino students who do graduate from high school in America will read, write, and do math at about an eighth-grade level.[7]

At Teach For America, we have trained and supported almost twenty-five thousand teachers in communities and schools where the achievement gap is most pronounced. Our teachers have worked with nearly 3 million children living at or near the poverty line, the vast majority of whom are African American or Latino students who are performing well below their peers in higher-income neighborhoods. From this vantage point, we have the opportunity to learn about the distinguishing methods of teachers whose students are demonstrating dramatic academic achievement.

# Defining Teacher Effectiveness in Terms of Student Learning

Imagine that you are joining us on this day to observe two particular first-year teachers. Both have come into the classroom with an impressive record of accomplishments in college. They seem to have similarly strong critical thinking, communication, and organizational skills. They teach the same grade and subject matter, right across the hall from each other. The first teacher, according to records from previous observations and data, is a solid new teacher. Struggling a little bit with classroom management, this teacher has a good rapport with the students, and the classroom has a generally productive atmosphere. According to the district's midyear assessments, halfway through the school year, the students in this classroom are on pace to gain about a year's worth of academic skills—a feat that many people view as admirable in light of all the challenges facing students and teachers in high-poverty schools.

Across the hall, however, something extraordinary is happening. According to the same previous observers and data, every student in this teacher's classroom is on pace to gain almost three years of academic growth. This teacher is exceeding expectations for what any teacher—much less a new teacher—should be able to accomplish with her students. No one would suggest these dramatic results are "pretty good given all the challenges." Student learning in this classroom is, on an absolute scale, phenomenal.

At Teach For America, we define and measure our teachers' success in terms of how much their students learn. Our mission is to end educational inequity, to end the travesty that in our country where a child is born determines his or her educational outcomes and life prospects. We have seen that significant academic achievement is uniquely powerful in expanding life opportunities for our students. We therefore seek success on the same terms—measurable academic achievement—that define the disparities between children in low-income communities and their counterparts in higher-income communities.

By gathering and evaluating data on student achievement from thousands of teachers' classrooms, we are able to view our teachers on a spectrum of effectiveness, from those who are struggling mightily to make any progress at all with their students, to those who are forging a path to dramatic academic progress. (An overview of our system of defining, measuring, and tracking students' academic achievement is included as Appendix D.)

# What the Most Effective Teachers in Low-Income Communities Are Doing Differently

As we walk down the hall, we think about the different academic trajectories of students in these two classrooms. We know that the students on one side of the hall may be getting on track for honors classes, Advanced Placement courses, additional education opportunities, and perhaps college. The other room of students, even with their solid efforts, will end the year just as far behind as they were when the school year began.

Knowing only that one teacher's students are making decent academic gains and the other teacher's students are making phenomenal academic progress, we stand between the two classrooms wondering what distinguishes these two teachers. What are extraordinarily successful teachers in our nation's most challenging contexts doing differently? What does it take to erase the achievement gap for a classroom full of students?

Twenty years ago when Teach For America was just getting started, we heard of a few celebrated teachers in low-income communities who were ensuring that their students were achieving at the same levels as students in economically privileged communities. Many people assumed that those few teachers were "born to teach"—superstars whose success was a mysterious anomaly. However, as hundreds and then thousands of our teachers struggled for day-to-day progress with their students, at first a few and then more and more of them figured out how to lead their students to dramatic academic success in some of the nation's most challenging contexts.

## Our Ongoing Investigation

We first enter the classroom of the teacher with the good but not extraordinary results. The teacher is working hard, pushing through the lesson, trying to keep students focused on the subject matter. Some students seem a little distracted, but most of the time they are paying attention and following the teacher's instructions. The teacher knows the material, clearly knows how to plan lessons and how to communicate instructions, and is positive and warm in tone and affect. Occasionally students misbehave, and the teacher addresses the problem, with some success. The overwhelming sense in the room is that the teacher is doing the right things and trying hard. We see indicators of student learning, but we also have the sense that the students may simply be going through the motions of being at school. After ten minutes, we leave.

Across the hall, we instantly sense a difference. Even as we cross the door's threshold, without the teacher or other students seeming to notice or care, a student pops up and escorts us to an observer's table at the back of the room, opens a notebook, and in a whisper shows us the learning goals for the day. He then hustles back to his seat, his hand shooting up to contribute to the class discussion. Even before we have figured out what the lesson is about, we feel ourselves leaning forward with the students to hear the teacher's hushed secrets. With some effort, we shift our focus from the teacher's instruction to the room itself. We notice that the giant 2s all over the wall are also on the cover of the notebook in our hand. We see a banner above the chalkboard. The banner explains that the 2s signify the two years' worth of academic growth that students are committed to making in this classroom. We watch the students and notice that every time the teacher asks a question, every child holds up some kind of hand signal. The teacher excitedly nods and asks another question. The teacher praises students' efforts, and we wonder what she is marking so frequently on the clipboard in her hand. Almost imperceptibly, subgroups of students shift from one exercise to another, and the teacher seamlessly moves among those groups. Now every student is working independently. In the span of just four minutes, we see two different pairs of students lean together and help each other. Every action by every person in the room seems completely purposeful. The sense of urgency is thick. We hear the teacher double-checking with students about attending tutoring after school. After what we think is ten minutes, we realize fifty minutes have actually passed.

For two decades, Teach For America has been learning about what distinguishes highly effective teachers in low-income communities. We frequently observe teachers in person and on video, for example, to gather qualitative evidence of their actions in and around the classroom. We interview them and facilitate reflection about their processes, purposes, and beliefs. We review teachers' planning materials, assessments, and student work. We survey teachers in our program at least four times a year about what training and support structures are most influential in their teaching practice. (A closer look at how we train and support our teachers is in Appendix C, and an overview of how we learn about our teachers' actions is in Appendix D.)

When we put all this information about what teachers do, know, and believe alongside what we know about how much their students are learning, we see common patterns in the approach of the most effective teachers. We see highly effective teachers embodying the same principles employed by successful leaders in any challenging context—principles we call *Teaching As Leadership.*

## Teaching As Leadership

Through observations, interviews, and surveys, we have literally and figuratively stood in thousands of halls between teachers who are getting merely good results from their students and teachers whose students are making dramatic, life-changing progress. This book describes what we are learning from the teachers whose students overcome inordinate challenges to achieve dramatic academic success.

Distilled to their essence, our findings indicate that six general principles distinguish the actions of highly effective teachers from those who are merely solid or struggling—principles one would find embodied by any successful leader in any challenging context. These are teachers who:

| Set big goals | that are ambitious, measurable, and meaningful for their students |
|---|---|
| Invest students and their families | through a variety of strategies to work hard to reach those ambitious goals |
| Plan purposefully | by focusing on where students are headed, how success will be defined, and what path to students' growth is most efficient |
| Execute effectively | by monitoring progress and adjusting course to ensure that every action contributes to student learning |
| Continuously increase effectiveness | by reflecting critically on their progress, identifying root causes of problems, and implementing solutions |
| Work relentlessly | in light of their conviction that they have the power to work past obstacles for student learning |

These six ideas make up Teaching As Leadership, a framework of principles and teacher actions distinguishing teachers whose students, despite starting behind and facing huge challenges, are demonstrating tremendous academic gains.

## A Starting Premise: Teachers Can Close the Gap

In 1966, the U.S. Office of Education released a landmark government report (commonly known as the Coleman Report)[8] contending that factors other than school (like children's socioeconomic background and home life) account for 90 percent of their achievement in school.[9] According to many, this report fostered a perspective absolving teachers and schools from responsibility for students' success or failure, encouraging a disempowering tendency to look "outside their own sphere of influence for reasons why students are not succeeding."[10] For four decades, this outlook has been a persistent element of our nation's collective consciousness.[11] Some people continue to doubt the impact that schools and teachers can have in the quest for educational equity, and others doubt that goal can ever be reached.

The teachers you will meet in this book reject that view. With hard work, they declare their conviction that their students can make dramatic progress despite the burdens of poverty. Through their students' accomplishments, they prove that achievement gap statistics need not be destiny. Highly effective teachers in low-income communities are showing that teachers and schools can be a major force in the quest for educational equity in America.

Seeing firsthand evidence of this truth is one of the great privileges of our work and the impetus for writing this book. We share these teachers' rejection of the cynical ideology that was unintentionally created by the Coleman Report. Every day we see teachers disproving its conclusion with their students' success. We see the success of the teachers you will meet in this book, teachers like these exemplars:

- **Josh Biber,** whose fifth-grade students in Phoenix started the year with a host of challenges. Some had been chronically truant the previous year, missing over forty days of school. Some had just immigrated and spoke little English; others, because of their families' needs, had been to four schools in two years. They walked into his classroom reading, on average, over two years below grade level; only three were reading on grade level. In fact, some of his students were barely literate despite having received A's and B's the prior year. Mr. Biber realized his students had been ushered through a system of low expectations and even lower achievement. And yet by the end of Mr. Biber's first year of teaching, fifteen of his twenty-seven students were reading on grade level. On average, his class had achieved over two years of growth in literacy skills. In the last weeks of school, his students celebrated surpassing their goal of 80 percent mastery of fifth-grade math objectives. In his second year, nine of Mr. Biber's students started the year reading below the fifth-grade level, but by February, every one of those students had caught up, and all but six had moved ahead to tackle sixth-grade literacy objectives. In addition, in math, Mr. Biber's students were able to celebrate averaging 85 percent mastery of the fifth-grade math objectives on the District Quarterly Math Assessments that year. Over two years, Mr. Biber and his team of colleagues more than tripled the percentage of students passing the math test and more than doubled the percent of students passing the reading exam.

- **Felicia Cuesta,** whose seventh-grade remedial English students in Los Angeles were placed together in her class because they were so far behind. They started the year reading, on average, on a mid-third-grade level. The previous year, this group of students had had no permanent teacher, just a series of substitutes. Her students, on average, had scored below the fifteenth percentile on the state assessments. She was told that because they were so far behind, they would be exempt from the grade-level assessment. And yet Ms. Cuesta insisted that her students be held to seventh-grade standards. After a year of difficult work, she administered the assessments, and fifty-one of her fifty-nine students scored at the mastery or exemplary level for seventh

grade. Two-thirds scored high enough on the district's reading fluency test to leave the remedial program for a mainstream English class.

- **Anjali Kulkarni,** whose second graders in New York City had a range of disabilities and entered her class between two and three years below grade level in literacy skills. An administrator called her class "the most challenging of the seventy-four classes in the school." Undeterred, Ms. Kulkarni decided that by the end of the year, her students would be "taken seriously not only in academic settings but also in social settings." In her first year, her students on average grew 1.6 years in reading skills according to the Fountas and Pinnell system of leveled readers and assessments. In math, according to school assessments, they demonstrated mastery of all twenty-eight second-grade math standards. They progressed in social situations as well. Ms. Kulkarni described to us with pride the moment in March when David, as line leader, turned to the rest of the class and announced, "Ladies and gentlemen, we will not be walking into the hallway until we can behave like second graders."

• **Jacob Lessem,** whose high school math and science students on the Zuni Pueblo in New Mexico struggled against the burdens of poverty. Some had significant work responsibilities to help their families make ends meet. Some suffered from health and nutrition problems. Virtually all of his students came to his classes lagging behind academic expectations for their grade. And yet nine months later, Mr. Lessem's "basic math" students had made, on average, two years' worth of academic progress, and many of them were able to skip Basic Math II and get back on track. His physics students completed the first Advanced Placement science course in the school's history. His robotics team, made up of students from all over the school and advised by a NASA scientist, completed a national competition. Although the team's robot did not win the competition, many of Mr. Lessem's students altered their aspirations and chose to attend four-year colleges, some studying engineering.

As we consider the dramatically disparate academic performance of students in low-income versus higher-income neighborhoods, teachers like Mr. Biber, Ms. Cuesta, Ms. Kulkarni, and

## ▶ OUR FOCUS ON THE IMPACT OF NEW TEACHERS

**TEACH FOR AMERICA SUPPORTS** thousands of its alumni who continue to work on school campuses, but the primary focus of our training and support, and of the inquiries that fueled this book, has been first- and second-year teachers.

In focusing on the power of new teachers to lead students to dramatic academic gains, we do not dismiss the value of experience for educators in difficult contexts. Our data show more second-year teachers making dramatic gains with their students than first-year teachers and thus align with research suggesting that teachers improve with time and experience.[12] While recent research is indicating that the learning curve for teachers may be shorter than we once thought,[13] we have yet to meet a teacher who does not say he or she improved in his or her first day, month, year, or decade of teaching.

At the same time, we (and external researchers performing rigorous research on our teachers) have seen that some new teachers like those featured in this book, even in their first and second years in the classroom, are having a profound impact on student learning.

Mr. Lessem deny us the rationalization that the achievement gap "is just the way it is." Even before we ask what these highly effective teachers are doing differently, we see that whatever they are doing is changing the lives of their students, and that students' success is not something predetermined by students' socioeconomic conditions.

The highly effective teachers we work with inspire our conviction that educational inequity is a problem that can be solved. They demonstrate that teachers can be a powerful force for closing the achievement gap.

A growing body of research verifies this promising insight.[14] Over the past decade, study after study has indicated that "the schools that are highly effective produce results that almost entirely overcome the effects of student background."[15] One study found that low-achieving students with least-effective teachers gained about fourteen points per year on state assessments while the same students with the most effective teachers gained more than fifty-three points.[16] Another found that if the yearly differences in learning in the strongest classrooms were to accumulate, "having a top-quartile teacher rather than a bottom-quartile teacher four years in a row would be enough to close the black-white test score gap."[17]

In the words of analysts Kati Haycock and Heather Peske at Education Trust, "Differences of this magnitude—50 percentile points in just three years—are stunning. For an individual child, it means the difference between a 'remedial' label and placement in the accelerated or even gifted track. And the difference between entry into a selective college and a lifetime of low-paying, menial work."[18]

The belief that teachers can make that difference is deeply ingrained in the actions of highly effective teachers from which the Teaching As Leadership framework is derived. The teachers you will meet in this book begin with the conviction that we, as teachers, have enough influence in our students' lives to put them on a different academic trajectory toward greater opportunities and options in life.

## Race, Socioeconomic Status, Diversity and Teaching As Leadership

Issues of race, socioeconomic status, and diversity permeate this exploration of what it takes to close the achievement gap in our classrooms. Over 90 percent of the students our teachers work with are African American or Latino. In some of our classrooms, virtually all of our students are Native American or Native Hawaiian. Almost all of our students live at or near the poverty line and qualify for free or reduced-price lunch.

Not only are we all surrounded and affected by negative messages about our students and their potential to succeed, but we may also experience dynamics related to race and socioeconomic status in our work as teachers in low-income communities. If we share racial identity with our students or have grown up or worked in low-income communities previously, we may be surprised or unsettled by a mix of perceived and real dynamics of difference we experience with our students and their families. For teachers who are white, working to close the achievement gap may be the first time some element of their identity makes them (in some sense) a member of a minority group, and they may experience a new and perhaps uncomfortable awareness of their own race and background as they work in their new community. Meanwhile, our students are developing their own sense of identity as we work to shape their confidence that they can succeed with hard work. All of these complex dynamics combine to suggest that how we think about who we are in relationship to our students matters to how and what they learn from us.

Because race and socioeconomic status, and the dynamics of difference they generate, are so integral to the quest for education equity, these issues are fundamental to the Teaching As Leadership framework. They undergird discussions of maintaining high expectations and investing students and families in working hard to achieve academic success. They arise as we build relationships and collaborate with students, families, and colleagues in our collective pursuit of building a welcoming environment for our students and making well-informed instructional decisions. At the same time, our own awareness of how we experience and respond to issues of race and socioeconomic status can have implications for our continuous improvement and persistence in the face of obstacles and failures. For all of these reasons, issues related to race and socioeconomic status are inextricable from the Teaching As Leadership framework and are discussed in this book.

As members of a society that perpetuates low expectations for the children in our schools, whatever our own race or socioeconomic background, we may bring to our classrooms conscious and subconscious biases and prejudices about our students. Sometimes those perspectives can manifest as sympathetic, yet ultimately harmful, excuses for our students' underperformance. Some teachers attempt to compensate for those hidden biases with figurative "color-blindness" (represented by the well-intentioned comment, "I don't see color; I see children."). In our experience, that approach is at best misguided. The most effective teachers are in fact aware of their students' unique backgrounds and perspectives, and they capitalize on opportunities to acknowledge and celebrate those elements of their students' identity in the natural course of their leadership. Whether working with families in the tobacco hills of North Carolina, or with stressed but determined colleagues in Oakland, or with tribal elders of the Navajo Nation, many of the teachers who are seeing the most dramatic achievements from their students are those who are respectfully engaging and aligning their actions with students' background, community, and culture.[19]

What we are learning about how those teachers work has been informed by a host of important diversity-related concepts, including racial identity theory, cultural learning styles, and notions of multicultural education. We also see, in the classrooms we visit, common approaches among teachers who build relationships and collaborate well across lines of difference like race, ethnicity, socioeconomic status, experience, background, culture, or language. Through dozens of interviews with a diverse group of teachers, staff members, professors, principals, and researchers, and through hundreds of surveys with first- and second-year teachers, we have identified clusters of skills that seem to be critical to working across those lines of difference. Certainly the full story of how and why some teachers work well across lines of difference is a complicated one, but part of that story seems to be that effective teachers share these qualities and abilities:

- *An ability to suspend judgment.* They have the ability to identify moments when they might be unfairly judging someone's competence, commitment, effort level, or way of doing things and to suspend judgment so that they can check their biases and ensure their interpretation of tough situations is objective and productive.

- *Asset-based thinking.* These teachers have the ability to consciously search for and focus on the positive aspects of a person or situation, and build on an individual's strengths, even when they are not immediately apparent.

- *A strong locus of control and growth mindset.* These teachers demonstrate the ability to identify and relentlessly attack the problems that are within their control and worth solving, to avoid obsessing about the ones that are not, and to conceive of setbacks as opportunities for personal learning.

- *Interpersonal awareness.* They build trust and deepen relationships with others by recognizing the limits of their own perspective and seeking to understand others' point of view.

Because matters of diversity and working across lines of difference are such a fundamental part of highly effective teaching, we will invite you into discussions of these skills at various points in this book.

## The Purpose of Teaching As Leadership

An organizing framework for the knowledge, skills, and mindsets new teachers must possess, the six principles of Teaching As Leadership offer teachers a path to extraordinary academic achievement for students in low-income communities. By gathering and communicating the replicable actions of highly effective teachers in some of America's most challenging contexts, we aspire to accelerate learning for students who are behind academically.

We are not the first to ask what we can learn from exceptional teachers. A number of researchers and scholars have contributed to the ongoing quest

---

> ▶ **SEEKING A GENERAL PEDAGOGICAL FRAMEWORK**

**To meet the needs** of our students and schools, we place a premium on the knowledge, skills, and strategies that can be used to teach any grade or subject matter. And our studies indicate that wherever we see extraordinary achievement, we will find these six principles, whether it is in a kindergarten classroom, a self-contained classroom of fifth graders with disabilities, or a high school chemistry lab. These findings do not diminish the huge importance of pedagogical content knowledge but rather reflect our investment in seeking universally applicable strategies that correlate with success across all grades and subjects.

to spread the practices of teachers whose students are succeeding even as they face great challenges. While most of what is contained in this book is distilled from our experiences working with teachers in low-income communities across the country, it is also built on and informed by those who are asking similar questions and sharing their findings. Not surprisingly, when we study our most effective teachers, we find some well-established elements of pedagogical theory. This book enters, rather than creates, a critically important conversation.

A painful reality is that too few teachers—both within the Teach For America community and in the broader population of teachers in high-poverty areas—are acting in ways that are transforming students' life prospects through extraordinary academic achievement. Our purpose in sharing these findings is to accelerate our collective progress to a day when every child, regardless of race, ethnicity, or socioeconomic status, has the opportunity to attain an excellent education.

## This Book's Structure and Organization

This book answers in six chapters the question, "What distinguishes highly effective teachers in low-income communities?" Each of the six chapters explores, with anecdote-driven and research-supported discussions, one of the six principles of leadership we see embodied by teachers who are leading their students to dramatic academic gains. Each chapter begins with a discussion of a general leadership principle demonstrated by highly effective teachers and then explores ways that principle manifests in teacher-specific actions in the classroom. (Throughout the text, students' names have been changed. A master list of the highly effective teachers introduced in this book—and their students' achievements—is included at the back of the book.)

The content of this book is also captured at a more granular level in a rubric, which is set out in Appendix A and available online. The Teaching As Leadership rubric offers both the specific actions that we see when teachers embody the principles in this book, as well as a grid of indicators we see as teachers grow and develop into highly effective classroom leaders.

The focus of this book is on a vision of excellent teaching that correlates with dramatic student achievement in low-income communities where the achievement gap is most severe. All of the many ways that new teachers *develop* into excellent teachers that produce dramatic student achievement is more than we can fit in this book (and more than we know). For readers who want to explore the details of "how," this book's companion Web site captures what we have learned so far about how to perform and improve on these teachers' actions in your own classroom. The site offers some step-by-step guides, common pitfalls that new teachers who are attempting these actions encounter, and annotated video clips of teachers performing the actions.

Also on the companion Web site is the *Ms. Lora Story*—a fictionalized narrative based on the true story of our teacher Aurora Lora as she strives to embody the Teaching As Leadership principles in her classroom in the Fifth Ward in Houston. This story covers essentially the same territory as the chapters of the text, but in a narrative format. Each chapter of this book concludes with an excerpt from that extended case study.

These various structures—the anecdote-driven text, the rubric, the online resources, the case study—are designed to translate what we are learning about what distinguishes highly effective teachers in low-income communities into actionable guidance for new teachers joining the fight for education equity.

This book is dedicated to those of you who are entering the classroom to fight educational inequity. By drawing on the proven insights of teachers across the country who are changing the academic trajectories of their students—teachers who are disproving the supposed inevitability of the achievement gap—you can maximize your own impact in the lives of your students. By focusing your hard work and leadership on ending the injustice of educational inequity, you can contribute to this conversation that, we are confident, will lead to a day when all children in this nation will have the opportunity to attain an excellent education.

## "THERE'S NO TURNING BACK NOW."

*An excerpt from Ms. Lora's Story, a case-study in Teaching As Leadership, available online at www.teachingasleadership.org.*

Ms. Lora stepped back into the hall, her room key in hand.

Following the school secretary's instructions, she walked right past the Cafetorium sign to the two-story wing. It was only her second stroll down this hall, but she was surprised by how quickly this tangle of motley-aged buildings went from primarily confusing to primarily small. Without children, the school felt cluttered but manageable, jumbled but cozy. And once inside Blair Elementary's walls, she found that she didn't think at all about the barbed wire outside them.

As Ms. Lora climbed the yellow, glossy-painted stairs of the classroom building, her book-box rocking on her thighs with each step, she tried to imagine the school bustling with children and teachers.

Ms. Lora turned right, her only choice, at the top of the stairs. Her steps echoed off of the blue lockers and shiny black floor as she made her way down the hall, monitoring the descending room numbers. She felt the gnawing nervousness in her gut return and accelerate. "There's no turning back now," she thought to herself as Room 210 came into view on her right.

There was actually no turning back months ago when she committed to teach in Houston, but Ms. Lora drew some amused comfort from mentally labeling each new landmark the point of no return. Accepting her assignment, then reading the teaching instruction books, then observing other teachers, then arriving at the summer training institute, then her first day of supervised teaching there—each was a major milestone. Each was a discrete step that helped her parse her trepidation into manageable pieces.

As it was happening, Ms. Lora knew that this first walk down the hall to Room 210 was one of those landmark events. She deliberately looked around in hopes of remembering the moment. Yet another point of no return.

Over the past few weeks, she had struggled and failed to hang on to fleeting flashes of confidence she had enjoyed on a few occasions during her intense preparations over the spring and summer. As the school year neared, she had been distancing herself from the Teach For America staff members who tried to reassure her that her "academic achievement and leadership" in college was going to translate into success for her students. She was positive that no fourth grader was going to care one bit that she got some scholarships for college or that she was a National Hispanic Scholar or led some student group. They would have no interest in the fact that she woke up to study at 5:30 AM and rarely slept before 1 AM to maintain both her grades and paycheck during the

*(continued on next page)*

last four years. Sure she was proud of her varied college experiences, but she just couldn't believe that a few months after graduation, she would be responsible for real children.

What confidence Ms. Lora could muster came not from her past accomplishments but instead from the internal engine that had driven her to achieve them. She knew that she was going to make this work, somehow. Her pride would not let her quit, so she would do whatever it took to be successful. Thus, part of the trepidation she felt in the doorway of Room 210 was fear of failure, but most of it was anxiety about embarking on the most challenging adventure of her life— one that she was told by experienced teachers promised gratifying rewards and devastating failures.

As she stepped across the threshold into Room 210, she swallowed hard and mumbled to herself again, "There's no turning back now." It was louder than she had intended, but hearing her own voice made her smile.

To her surprise and relief, she felt a wash of calm as she surveyed her classroom for the first time. Her mind methodically filled this empty space with all of the many details of her imagined classroom. She set down her box and keys and crossed her arms, savoring the room's reality.

A white-lined chalkboard dominated the room, wrapping around two of the four walls. One other wall, the one she faced as she stood in the classroom doorway, was all windows, starting above the long, low air conditioner on the floor. The windows overlooked the small faculty parking lot, and she could see her own car parked on the street.

Curiously, several pairs of scissors stuck out from the metal frames of the windows. Ms. Lora walked over and, with some effort, pulled one pair of scissors out of a gap in the metal frame.

The window startled Ms. Lora by jumping open. With even more effort, she pulled the spring-loaded window shut and crammed the pair of scissors back in its place to hold the window closed.

The street below the windows was quiet and gave the impression that it always was. Across the street in his yard, a man standing next to a shiny car shuffled back and forth as he talked on a cell phone.

The remaining wall of Room 210 was a series of tall, full-door cabinets flush against a wall of large, grid-set, painted bricks. Ms. Lora imagined her desk with its back to those cabinets. She imagined team-inspired tables and chairs clustered around the room. She imagined herself standing in front of that chalkboard with a room full of children.

The nervousness returned with a rush.

**Aurora Lora**

# 1

# Set Big Goals

**REFLECTING ON WHERE** their students are performing at the beginning of the year and holding high expectations for their true potential, highly effective teachers develop an ambitious and inspiring vision of where their students will be academically at the end of the year. They set big goals informed by that vision—goals that when reached will make a meaningful impact on students' academic trajectory and future opportunities.

SET BIG GOALS

INVEST STUDENTS AND THEIR FAMILIES

PLAN PURPOSEFULLY

EXECUTE EFFECTIVELY

CONTINUOUSLY INCREASE EFFECTIVENESS

WORK RELENTLESSLY

> *By the end of the year, my first graders will read, write, do math, and behave like third graders.*

**LIKE MANY OTHER NEW** teachers in underresourced schools, Crystal Jones was initially dismayed by her first graders' skills coming into her classroom. Many of them had not attended kindergarten, and few knew all of the letters of the alphabet. Some did not know how to hold a book. On their very first day of school ever, they were already behind.

Determined to put them on track for academic success in the future, she tapped into her students' obsession with wanting to be big kids. She rallied them around the idea that they could and would learn not just first-grade material this year, but also second-grade material.

**Crystal Jones,**
First Grade, Georgia

The day before spring break, Ms. Jones's first graders giddily "graduated" to second grade in a "pomp and circumstance" ceremony in her classroom. All of her students had earned those diplomas by having tested on a second-grade level. Her first graders proudly called themselves "second graders" for the rest of the year.

By year's end, 100 percent of Ms. Jones's students met or exceeded the first-grade reading standards. Despite beginning the year lagging well behind incoming first graders in higher-income communities, 90 percent of her students were now a full year or more ahead of state standards, reading on or above a third-grade level. The rest were reading on at least a second-grade level.

> *My students will think, speak, and write like world citizens as defined by our rubric, and 100 percent of them will pass the New York Regents Exam for Global History, earning a classroom average of at least 80 percent.*

**MR. DELHAGEN SAW THE** outrageous statistics of the achievement gap playing out in his students' lives. His students—most of them students of color whose families had immigrated from countries in the Caribbean and many of whom lived in or on the edge of poverty—were far behind in their academic progress and struggling to juggle school with significant responsibilities at home. He knew that the stakes in his classroom were high: passing the Regents Exam is a graduation requirement in New York State, and if his students did not graduate from high school, their life opportunities would be significantly limited.

> *All of my students will grow at least 1.5 years' worth of reading growth (as measured by the Developmental Reading Assessment) and will master at least 95 percent of ambitious, rigorous, and carefully tailored IEP [Individualized Education Program] goals, which are designed to move them toward the ultimate long-term goal of independent living.*

**MANY OF KATIE HILL'S** sixth-, seventh-, and eighth-grade students had been diagnosed with moderate to significant cognitive disabilities, with IQs in the thirties and forties. When she first met them, they were, on average, reading below a first-grade level, and some were still unfamiliar with all the letters of the alphabet. Most of them were unable to give personal information such as their parent or guardian's name, their phone number, their address, or their lunch identification number.

In addition to the challenges posed by their learning differences, Ms. Hill's students were seen by many as unable to learn basic academic and functional skills and incapable of ever living independently. Ms. Hill however, was determined to ensure that her students made significant gains in the knowledge, skills, and sense of self-efficacy and self-advocacy they would need for successful independent living.

Ms. Hill committed herself to achieving this big goal with her students and worked with students' families to rewrite their IEP goals to include these academic and functional targets. With these individualized big goals driving her every decision, her students made, on average, 1.6 years' worth of reading growth and approximately three years of growth in math by the end of the year. They also mastered 83 percent of the grade-level standards they were shooting for as a class. Under her leadership, in one year, her students made more academic progress than they had in their previous six to eight years combined.

**Katie Hill,** Middle School Special Education, North Carolina

**Taylor Delhagen,** High School Global History, New York

Passing this exam was a daunting challenge. Not only did his eleventh graders lack many basic skills (with some reading on a fifth-grade level), but Mr. Delhagen had only one year to teach two years' worth of material. He committed himself and his students to this audacious big goal.

At the end of the year, Mr. Delhagen's students had fulfilled his vision of becoming "global citizens," embodying the qualities of rigorous thinking, eloquent speaking, and effective writing he had set forth in the first weeks of school. On the Regents Exam, his students beat the city average for students in communities who took the same course over the traditional two years. His students outperformed every other class in the school taking any Regents Exam. Fifty-one of his fifty-seven students passed the exam on their first attempt, with a few students just missing a perfect score.

Students make dramatic academic progress when their teachers begin the year with a clear, ambitious vision of student success. Highly effective teachers know exactly where they want their students to be by the end of the year. Teachers like Ms. Jones, Ms. Hill, and Mr. Delhagen realize that a bold (and some might say crazy) vision of student success can actually foster student achievement.

Virtually any successful leader in any context tackles massive problems in this same way, starting with a mental picture of a new and better reality. The United States was the first nation to land on the moon, for example, *because* President Kennedy made the bold (and some said crazy) declaration that it would be. While most of us (including Ms. Jones, Ms. Hill, and Mr. Delhagen) might be reluctant to compare ourselves to President Kennedy, these teachers are in fact employing leadership techniques when they develop and communicate their vision of a different reality as a means of driving dramatic change. As James Kouzes and Barry Posner found in their worldwide study of qualities of leadership, successful leaders are able to *"envision the future,* gaze across the horizon of time and imagine the greater opportunities to come. They see something out ahead, vague as it might appear from a distance, and they imagine that extraordinary feats are possible and that the ordinary could be transformed into something noble. They are able to develop an ideal and unique image of the future for the common good."[1]

If you are a teacher working to close the achievement gap who wants to maximize your impact on your students' life opportunities, setting a big goal for student learning is a launching point for the single-minded focus and urgency that will drive your and your students' hard work throughout the school year.

## Foundations of Effective Goal Setting

Strong goals are founded on three ideas. First, like all other strong leaders, highly effective teachers insist on defining and measuring achievement so that progress and success are clear. In our context, that principle takes the form of ambitious standards—aligned and quantifiable goals—targets that help students see their progress and appreciate the benefits of their hard work.

Second, the highly effective teachers we have studied expect the best of those they are leading. In our context, this means demanding and seeing that their students reach their full potential, holding high expectations that actually raise student performance. The best teachers, in our experience, refuse to accept and instead set out to disprove the myth that students in low-income communities are destined for lower achievement and fewer opportunities than children in higher-income communities.

Third, like other great leaders, strong teachers are keenly aware of their constituents' (in this case, their students') needs and desires. These teachers not only seek to meet those inherent interests and motivations; they also find ways to build them into their vision of success to make it all the more inspiring to their students.

We will engage these three leadership tenets in two passes. First, we will explore the purposes and power of big goals. Then, to make these ideas more concrete, we will revisit these tenets through the processes and reflections of highly effective teachers as they design the big goals for their classrooms.

## Inspiring Strong Results with Measurable Outcomes

The big goals that are introduced in this chapter are measurable. Ms. Jones, Ms. Hill, and Mr. Delhagen recognize that success must be defined in a way that makes clear when progress is or is not being made and when success has been achieved. Strong and highly effective teachers see the important benefits of having a clear, objective destination in mind:

- *By making clear the destination, big goals help focus and align the efforts of many individuals.* When we talk to successful teachers about why they put so much energy into developing and implementing an ambitious big goal, the responses often take the form of analogies: "to keep us on the same page," "so everyone knows where we are headed," "so we can work as a team," or—a favorite—"the big goal is a litmus test for everything you do." A number of teachers, like Erin Wahler, a fifth-grade teacher in Zuni, New Mexico, describe how virtually every conversation they have with a student about changing performance starts with a series of questions about how the student's actions are or are not contributing to achieving ambitious academic goals. Eventually students begin to adopt this approach without prompting, asking themselves, "What am I doing to help us reach our goals?" These teachers are telling us exactly what management and leadership experts say: "Vision plays a key role in producing useful change by helping to direct, align, and inspire actions on the part of large numbers of people. Without an appropriate vision, a transformation effort can easily dissolve into a list of confusing, incompatible, and time-consuming projects that go in the wrong direction or nowhere at all."[2]

- *The timeline and deadline inherent in setting a measurable goal bring urgency to you and your team's efforts.* Jess Bialecki shared with us the influences big goals had on her daily intensity when she came to realize that her first graders were not progressing fast enough. When she calculated forward the progress her students had made, she was initially "devastated" to realize that their progress was not on pace to reach her goals. She decided she had to change course and increase her efforts: "Transitions needed to be tighter, restroom breaks had to be transformed into learning opportunities, literacy centers needed to be more purposeful, and even snack time had to double as sight-word game time," she said. Ms. Bialecki says that her students initially balked at the changes to the routines to which they had become accustomed, but as they witnessed their own growth under their new schedule, attitudes changed and investment in the big goal skyrocketed. Ms. Bialecki explained, "I soon found that the roles had reversed, and my students were the ones holding me accountable for maintaining our sense of urgency. They reminded me when I forgot our sight-word cards when lining up for lunch or complained when their classmates took too long during transitions."

## ▶ MEASURABLE OUTCOMES IN OTHER SECTORS

**IT IS HARD TO IMAGINE** a successful politician, coach, or business leader acting without quantifiable definitions of success, be those votes, wins, or dollars. Many great accomplishments in any sector of society began with an articulation of measurable outcomes.

Consider the Montgomery bus boycott, which started in 1955. When Rosa Parks was arrested, community leaders did not simply call for a boycott of the bus system. They called for a boycott of the bus system *until three objective conditions were met:* African American riders would not have to give up their seats to white riders, they would not have to pay their money at the front of the bus and then get off to enter the back door of the bus, and buses would stop as frequently in African American neighborhoods as they did in white ones. This specificity sustained the community's sacrifices and determination for 381 days, when all of those goals were finally met.

The world of business provides many examples of the power of clear measures of success. Jim Collins and Jerry Porras offer Boeing's work on the 727 as one example. When Boeing sought to become the dominant player in the commercial aircraft industry, the company did not say to its engineers, "Let's become the best." Instead it set out to "build a jet that can land on runway 4–22 at La Guardia Airport (only 4,860 feet long—much too short for any existing passenger jet) *and* be able to fly nonstop from New York to Miami *and* be wide enough for six-abreast seating *and* have a capacity of 131 passengers, *and* meet Boeing's high standards of indestructibility."[3] While many observers thought that goal was impossible, Boeing's engineers were motivated and pushed by the goal's boldness, and they were also united and informed by its precision and clarity. They rallied for one of the greatest feats of engineering in history, creating the plane that became the standard for the airline industry.[4]

As one more example, when Steven Case's little-known company, AOL, became the standard bearer of the fledgling Internet industry, he explained that the key was setting the audacious goal of signing up 1 million subscribers. Case remembers that with this objective, measurable goal in mind, people began to work differently, with more focus and urgency, making innovative choices with the big goal in mind, and the numbers of subscribers began to climb at record rates. Case recalls, "It wasn't exactly the equivalent of 'Let's put a man on the moon,' but for us this march to a million was a big deal. . . . If we got to a million, we felt that kind of put us in the big leagues, so we were on this march to a million, and we got there."[5]

• *Measurable targets offer a benchmark against which a teacher can evaluate his or her own effectiveness.* Seeing progress is beneficial to more than students. A distinguishing characteristic of highly effective teachers is their insistence on constantly increasing their effectiveness. The big goal serves as a concrete benchmark against which to measure student learning and thereby gain insights about a teacher's strengths and weaknesses. (See Chapter Five.)

Thus, when a teacher states an unmeasurable goal like, "We will learn as much as we can," that noble but subjective idea offers none of the urgency, focus, efficiency, or alignment[6] that we see when a vision is clearly and objectively expressed: "Every student in my class will score at least a 3 on the AP exam" or "My students will read on a fifth-grade level."

▶ **EXAMPLES OF MEASURABLE AND NOT MEASURABLE ACADEMIC GOALS**

| Measurable | Not Measurable |
|---|---|
| "All students will demonstrate at least 85 percent proficiency of the state's fourth-grade math standards as measured by the state's end-of-year assessment." | "All students will improve their math skills." |
| "My students will each write a five-paragraph persuasive essay that scores a 4 or 5 on the state's sixth-grade writing rubric." | "My students are going to write great persuasive essays by the end of the year." |
| "My students are all going to score a 3 or higher on the Advanced Placement exam." | "Every student is going to do his or her best on the Advanced Placement exam." |

## Defining Academic Achievement with Rigorous Learning Standards

Highly effective teachers in low-income communities are determined to give their students opportunities comparable to those enjoyed by children in higher-income areas. They know that means ensuring their students receive an excellent education, with all the academic skills, enrichment, and character-shaping experiences that come from engaging in a rich and challenging pursuit of the ideas and skills necessary to succeed in college and in life.

For teachers striving to close the achievement gap in low-income communities, quantifying success means defining and measuring how much our students learn. Highly effective teachers recognize that academic achievement is both a quantifiable indicator of student progress and a key that opens doors to broader educational, occupational, and life opportunities for children growing up in poverty. So for teachers committed to changing their students' life paths, the ultimate measure of success is their students' measurable academic achievement as defined by rigorous learning standards.

In our context, achievement is defined by learning standards—guidelines that set out what knowledge and skills students are expected to demonstrate, grade by grade and subject by subject. Developed by districts, states, and national groups, these standards help teachers determine where their students are at the beginning of the year and how much progress they have made over the year.

### ▶ MEASURING LEARNING WITH STANDARDIZED TESTS

**ALIGNING TEACHERS' DEFINITIONS OF SUCCESS** with students' academic growth does not equate to teaching to standardized tests that value rote memorization over more meaningful critical thinking skills. In fact, our focus on academic achievement only increases our obligation to ensure that how we assess academic growth captures meaningful learning. Even as we need to develop more rigorous and authentic assessments, the tests we have provide useful information about students' knowledge and skills, and we have to use that information for all it is worth. In our experience, the path to excellence and opportunity for our students embraces and improves—rather than rejects—assessments that measure student achievement.

### ▶ THE DEBATE OVER LEARNING STANDARDS

**THE STANDARDS MOVEMENT IN** education has been both welcomed and criticized. Some teachers are concerned that learning standards and the tests they spawn limit teachers' judgment and creativity. Some teachers extol the benefits of standards and appreciate the guidance they give about what students must learn. In our quest for educational equity, learning standards can play a key role in ensuring that student learning in low-income communities is comparable to student learning in higher-income areas.

Whatever your view of learning standards, all states and districts now use them to guide instruction, and it is important to think about your role as a teacher within that reality.

For example, according to state education agencies, a tenth-grade geometry student in Texas should be able to "use logical reasoning to prove statements are true and find counter-examples to disprove statements that are false."[7] A second grader in California should, by the end of the year, be able to "generate alternative endings to plots and identify the reason or reasons for, and the impact of, the alternatives."[8] A seventh grader studying geography in South Dakota should be able to "describe the impact of the natural environment on settlement patterns."[9]

Although not all learning standards are as rigorous as some teachers would like, they do have a special role in the fight for educational equity in that they (and the assessments they generate) provide a standard yardstick for student learning. A lack of such standards and data in the past has been part of what allowed the achievement gap to fester and grow.

The key point is that learning standards help define the academic achievement we seek for our students and are therefore centrally important to setting big goals. When Mariel Elguero, a fifth-grade reading teacher in Newark, New Jersey, works with her team of colleagues to set a target of two years of growth in reading skills for each of her students, that target has specific meaning according to the New Jersey learning standards. By referring to those standards (available online and elsewhere), Ms. Elguero found a breakdown of the specific skills and growth her students must demonstrate to have made two years of progress. Her analysis of those standards revealed a dozen or so essential skills and strategies that all involved knowing when you are missing comprehension as a reader and being able to independently apply strategies to resolve those misunderstandings. This realization was the foundation for Ms. Elguero's big goal and served as a useful framework as she planned the year.

In rare cases, you may find that your district or school does not have official learning standards for your courses. In this situation, you will have to do the best you can to derive learning standards from other respected sources. Arianne Kerr, for example, discovered that her district in Tennessee did not have clear learning standards to define what her English as a Second Language (ESL) students needed to learn. "I did not realize how much of my position as a teacher would involve research—Internet research, making district and regional connections, finding professional organizations and conferences, etc.," Ms. Kerr recalls. She immersed herself in relevant standards from other districts and states, deriving from them a list of objectives that she used to shape her big goals and plan her course. The learning standards Ms. Kerr developed not only became the backbone of her big goals, but earned her a new role as ESL coordinator at her school.

In most cases, of course, learning standards are available to you as a starting point to guide to what your students should understand and be able to do. The most effective big goals are built on these well-established learning expectations, not on your teacher's intuition, interests, or assumptions about what students should learn.

---

### ▶ COMMON PITFALLS FOR TEACHERS ENGAGING LEARNING STANDARDS

**IN OUR EXPERIENCE, TWO** errors characterize less effective teachers' engagement of learning standards as they develop big goals:

1. *Preconceived notions.* Less effective teachers may approach the big goal design process with preconceived notions of what *they* want to teach (perhaps because they remember learning some concept in this grade when they were in school, or they have an affinity for some particular subject or skill) instead of using the standards to determine what students need to learn. These teachers incorrectly see learning standards as informing their preconceived notions instead of *resetting* their assumptions about what students need to learn. Simply stated, teachers can and do teach more than the learning standards, but effective big goals start from them.

2. *Complexity.* Less effective teachers may start to engage with the standards but may be intimidated by the standards' complexity and give up before fully appreciating the guidance they offer. Learning standards are not always easy to use but highly effective teachers attest to the benefits that come from working hard to understand them.

Thus, rigorous learning standards (and assessments that demonstrate student mastery of those standards) play a central role in designing big goals. They tell us exactly what, at a minimum, our students must learn, and they give us objective bases for evaluating that learning. In our studies of more effective and less effective teachers, we have seen that teachers who do not engage with learning standards are inclined to develop big goals that evade measurement and therefore cannot influence teachers' and students' behavior in ways that accelerate achievement.

### Building Students' Love of Learning, Persistence, Self-Esteem, and Other Empowering Dispositions, Skills, and Mindsets

Many teachers seek to instill in students certain values, dispositions, and life skills that will support students' hard work and success in the long term—concepts like resilience, love of learning, respect for others, self-advocacy, and independence. While these concepts are sometimes articulated as separate big goals, highly effective teachers emphasize that academic achievement is an integral part of achieving goals and cannot actually be separated from them. One cannot simply tell students to have self-esteem, or to be persistent, or to love learning; rather, these important characteristics are most effectively developed through the pursuit of something difficult and valuable—academic achievement. One effective teacher, Karen Fierst, explained:

> I have found that a child's self-perception and motivation are so intertwined with academic achievement that it is nearly impossible to address either one exclusively. For a student to make significant academic gains, they must internalize the desire to grow and develop the confidence to take academic risks. However, in order for a student to develop that intrinsic motivation and self-confidence, they must experience some success with academics.

Highly effective teachers' focus on empowering traits comes from their insistence that these traits have a meaningful long-term impact on students' lives. These teachers are asking themselves, "What accomplishments and areas of growth will most open opportunities for students?" With that question in mind, Mr. Delhagen combined his strictly academic goal (passing the Regents Global History Exam) with his vision of effective thinking, writing, and communicating to help his students develop into global citizens. Ms. Jones, in her goal that her students would "read, write, do math, and *behave* like third graders," similarly developed and shared with her students specific indicators of behavior, related in large part to cooperation, collaboration, and respect, that she sought to develop alongside academic skills.

As we see modeled by these teachers, the less tangible nature of such longer-term dispositions, mindsets, and skills does not mean they cannot be tracked and, in some sense, measured. In fact, if these ideas are going to be infused into a big goal, you must have a way to know that you are making progress toward them.

Mekia Love, a nationally recognized reading teacher in Washington, D.C., sets individualized, quantifiable literacy goals for each of her students but also frames them in her broader vision of "creating life-long readers." This is a trait she believes is a key to her students' opportunities and fulfillment in life. In order for both Ms. Love and her students to track their progress toward creating life-long readers, Ms. Love developed a system of specific and objective indicators (like students' self-driven requests for books, students' own explanations of their interest in reading, the time students are engaged with a book). By setting specific quantifiable targets for and monitoring each of those indicators, she was able to demonstrate progress and success on what would otherwise be a subjective notion.

Strong teachers—because they know that transparency and tracking progress add focus and urgency to their and their students' efforts—find a way to make aims like self-esteem, writing skills, "love of reading," or "access to high-performing high schools" specific and objective. These teachers—like Ms. Love, Mr. Delhagen, and Ms. Jones—ask themselves what concrete indicators of resilience or independence or "love of learning" they want to see in their students by the end of the year and work them into their big goals.

In our experience, less effective teachers may sometimes assume that because a measurement system may be imperfect or difficult, then it must be wrong or impossible. As Jim Collins reminds us in his studies of effective for-profit and nonprofit organizations,

> To throw our hands up and say, "But we cannot measure performance in the social sectors the way you can in a business" is simply lack of discipline. All indicators are flawed, whether qualitative or quantitative. Test scores are flawed, mammograms are flawed, crime data are flawed, customer service data are flawed, patient-outcome data are flawed. What matters is not finding the perfect indicator, but settling upon a consistent and intelligent method of assessing your output results, and then tracking your trajectory with rigor. What do you mean by great performance? Have you established a baseline? Are you improving? If not, why not? How can you improve even faster toward your audacious goals?[10]

To drive this point home, Collins offers the helpful example of the Cleveland Orchestra, which defined its own success in terms of "artistic excellence." Obviously tracking progress toward artistic excellence is tricky, and simply going with any subjective determination of artistic excellence negates the purposes of setting a goal in the first place. Subjective, after-the-fact opinions offer no destination against which to track progress and success and provide no urgency or focus.

Given the subjective nature of "artistic excellence," the orchestra's leaders developed a series of indicators that would serve as proxies for that vision. They tallied and tracked standing ovations, the range of pieces they could play with perfection, invitations to the most prestigious music festivals, demand for tickets, other orchestras' imitation of their style, and the number of composers seeking out the Cleveland Orchestra to debut new compositions. As Collins reminds us, those factors are not perfect, but they are good indicators of success. With those proxy indicators, the leaders of the orchestra were able to reap the same benefits as with more quantitative measures used in other endeavors.[11]

Many teachers, in their big goal design, face some version of the Cleveland Orchestra problem. While some aspects of our goals (for example, "Every student will master 80 percent of the North Carolina chemistry standards as measured by the state assessment") are obviously measurable, some other aims (for example, "Students' writing skills will improve by X amount" or "Students will become stronger critical thinkers") require development of proxy indicators, rubrics, or other means to ensure clear progress tracking is possible.

## Inspiring High Performance with High Expectations

*Leaders expect the best of the people around them.*

— Warren Bennis[12]

Without exception, the strongest teachers we have studied tap into an amazing phenomenon of human psychology: the self-fulfilling prophecy of high expectations. These teachers recognize that we get from our students what we expect from them. These teachers' every action is driven by the insight that high expectations cause high achievement.

In the words of a first-grade teacher in Phoenix, "Every time I have raised the expectations in my classroom, students have also raised their performance." Another teacher summarized

> ▶ **RESEARCH ON THE SELF-FULFILLING PROPHECY OF HIGH EXPECTATIONS**
>
> **CALLED BY SOME THE** "Pygmalion" effect (after the mythical ancient Greek sculptor whose love for his statue made her come to life), the "self-fulfilling prophecy of high expectations" has been verified by researchers.[13] In one landmark study, teachers were told by researchers that certain students in their classes had performed well on a test that predicts intellectual growth. In truth, these students had been randomly selected by the researchers to be described as high performing for the purposes of the experiment. These students were actually distinguished only by their teachers' expectations for their performance. Eight months later, those randomly selected students described to the teachers as high performing had significantly outperformed their peers on IQ tests, showing an increase of an average of twelve points on an IQ exam (while other students had grown an average of eight points). And the teachers themselves consistently

the idea like this: "The biggest obstacle to my students' success is actually low expectations. Too many of us, as teachers, do not expect them to succeed, so they do not. Too many students do not expect themselves to succeed, so they do not. When my students are expected to perform at high levels, they absolutely do."

While the self-fulfilling prophecy of high expectations is well established by research, in our experience, the most compelling evidence of this idea's power comes from the many testimonials we receive from strong teachers. Crystal Brakke, for example, is a teacher who in her first year teaching eighth grade in Henderson, North Carolina, took her students from almost 70 percent failing the state literacy assessment to over 80 percent passing it. Ms. Brakke shares how her high expectations helped change the academic trajectory of one particularly challenging student.

"The Wilson," the self-appointed nickname of a young man named Scott, was a living legend at Henderson Middle School. He was nearly sixteen years old and had already spent three years at the middle school. The crowds would part in the hallways for him. He ruled the school, and he knew it. He also knew that, probably quite realistically, he would be promoted to high school no matter what he did this school year—we just couldn't keep him in middle school another year. So my second-period class quickly became his personal playground . . . and I realized that if I didn't do something soon, the year would be lost for both him and the other twenty students I needed to teach. . . . Scott wasn't ready for high school—he was reading at a fifth-grade level.

So I got together with the other teachers on my team, who were facing their own struggles with Scott, and we came up with a plan that was supported by both Scott's grandmother (his guardian) and his older brother, Richard, whom he idolized. We called him into a team

described the "bloomer" students as better behaved, more academically curious, more likely to succeed, and more friendly than other students in the class.[14] Researcher Robert Marzano summarizes this body of research:

> A teacher's beliefs about students' chances of success in school influence the teacher's actions with students, which in turn influence students' achievement. If the teacher believes students can succeed, she tends to behave in ways that help them succeed. If the teacher believes that students cannot succeed, she unwittingly tends to behave in ways that subvert student success or at least do not facilitate student success. This is perhaps one of the most powerful hidden dynamics of teaching because it is typically an unconscious activity.[15]

meeting, and he sauntered in, ready for whatever we could give him—in-school suspension, after-school detention. He'd seen it all before. Instead, I told him that his schedule had changed: he would now be coming to my class first period and working with the cluster of "gifted and talented" students in that class. Honestly, you could see the color draining from his face. I explained that I realized what the problem was—that it wasn't him; it was me. I wasn't teaching him what he needed; wasn't teaching to his level and expecting from him what I knew he was capable of doing. That's when he just flat out called me "crazy."

But the next day, Scott came to my first-period class. He sat down, and didn't say a word for the next ninety minutes. That's when I knew we were on to something. I can tell you for certain that progress came slowly, very slowly. Some days I had to fight just for him to keep his head up, but then one day, he brought a pen and pencil to class. I almost cried, I was so excited. Another day, he raised his hand to answer a question. He had started participating, and that was the end of behavior problems with "The Wilson."

By January, he was just another kid in my class and was sharing insights into *Romeo and Juliet* that made my jaw drop. My favorite memory from that year came when one of the seventh-grade teachers approached me after a staff meeting, asking, "What are you doing up there with Scott Wilson?" It turns out that "The Wilson" had made a visit to the seventh-grade hallway to chat with some of his old teachers and let them know that we finally figured it out: he's gifted.

Another highly effective teacher, Brent Maddin, saw the power of setting and maintaining high expectations for student performance in his science classes in south Louisiana. Sometimes Mr. Maddin's high expectations took the form of a low grade for a student who was not used to getting them (see table below).

Virtually every highly effective teacher we work with has similar stories of the power of expectations, starting with the expectations they set for all their students in the form of ambitious academic goals. At the same time, most of those strong teachers also have

| Mr. Maddin's Perspective | The Student's Perspective |
| --- | --- |
| When Jeohn turned in his science fair project, it looked absolutely beautiful. But when I really looked at the work, it was substandard. He had cut corners and not put much effort into it. Not much learning had happened even though he had known the expectations. Our project evaluation rubric was much more about the science than the aesthetics, and even though it looked good superficially, I knew he could do so much better. | I got a D on my science fair project. I had never gotten a D before. I always got A's. And I always won with my science fair projects. I was pretty upset about it. But when I sat down and talked to Mr. Maddin about it, he showed me there was a whole lot more I could have done. He showed me what success really looks like. He showed me what I was capable of. He was disappointed that I hadn't worked hard, and I became disappointed too. |

| Mr. Maddin's Perspective | The Student's Perspective |
|---|---|
| I knew I was going to take a lot of flak from people, and I did. Both Jeohn and his mother came in and said, "You can't do this. This project would get an A in any other class. This project looks better than any of those others." | It was just a science fair project, but that was a lesson that translated into life, college, everything. That D made me realize that there could be a different standard. And I saw that it was hard for Mr. Maddin sometimes. He would give kids an F while others would give them an A and some people would be really mad, but once kids saw the bigger picture, they weren't bitter. |
| Jeohn's project might have done well in another class, but our standards were high, and also clear. Many of his classmates had in fact met those expectations, even though the product was not as pretty as Jeohn's. | |
| That was a moment when Jeohn suddenly just got it. He knew he could do better. He knew I wasn't going to accept less than his best. I think it was a real turning point. He knew he could perform to the high standard I had set, and he decided he would. | It took a lot of courage and determination and tenacity from Mr. Maddin to stand up to students and colleagues when they questioned the standard he was setting. I certainly wouldn't be where I am today if I hadn't encountered him in high school.

*Jeohn went on to attend Yale and is now in the foreign service.* |

counterexamples of times when they, for one reason or another, let slip their high expectations in ways that undermined student progress.

## Cutting Through the "Smog" of Low Expectations

The fact that many strong teachers describe their struggles to establish and maintain high expectations for their students reminds us that acting on our students' true potential takes a strong commitment, affirmative work, and constant vigilance against powerful influences all around us. We live under a barrage of negative messages about our students that can, if we are not working against them, gradually erode our belief in our students' potential.

Beverly Tatum, president of Spelman College, psychologist, and author of *Why Are All the Black Kids Sitting Together in the Cafeteria?* uses smog as an analogy for the racial bias all around us.[16] The same analogy is appropriate for the closely related and constantly present low expectations that we as a society have for children in low-income communities. She writes, "Sometimes it is so thick it is visible, other times it is less apparent, but always, day in and day out, we are breathing it in. None of us would introduce ourselves as 'smog-breathers'. . . but if we live in a smoggy place, how can we avoid breathing the air?"[17]

One key form of that "smog" is the media messages we consume every day. Most of us are probably aware, at least in a general sense, that popular media portrayals of people living in poverty and people of color are rife with negative stereotypes.[18] African American and Hispanic youth (especially boys) are, on the news, on television shows, and in movies, often portrayed as violent, criminal, lazy, and uninterested in academic success.[19] A number of

▶ HOW THE GENERAL PUBLIC SEES THE
ACHIEVEMENT GAP AND ITS CAUSES

**THE GENERAL PUBLIC BLAMES** our students and their families for the achievement gap in America. In a Phi Beta Kappa/Gallup survey, the general public pointed to lack of parental involvement, home life and upbringing, and lack of interest on the part of students themselves as the three most important factors in creating the gap.[21]

When we ask precisely the same questions of our teachers who are actually working around and against the achievement gap every day, we get very different answers. These teachers respond that a leading cause of the achievement gap is low expectations of students. They suggest that all of us—teachers, students' families, and students themselves—simply do not expect enough of students in low-income communities.[22]

"I think that one of the public's biggest misunderstandings is that students in the communities and schools where we teach do not have the desire or the ability to learn and perform at the same level as students from more affluent communities," responded a middle school English teacher in Philadelphia.[23]

The complete report on these surveys of our teachers about the causes and solutions of the achievement gap is available online.

 teachingasleadership.org

studies demonstrate that African American and Hispanic people are overrepresented as criminals on the news and underrepresented as victims.[20]

Television and movie portrayals similarly misrepresent students' demographics. One study found that in movies, African Americans are much more frequently cast in roles "involving physical action or buffoonery than those that rely on close audience identification with a complicated, dramatic problem faced by a main character,"[24] and another found that Hispanics are typically cast in caricatured roles with negative associations.[25] The rare instances of modern Native Americans represented in film and television tend to be "militant activists or alcoholics."[26] In commercials, people of color use computers less often than whites, and white males hold a virtual monopoly on positions requiring technological expertise.[27]

These media-perpetuated stereotypes are arguably both a cause and effect of the general public's doubts and fears about our students. Whatever the cause and effect, we experience the smog of low expectations at every turn.

Sometimes we breathe that smog through personal interactions, like when a stranger stops Crystal Brakke in Wal-Mart as she buys school supplies to say how sorry she is that Ms. Brakke has to work with "those kids at that school." Or when a cynical school administrator suggests that second-grade teacher Alaina Moonves stick to "finger painting and puppets" with her students with special needs. Or when Chancellor of District of

Columbia Schools, Michelle Rhee, is told by a teacher to slow down her reforms because "you can't teach pigs to fly."

Sometimes that smog is part of the system in which we work, as when ESL teacher Stephen Ready's students were not tested for Gifted and Talented programs. Or when Kate Sobel's school in a low-income neighborhood is "recognized" and celebrated because students earned a 3 on a ten-point assessment (but such celebrations happen in wealthy districts when students earn a 10). Or when Lisa Barrett inherits a new student with the IEP goal "to prove himself to be a helpful, outgoing student." Or when a student has to bring his parents to school to convince a counselor to move him from a floor-covering class into Spanish as he requested.[28]

Sometimes the same corrosive messages about our students come in the form of well-intended but nonetheless damaging praise for us as teachers. When we receive a compliment on our patience, bravery, or generosity for "dealing" with those difficult and needy students, what is that saying about our students? Of course, the work of teachers in low-income communities is difficult, and many students are in great need, but sometimes the motivation for appreciating a teacher is not actually the burden of those external difficulties but is instead negative assumptions about students' potential.

We, as teachers, can be consciously and subconsciously affected by those comments, structures, and compliments in at least two ways. First, we may begin to believe that merely exceeding those low expectations of our students is success. But given the high stakes for our students, learning more than last year cannot be enough. Because we know our students can excel on the absolute scale used in well-resourced and high-performing schools and because we know they are so far behind those students, the same absolute bar used for students in higher-income communities must be our bar as well.

Second, the inundating smog of low expectations around us can shift our primary focus from our students' potential to learn to the challenges that these students face. The unfortunate reality of our society is that violence, drug use, unemployment, malnutrition, and other symptoms of poverty do have higher incidence in low-income communities than in higher-income communities.[29] The unfortunate reality is that children in low-income communities, the vast majority of whom are children of color, are statistically more likely to fail, drop out, and be incarcerated than children in wealthier communities.[30] Highly effective teachers, however, realize that those realities do not change their students' potential to succeed. They may require hard work to navigate, but they do not make these students any less capable of achieving success.

Imagine for a moment the "smog" at play when Ms. Brakke wrestled with how to handle "The Wilson" in her second year at Henderson Middle School. As a "young black male"— a phrase that one study of *Time* and *Newsweek* cover stories found to be synonymous with "criminal"[31]—Scott Wilson fit a stereotype that both Scott and Ms. Brakke encountered every day. As a student who had failed several years previously, Scott had a reputation among many teachers as someone who could not succeed. And in Scott's bullying and misbehavior, he could be seen to validate various negative assumptions others were making about him. And yet from within this smog of low expectations, Ms. Brakke, like all other highly effective teachers, worked to maintain her high expectations of Scott Wilson:

> There were definitely times when I was discouraged, when people, besides Scott himself, told me I was crazy for moving him to my advanced class. Some of his previous teachers, some of his classmates—even some of his friends—told me that it just wasn't going to work. He couldn't cut it in a regular class, there was no way he could make it in a more challenging one, they said. I just kept going back to this thought in my head: that I honestly didn't believe that, and there was no reason to expect something different for him than for any of my other students. We had to get to our goal of every student reaching 80 percent mastery of the literacy standards, and that included Scott. I wasn't doing my job if I put him off to the side.

Scholar Sonia Nieto refers to the hidden curriculum in our classrooms—"those subtle and not-so-subtle messages that, although not part of the intended curriculum, may nevertheless have an impact on students." Nieto points out through research and examples that our expectations of our students are one key element of that hidden, and powerful, curriculum. The highly effective teachers we work with, teachers like Ms. Brakke, take to heart Nieto's warning that "many times, unintentional discrimination is practiced by well-meaning teachers."[32] They work diligently to check and preserve their high expectations for their students against the smog of degrading messages around them.

Thus, maintaining our high expectations requires affirmative work and commitment. When we cut through the smog of low expectations, big goals are at the center of that hard work and commitment. For strong teachers, setting big goals is a public declaration—to their students, themselves, and others—of their commitment to fulfill students' potential. Successful teachers use this public pledge as an inoculation against the degrading influences of the doubts they hear, and may sometimes have, about their students.

### Turning High Expectations into Ambitious Big Goals

High expectations drive a big goal's design even as teachers seek a realistic and informed understanding of what their students can learn in the time available. Highly effective teachers develop a well-considered opinion of what their students, with great effort, can accomplish. They then factor that understanding into their big goals. Note that feasibility, therefore, is not a generic check on ambitiousness but rather a call for well-informed ambitiousness.

In our conversations, strong teachers suggested four important sources for pinpointing the frontier of ambitious and feasible for their students:

| Relevant learning standards | Sometimes you may find yourself working with more than one set of standards. Experienced educators you work with will have opinions about which learning standards are more and less rigorous. By studying those standards and assessments, you will gain insights that help you calibrate the ambitiousness of your own academic goals for your students. |
| --- | --- |
| Evidence of your students' prior academic achievement | Sometimes you can obtain access to your students' prior academic achievement before the school year starts. Many teachers often also find or design diagnostic assessments to clearly understand what students know and can do at the beginning of the year. |
| Levels of achievement reached by students in higher-income communities | "Excellent school visits" (when a teacher gets to see what other students are achieving) are often inspiring catalysts for ambitious goals. |
| Levels of achievement reached by the strongest of your fellow teachers and predecessors | What is the higher end of academic gains achieved by students who previously came into this grade level and subject as far behind as your students are? Your best source for these data are often strong teachers in high-performing schools. Find those teachers teaching your grade or subject who seem to have clear goals themselves, and discuss their students' achievement and the challenges to that achievement. Find teachers with a proven record of dramatic academic gains for their students and ask them to describe those gains. |

These considerations, taken together, help a teacher make an informed judgment that a big goal is both ambitious and feasible.

One implication of ensuring that big goals are ambitious and feasible for all students is the need to individualize goals. When students begin the year with dramatically different prior knowledge and skills, or different interests and motivations, or different experiences and learning styles, excellent teachers design big goals that reflect those differences. Mariel Elguero, for example, the fifth-grade teacher whose big goal is in part to improve students' reading levels by two years, must know each student's literacy skills at the beginning of the year in order to make her growth goal meaningful. While all of her fifth graders should be reading chapter books like *Harry Potter*, her diagnostics indicate that some would struggle with *Magic Tree House* books, and some would even struggle with advanced Dr. Seuss books. By looking forward from a student's starting point to where two grade levels of growth would take the student, Ms. Elguero in effect creates individualized goals for each student.

Other big goals aspire to some absolute end that does not depend on where students start: Mr. Delhagen's determination that all his students would pass the Regents Global History Exam or Ms. Jones's vision that all her students would "read, write, do math, and behave like third graders" are examples of mastery goals that are independent of where students begin. Mastery goals, of

▶ **DOES THE GOAL GRAB YOU IN THE GUT?**

**A COMMON QUALITY** of effective big goals is that they are exciting to both the students and the teacher. Not only did Ms. Jones's goals bring alignment and urgency to her and her students' efforts, but her students were also inspired by the idea that their academic skills and behavior would compete with the big kids upstairs. As Collins and Porras found in their studies of extraordinarily successful organizations, the best big goals are those that constituents instantly understand and that "reach out and grab them in the gut."[33]

Big goals prove to be critical motivators in the face of great difficulty. In fact, one extensive study of leadership found that clear big goals are especially important for helping people stay the course when the leader and organization faced tough challenges.[34]

In our context, the power of big goals to sustain effort is hugely important given the debilitating challenges we may face in our quest to put our students on a new academic track. The harsh reality is that some (certainly not all) of the schools where the achievement gap is most prominent are dysfunctional settings. We may face unforeseen surprises (perhaps five more students have just been assigned to your classroom in the middle of the semester), exhaustion (perhaps neither you nor your students slept enough last night), disruptive administrative demands (perhaps attendance records must be handed over halfway through your class), or seemingly impossible challenges (perhaps your eighth graders read on a third-grade level). Teachers working to change the life paths of children in low-income communities face potentially frustrating obstacles along the way. Highly effective teachers report that having the clear vision of victory down the road helps them keep all those daily challenges in perspective and keep working hard.

course, run the risk of underachievement for students who start the year ahead of others and may need to be individualized accordingly. Either a growth or a mastery model can be a powerful driver of student achievement. In our experience, the key is whether the teacher is asking, "Does this goal realistically maximize the potential for every student in the class?"

With either growth or mastery goals, individualization can sometimes be an effective substrategy of setting big goals. As Sara Egli, a teacher in Phoenix, explains:

"Each month I update the personalized big goal signs on each student's desk. Juan's February goals were to read ninety-two words in one minute and to count by threes to ninety-nine. George was working on reading eighteen words in one minute, and counting by ones to fifty. They each met both goals. It was pretty powerful to see Juan and George stand in front of the class to receive their class cheer together last week. Both students beamed with pride as their peers congratulated them. . . . Class averages are great in some situations, but I know that personalized monthly big goals have kept both of these students motivated to work hard to achieve."

## ▶ BELIEVING IN OUR GOALS EVEN WHEN WE MISS THEM

**MARTIN WINCHESTER, AN AWARD-WINNING** veteran teacher in the Rio Grande Valley of Texas, sets a number of big goals for his students. Reaching one of those—that 100% of students will pass the state assessment—has just barely eluded him, but he has no regrets about setting it:

"In eleven years of teaching, I've had 99 percent of my students pass the state assessment four consecutive years in a row, and I've averaged 95 percent over the last six years, but never every single student. And you know, I'm proud of those numbers, and at the same time each year's failure truly, truly hurts. But you know what? At the beginning of every one of those years, and at the beginning of every year I teach, I honestly believed and will believe that THIS is the year we're going to get every single one of them to pass the test on the first take. Seriously, I've never described that goal to my students without absolutely, completely believing we were going to get there. How could I ever be satisfied with aiming for 90 percent or 95 percent passing? . . . Sure, there are days in the year when I struggle with doubts, but when that happens, I reach deep inside myself and make myself believe we're going to do it. . . . I have to be able to look every one of my students in the eye and say with conviction that we can do this together. If I didn't believe it, even for one brief moment, they would see right through me."

Mr. Winchester believes that "90 percent of the value of the big goal is the motivating power of high expectations." In his experience, the value that comes from setting high expectations and acting on them, even if you don't quite meet your goal, far outweighs any damage that missing the goal can have—especially when the teacher is tracking and celebrating progress along the way. "The key to dramatic academic progress is students' belief in their own ability to do it," Mr. Winchester says. "The key to their belief in their own ability, is *my* belief in their ability. I'm going to keep setting ambitious goals knowing, in my heart, that we can and will reach them."

Whether you are individualizing student goals or not, the stakes in the difficult and imperfect search for an informed ambitiousness are high. If we underestimate the potential of our students to master rigorous content, we contribute to the low expectations that drive educational inequity in the first place. Yet setting a goal that is impossible for students to reach even with extraordinarily hard work might further undermine students' shaky confidence, cementing their impression that effort does not lead to achievement and that they are "not smart" enough to achieve in school.

Most of the highly effective teachers we work with acknowledge the heavy burden of those high stakes and difficult tensions. At the same time, they express a sense of empowerment and inspiration that comes from deciding on a vision and doing everything they can to lead students to it.

## Leading with Students' Needs and Interests

A teacher's vision of the future must also take into consideration students' visions of the future. The most effective big goals are those that build on students' desires and motivations. They have meaning in students' lives, even if the teacher has to do some work to ensure every student appreciates that meaning (see Chapter Two). As Mekia Love told us, "You have to really ask why those academic targets are so important to you and your kids, and the answers to that question will help shape how you articulate your big goals."

In their massive study of leadership across all sectors, Kouzes and Posner made this same observation: "What people really want to hear is not simply the leader's vision. They want to hear about their own aspirations. They want to hear how their dreams will come true and their hopes will be fulfilled. They want to see themselves in the picture of the future that the leader is painting. The very best leaders understand that their key task is inspiring shared vision, not selling their own idiosyncratic view of the world."[35]

Katie Pierce, a successful teacher in New York City, shared with us a story about an experience with her students' families that showed her the importance of seeking the meaning behind her big goals. When one of her students' fathers articulated the value of his child's learning to him and his family, Ms. Pierce realized that all the benefits of big goals are magnified when the goal is closely tied to students' deepest aspirations:

At the end of my first year I set up an awards ceremony for our "Academy of Scholars." I wanted to recognize my ESL social studies students for meeting our big goal that all students would reach at least 80 percent mastery of the state social studies standards. I was also celebrating the students in my Spanish class (for Spanish speakers) who had scored 80 or higher on all ten of their writing projects.

My coteacher and I had invited the students' families, and we all had a fabulous potluck dinner before the awards ceremony. Our "decorating crew" of students had the school cafeteria just covered in streamers, the tables set with tablecloths and confetti, and a big banner that read, "*Bienvenidos, estudiantes y familias.*" Families came bearing *pollo horneado* (baked chicken), *moro* (Dominican rice and beans dish), more *pollo horneado*, more rice and beans, *pozole mexicano*, salads and desserts. The students looked dashing in their dress clothes: Aiden in a three-piece suit; Sonali in a kid's-sized evening gown with her shoulders absolutely smothered in gold glitter. We listened to music, ate dinner, and took photo after photo after photo, before heading into the auditorium for the awards ceremony and poetry recitation performance by the students.

During the ceremony, one of my students' fathers asked if he could speak. He stood up and said, in Spanish, "I feel like so many people here look at us and think, 'They don't even speak English; they'll probably just stay cutting fruit to sell on the street.' And up until this year, I have always thought that my son would, like me, cut fruit for a living. But after this year, my son and I do not believe that. I believe that my son, and any child in this room, can go to any university he or she wishes to, and can become anyone he or she wishes to become. Thank you, teachers, for reminding us that our children's education is our future."

For me, that was the moment I started thinking of big goals as not just about meeting numerical targets but also about the reason for meeting those targets. I decided that what I really wanted the next year was for every parent to feel like that father did. I sat down to redesign my big goals so that by the end of the year, my students would deeply understand the connection between their education and whatever it is they want to become.

When teachers like Ms. Pierce and Ms. Love ask themselves, "Why are these accomplishments important?" they uncover context and meaning that actually shapes their vision of what must be accomplished, making the resulting big goal all the more powerful for their students. In the words of Kouzes and Posner about all successful leaders, "They liberate the vision that's already in their constituents. They awaken dreams, breathe life into them, and arouse the belief that we can achieve something grand."[36]

# The Qualities of Effective Big Goals in Action

When a teacher combines the urgency and focus of measurable outputs with the motivation of high expectations with the direct relevance of students' interests and needs, the teacher creates a big goal that drives extraordinary accomplishments. The remainder of this chapter will revisit these ideas from the perspective of the highly effective teachers who are implementing them for the benefit of their students.

As a starting point for parsing and exploring those qualities as they play out in designing big goals, we will share how Gillette Eckler, a highly effective fourth-grade teacher in Brooklyn, approached the vision-setting process.

**WHEN GILLETTE ECKLER MET HER FOURTH GRADERS** in Brooklyn on the first day of school, they were reading, on average, on a second-grade level. In math, her students were even further behind, unable to add and subtract numbers of more than one digit. According to state standards, they should have been learning multiple methods of multiplying two-digit numbers by two-digit numbers.[37]

*Ms. Eckler administered diagnostics to gauge her students' starting academic needs and strengths.*

Shocked and disturbed by those realities, Ms. Eckler took some time to reflect on her students' potential and the challenges facing them. She played out in her mind what was going to happen to her children if they stayed on their current academic path. Without aggressive intervention, her students would contribute to the ugly statistics that drove her to teach in the first place.

*Her thinking about her big goal is driven by her desire to have a meaningful impact in students' lives.*

Ms. Eckler determined that her students must master the reading, writing, and math skills that would open opportunities down the road. So she set out to gain a thorough understanding of what academic skills her children needed and what skills they lacked. She studied her district's learning standards, as well as her students' diagnostic assessments and records of previous academic performance. Ms. Eckler reached out to veteran teachers who had had success with teaching literacy in her school.

Ms. Eckler also recognized that while dramatic academic growth was a critical element of broadening her students' choices in life, it would not be enough if she wanted

*She consults the standards and veteran teachers to gain an understanding of what would be ambitious for her students.*

to put her students on a path to greater opportunities. She saw that her students and their families lacked knowledge of and access to the often complicated admissions processes for high-performing magnet, charter, and private schools that are available to students in wealthier neighborhoods. She was bothered by the reality that her students were not on track to attend special schools for visual arts, theater, music, dance, technology, mathematics, science, and other specific studies that students from other neighborhoods had access to. She saw that her students needed not only academic skills but bureaucratic and political access to the opportunities those skills could generate. In Ms. Eckler's words:

*Ms. Eckler thinks about the particular pathways to opportunity in front of her students.*

"My students deserve the best educational opportunities. . . . I want my students to make educated choices about furthering their schooling. These schools provide my students with challenging, hard-working, structured environments where they can pursue specific talents and interests or determine what those talents and interests are and be on the college-bound track in life. They provide extracurricular activities such as drama clubs, choirs, orchestras, sports teams such as running and soccer clubs, robotics, filmmaking, and so on, to provide a well-rounded education that focuses on all aspects of student achievement. These are the schools that my students deserve to know about and have the chance to attend, the path on which they deserve to travel.

> Her thinking about big goals is driven by her belief in their potential to succeed.

This vision of an alternate future for her students became Ms. Eckler's big goal. She committed to creating a new reality in which students would gain academic skills, the administrative knowledge and access, and the self-confidence and perseverance they needed to compete for prestigious middle schools. She set clear, measurable targets for her students' mastery of the state math standards. She determined that each student in her class would advance nine reading levels on the system her school used to calibrate reading passages (a gain that was the equivalent of well over two years of reading growth). She pledged that her students would have opportunities to attend excellent middle schools across the city.

> She ensures that her students' growth toward the goal will be measurable and transparent.

With this vision in mind, Ms. Eckler entered her classroom energized, focused, and in a hurry. She laid out her vision to her students, investing them in the opportunities that would come with achieving those aims. Ms. Eckler recalls that while her students were inherently motivated by the idea of competing for admission to top middle schools, she was careful and methodical in developing each student's "nine levels growth" reading goal. During the first week, she individually diagnosed each child's skills and met with that child to set short-term goals for moving up one reading level. As students came to understand how the system worked and how much work was necessary to move up a level, she rallied them around the ambitious target of advancing nine levels. In time, her students became as fired up as she was.

> Ms. Eckler taps into students' existing desire to attend top middle schools.

Not surprisingly, Ms. Eckler's clear vision of success for her students drove every decision and strategy in her classroom. She and her students created systems for tracking and celebrating their progress. She invested her students' families in the goals and the work it would take to achieve them. A palpable sense of urgency overtook her classroom.

> She recognizes that students' families must be invested in the big goal.

*(continued on next page)*

In that goal-driven arena, Ms. Eckler's students exceeded all expectations. Not only did her fourth graders grow an average of over two years in reading in just one year, not only did every single student pass the English Language Arts New York State Exam, and not only did the students end the year with 90.08 percent mastery of state math objectives, but after Ms. Eckler convinced her principal to let her move with her students to the fifth grade, their rate of progress continued for another year, and many of her students left her classroom ahead of grade level. Meanwhile, true to her goal, Ms. Eckler became an expert on middle school admissions processes, shepherding each of her students through the Byzantine time lines and paperwork (and even obtaining extensions for her students when a key deadline for some schools was changed but communicated to her students' families on short notice).

Because Ms. Eckler developed a clear vision of success, her students were able to work toward and reach it. They went on to compete for and attend some of the most prestigious and demanding middle schools in New York, including the Academy of Arts and Letters, Philippa Schuyler Middle School, the Eagle Academy for Boys, and other Gifted and Talented and science and tech schools.

By methodically building a big goal that will have a meaningful impact on students' lives, Ms. Eckler illustrates the key issues that all highly effective teachers consider as they set a vision of student success. Powerful big goals that meet the criteria of measurability, ambitiousness, and meaning are developed by considering four questions (Figure 1.1):

1. What measurable academic progress should my students achieve?

2. What traits, mindsets, and skills will best serve my students?

3. What pathways to opportunity are in front of my students that should inform the big goal?

4. What student interests and motivations could shape the big goal?

While every highly effective teacher we have worked with has strong academic aims in his or her big goals (academic achievement is, after all, our definition of "highly effective"), the other three questions are more and less emphasized by different teachers in different contexts. The fundamental tenets of big goal setting (measurability, high expectations, constituents' interests) appear throughout highly effective teachers' engagement with these questions.

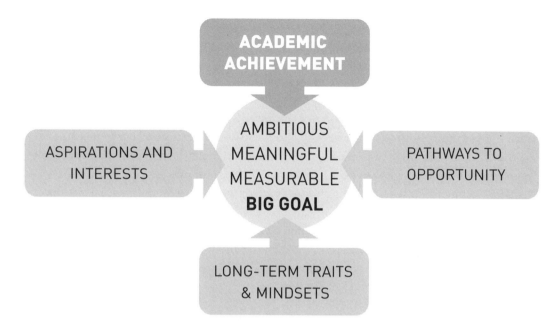

Figure 1.1  Considerations that Influence Big Goals

## What Measurable Academic Progress Should My Students Achieve?

In our experience, this question about measurable academic progress leads teachers to inform themselves about students' academic proficiency at the beginning of the year, deeply engage learning standards, understand where students on the other end of the achievement gap are performing, and develop ambitious and measurable targets for academic performance by the end of the year.

For example, Katie Hill, the North Carolina teacher whose middle school students with cognitive learning disabilities improved their literacy skills dramatically, navigated a number of challenges before the school year even began to understand what accomplishments should define success for her students. She began by studying the state's alternative learning standards for children in special education. (These are standards for the very small fraction of students—1 to 2 percent of all students, or 10 to 20 percent of students with disabilities—who are exempt from state testing requirements. The vast majority of students with disabilities are held accountable to the same general education standards as their peers in general education.) Ms. Hill supplemented her understanding of those alternative standards with a deep engagement of the general education standards for pre-K through third grade, on the theory that her incoming students would probably be relatively low functioning in terms of literacy and math and she needed to understand how the foundational learning goals all fit together.

Once she met her students, Ms. Hill invested considerable time diagnosing their knowledge and skills. Given that students' disabilities can sometimes lead to inconsistent performance on assessments, she repeated all diagnostic assessments three times to ensure she was getting an accurate picture of proficiency. She found her students were reading on average at a kindergarten to first-grade reading level. Some knew the letters of the alphabet but could give the sounds of only about 70 percent of the letters. None of her students could rhyme words. None could tell time. Some were able to identify different coins, but none could compare their values. Most of her students did not understand the concept of subtraction. To prepare herself to design well-informed big goals, Ms. Hill met with the students' families to understand their sense of their children's strengths and needs and their wishes for their children's functional goals.

For Ms. Hill, the key to her success was not, however, all of this preparation. "I think the most important thing I did was walk into the school year with the assumption and expectation that my students could and would learn," she says. "Immediately, I could see that my students had strong work ethics and an incredible desire to learn and succeed. I could not let

---

▶ **THREE WAYS TO MEASURE ACADEMIC PROGRESS**

*Academic growth.* Improvement in student skills from the beginning of the year to the end of the year. This measurement is most appropriate when the learning standards call for skill development (for example, in reading or writing or math) that builds along a continuous spectrum of growth.

*Learning goal mastery.* Attainment of grade-level expectations (mastery of standard). For some classrooms, especially where discrete knowledge of content is being taught rather than a spectrum of fundamental skills, mastery of X percent of content objectives serves as a useful learning target. (Sometimes for students with special needs, IEP goal mastery is used for these benchmarks.)

*Gap-Reduction Targets.* This refers to reducing the difference between the performance level of your students and the students in high-performing schools ("distance to high performers"). Where available data lend themselves to these comparisons, you may be able to view your students' academic achievement as compared to the academic achievement occurring in better-resourced schools in higher-income communities.

them down by setting the bar too low for them. After looking over their files and speaking with their parents extensively, I got a sense of how much they had learned in the past, how quickly, and what strategies worked."

With that information in mind, Ms. Hill was able to determine where her students fit on the broad continuum of learning outlined by the standards. And in the spirit of special education (and in a way that many highly effective teachers do in general education), she individualized students' math and writing goals around the aim of growing approximately 1.5-grade levels. She set out to revise her students IEPs to make sure they were appropriate and ambitious for each student: "In order to do so, I used lower elementary standards and North Carolina's Extended Content Standards to create a curriculum map that would allow me to place students on a spectrum of highly prioritized math and literacy standards that contribute to the future of my students' long-term transitional goals of independent living and employment."

Although she dramatically increased the rigor of all of her students' IEP goals as part of this goal-setting process, all of her students met those goals by halfway through the year. Under Ms. Hill's leadership, her students' academic growth in their first semester rivaled all the literacy and math progress they had made previously in all their years of school. As Ms. Hill explains, this progress meant that "I have had to revamp my big goal to ensure that it remains an ambitious and relevant goal for my students. I have done so by changing my students' IEP goals to move them further along the continuum and include more abstract math concepts, coupled with writing focused on content-specific subjects." Ms. Hill's approach reminds us that big goals serve as a target to drive urgency and focus, and if changing realities (like unprecedented student achievement) diminish the utility of the big goals in that regard, they may need to be adjusted.

Like Ms. Hill, but in the context of high school history, Mr. Delhagen also asked himself, "What academic achievement should define success for my students?" Facing the daunting reality that global history was usually taught over two years but that he was assigned to teach it in just one year, Mr. Delhagen set out to fully understand everything about the learning goals covered by the Regents Exam. After studying one copy of the exam, he recalls that his reaction was, "Whoa! This covers everything from the neolithic revolution to 9/11. This is a bus tour!" To help make sense of that massive breadth of history, Mr. Delhagen got his hands on fifteen past global history exams and made a spreadsheet to analyze the key ideas and themes of the course.

Mr. Delhagen made all of his investigation transparent to his students. Based on previous experience teaching and his consultations with his students, he decided that a goal of an 80 percent average and 100 percent passing on the exam would be challenging but realistic. He and his students called this goal the *quantitative goal*, and he discussed with them the benefits of having this hard target to "make it easy to see if we're on track."

▶ **COMMON PITFALLS TO AVOID WITH BIG GOALS**

| | |
|---|---|
| **"Set it and forget it"** | Big goals influence student performance only if they are made a central element of the classroom experience. In particular, you need to establish systems that make transparent your students' progress toward the big goal. (See Chapter Two.) |
| **Reflexive adoption of others' goals** | While you should not have to "reinvent the wheel," given all the considerations that inform big goals, you should bring your own thinking to whatever big goal models you borrow from others. |
| **"X percent of students will"** | Big goals must apply to all students. If your big goal gives you an incentive to underserve some fraction of the class, it is a bad big goal. |

This academic achievement also was part of Mr. Delhagen's consideration of his students' pathways to opportunity, as every student wanted to graduate from high school, and, since a prerequisite for graduation was passing the Regents Exam, his students were inherently motivated by the goal of success on the exam.

## What Traits and Mindsets Will Best Serve My Students?

Like all the other teachers featured in this chapter, Mr. Delhagen believed that his students needed and deserved even more than academic achievement. In his case, it was interactions with his students that sparked his commitment to add other trait and mindset goals to his determination that they would all pass the Regents Global History Exam.

As he studied the learning standards and assessments, Mr. Delhagen noticed a theme of the value of citizenship in human interactions and governance. That theme, he thought, was starkly juxtaposed with some of the behaviors and problems he was seeing in his school, especially among young men. Mr. Delhagen was particularly influenced by one student who came to him to discuss the disrespectful way some of his male classmates were acting toward female students. "That's not how good citizens behave," the student said.

Inspired by his students and the subject matter before him, Mr. Delhagen determined that his students would also learn to think, write, and speak like world citizens. Mr. Delhagen faced a Cleveland Orchestra problem. While on their face those aims were too vague to change student behavior and mindsets, Mr. Delhagen had in mind particular behaviors and mindsets he wanted to develop. He set out to involve his students in objectively defining them. Together he and his students designed an "accountable talk" rubric that delineated the qualities of world citizenship and offered specific indicators of students who are accountable to the learning community, to knowledge, and to rigorous thinking:

▶ **ACCOUNTABLE TALK: HOW WE ARE TALKING TO EACH OTHER**

| Accountable to Learning Community | Accountable to Knowledge | Accountable to Rigorous Thinking |
|---|---|---|
| **Students** | **Students** | **Students** |
| Are engaged in talk | Make use of specific and accurate knowledge | Use rational strategies to present arguments and draw conclusions |
| Are listening attentively to one another | Provide evidence for claims and arguments | Construct explanations and test understanding of concepts |
| Elaborate and build on ideas and each other's contributions | Recognize the kind of knowledge or framework required to address a topic | Challenge the quality of each other's reasoning |
| Ask each other questions aimed at clarifying or expanding a proposition | | |

By evaluating and tracking students' progress on these indicators, Mr. Delhagen so infused these values in the classroom that classroom management was effectively taken over by students who would ask each other questions from the accountable talk rubric when they got off task.

## What Pathways to Student Opportunity Should Inform My Big Goal?

Sometimes a particular academic milestone in a student's future influences the design of a big goal. Imagine that your students are scheduled to sit for an assessment that covers your class's subject matter and success on that assessment will influence students' educational opportunities. Most highly effective teachers would incorporate success on that assessment into their big goal design. For example, perhaps a certain score on a certain exam will make students competitive for high-performing middle schools (as was the case with Ms. Eckler's students), or perhaps achievement of certain ambitious language arts goals will move ESL students out of a remedial English track (as was the case with the students of Felicia Cuesta, an English teacher in Los Angeles), or perhaps high school sophomores' writing skills are not strong enough to write an exemplary college-level essay (as was the case in Eric Thomas's tenth-grade English class in Baltimore). These unique realities allow teachers to connect big goals to pathways of opportunity in their students' future.

Eric Scroggins led his eighth graders in the South Bronx to academic success that earned them high school credit and, for some students, scholarships to high-performing high schools.

He described his realization that the impact his students' learning could have on their future opportunities should shape his big goals:

> During the spring of my first year of teaching, I had dinner with the director of the science department for public schools in Scarsdale [a high-performing district in a well-resourced community] and learned that the eighth-grade science honor students there were expected to take the Earth Science Regents Exam at the end of the year. I knew that if those students did well on this test, they'd have different choices for high school, which would put them on a different track for college. I thought, "The kids on track to go to the best schools take the Earth Science Regents Exam in eighth grade, and that is what my kids will do." It became clear to me that equality for my students in the Bronx meant the opportunity to take this exam for high school credit.

While these landmark hurdles are less frequent in elementary school, the same idea applies. For example, some elementary teachers see that their students will be tracked into regular or honors classes starting in sixth grade. Or they see that their students with disabilities, or who are learning English as a Second Language, can earn their way onto different tracks with certain levels of performance. These teachers therefore look carefully at what level of performance is necessary for that particular trajectory and aim for it.

## What Student Interests and Motivations Could Shape the Big Goal?

Another implication of thinking about making big goals meaningful to students is considering what lights a fire for our students. Is there a way to connect our vision of ambitious achievement to students' desires so that we can instantly excite students about the big goal? (If so, the big goal will give you a jump-start on investing students in working hard toward accomplishing it, as discussed in Chapter Two.)

Some elementary school teachers leverage their students' intense, inherent desire to be thought of as "big kids." For Ms. Jones, a conversation with her students inspired this strategy.

Ms. Jones remembers thinking to herself that she wanted a big goal "that sounded a little crazy." She wanted to shake up her students and their families and inspire them to a big and meaningful achievement. Her first idea was to aim for one-and-a-half years of growth for each student, but as she talked to her students about that goal, she knew that *she* was excited about it but her students had no idea what she was talking about. She wanted a goal they could understand and own themselves, and that really excited them.

A few weeks into school, she hosted a "town hall" meeting with her students.

"We're going to talk about all of the amazing things we are going to learn this year, but first I want to hear from you all. So tell me, how smart do you all want to get this year?" she asked her first graders.

One girl stood up beside her desk, put her hands on her hips, and announced, "I want to be a third grader!"

The rest of the class erupted with oohs and aahs. Every head in the room was nodding excitedly.

"Why?" Ms. Jones asked. "Why do you want to be third graders?"

The whole class began to speak at once. It turns out that many of her students had older siblings, and all of her students watched the older kids with great admiration and envy. One student, who had a sister in third grade, explained, "Upstairs [where the third grade is] they read books, and they do math."

Again, the room erupted with excited affirmation of that assessment. These children desperately wanted to be like those older kids.

Reflecting on that conversation, Ms. Jones realized that her "crazy" goal could be to turn her first graders into third graders. But she had a lot of questions to answer first. What do students have to be able to do to begin third grade? What are the reading, writing, and math skills that indicate students are "third graders"? Ms. Jones dug into the Georgia state performance standards for first and second grades. She huddled with her teaching coach and other veteran teachers. She asked for a meeting with an excellent third-grade teacher at her school, who agreed to advise Ms. Jones on how to alter her teaching materials so they prepared students for third grade. She obtained and studied the state assessments for second and third grades.

Ultimately, Ms. Jones learned that getting students to a third-grade level—instead of merely a second-grade level—usually meant increased depth on a discrete list of skills, rather than teaching additional skills. That is, instead of just teaching number sense to the tens place, she would need to go to the thousandths place. Instead of teaching students to write sentences, she would need to teach them to write a series of sentences to make paragraphs. For each of the concepts in her first-grade curriculum, she looked at the second- and third-grade versions and pushed her planning further.

Through this exploration, Ms. Jones came to believe that a big goal around getting her children, most of whom were performing below first-grade level, ready for third grade was in fact "crazy." But she also became convinced that that vision was in fact possible. It was going to require very hard work, but she found the idea intensely motivating for herself, not to mention the students. When she unveiled this new big goal to the children, they were overwhelmed with excited pride. They were inspired to do whatever Ms. Jones asked if she could make them third graders.

We see similar patterns among other strong teachers in all grade levels and subject matter. Some secondary teachers work with their students' inclination to respond to peer pressure, using both a sense of team and a sense of competition (perhaps with a well-resourced rival school, for example) to frame academic achievement. One high school teacher, Chris Ott, established a "competition" with eighth graders' performance in the United Kingdom. Some special education teachers hook into a student's interest in an inclusion or mainstream setting, connecting academic accomplishment

> The Teaching As Leadership rubric (see Appendix A) describes the specific teacher actions that indicate a teacher is setting big goals.

to opportunities for autonomy and responsibility. Those are just a few of many examples of ways that teachers draw on the inherent motivations of their students to shape their big goals.

# Conclusion: Key Ideas and Next Questions

## Key Ideas

In our experience, highly effective teachers believe these key ideas are a foundation for leading students to overcome great odds and make dramatic academic achievement:

- Effective big goals draw on three principles of strong leadership: an insistence on measurable outcomes, expecting the best of those around you, and informing your vision with the aspirations of your constituents.

- Big goals maximize student learning by aligning the effort of the teacher, students, and their families and by bringing urgency and focus to learning. Well-designed big goals can be inspiring and motivating to teachers and students.

- Effective big goals are measurable, ambitious, and meaningful to students' lives.

- The core academic element of any big goal must be aligned with rigorous learning standards.

- Highly effective teachers develop their big goals by asking themselves several questions:

  ○ What measurable academic progress should my students achieve?

  ○ What measurable traits, mindsets, and skills will best serve my students?

  ○ What pathways to opportunity are in front of my students that should inform the big goal?

  ○ What student interests and motivations could shape the big goal?

---

 teachingasleadership.org

The Teaching As Leadership rubric articulates indicators of effective goal setting. More guidance on how to develop big goals is available online, including:

- Additional specific indicators of strong big goals

- Annotated examples of effective big goals from a variety of grades and subject matter

- Common pitfalls that often trip up new teachers as they are designing big goals

## Next Questions

With these ideas in mind, you are ready to consider a whole range of critically important questions for the benefit of your students:

- How can I access and digest the learning standards that apply to my students, and how do those standards shape my vision for my students' success?

- What are the concrete connections between my students' academic achievement and broadened opportunities, and how should those connections inform my goal setting?

- How should I evaluate or design assessments that will ensure my students have met the big goal? How can I ensure that my assessments are rigorous and reflect the full extent of my students' progress? (See Chapter Three.)

- What sorts of big goals have teachers in my grade and subject area used with success, and how might those be applicable or not applicable for my students?

- How can I ensure that each of my students individually feels the benefits (in terms of urgency, focus, inspiration, clarity) of my classwide big goals?

## "WHY DO PEOPLE SET BIG GOALS?"

 teachingasleadership.org

*An excerpt from Ms. Lora's Story, a case study in Teaching As Leadership, available online at www.teachingasleadership.org.*

"Lourdes, would you mind sharing what you wrote in your journal this morning?"

As she often did, Lourdes raised her hand even though she had just been called on. She then lowered her hand and read quietly, "My goal is to be a doctor or a dancer. My sister's goal is to be a police but not mine."

"Thank you, Lourdes. Chris, would you share your journal entry with us?"

Ms. Lora tried to alternate between stronger and weaker writers.

"My goal is to be a boxer. I made my goal already, but I want to be a real boxer. I will practice a lot and will training-box with my uncle this summer."

Ms. Lora elicited several other examples. Beto's goal was to "play soccer so good I get paid." Tanya, standing by her desk and in a voice much louder than necessary, offered that her goal was to be a veterinarian.

After a few minutes, as she had promised, Ms. Lora read her own entry to the class. The students listened intently. They were naturally hungry for information about their teacher's personal interests.

"My goal is to become a student again," Ms. Lora read from her own tattered spiral notebook. "I would like to return to school to learn about being a principal, like Dr. Werner, or a superintendent, like Dr. Page. A principal is a boss of teachers, and a superintendent is a boss of principals. I think my biggest goal is to be a student at Harvard University. Harvard is a college in Massachusetts. In high school, I always dreamed of going to Harvard, but I lacked confidence and never did apply. Now I regret that I did not try to go there. Even if I had not gotten into Harvard, I wish I had tried. After I have been a teacher for a few years, I might apply to Harvard or some other school to learn to become a principal or a superintendent."

After briefly entertaining several questions from the students about Harvard ("Is it far away?" "Does it have a football team?" "What do people eat there?"), Ms. Lora began what she had come to consider the most important conversation in each of her years of teaching. Over the course of several weeks at the beginning of the school year, she discussed with the students the importance of setting and working toward goals. And she had discovered that it was vitally important, and immensely rewarding, to actually teach those ideas—just like any other difficult academic objective.

"Can anyone tell me why he or she thinks people set goals?" she asked. Several hands slowly rose. "Yes, Jasmine. What do you think? Why do people set goals?"

For the next fifteen minutes, and each day during the next few weeks, Ms. Lora would start the long road to indoctrinating her students into a goal-oriented mindset. She moved slowly and stopped frequently at concrete examples, but she kept her students' minds thinking about ideas like tracking their progress toward a goal, pacing that progress, and working hard every day to reach that goal. Drawing on the students' own examples, she emphasized the hard work and focus that it would take to become a doctor, a dancer, a boxer, a lawyer, a soccer player, a firefighter, and a teacher. Students drew "challenge maps" to articulate the obstacles they might encounter on the way to reaching their goals. They added the words *ambitious, realistic, and persistence* to the class word wall. Hilario offered that the Blair Elementary Learner's Creed was a kind of goal that you set every day. The excitement about setting and achieving goals gradually built, stoked by Ms. Lora's excited anticipation for the day when, as a class and individually, they would set their own academic goals for the year.

This morning, Ms. Lora's objective was just to plant the seed of need. She wanted her students to start to feel that without a clear goal, they would be lost.

"That's great thinking, Jasmine," she said. "You're right. Some people set goals so they can know when they are finished. Let's think of some examples of that idea. Can anyone tell me about a situation in which people might like to have a clear goal so they know when they are finished working hard?"

# 2

# Invest Students and Their Families

**HIGHLY EFFECTIVE TEACHERS** invest students in working hard for extraordinary academic achievement. With the help of students' families and other influencers, these teachers convince their students that they can reach their big goals if they work hard enough, and that doing so will make a real difference in their lives.

SET BIG GOALS 1

INVEST STUDENTS AND THEIR FAMILIES 2

PLAN PURPOSEFULLY 3

EXECUTE EFFECTIVELY 4

CONTINUOUSLY INCREASE EFFECTIVENESS 5

WORK RELENTLESSLY 6

**Brian Wallace,**
Fourth-Grade Self-
Contained Special
Education, New York

*"Nothing was going to hold her back from getting there—even me."*

**I'LL NEVER FORGET THE** way that Melia used to beg me to reassess her reading level, even if the next assessment wasn't scheduled for another month. Every time she would improve her time on a fluency passage or successfully decode an unfamiliar word, she would say, "See, Mr. Wallace? I'm ready to move up another level. Get out the stuff and test me now." Melia was so invested in becoming a stronger reader and so invested in meeting her goal that absolutely nothing was going to hold her back from getting there—even me. But this didn't just happen on its own. It took constant reinforcement of her efforts, setting small and attainable benchmarks along the way that would allow her to experience success, giving targeted and meaningful praise, and really celebrating even the smallest step toward the goal.

*"The progress and urgency in the classroom built to a fever pitch."*

**I DID EVERYTHING I** could to invest my students in working hard to succeed. I built strong relationships with my students, and they called my home phone nightly to talk through homework problems or share stories about our lives. We talked about the value of hard work, and I talked to them about the achievement gap. We rallied around the idea that we would prove the world wrong. I modeled the hard work I wanted to see in them: I was often the first to school and the last to leave. I taught my students on Saturdays. We entered science fairs and state-sponsored reading, writing, and math competitions. The progress and urgency in the classroom built to a fever pitch. I saw my fourth and fifth graders "tutoring" each other. They were not just making great progress; they demanded more.

On the day our state test scores came back, every child watched as I opened the envelope. When I told them—a group of students who had been, in effect, academic kindergartners, first graders, and second graders the year before—that they were on grade level in literacy and over half-a-year *ahead* in their math skills, absolute pandemonium ensued. It was a highlight of my life.

And then one student quieted us all down to point out a harsh reality. "But, Mr. Griffith," Darnell said, "isn't that where we were supposed to be all along? We worked so hard, and we did everything just to catch up. We're not even far ahead. I don't get why we are celebrating. We are just as smart as all those other kids that we faced in all those competitions, but we didn't know it before." As hard as it was to hear that truth, I knew in that moment that these kids *got it.* They were going to keep working hard.

**Kwame Griffith,**
Fourth and Fifth
Grades, Texas

*"Over the next month, I revised my whole-class investment system and also implemented an individual investment system for Joanna. The results were tremendous."*

**JOANNA WAS** . . . disruptive during whole group lessons, mean to other students, and outwardly defiant toward adults. I realized that in order for Joanna to make progress and meet our big goals, she needed . . . to understand what she was learning and why she was learning it. Over the next month, I revised my whole-class investment system and also implemented an individual investment system for Joanna. The results were tremendous; not only was Joanna thrilled to earn balloons by working hard in our class system and "Hello Kitty" stickers by working hard on her own investment system, but she also truly understood the concept of hard work. Soon, when she became disruptive, all I had to say was, "Joanna, you need to work hard so that you can learn," and she would immediately fix her behavior. I knew she had completely internalized the message when one day on the carpet, she turned to a peer who was being disruptive and said, "C'mon, Matt! Sit up so that you can learn!" and Matt immediately fixed his behavior.

**Jennifer Rosenbaum,**
Prekindergarten,
Washington, D.C.

**Erin Wahler,** Fifth
Grade, New Mexico

*"What a long way my students had come."*

**AS I TURNED AROUND** from writing the day's math objective on the board, I noticed a student's empty seat. I knew no one was absent today, so I glanced around the room and saw Jarod approaching the classroom consequence chart.

"Ms. Wahler," he said, "I can't find my problems-of-the week sheet." As he said this, he moved his clip from "ready to learn!" to "need to focus" on the expectations chart, unprompted! "I know I'm not prepared, but I'll look at Orlando's sheet until I find mine," Jarod explained.

What a long way my students had come from having consequences applied by the teacher when a rule is broken. I now see consistent evidence that students are monitoring their own behavior, accepting responsibility for mistakes, and finding ways to solve problems in a continuous effort to achieve their goals.

Outraged by a statistic that only one in ten of his students is likely to graduate from college, Joseph Almeida insists that his fifth graders in New York will both catch up academically and

come to *expect* to attend college just like kids in wealthier neighborhoods. He welcomes them on the first day of school by handing them a mock college acceptance letter as "Pomp and Circumstance" fills the room. Soon he has his students writing real letters to real admissions officers at the nation's top universities, and his students are thrilled to receive personal responses of encouragement from schools like Harvard, Yale, Stanford, and Princeton. To cement his vision of success in his students, Mr. Almeida took his fifth graders to Georgetown University in Washington, D.C., where they attended classes, met with professors, and toured the dorms.

**Joseph Almeida,** Fifth Grade, New York

Back at school, Mr. Almeida established a monthly Parents' Learning Night, conducted in Spanish and English, to preview class content for families. He makes about twenty calls each week to parents to celebrate their children's progress and accomplishments, thereby fostering a reinforcing web of support around his students. As Mr. Almeida's students adopted his vision as their own, they began to work harder and achieve more than they ever had before. He celebrated that hard work by taking them bowling, to Madison Square Garden for basketball games, and to a jazz concert at the Apollo Theater.

By the end of the year, Mr. Almeida's students earned the highest average in the school on the statewide mathematics test and second-highest English/language arts scores. One student's mother wrote a note to him:

> For some time now, [my son] and I have been talking about college. He wants to attend Georgetown, I want him to stay closer to home. . . . Going to Georgetown and seeing all the possibilities that lay ahead for my son has driven me to become a better parent. I promise that I will work even harder towards his educational success. . . . If every teacher were like you the possibilities would be endless for every student.

"Investing our students" means developing their desire for academic success and their belief in their ability to achieve it. In highly effective teachers' classrooms like Mr. Almeida's, we see students who have adopted ambitious goals as their own and are working with intense urgency and focus to succeed in school. We see students who, like their teachers, are on a mission to catch up with students in wealthier neighborhoods and to access the opportunities that too often are out of their reach. We see teachers who ensure their students are invested in working hard to learn. We see leaders who recognize that their own success depends on constituents' sharing not just the leader's vision but also the leader's motivation to reach the ambitious goals.

Mr. Almeida and leaders like him demonstrate not only the power of fully investing students in striving for ambitious goals but also the variety of strategies that drive that investment. In our experience, the most successful teachers are those who build strong personal relationships based on trust and high expectations, model and market the hard work necessary to achieve the big goals, and deliberately create a community of support and encouragement to drive individuals' effort.

# Key Elements of Investment

We have studied the actions of teachers whose students monitor and manage their own behavior, bemoan an unexpected loss of learning time, and on their own initiative reach out to help their classmates learn. In our experience, these teachers share two general mindsets about investing students.

First, these teachers take responsibility for convincing students they can and want to learn. These teachers recognize that their big goals will remain out of reach if their students do not see the value in academic achievement and that hard work will lead to success. Second, these teachers, like all other strong leaders, expand their influence on their students by ensuring that students' families, coaches, other teachers, religious leaders, and any other influencers are all aligned in building students' investment. Highly effective teachers recognize that achieving the big goal is too big a task to take on alone and that students are most likely to change their beliefs and behavior when they hear consistent messages in all facets of their lives.

## Shaping Students' Mindsets

*If you want to build a ship, don't herd people together to collect wood and don't assign them tasks and work, but rather teach them to long for the endless immensity of the sea.*

— Antoine de Saint-Exupéry, aviation pioneer and author

Many highly successful teachers (and education experts) boil the idea of student investment down to two factors: students' belief that they are *able* to achieve at high levels alongside their *desire* to do so.[1] Stated more simply,

Student investment = "I can" × "I want"

For any endeavor, consciously or not, students are asking themselves, "Can I do this?" and "Do I want to do this?"[2] Your responsibility is to be sure that every student answers yes to both questions. When your students internalize those perspectives and become invested in working hard to reach ambitious goals, they are not only receptive to, but also eager for, instructional leadership. With invested students, your potential for influence expands dramatically. With uninvested students, your efforts will lead to very little learning.

Leading our students to realize they can and want to achieve may be challenging. Those who take on and win this battle for the hearts and minds of their students treat that quest as a major undertaking, on the order of instructional planning or classroom management, and a task worthy of careful planning and considerable attention.

### Why Some Students Resist Investment

Working as a teacher in a low-income community often means serving many students who have experienced little previous success in school. It means working with students who, even at a young age, realize their academic skills are lagging. It means working with students who themselves live in a smog of low expectations—the same smog that threatens to degrade our own belief in our students' ability to succeed.

Our students frequently hear and see negative representations of people who share important elements of their identity: race, socioeconomic status, culture, or language. Rather than the high expectations that we know drive high performance, "children may bring to the classroom a lifetime of being told that they are failures, or even worse, that they are developmentally disabled."[3] These realities can lead students to be resistant to or dismissive of committing to the hard work necessary for dramatic achievement. Stephanie Crement, a reading specialist in East Palo Alto, California, shared the view of many new teachers when she said, "Before entering my classroom, I knew that low expectations and negative stereotypes for my students existed, but I was surprised by the extent to which my students had internalized them."

**RESEARCHER CLAUDE STEELE FOUND** in a series of experiments that African American students score lower on tests they are told are tests of intellectual ability. He calls this phenomenon "stereotype threat" and suggests that when a student experiences the additional anxiety of validating others' negative expectations, students' performance is diminished.[4] The same "stereotype threat" has been found to affect white males who—cognizant of the stereotype that Asian Americans perform well academically—tend to perform less well when given a test in a room full of Asian Americans.[5]

Virtually every teacher we have worked with has stories like one shared by Jessica Hancox, a third-grade teacher in North Carolina. Ms. Hancox had a student, Paul, who some had said was "unteachable." Paul had been expelled from two schools for misbehavior and was not only years behind academically but also years older than the other students in his grade. Paul had interpreted his experiences to mean that no amount of effort would change his level of success in school, an interpretation that Ms. Hancox believes was understandable given those circumstances.

Ms. Hancox determined that changing Paul's mindset and convincing him that he could in fact succeed with hard work was essential to bringing him out of his defensive stance. Using a variety of investment strategies that will be explored in this chapter (like graphing progress, making connections between the work and the rest of a student's life, and emphasizing key messages around effort and success), Ms. Hancox worked to alter the way Paul thought about school. She sought every opportunity to show him how his hard work was paying off.

"I can still remember the smile he tried to hide when he got his first 100 percent on an assessment in my class," she says, and goes on to add:

> He ultimately began to realize that the more effort he put in, the more successful he'd be in class. He was an extremely bright student, and accomplished a lot academically once he realized his potential for doing so. He ultimately earned one of the highest test scores [on the state assessment] in the entire grade that year . . . all because he learned to believe in himself.

Ms. Hancox's student responded to his previous lack of success in school by acting out and convincing himself that academic success was beyond his reach anyway. Other students, like a particularly withdrawn girl in Anne Lyneis's second-grade class in Louisiana, respond differently to similar experiences. At first, Ms. Lyneis's student seems nothing like Paul, but when we look more closely, we see that the two students present the same debilitating mindset. Ms. Lyneis recalls:

> I remember the first day of school when Hannah's mom came to meet with me. She explained that Hannah had repeated the first grade two times and still couldn't read. Her mom asked about referring her to special education. . . . Hannah was a shy, timid girl—a girl whose desire to learn had been crushed by so much failure. She never participated, she rarely asked for help, and she was insecure about everything that she did. And her mom was right; she was entering the second grade on a beginning-of-first-grade reading level.
>
> Over the first few weeks of school, I spent a lot of time getting to know Hannah. I was able to figure out through diagnostics exactly what she needed to learn so that I could teach her something that she could be successful with. I would ask her questions during read-aloud or math in order to build her self-confidence. Slowly, with success, Hannah started to become more confident with herself and believed she could do it. She was eager to pick out books from the basket I had set aside for her because she could successfully read them. She no longer participated just when I called on her for questions I knew she could answer, but she always raised her hand and didn't shy away when she got answers wrong.
>
> Her mom called a few months into school explaining how much of a difference she noticed in her daughter, how confident she was with everything she did at home, and how proud she was of her. A few weeks later when I called her back to share with her that Hannah had grown 1.45 years in reading skills in the first six months of school and was now reading on a second-grade level, her mother started to cry.

Ultimately both Ms. Hancox's and Ms. Lyneis's stories are about the power of high expectations: a teacher who expects more from students gets more from them.

These two stories represent a sadly prevalent theme we have seen with students who are performing far behind their potential. All too often, our students' educational experiences are influenced by low expectations, failed efforts, and unsupported academic struggles. Sometimes those realities have backed them into a self-protective psychological posture. Rather than feel responsible for their low performance, these students have adopted an alternative perspective: that they simply cannot learn. Such students may, consciously or not, be telling themselves, "The world is made up of kids who are good at school and kids who are bad at school. I am bad at school. There is nothing I can do about it." Our students sometimes find sanctuary in these debilitating thoughts.

A tendency of students who are academically underperforming to see themselves as inherently "bad at school" is well documented by educational psychologists and researchers and has profound implications for our work with children on the low end of the achievement gap.[6] Children who work hard and achieve academic success are inclined to be those who view ability or intelligence as a malleable quality. That is, they see intelligence as something you earn, not something you are. These students are therefore more likely to tackle risky, challenging tasks and rebound from failures by redoubling their efforts.[7] Conversely, low achievers usually see their ability as fixed, and thus they tend to choose easier assignments and be less resilient about failures.

Carol Dweck, an expert on student motivation theory, describes the two opposing theories of intelligence. A theory of fixed intelligence, she says, can make students more worried about looking smart than actually learning:

> Effort, difficulty, setbacks, or higher-performing peers call their intelligence into question—even for those who have high confidence in their intelligence. In fact, students [who believe in fixed intelligence] will readily pass up valuable learning opportunities if these opportunities might reveal inadequacies or entail errors—and they readily disengage from tasks that pose obstacles, even if they were pursuing them successfully shortly before.[8]

Meanwhile, other students hold the opposing view of intelligence: that it is malleable. From that perspective, "intelligence is not a fixed trait they simply possess, but something they can cultivate through learning," so students want to learn. "Why waste time worrying

▶ **STUDENTS WHO BELIEVE INTELLIGENCE IS. . .**

| Fixed | Malleable |
|---|---|
| Do not believe hard work correlates with success | Believe "smart" is earned with hard work |
| Choose easier assignments | Are more likely to tackle challenges |
| Give up when they fail | Learn from mistakes |

about looking smart or dumb, when you could be becoming smarter?" explains Dweck. "And in fact students with this view will readily sacrifice opportunities to look smart in favor of opportunities to learn something new." For these students, becoming smarter means "engaging fully in new tasks, exerting effort to master something, stretching their skills, and putting their knowledge to good use."[9]

One of Dweck's experiments brings these contrasting worldviews to life in the same way they come to life in classrooms. Fifth graders were given a set of solvable problems, followed by a set of problems far too difficult for students their age. The students' responses to the second set of problems fell into two categories, mirroring the two theories of intelligence. One group of children, whom psychological tests showed to believe intelligence is fixed, became sullen, frustrated, and critical of their abilities, making statements like, "I never had a very good memory"—despite the fact that they had experienced a string of successes just a few moments earlier. The second group of children, who believed intelligence is malleable, gave themselves pep talks, issued themselves self-pacing instructions ("slow down and you'll get it"), tried to apply strategies from previous problems, and made self-motivating statements like "I love a challenge" and "mistakes are our friend." When all the students were faced with new, manageably difficult problems, the first group of students, now impaired by feelings of incompetence, were much less likely to try to solve the problems than the other children.[10]

> ▶ **INSTILLING BELIEF IN MALLEABLE INTELLIGENCE**
>
> **YOU WILL LIKELY NEED** to transform some, and maybe many, students' mindsets from a fixed intelligence perspective to a malleable intelligence perspective—a responsibility that arises in small and large ways every day:
>
> - Rather than praising students for being "naturally good" at something, successful teachers praise children for "learning" and for their great effort, and then they celebrate the accomplishments of that effort.
> - Instead of making statements like "You have a good memory," these teachers emphasize that students "listened carefully."
> - Instead of just talking about effort, these teachers quantify (and sometimes even graph) students' efforts, creating structures in their classroom systems that surround the students with this idea that effort leads to success.
>
> In fact, many of the highly successful teachers we studied explicitly discuss, in age-appropriate ways, malleable intelligence with their students. For example, they might talk about the brain as a tool that must be exercised and developed. Experts recommend the same approach: "Teach students about the dynamics of motivation and how those dynamics affect them."[11]

Clearly these insights have implications for a teacher whose children have experienced little previous success in school. One researcher summarized those implications:

> If students believe their failures occur for a lack of trying, then they are more likely to remain optimistic about succeeding in the future. For another thing, trying hard is known to increase pride in success and to offset feelings of guilt at having failed. And, perhaps, most important of all, the emphasis on the role of effort in achievement is justified because it is widely believed that student effort is modifiable through the actions of teachers.[12]

## Collaborating with Students' Families and Influencers

Highly effective teachers also recognize that changing students' beliefs about learning requires the help of other influential people in students' lives—influencers such as coaches, ministers, friends, and other teachers. To maximize students' learning, these teachers invest families and other influencers in helping students work toward the big goal. Collaborating with such partners, these teachers create a network of well-aligned messages that reinforce the benefits of hard work and the value of achieving the big goal.

Atlanta teacher Tanya Morgan Dixon embodied this idea when she rallied her students' families in response to the difficult news that many of her ninth graders were failing. The following reflection, originally published in a teacher newsletter, introduces some of the strategies and perspectives of teachers who increase student learning by involving students' families in their classrooms:

> At the end of the first term of the . . . academic school year, more than half of my ninth-grade students were failing at least three core classes. Twenty-two out of twenty-four students in my homeroom were failing science. Nearly all of the students felt defeated by the academic standards and social responsibility of high school.
>
> On Tuesday afternoon the four teachers of my ninth-grade team met for our routine paperwork and logistics sessions. Although this Tuesday's meeting was extremely productive, it was far from routine. All four teachers, including myself, brandished cracked smiles atop broken ambition. We were all cordial but noticeably downtrodden. The mid-term grades had definitely had an effect on us. After fifteen minutes of formalities, I rolled backward and sighed, "We're failing."
>
> After several minutes of superfluous blame, targeting the "system," the eighth-grade teachers, and even society at large, our concern and professional responsibility led to productive brainstorming. We decided to try an emergency parents' meeting. This plan was ambitious because the previous meeting yielded 2 out of 120 parents. Although we faced the monsters of complacency, discouragement, and inflexible work schedules, we were determined to try and initiate change.

First, we produced a list of students in jeopardy of failure, then mailed letters to parents and sent letters home with students that simply read, "Your child is failing the ninth grade." We then called every parent and gave them an option of a daytime meeting or an evening meeting. Our hard work paid off. We had two meetings full of concerned members of our community.

The meetings were conducted like town hall meetings. We had mothers, fathers, aunts, uncles, grandfathers, social workers, teachers, and students openly talking about how we, as a community, can succeed. We launched our "Team C Student Improvement Plan."

The Team C Student Improvement Plan was an improvement strategy of collective work and responsibility. In this plan, we initiated parent-run after-school reading workshops, designated homework areas at home, supervised study time, weekly progress reports (including academic, attendance, and conduct information), at least one parent classroom visit per semester, student achievement contracts, after-school tutorials, and, most important, constant teacher-student-parent communication.

Although this was only one step in the collective movement to ensure that students succeeded, it was a giant step in the right direction. . . . Hopelessness was being boldly confronted at South Atlanta High School: parents had not given up on their children, teachers still believed in their students, and students were starting to believe in themselves. And most important, the community had not given up on its future.

Even with significant turnover among science teachers, including three different long-term substitutes, Mrs. Morgan Dixon's ninth-grade student attendance and achievement jumped significantly that year, demonstrating greater improvement than any other team in the school.

Mrs. Morgan Dixon's story vividly illustrates a number of the benefits of making students' families an integral part of the team working for student success. First, as they did for Mrs. Morgan Dixon, students' families can offer additional hands and energy to do what needs to be done, whether that is tutoring a small group of students, building a bookshelf for the new in-class library, advocating before the school board for more resources for the science lab, or chaperoning students on a trip to hear an author speak. At the same time, Mrs. Morgan Dixon's engagement with students' families and influencers provided her with a vantage point on a student's interests and background that informs and improves her instructional choices. Perhaps by engaging a student's family, you may learn that his grandparents live in Haiti, that his mother works in the evenings, and that his brother is in college. All of these facts could help shape assignments and instructional methods to appeal to the students' interests.

Most important, perhaps, Mrs. Morgan Dixon's engagement with students' families increases student investment by aligning the messages a student is hearing from significant

**Tanya Morgan Dixon,**
High School History,
Georgia

people in his or her life. From media, peers, and other sources, students are exposed to negative messages. Great teachers rally a student's influencers to take on, and beat, those negative messages.

When we look at how teachers who are enjoying these benefits approach collaborating with student families, we see clear patterns. Highly effective teachers like Mrs. Morgan Dixon assume responsibility for investing families, recognizing that family members and influencers have valuable contributions to make to the collective quest for student success. The most successful teachers we work with build family investment on a foundation of effective communication with students' family members.

### Defining "Family and Influencers" Broadly

Strong teachers seek to partner with anyone who can influence a student's mindset about school and hard work, a list that starts but does not end with family members.

When first-grade Los Angeles teacher Kate Sobel realized that one of her struggling students was hearing nothing all day but negative commentary on his behavior (including from her), she set out to discover all the people with whom he interacted each day, from his mother to his cousin to the physical education teacher. She invested all of them in a vision of his academic success and asked them to respond to his behavioral challenges with comments and questions about his *academic* efforts. She went so far as to regularly send around a mini-newsletter that offered concrete talking points on the child's academic progress. When he went to his physical education class, for instance, the instructor could comment on his recent success on a writing project. Ms. Sobel herself committed to responding to the student's misbehavior with a comment about its impact on his learning. In just weeks, the whole team of influencers around this child was thrilled to see radical change in his behavior, attitude, and success.

Many of our teachers, like Ms. Sobel, have found that sometimes non-family members, such as a coach, a friend, or a pastor, are just as important to invest in students' progress as family members. Talla Rittenhouse, a high school math teacher in Philadelphia, explains: "I found that every student had an influential person in his or her life; I just had to get to know each student to find out who that person was." When Ms. Rittenhouse realized that one of her struggling students greatly admired his basketball coach, she sent the coach a daily report. The coach discussed the student's performance with the student every day. "I know this worked," Ms. Rittenhouse says, "because Gerald went from skipping school every other day to getting an academic scholarship for college."

### Assuming Responsibility for Family Involvement

A clear theme of Mrs. Morgan Dixon's story is that she and her colleagues *created* family involvement. We see this pattern in all highly effective teachers' classrooms: a teacher's outreach is what ultimately drives family and influencer investment. Research findings verify this idea: "Nothing motivates a child more than when learning is valued by schools and families/community working together in partnership. . . . These forms of involvement do not happen by accident or even by invitation. They happen by explicit strategic intervention."[13]

As with so many other elements of effective teaching, we see that teachers who draw in students' families demonstrate a strong internal locus of control by assuming that they can and must engage student families in student learning. (This perspective, discussed in the Introduction and explored in more depth in Chapter Six, has proven to be a key approach of teachers who work well across lines of racial or socioeconomic difference.)

Contrast the excerpts from two interviews shown here. Both teachers are describing their experience reaching out to students' families. The first quotation is from a teacher who does not have a strong locus of control. The second teacher does. The contrast is not just that the second teacher takes an asset-based perspective of students' families. The second teacher also realizes that the lack of communication with home is a challenge, and she takes whatever action is necessary to overcome it.

| Weak Internal Locus of Control | Strong Internal Locus of Control |
|---|---|
| There would be kids, I was like, I'm going to go home and call their parents tonight, and I'd call, and it wouldn't be the right phone number. And I'd ask the kid, "Do you have a more current phone number than this?"<br><br>And they'd be like, "Oh, not right now; my phone's shut off." I would say with . . . 50 percent of my kids . . . their phone numbers changed throughout the year. They didn't have the same phone number because their phones got disconnected or they moved . . . I had regular contact with [about 10 percent of my students'] parents. | My students' parents worked constantly. Most of my kids, when they went home, their parents weren't there, because they're around-the-clock working. That was what made it difficult, you know, phones not being connected, so I couldn't even call parents. . . . I think something that I figured out, and another teacher of mine in my cluster, we just decided . . . we would just start taking kids home, and we would wait at home until the parent came home, and we would just make home visits constantly. If we needed to go meet a parent at work or wherever, we just made it happen.<br><br>I knew that if that was what was going to help my student out, then I would go and do that. I would take them home and wait at home, or meet Mom wherever she needed to be met. Or talk to whoever I needed to talk to, and however it needed to get done. . . . |

Highly effective teachers' interactions with students' families and influencers demonstrate that assuming responsibility for those relationships leads to creative and productive strategic interventions. A teacher might be hosting curriculum nights during which family members come and enjoy lively mini-lessons on the objectives their students are learning. A student's grandmother might be regularly attending reading workshops to work with small groups of students and reinforce comprehension strategies. A teacher might be sitting down with the youth director of a local church to discuss the challenges of students' fixed-intelligence perspective and to brainstorm ways to work together to change it. While the particular methods that highly effective teachers use vary, all are intended to invest students' families and other influencers in the hard work necessary for the students to reach the ambitious academic goals.

### Recognizing the Contributions of Students' Families

Some of the same dynamics of race, class, culture, and language stereotypes that perpetuate low expectations also fuel a prevailing public assumption that families in low-income communities do not care about education.[14] Our teachers' experiences debunk that bias. One seventh-grade English and social studies teacher in San Mateo, California, wrote in an anonymous survey response,

> I constantly hear blame being placed on parents who "just don't care," and have found that this is simply not the case. I had parents lined up outside my classroom until 9:00 P.M. on a conference day that had no earlier notification. Parents are constantly calling me at home or stopping by to check up on their child. The ones who appear to be "not as involved" have all had very extenuating circumstances (disability, difficult work schedule, etc.).

Another teacher admits that he brought to his classroom an ill-informed assumption that students' families and others did not care, but he immediately saw a different reality:

> Initially I was under the impression that community members, parents, and teachers were not concerned with the academic progress of the community's children. I quickly learned that . . . their hopes, dreams, and aspirations were far-reaching, and not limited to the poverty conditions that surrounded them. After inviting parents to a "report card dinner," I quickly realized that we as a community were all in this together.

To be clear, the most effective teachers we work with do not stop at realizing that students' families want to be involved. These teachers also see their students' families as "funds of knowledge,"

> ▶ **RESEARCH ON ASSET-BASED VIEWS OF FAMILIES**
>
> **RATHER THAN HAVING TEACHERS** make a home visit to dispense knowledge, a study in Arizona had teachers enter the home as learners. They asked questions during a visit in order to find out more about the skills, topics, and interests shared and emphasized within the family. Because family members' abilities may or may not be related to their current employment, teachers would invite them to share stories not only about their work, but also hobbies, previous jobs, or the skills for which relatives rely on them. The teachers participating in the study found a range of proficiencies in students' families, from agronomy to soil and irrigation systems, to transborder marketing and ethnobotanical expertise. A teacher might, for example, access the "funds of knowledge" (to use some researchers' phrase) found in the household when making plans for curriculum units in social studies, math, science, language arts, and other subjects. This asset-based perspective acknowledges a family member's experiences and skills as valuable, and participating teachers report that the families feel an increased sense of comfort with and connection to the school.[15]

as possessing experiences, insights, skills, and perspectives that can be harvested to increase all students' learning. Such a mindset has far-ranging positive consequences for a classroom leader, especially when contrasted with a teacher who fixates on perceived shortcomings of his or her students and their families. We have seen that teachers who have an asset-based view of their students' families frequently invite family members to their classroom, whether to help translate a letter home, to monitor a science experiment, to speak about the importance of perseverance. We see that these teachers are able to quickly build meaningful relationships that provide them with support when difficult classroom management issues arise. Most important, they are able to build a team around their students that shares the work of investing them in dramatic academic success.

Maia Heyck-Merlin, as a fourth-grade teacher of African American students in an impoverished community in Louisiana, committed herself to a mental exercise that ensured she took an asset-based view of her students' families and worked to be aware of personal biases she was bringing to those interactions:

> I remember it was really hard to prevent making assumptions of why occasionally parents would be late or not show up to parent-teacher conferences. It scared me to realize that I would be more generous and "understanding" of those parents from higher-income communities. To combat this, I actually used an envisioning exercise where all of my parents were huge company CEOs who were extremely busy with multiple meetings, and thought of how I would react in that same situation in a more affluent environment and what assumptions I would make about those parents in a suburban community. That allowed me to maintain very high expectations of my parents, but at the same time understand that they had multiple things they were juggling—and it didn't matter if the job was president of Xerox or cleaning the riverboat casinos or working for a local real estate company—they still had the best interests of their students in mind. And it worked. With the right amount of persistence, I had extremely high parent turnout for my conferences. And it didn't matter if we had to reschedule or if I had to make a home visit or arrive at school early. It's what any good teacher would do.

When teachers assume the best of their students' families, they can tap into a world of knowledge and experience for the benefit of their students. Teachers like Ms. Heyck-Merlin are constantly asking, "How can the experience, wisdom, knowledge, and skills of my students' families further our progress toward our goals?"

Perhaps not surprisingly, both our teachers and education researchers find that one of the most powerful contributions students' families can make is to reinforce healthy intelligence theories. Researcher Janine Bempechat notes that "several studies of successful adults from minority groups indicate that motivational support from parents—statements that stress the value of effort or of education—may be even more important for poor or minority children than whether the parents can help with homework."[16]

Despite all the contributions they can make to student learning, research suggests that students' families in low-income communities are less likely to be involved in their children's schooling.[17] Sociologist Annette Lareau refutes, however, the assumption that parents in low-income communities care less about education. Her research shows that almost all parents—whether in low-income or high-income areas and whether or not they are actively involved in school—believe in the value of attaining a high school diploma and are deeply upset by their children's educational failures. She found, however, that parents in low-income communities were less involved because they had less academic experience, fewer resources, and fewer connections. They may also have had less success or fewer positive experiences in school themselves—factors that may inhibit their involvement: "Upper-middle-class parents had much more information about the educational process in general and about the specifics of their children's school-site experience than did working-class parents."[18]

These realities—that because of cultural distance, prior bad experiences, or intimidation our students' families may be uncomfortable engaging with our school, our classroom, or us—emphasize the importance of our ability to work well across lines of cultural, socioeconomic, and racial differences. Conscious and subconscious biases related to race, class, and culture have the potential to lead us to unfairly judge parents' and guardians' competence, their commitment to their children's academic success, or their way of doing things, but some teachers demonstrate that they can work through and past those biases to build strong, fruitful relationships for the sake of student learning. In our interviews and observations, we have seen that those teachers are particularly self-aware, constantly considering how they are being heard

---

### ▶ INVOLVING STUDENTS' FAMILIES AND INFLUENCERS IN ACADEMIC CONTENT

**ATLANTA TEACHER DIANA ELLSWORTH** found that by ensuring parents understood what their children were learning and how it would be assessed, she caused motivating conversations between students and parents that vaulted her students' academic growth to new heights:

> Many parents knew that their students had to take a big fifth-grade writing test, but few knew what scores meant . . . and fewer still had any idea what specifically it took to get a mystical 4, 5, or 6. Hosting a parent workshop gave my students an opportunity to show their parents that they not only knew what it took but also understood their areas of strength and those where they needed improvement, not only that they themselves cared about the test but also that it was within their reach to write the "Wow!" paper for which they were striving. I'd like to say I did it, but, no, my students invested their parents in the test and their progress toward an articulated goal. Their parents understood and genuinely celebrated the results when the school had the largest percentage of students scoring at the highest two levels of any inner-city school within Atlanta Public Schools.

and perceived, a skill that helps them identify moments when they might be unfairly judging their students or their students' families. At that point, they stop, check their perspective, and reset their outlook with the reality before them. Even when a teacher shares some elements of identity with students' family members, other differences (race, ethnicity, language, socioeconomic status, culture, sexual orientation, educational background, community connections, age, position of influence) may influence interactions.

Monique Cueto-Potts, who called the families of her students in New York City at least every two weeks, says that the relationship of all teachers with students' families should be governed by a simple truth: "We want the same things for our kids . . . we want them to have opportunities and choices in life."

## Communicating with Students' Families

The currency of strong teachers' engagement with students' families is thorough and frequent communication. As researchers have found, "specific vehicles must be established to facilitate the flow of information to and from the school."[19] In our experience, the teachers who have the most involved families and influencers are those who create systems to communicate what is happening in class and why, as well as how those who care about the students can help foster student growth. In the words of one teacher, "Constant feedback and communication [with parents] enables my students to feel as if they are part of a strong network that is working feverishly for their benefit."

Sometimes highly effective teachers even bring students' families and influencers together to learn what students are learning. When fifth-grade teacher Joseph Almeida heard families say they wished they could do more to help their children learn but did not understand or remember the material themselves, he instituted Parents' Learning Nights. Now he hosts students' influencers in classes once a month to preview the mathematics content he will be covering in the following month:

> I explain how I teach it and multiple ways that the problem can be done. Because many of the parents speak Spanish, I will have my [PowerPoint] slides in English and translated into Spanish. The best part about this is that both students and their parents come to these nights, so the students are gaining exposure to the material before it is taught during the school day and parents and their [children] are learning the material together. Approximately fifteen parents attend per month. This has contributed to the high achievement in mathematics.

Methods of communication employed by strong teachers are hugely varied and creative. If you were to join us in our visit to Melissa Simon's classroom, you would see, for example, students keeping detailed binders to show their family in which they have identified both their best pieces of work and work that needs improvement. You would see students preparing and practicing how to explain their academic progress to their families, and several times a year (after the students have sent out announcement letters) you would see students leading parent-teacher conferences. You would also notice that Ms. Simon has enlisted parents and guardians in checking the students' English homework and reading with children every evening as recorded in the reading log. And you would likely notice that Ms. Simon is not only making calls to students' families but frequently receiving them as well.

Victor Wakefield, another teacher focused on family investment, implements a menu of communication strategies in his sixth- and seventh-grade language arts classes to "keep . . . communication constant between home and the classroom." We see many of his team's strategies in the most successful classrooms:

- *Weekly newsletter.* He sends a weekly newsletter with the major academic, logistical, and cultural events for the week. He provides incentives for students to bring back the newsletters signed by their parents.

- *Homework agenda.* The newsletter includes a weekly homework agenda that outlines the assignments for the upcoming week from all four teachers on the sixth- and seventh-grade team.

- *Electronic communication.* He sends e-mails regularly to invite additional interactions (and follows up with written notices for families without computers). For example, he sent a contact list of all of the classroom families.

- *Tracking folder for assessments.* Students maintain a tracking folder with all of their assessments and a graph of progress on the assessments. This folder is shared with parents at parent-teacher conferences.

- *Biweekly progress reports.* Together as a team, the four teachers working with his students send home biweekly progress reports to be signed by a family member.

- *Open invitation to the classroom.* Parents are invited and encouraged to come to the class any time to check on their students or observe the type of work they are doing.

- *Shout-Outs.* He puts "shout-outs" (celebrating specific accomplishments of particular students) in the newsletter for A grades on weekly quizzes and for growth and proficiency on standardized assessments.

- *Celebratory calls.* Every A that is earned on a weekly quiz earns a celebratory call to whomever the student wishes. All the student has to do is submit the names and phone numbers of the people for the teacher to call when they receive their A.

The key idea here is not that any one of these particular strategies is best or must be used. Rather, it is that highly effective teachers recognize they are more likely to reach their goals when they communicate and collaborate with students' families and influencers. Not all teachers, certainly, can adopt Taylor Delhagen's ritual of riding his bike through the neighborhood, sometimes stopping at students' homes to make sure they are going to be on time to first period and to get a face-to-face check-in with parents. (Or his ritual of strapping a box of pancakes to his bike on Saturdays for attendees of his Saturday classes.) Not all teachers would want to adopt Kevin Lohela's tactic of printing his cell phone number and e-mail address on the bottom of every progress report. (In his classroom, open communication was the norm, and he had 100 percent attendance at his parent-teacher conferences during the year.) Not all teachers will want to employ Justin Minkel's strategy of hosting a night at school for students' families to learn methods of reading instruction to use with their children at home.

All highly effective teachers will, however, build a toolbox of communication strategies that match their style, students, and needs. Summarizing these ideas, teacher Veronica Ruelas captures the importance and power of involving students' families and influencers:

> I believe beyond a doubt that every parent/guardian is invested in their child's learning. I have come to make myself believe this. I have found that when I believe this, I work even harder to ensure that I am reaching all parents/guardians. They have come to expect this from me and should expect the amount of communication they have with me from all of their children's educators. I hold meetings at the beginning of the year explaining what options their children have for high school and explaining what their role is in advocating for their children. I send home parent surveys, document all parent/guardian communication to ensure that I am making positive contact, and send home progress reports every two weeks that list grades. I also e-mail, text, call, write monthly newsletters, meet in the morning, meet in the evening, and send personal thank-you letters, all to enlist their help.

> My parents/guardians are my greatest influencers. They are their child's first educator, and I consider them partners in educating their children. Yes, there are times when I do close to *everything* to communicate with a parent/guardian and it does not work. But just as I am about to give up, I stop myself and find an aunt, uncle, brother, sister, cousin who I can work with. I need to invest students' influencers in this way, because when the students move on, I want them to have developed the skills and strategies to advocate for themselves, to know what they should expect from their education and their future teachers.

# Strategies for Investing Students

Leading your students to realize that they can and want to achieve ambitious academic goals is hard work, especially when they come to your classroom doubting that effort correlates with success. We have learned that this hard work yields huge returns for teachers who are fighting for increased opportunities for their students.

We see varied and creative investment tactics in our most effective teachers' classrooms. Here we will highlight some of the most powerful ones:

| A Welcoming Environment | A Culture of Achievement | Instruction and Learning |
| --- | --- | --- |
| Building relationships with students | Promoting values that drive student investment | Establishing the relevance of content |
| Creating a sense of community in the classroom | Making progress transparent and celebrating success | Teaching at the frontier of student ability |
| | Purposefully employing role models | Empowering students with choice and responsibility |

Additional guidance in the form of how-to guides, common pitfalls, and more exemplary (and less exemplary) models of investment strategies are available online: www.teachingasleadership.org.

## Creating a Welcoming Environment to Increase Student Investment

Justin May's students in pre–Katrina New Orleans came to his first-grade classroom from one of three major housing projects served by his school. He recalls a report that indicated a high incidence of post-traumatic stress disorder in children in these projects from having witnessed violence and crime in their neighborhood. Some of his students arrived at his door without shoes and socks or without having had breakfast that morning or dinner the night before. And even in first grade, all of them arrived at his classroom already behind their peers in other schools.

It is easy to jump to the conclusion that we simply cannot teach children effectively who come to school hungry, or sick, or tired, or scared. In reality, however, we cannot teach children effectively *while* they are hungry, or sick, or tired, or scared. Highly effective teachers like Mr. May show that even in these most challenging environments, we have the power to create a warm and welcoming space in our classroom where students can escape some of the distracting burdens of poverty, a space where they want to, and can, learn.

Mr. May addressed his students' needs head-on. He began by calling parents, visiting students' homes, and inviting students' families to school in order to build relationships with the families—a strategy that not only helped him learn students' needs but showed students that he cared for them. Mr. May found that some of his students were genuinely afraid of school and teachers, and he did everything he could to ameliorate this feeling: from creating a visually welcoming space, to hosting morning meetings to talk about feelings, to crouching down at students' level to communicate with them eye-to-eye. (Mr. May realized his six-foot-four frame intimidated his children.) He invested time in getting to know them and showing he cared about them. When he could, he took care of basic needs to make his students feel comfortable, working with local churches and organizations to provide them uniforms, shoes if they didn't have them, and snacks. He let them see him make mistakes and he took part in Apology Time alongside his students. He taught them how to resolve disagreements. As Mr. May would put it, he simply loved his children for who they were. Whatever the challenges they faced outside school, Mr. May created a space where both he and his students wanted to be and could be themselves.

Although all of his students started the year behind, eight of Mr. May's twenty-four first graders were reading on a third-grade level by the end of his first year of teaching. Thirteen others were ready for second grade. The three who were still behind were making great progress and were continuing to work with Mr. May to catch up.

The burdens of poverty are just one subset of many pressures that can interfere with the affirmation and comfort students need to take academic risks and learn. Sometimes the inhibitors are other students (through teasing or pressure) or teachers (through conscious and unconscious actions and inactions). Even the best teachers have seen firsthand the debilitating effects of students' feeling unwelcome in their own classroom. Perhaps a student has been called a derogatory name by a classmate; or a student is self-conscious because her clothes are more worn than someone else's; or some aspect of a student's identity (Latino, gay, female, something else) causes the student to feel isolated from others; or a student picks up on a teacher's subtle preference for a particular group.

In each of these cases, the student's energy is diverted by the emotional and social worries of feeling isolated and alone. Highly effective teachers not only create an environment that diminishes the chances that students' energy will be diverted in this way but also create an environment that affirmatively strengthens students' self-confidence and esteem. Thus, students are empowered to fend off affronts to their self-confidence and focus on working hard toward ambitious academic progress. As New Mexico first-grade teacher Christine Probasco put it, "When the classroom is an emotionally and physically safe place for students, authentic learning can begin."

Experts also draw a direct line between a welcoming, emotionally supportive environment and student learning. In his observations of thousands of teachers, for example, researcher Robert Pianta found that emotional support in the classroom correlates with closing the achievement gap, growth in students' functioning, and growth in reading and math achievement.[20]

In our experience, a key to creating an emotionally and physically safe place for students is building relationships with and among students.

### Building Relationships with Students

Some popular conceptions of leadership emphasize the importance of emotional distance between a leader and constituents. Our experiences with classroom leaders, like some other recent studies, challenge that conventional wisdom.

A massive cross-sector study of effective organizations and individuals by Gallup did find that over-involvement between leaders (or service providers) and constituents can correlate with poor performance, but it also found that purposeful emotional engagement with constituents distinguishes many of the most effective individuals from moderately effective ones. For example, in the case of nurses:

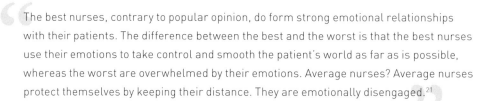

> The best nurses, contrary to popular opinion, do form strong emotional relationships with their patients. The difference between the best and the worst is that the best nurses use their emotions to take control and smooth the patient's world as far as is possible, whereas the worst are overwhelmed by their emotions. Average nurses? Average nurses protect themselves by keeping their distance. They are emotionally disengaged.[21]

We see a similar pattern in exceptional and average teachers' classrooms. Those whose students are making dramatic gains build strong, close, and purposeful relationships. They learn who their students are, what they believe, and where they come from. These teachers harness that emotional engagement and the knowledge it produces to drive student investment and, in turn, increase students' academic achievement.

The work of a pair of teachers in rural North Carolina helps make this point. Tammi Sutton and Caleb Dolan worked together to increase their middle school students' achievement so dramatically that their principal credited them with moving their small middle school from the lowest quartile of the state's accountability ranking to a top quartile ranking of "exemplary." Their classes scored so high on state assessments that they changed the school's average score dramatically. And according to the principal, their example inspired other teachers to do better.

When we talked to Ms. Sutton and Mr. Dolan, it became clear that building relationships with and learning all they could about their students was a key element of success. They took every opportunity they could find to learn what made their students tick, because, Ms. Sutton says, "It was vital for me to remember that I was not just a language arts or social studies teacher. Before and long after I taught novels and grammar, I would be teaching students. In order for us to be most successful during the school year, I would have to really get to know my students and their families beyond the traditional walls of our classroom or even school building. By spending time together, we forged bonds that would help us in countless ways on the hardest days of class and well beyond the school year." Ms. Sutton and Mr. Dolan attended church dinners, cookouts, and were even invited on family trips.

Students identify a teacher's care and concern as the number one factor that influences their learning.[22] Students who feel personally cared for by their teacher are freed up to pursue other needs, like achievement and success. Moreover, building relationships is a means of building trust—trust that you will support and not belittle a student's efforts, trust that your interest in a student will be sustained in hard times, and trust that you yourself are invested in the student's success. This trust between you and your students is at the root of students' willingness to take academic risks, try new skills, and learn from mistakes. In the words of a pair of experts on relationships in schools, "Trusting student-teacher relations are essential for learning."[23]

As with investing families, highly effective teachers take numerous approaches to building relationships and trust with students. Los Angeles middle school science teacher Nisha Wadhwani told us, "There's no general recipe for building relationships, and it takes a lot of time on the teacher's part." Ms. Wadhwani herself changes her methods frequently, including how often she writes personalized notes to her students, cheers for students at basketball and football games, and decorates the walls with pictures of her students. Below we provide some additional examples to inspire your own system of relationship building to serve as a foundation for student investment in high academic achievement:

- *Information gathering, surveys, and sharing.* Many of the highly effective teachers we have studied begin the year with informal conversations, surveys, or other structures that ask students to share information about themselves. (Some teachers send surveys to students' families as well.) These tools quickly harvest useful, trust-building information about students' lives and interests. Jane Winfield, a global history teacher at an alternative high school in New York City, tells us, "It's so important to get to know students personally, not just what their past Regents scores were. The more I know about them (and the more they know about me), the more they trust me. At the beginning of the year, I ask students to write about three people who are important to them, and about three important events in their lives. Thus, I learn that Andrea has a one-year-old baby or that Stephen just got out of prison or that Cori was tormented at her last school for being openly gay. Their responses help me to understand them as people, and I learn even more as I later pull them aside and ask them questions about their responses. This allows us to build trust, and it helps me figure out how to connect what we're doing to what matters most to them."

- *Individualized notes and e-mail conversations.* A. J. Nagaraj, a high school social studies teacher in Hawaii, used the results of his early surveys with students to start up correspondence with each student about interests they had in common. "Sometimes these links were superficial (e.g., we enjoyed the same television shows) and other times they were more substantive (e.g., we both had similar relationships with our siblings)," Mr. Nagaraj said. "I found that these letters increased student investment because they simultaneously (1) proved to my students the degree to which I was interested in their lives, (2) demonstrated that my background was not as different from theirs as they may have initially assumed and (3) conveyed that I was willing to share my life with them before I expected them to share theirs with me."

- *Spending time together in and around school.* Emily Kronemeyer started a "lunch bunch" with her elementary students in Phoenix. She invites two or three students at a time to have lunch with her in the classroom. During that time, they listen to music, play games, and talk about their interests. Ms. Kronemeyer also makes a point of frequently eating in the cafeteria with her students, playing on the playground with them at recess periodically, and sometimes walking students home from school (which, she notes, is a chance to connect with students' families as well). "Taking the time to get to know my students and their lives outside the classroom showed that I was invested and interested in them not just as students but as individuals," she says. "I found that when they knew that I cared about them, I could push and challenge them further because they knew I believed they could do it."

- *Sponsoring student activities.* Teachers build relationships through involvement with student activities (sports, student councils, clubs, and others), both in and out of school. One teacher, LesLee Bickford, put together and coached a basketball team so that she could spend more time with her students who loved basketball. In the same spirit, Alexis Hanson, after learning about Students Run L.A., an organization that trains students for marathons, started a training group at her school, giving her lots of quality time running with some of her high school biology students. The relationships she developed through the training group, along with the substantial efforts of her many dedicated colleagues, had an amazingly positive impact on her students. One student, for example, who started the year withdrawn, low performing, and with some drug problems, demonstrated dramatically increased investment in class (and became a healthier person). Another student began passing his classes for the first time in high school after he joined Ms. Hanson in the training program.

- *Engaging students outside of school.* For many teachers, building relationships with students frequently takes them into their community as they search out the places where their students are congregating. That can mean eating at a restaurant where students work or attending a county fair where students are likely to be. "Your school is a community within an even greater community," Christopher Ruszkowski, a teacher in Miami, says. "Kids play sports, go to church, go shopping. I attend many games and concerts, family outings, and live near my school. Living in or close to your community is a wonderful opportunity—I bump into my kids and their parents at the grocery store. Living in and becoming involved in my community has led to some very strong bonds with my students."

- *Making yourself available to students.* Many successful teachers invite students to contact them beyond the school day. We have seen, for example, teachers giving out refrigerator magnets with contact information on them, printing their phone number on homework, and hosting homework jam sessions at a local McDonald's.

## Creating a Sense of Community in the Classroom

In addition to relationships between the teacher and students, relationships among students are critical to maximizing student learning. As a teacher in New Orleans, Jess Bialecki saw many students struggle with distractions and burdens of poverty, inspiring her to work hard to create within the four walls of her classroom a warm, affirming, and protective space for children to learn:

 My students attend a school composed entirely of temporary modular buildings in a neighborhood that remains virtually abandoned three years after Hurricane Katrina. Needless to say, it is not the most welcoming environment in which to learn and grow. Thus, one of my highest priorities at the start of the school year was to create an environment in which my students felt safe and valued. This involved tremendous investments from the outset in both the physical design as well as the social/emotional climate of my classroom. I wanted my students to have access to an extensive classroom library that included a comfortable and appealing space for them to read their favorite books independently, complete with couches, rocking chairs, and stuffed animal reading buddies. To do this, I needed to reach out to my personal network of friends and family to solicit donations of children's books; once I did, I was astonished by the outpouring of generosity and many hundreds of high-quality books we received.

I knew it was important for my students to develop strong and positive self-images, so I hung up color photos of each child around the room along with work samples that they had identified as their "best." I wanted my students to have access to the same caliber of learning materials as their peers in higher-income areas, so I obtained over two thousand dollars in outside grants for hands-on resources for math and literacy centers. However, I didn't just make investments in the physical aspects of our classroom; I also invested a great deal of time and energy into making our room a caring and emotionally safe space for my students. Much of this was accomplished in the first six weeks of school, during which I devoted a significant amount of class time to a variety of getting-to-know-you and community-building activities. And these activities continued throughout the year. At the end of the day during snack time, I gave each of my students the opportunity to offer a "thumbs up" or a "delta" to anyone in the class. A "thumbs up" is a positive comment on something—big or small—that a classmate (or teacher) did that day, and a "delta" is something the person would like to see changed in the future.

It was clear that my investments paid off. Before long, my students looked forward to coming to school each day and frequently talked about how much they would miss our classroom before holiday breaks and even weekends. When given the opportunity, they proudly showed off the highlights of our classroom to their friends from other classes, their family members, and school staff members. Furthermore, our classroom community grew to be extremely closely knit. My students were quick to celebrate their peers' achievements or offer assistance when someone was having a difficult day.

Like all other successful teachers, Ms. Bialecki charts a path to a welcoming environment by purposefully planning for and creating a sense of community where students respect and support each other. For her, the ultimate sign of success in building relationships among students is students taking care of each other and encouraging each other's learning:

My class during my first year of teaching included two students with moderate to severe disabilities, including a first grader with autism who received virtually no services from the overburdened special education department at our school. This student, Daniel, began the year crawling on the floor and singing at the top of his lungs for most of the school day. As challenging as this was for me, I knew that I had to send a message to my students that Daniel was an integral member of our class who could and would contribute to our collective growth. I sought out every opportunity to praise Daniel for a positive behavior—no matter how small—and did my best to set him up for success in cooperative learning situations. My students took notice of my deep respect for Daniel's abilities. . . . Serving as Daniel's buddy on an assignment became our most valued job, and students squabbled over who would get to hold Daniel's hand in line or push him on his favorite swing at recess. I knew I had been successful in creating a supportive classroom climate when my students began coming up to me during independent work time, beaming, to tell me about something positive that they had seen Daniel do.

Like Ms. Bialecki, highly effective teachers use a whole range of methods to build unity and interdependence in their classroom. This community setting ensures that students do not feel isolated or alienated and that they have a sense of belonging that allows them to fully and unselfconsciously try, possibly fail, and thereby learn to master challenging concepts and skills.

Here is an introduction to the most common and important strategies for building community we see in highly effective classrooms:

- *Fostering an inclusive and positive atmosphere.* Creating a welcoming sense of community starts with the teacher's positive and inclusive tone with students. Whether in a kindergarten or high school classroom, we often see strong teachers standing in the doorway, greeting every entering student with a personalized welcome: "Brenda! Welcome back! How did your game go last night?" Or "Joshua. How are you? High-five today? High-five! Welcome to class. The 'Do Now' is on the board." Or "Robert—where's the smile I like so much? I need it today. Wait, wait, wait—there it is! Welcome back, Robert. I'm glad you're here today!" Our point is not that every teacher should greet every student at the door in this way (although that is a great practice), but that the spirit of welcome and warmth embodied in that ritual needs to pervade the classroom all the time. Highly effective teachers use a variety of tactics to foster this positive atmosphere. When we observe their classrooms, we see that these teachers:

- Make a point of saying something personal and positive to every student every day.

- Use a mature and respectful tone with students.

- Model the ways that people interact in strong, healthy relationships—from always saying "please" and "thank you" to stating explicitly and nonjudgmentally the specific behavior that is appreciated or needs to change.

- Avoid sarcasm and teasing, remaining hypersensitive to students' feelings—especially with younger children, English language learners, or other groups for whom misunderstandings are likely.

- Remain authentic by speaking and teaching as one's self, not in an affected or adopted persona.

- Make discussions of the classroom's culture and atmosphere a regular part of interactions with students.

- *Building relationships among students.* When members of the class know each other well, they are far more likely to value and respect each other, to feel valued and respected by others, and thus be less burdened by social and emotional anxieties that compete with a focus on learning. Highly effective teachers therefore do not leave student relationships to chance. They create multiple overlapping opportunities for students to build relationships so that everyone feels connected and included in the classroom. In our observations of these teachers, we see that they often:

- Help students share and celebrate one another's work and progress in class.

- Facilitate interactions among students who may not know each other.

- Talk about the vision for community in the classroom.

- Forgo empty icebreakers in favor of joint problem solving and collaborative work toward learning objectives.

- Hold community meetings.

- Acknowledge student birthdays.

- Model the language of cooperation.

- Reinforce the notion that all ideas in the community are respected and valued.

- Plan for the arrival of new students to the classroom—for example, by assigning a friend to each new student to provide support, guidance, and leadership.

- *Teaching, modeling, and expecting tolerance and inclusion.* All classrooms include student diversity and difference. Beyond obvious axes of race, ethnicity, and gender, students have varied skills and abilities, prior knowledge, background experiences, aspirations and interests, and confidence and sensitivities. Like all of us, students need help navigating those dynamics of difference.

Highly effective teachers enter the classroom with the starting assumption that students are interested in, if not fascinated by, differences between themselves and others. As children are developing their own identity, they are keenly aware of others' identities. As one pair of researchers suggests, "Our work in schools is identity work."[24] With this premise in mind (and in ways that are informed by the age, interests, and perspectives of their students), successful teachers teach social and interpersonal skills that allow students to appreciate diversity.

An unfortunate reality is that students often reflect the tensions they perceive in the world around them. Sometimes those tensions manifest in classrooms in ways that make all of us feel uncomfortable and unwelcome. In fact, on surveys, teachers tell us that personal insults—from student to teacher and from student to student—are one of the most surprising aspects of their time in the classroom and one of the most challenging situations to handle.

The most effective teachers we have studied teach values of respect and tolerance, and they model those values with swift, consistent responses to insensitivity. We have captured some of the patterns we see in highly effective classrooms:

**TEACHING TOLERANCE**

- Draw opportunities to teach principles of tolerance from the curriculum in literature choices, reflections on historical events, writing projects, and so forth.

- Draw opportunities to teach principles of tolerance from current events in both the news and students' lives.

- Model in role plays and day-to-day interactions the responses to insensitivity that are desirable.

**RESPONDING TO INSENSITIVITY**

- All insensitive comments, including those made in humor, can threaten students' sense of affirmation and ability to learn.

- Many insensitive comments are teachable moments, worthy of broader class discussion.

- In cases where insensitivity violates class or school rules, consequences must be clear, predictable, and consistent.

- *Empowering students with conflict resolution skills and systems.* Highly productive classrooms have systems for resolving tensions among students so that conflicts are handled quickly and effectively, without distracting or lingering effects that disrupt learning. For example, some teachers develop procedures by which two students can sit down to work out some tension, perhaps at a special table or space in the room (sometimes with the teacher's guidance or oversight). In other cases, teachers might bring problems to the entire class, often using the problem-solving process as a chance to model what the teacher would like students to do on their own. Annie Lewis, a highly successful Baltimore teacher, describes the sense of community she aimed for in her classroom:

> When conflicts arise in class, I ask the whole class, "How are we going to solve this?" Sometimes the whole class has to be involved, and we'll sit in a circle and discuss the problem. Other times the students involved in the conflict go to the back carpet and talk it out. My students have become so good at this that I usually just have to go check in with them to see how they've resolved it. The key is getting the kids to buy into the shared vision of what they want our class to be, and then to really think about what it takes to make that vision a reality. We have talked so much about wanting a classroom in which they have friends, people are kind to them, classmates help each other, etc., that they really want it. Having this shared vision helps us want to work out conflicts instead of getting stuck on them.

Whatever community-building strategies a highly effective teacher is employing, he or she treats these social skills in the same way as academic skills—as discrete objectives needing to be diagnosed, introduced, practiced, and assessed for mastery. In the words of Melissa Storm, who taught special education in south Louisiana, "Social skills must be taught like anything else. We cannot assume that a student comes to school understanding how to resolve conflict, avoid fighting, or be respectful to other students. We must lead discussions about these skills and directly teach them to students, providing modeling and opportunities for students to practice." Strong teachers recognize that they set the tone and expectations for student interactions, just as they do for academic performance.

This notion that we as teachers and as a society ultimately determine how students think about differences and conflicts among us is driven home by Kristy Marshall, a teacher with a physical difference:

> I was born with Poland's Syndrome, and as a result, my right hand did not fully develop in my mother's womb. As a child, I had no idea I was different until I encountered a world that did not know how to treat people who were physically or mentally different from what society deems as the norm. One of my many reasons for [becoming a teacher] was to ensure that regardless of one's difference, every child has the same opportunities.

I taught first-grade English as a Second Language. I vividly recall preparing for my first day, daunted by the thought of how students would react to my hand. Goodness, I was twenty-one years old and still succumbed to the pressure of image and beauty as defined by our society. Looking back, I cannot believe that I was worried about what six-year-olds would think, say, or do for that matter.

I walked into my classroom the first day of school with my number one classroom management tool. I introduced myself and gave each of them a chance to meet and greet each other and then went on to explain and model how they would know it was time to stop, look, and listen. I clapped twice and told them to repeat after me. At that moment, I looked at the class, and each of them had one fist (modeling my withered right hand) and one hand clapping back at me. My teaching moment began right there. However, it was not their lesson but my lesson.

My entire life I took each child's actions and words (from when I was growing up) . . . personally, as children do. I let those children I encountered define how other children and people would perceive my difference. As an adult, I realized that my students were merely modeling their teacher. At that instant, I realized the innocence of a child and, in reality,

---

### ▶ A MINI CASE-STUDY IN HANDLING INTOLERANCE

**ALL LINES OF DIFFERENCE,** including race, gender, age, religion, and background, can affect classroom interactions. One source of tension some teachers see and experience arises out of differences (real or perceived) in sexual orientation. Our conversations with and survey responses from teachers who are gay offer a personal and instructive view of the discomfort and challenge of addressing any insensitive comments in class.

One teacher, who identifies himself as a gay, white male, recalled for us feeling hurt and uncomfortable as his students used the word *faggot* and worrying about the pain students' derogatory comments might be causing other students who might be gay or have gay friends or relatives. At first he says he lacked the sense of authority and confidence to respond. And in retrospect, he may have underestimated his students' potential to refine their behavior or understand why their comments might be offensive. Of course, his hesitation was deeply enmeshed with complex social dynamics of disapproval of his identity as gay: "I was also afraid of calling students out for using those words because I was afraid of . . . what implications that had for . . . how they perceived me," he says. "And I wasn't going to be out to my students, and I didn't want to have to deal with that kind of stuff, and I was already having enough trouble as it was."

Another teacher, who identifies as a white lesbian, described similar tensions in her classroom at the beginning of the year and the learning curve she traveled to address

humanity. I understood that every single child who scoffed at me, or ridiculed me, did not know any better. They had never seen anyone with a hand like mine, and more important, no one taught them how to treat people and to approach people who are different from them. The students saw me for me: as a classroom teacher with or without a hand.

Violence and bullying is prevalent in our schools, and often I received the brunt of it growing up. Yet in my classroom, there was no bullying, violence, hatred, or even an "I can't," because being different was okay in Room 17. Teachers need to teach their students that difference, diversity, and uniqueness are welcomed and encouraged. Open dialogue needs to occur, and students should feel comfortable asking people who are not like them questions to further educate themselves. As a white teacher—even a white woman—I could never, and will never, understand personally what it feels like to grow up in our society as a minority in terms of race, yet I have a responsibility to educate myself on the perspective of a black person by asking questions and generating conversations about race. I was a minority in some sense, and in my classroom, if my students were curious about someone or something, they asked. Violence, bullying, and hatred will be prevented in our schools only if students feel comfortable asking questions and sharing their feelings with each other.

them. Her first and admittedly not very effective response was to shut down discussions about homosexuality entirely. She prohibited her students from using the word *gay* because they were using it in a derogatory way. The problem was that her students could not explain "why that would be a not okay thing to do, other than maybe a teacher might yell at you."

As time went on, the teacher saw herself as capable of changing the way her students used the word *gay*, and she committed to understanding why her students were saying it without being conscious of their intentions. She thereby exhibited both the locus of control and interpersonal awareness skills we see in teachers who work well across lines of difference. She became convinced her students had the maturity to talk about particularly difficult subjects (asset-based thinking). With these skills, she was able to have direct conversations with her class as a whole and one-on-one with students about what *gay* means and why using the word might hurt someone's feelings.

This more direct and open approach enabled her to use moments of insensitivity as catalysts for teaching tolerance and building inclusiveness in her classroom. The safe and welcoming environment she created gave all students—even those who might have been questioning their sexuality or worried about being teased for being different for another reason—the feeling that they did not have to worry about being teased and were liberated to learn.

To summarize, creating a welcoming environment is a major component of investing students in working hard. Students must feel safe and affirmed in order to take the risks necessary to try, fail, and learn. We see in highly effective teachers' practice two strategies for creating a welcoming environment. First, they use a variety of ways to spend time with and get to know their students in order to build a relationship of trust. Second, these teachers build a sense of community in the classroom by fostering an inclusive and positive atmosphere, creating relationships among the students, teaching principles and values of tolerance and inclusion, and implementing effective, student-driven systems of conflict resolution.

Consider one more story about a welcoming environment, this one from Sara Egli, a first-grade teacher in Phoenix:

> At the end of the day each day our class participates in "community circle." This is a time when students are able to express appreciations of or concerns for events that occurred at school that day. Earlier this year, we were running late in preparing for dismissal one afternoon. I announced that we would not have time for community circle that day and would have to skip it. I saw Melanie's sad expression from across the room. I asked her if she was okay. She nodded, but asked if she could leave her table group to speak to Nic. I gave her permission. She approached Nic and invited him to the classroom "peace table," a table where my students share "I messages" and engage in conflict resolution. Nic is typically a very passive and focused student. He is rarely involved in conflict, so I was surprised when Melanie took him there. I really like to hear their conversations at the peace table, so I moved within range to hear their interaction. Melanie began, "Nic, since community circle is cancelled today I want to give you an 'I message.'" Nic looked very alarmed. Melanie continued, "I appreciate today, when I fell down in the cafeteria and you picked up my tray." Nic beamed and said, "You're welcome." They shook hands and returned to their desks. The act of kindness was simple, but I was proud of them. And then I realized that if my students can be so supportive of one another at school, then my job is that much easier. When school is a safe and welcoming environment, then my kids will be ready to learn.

## Developing a Culture of Achievement

*I got a brain so big like the sun*
*Hope you got a mind full of knowledge, I wanna learn*
*Slap the ignorance, change it now to "know"*
*Bulldog where's your book? We've got so far to go*
*We know how to read, we know how to write*
*We can go back home and keep the knowledge still in mind*

— Student-developed class creed in Nisha Wadhwani's
junior high class of at-risk students

Highly effective teachers recognize that in the quest to invest students in academic achievement, we face tough competition from a barrage of low expectations, stereotypes, and problematic distractions, all of which influence students' mindsets, choices, and actions. "Students want to be both significant and a part of something greater than themselves," says Tyson Kane, a high school biology teacher in Los Angeles. "There are many distractions that offer students these two ingredients, but many do so in an unhealthy way. As an educator, if I can create a culture of performance which students value more than other distractions around them, 80 percent of the battle for educational equity is won."

This battle for the hearts and minds of students plays out in a variety of ways in highly effective classrooms. We see, for example, successful teachers acting like aggressive marketers, identifying productive ideas and values and surrounding their students with them. We see teachers going to great lengths to ensure that their students can see tangible evidence of their own learning, which also has a huge impact on student motivation and investment. These teachers employ role models to reinforce the idea that hard work will lead to success. Taken altogether, these strategies create a culture of achievement, in which students share a teacher's love of learning and desire to succeed.

## Promoting Values That Drive Student Investment

While the particular messages teachers use to reinforce student investment vary, those messages generally relate to three critically important ideas:

### ▶ ACADEMIC ACHIEVEMENT IS HIGHLY VALUABLE

**A TEACHER MUST EXPRESSLY** reinforce the "I want" of student investment. Marketing this idea to students sets the foundation for ongoing conversations about the ability for academic success to generate opportunities they want and need.

**SAMPLE MESSAGES**
- "Academic Achievement = Opportunity."
- "Reading and writing opens doors."
- "Learning is the path to your dreams."

### ▶ HARD WORK LEADS TO ACADEMIC ACHIEVEMENT

**THIS IDEA GOES TO** the heart of fixed versus malleable intelligence. A teacher should take advantage of every opportunity to tell and show students the correlation between hard work and success.

**SAMPLE MESSAGES**
- "I think I can . . . I think I can . . . I think I can."
- "Work Hard. Get Smart."
- "We learn from mistakes."

*(continued on next page)*

▶ **ACHIEVEMENT REQUIRES TEAM EFFORT** *(continued)*

**STUDENTS' SENSE THAT THEY** are all in this together is often a critical driver of their hard work. Where students feel a sense of team, they are inclined to push, protect, and collaborate with their peers.

**SAMPLE MESSAGES**
- "We succeed together."
- "All-for-one and one-for-all."
- "Together Everyone Achieves More (T.E.A.M.)."

A number of factors—including the age of the students, a teacher's personal style, and the culture of the school—will influence what form these messages take. The key is to choose marketing strategies that fit the specifics of the context. The strength of the specific message a teacher sends is not in its words but in its effect on students' mindsets:

- *Class or team names or themes.* Some teachers, especially in younger grades, give their class or students a unifying team name, for example, "The A+ Class" (which reinforces the value of achievement) or "The Helping Hands Classroom" (which emphasizes collaboration and teamwork). You might name your high school room "The College Prep Class," as a way to communicate that your older students have the potential to go to college while also encouraging hard work. Students in Preston Smith's class are known as "scholars." Students in Danielle Neves's class come to identify themselves as hard-working learners as they pursue their class theme, "Excellence."

- *Class pledges.* Some teachers use an extended version of the class motto or theme as a class pledge. Most commonly in elementary classrooms, teachers use a pledge to make a ritual out of daily reminders of the core values of the classroom. Alongside the Pledge of Allegiance, we see students pledging to work hard, interact collaboratively, and maximize everyone's learning experience. While these pledges take many forms, students in Rachel Schankula's Mississippi Delta classroom recite their own creed daily:

> I believe in myself and my ability to do my best.
> I am intelligent. I am capable of greatness.
> I can learn. I will learn. I must learn.
> Today, I will listen. I will speak. I will see.
> I will think. I will feel. I will reason.
> I will read, and I will write.
> I will do all these things with one purpose in mind: to do my best.
> I am too smart to waste today.

- *Mottoes and signs.* We see in productive classrooms posters and mottoes communicating the idea that "Hard Work Leads to Success" or that "Mistakes ~~Helps~~ Help Us Learn." We see "Acts of Kindness" walls, or a T.E.A.M. (Together Everyone Achieves More) display, where a teacher or students post supportive actions of students or assignments in which students have collaborated to produce a high-quality product.

Schools in the Knowledge Is Power Program (KIPP)—a highly successful public charter system started by Houston teachers Michael Feinberg and Dave Levin—have a strong culture of achievement built in part on aggressive marketing of messages. Mr. Feinberg's description of that strategy offers helpful insights into how to approach this element of investing students:

> Students need to be set up for success before we place high expectations on them and hold them accountable to meet those expectations. Whether it is an academic skill or a preferred behavior, we need to reverse-engineer from the goal to uncover all of the ingredients necessary to achieving the goal. Then we must ensure that all of these ingredients are present in our teaching.
>
> At KIPP, the teachers have realized that before students can DO the actions we want them to do, they first have to be able to SAY those actions. Therefore, those actions and expectations need to be taught, explained, and constantly reviewed in our classrooms. By saying the actions and expectations, the students acknowledge the existence of this particular expectation, buy into the fairness of its existence, and realize their responsibility to maintain it. At KIPP, this translates into, "Say it, do it."
>
> Now, saying an expectation such as "work hard" or "be nice" is a great starting point. Getting students to agree with the importance of those phrases is another important step. As we've learned in our professional development efforts, however, teaching a concept one time to children does not guarantee mastery. We need to reach and teach from many different angles, and we need to review previous work in a spiral form to ensure long-term mastery. This is why KIPP has plastered its campuses with various sayings, slogans, values, rallying cries, and expectations. It is our assurance that all of our children are constantly bombarded by our positive expectations and values throughout the day—they hear it in class, and they see it wherever they happen to look (even when they're off task). On day one each year, we begin teaching such concepts as:
>
> 1. Team always beats individual.
> 2. There are no shortcuts.
> 3. Work hard. Be nice.
> 4. Climb the mountain to college in 20XX [the graduation year].
> 5. Focus.
> 6. Be the constant, not the variable.
> 7. Actions speak louder than words.
> 8. Time and place.
> 9. If you can't run with the Big Dogs, stay on the porch!
> 10. ALL of us WILL learn.

> . . . and many more to create productive classroom environments. These slogans and
> expectations are on the walls in our classrooms, are painted onto our sidewalks in
> between our modular buildings, hang from the ceiling over our covered walkways, deco-
> rate the windows in our front entrance, are on our letterhead, are on our bumper stickers,
> are on the students' uniforms, and if I could hire planes to sky-write these slogans, I'd do
> that, too. Children at KIPP are expected to learn, understand, and always remember what
> we ask them to do, and when they do the right thing, good things happen. A daily reminder
> is one small way that we as teachers make sure our students are set up to succeed. 99

Two conditions are met in classrooms where we see these messages and marketing tactics change student behavior and mindsets. First, every aspect of the classroom—the policies, systems, and design—is aligned with those messages. Second, the teacher's *actions* are faithfully aligned with those ideas.

The first condition, regarding classroom structure and design, represents a common pitfall for less effective teachers. Sometimes new teachers do not ensure that their classroom systems embody the messages on the wall. For messages to be meaningful every element of the classroom must align with them. If, for example, you have a banner hanging in your classroom that says, "Try, Try, Try Again: Effort Breeds Success," but your assessment policies do not allow students to keep working toward mastery and retake tests that they fail, the meaning of that critical message—and your own credibility as a leader of your students—is undermined. For Justin May, translating his messages about mistakes-as-learning-opportunities into policies meant designing an assignment system in which nothing was finished until every component was right. He explains that in his class, "Every mistake a student makes HAS to be fixed so that the student learns from it. Nothing is 'done' until it is perfect." Even with his first graders, he would circle, instead of correcting, problems in assignments and then work with students to fix those problems.

Similarly, Kristin Reidy, the Teacher of the Year in Arizona in 2007, works hard to ensure her message of teamwork aligns with her classroom design by means of her "GOAL" sessions (Great Opportunity to Achieve Learning). Any student who scores below 80 percent must come in for additional learning and then retake the assessments. Because the class progress-tracking system requires every student to master the objective before success is "published" on the wall, the entire class is invested in the GOAL sessions. Students who have passed the assessment already attend those sessions to help others achieve mastery. "It's pretty powerful," Ms. Reidy says. "Students correct each other's mistakes gently and encourage their peers to stay positive when frustration arises."

The second condition that ensures well-marketed messages will have their desired effect is that the teacher embodies those messages in his or her own actions. Simply stated, you have to walk the talk if you want students to truly internalize these ideas. To embody the idea that academic achievement is valuable, for example, teachers might make a show of hanging their college diploma above their desk, modeling the pride they want students to feel in their academic accomplishments. To embody the idea that we learn from mistakes, we see strong teachers making a public display of correcting and practicing their own spelling, reworking math problems, or sharing stories of times they have learned from errors.

Brian Wallace, a special education teacher in New York City, offers an example of practicing what he preaches in his attempt to market the concept that reading is fun and valuable. He was having a hard time inspiring a deep interest in reading in his students. He turned to a colleague for help, who started by asking him if his students had ever seen *him* read. He realized that they had not. So during silent reading time, instead of monitoring and enforcing reading, he picked up a book. The entire atmosphere in the classroom changed. "My students began to ask me about what I read," he says, "and I started doing some of the sharing at the end of the independent reading block that had previously been a huge struggle as I had to practically beg students to talk a little bit about the books that they were reading. Over time, not only were my students reading independently for longer periods of time, they actually started asking for more independent reading time and begged me to have the opportunity to share out and recommend their book to their classmates."

While we might recognize this modeling idea as particularly important with children, the fact is that studies of leadership in all contexts verify its universal efficacy. In their worldwide study of leadership, for example, Kouzes and Posner found that "leaders' deeds are far more important than their words when one wants to determine how serious leaders really are about what they say. Words and deeds must be consistent. Exemplary leaders go first. They go first by setting the example through daily actions that demonstrate they are deeply committed to their beliefs."[25]

## Making Progress Transparent

In addition to well-marketed messages about achievement, effort, and teamwork, we see another recurring pattern in most highly effective classrooms: the walls are often covered with visual representations of student progress in the form of line graphs, bar graphs, charts, and tables. Binders and folders are often filled with similar student-accessible representations of academic progress.

In Jenny Tan's third-grade classroom in Las Vegas, there are tracking charts for fluency; mastery of multiplication, addition, subtraction; number of books read; attendance; homework completion; and more. "I wanted my students to be constantly aware of their progress," she says. "I talked with individual students about putting in more effort to improve certain areas. When their hard work led to success, I made sure it was well documented as proof."

We see teachers using a range of methods to visually illustrate student progress, depending on student age, content taught, and other factors. Here is a random sampling:

- With older students, some teachers employ progress binders. Students themselves graph their upward trajectory on fluency or math skills or chemistry standards.

- One teacher made a habit of stapling a copy of each student's first diagnostic exam to each subsequent assessment so that the students could always look back and see their own growth.

- Simple or elaborate bulletin board systems map and track individual and classwide progress for students in all subjects.

- With younger students, some teachers use one sheet of paper on which students can collect stickers next to the class objectives they have mastered.

- One elementary teacher worked with her students to build "I Can" cans of accomplishments. When students master a skill, they write it ("I can multiply fractions" or "I can write a friendly letter") on a strip of paper and put it in the can. The teacher takes inventory of the students' cans periodically (or when students need a boost).

- Pamela Bookbinder, a New York City high school social studies teacher, set up a system online where her students and their families could get daily progress reports on academic achievement and behavioral performance. She noted that seeing their own progress has become a happy "compulsion" for her students. Some of them even check their progress maps from their cell phones during the day.

Why do we see so many concrete representations of student progress in classrooms where students are making dramatic academic gains? As we have investigated this pattern, we have come to realize that highly effective teachers are enjoying important benefits by making students' progress tangible with graphic representation. In several ways, these methods of illustrating progress contribute to a strong culture of achievement, which in turn fosters student investment.

Above all, highly effective teachers understand that students need to see their progress in order to believe they are progressing. All of us, and perhaps especially students who may not have experienced much success in school, are inspired by tangible signs of our own progress. Unfortunately, sometimes seeing our own intellectual growth can be difficult. Students may be dramatically improving their reading comprehension, or writing skills, or chemistry knowledge, and yet still feel they are not making progress. They therefore derive no benefit from the "I Can" component of investment, so teachers must find creative ways to illustrate progress and learning.

Although there is plenty of support in education research for the idea that illustrating progress begets more progress,[26] the most powerful endorsements come from the highly effective teachers who depend on this strategy. Felicia Cuesta, a teacher in Los Angeles who led her students to dramatic academic success, recalls that "independent tracking sheets revolutionized my class in terms of investment." She had her students fired up about working toward a goal, but she realized they were not connecting their daily hard work with the ultimate aim. To address the gap, she devised independent tracking sheets on which students recorded their performance on formative assessments. She saw her students more willing to work hard once they had evidence of the effects of their work.

Older students also scramble to get a glimpse of the latest broadcast of their progress toward mastering all of the particular learning standards. Over and over, we have evidence of even middle school and high school students rushing to see a new progress chart. One teacher, Veronica Ruelas, described this scene in her classroom of sixth, seventh, and eighth graders:

> I have a target board that holds the tests for the students who have mastered 80 percent on the previous week's assessment. The target board also lists the standard for the week that they have been assessed on. Students come in on Thursday and literally run to the board to see who has "made it." I will never forget the day that I had been doing this for about three weeks. One of my eighth-grade students went to the target board and realized he hadn't made it. He was visibly upset. My "coolest" student said, "That's okay, man, we'll figure out where you went wrong, and I can help you, because I made it. You'll get on next time."

In students' clamor for concrete indications of their success, we see the beginnings of an important journey from extrinsic to intrinsic motivations for learning. Early in the year, students' progress often earns them certain opportunities or incentives—lunch with the teacher, field trips, taking their progress tracker to the principal's office to get a word of encouragement and praise, dance parties, the chance to call parents during class to tell them about their progress. Highly effective teachers report that over time, students begin to internalize the value of academic achievement and take pride in the tangible signs of their academic growth rather than simply focusing on the more material and superficial rewards of grades and incentives.

Andrew Mandel, a teacher in the Rio Grande Valley, recalls that membership in his "English Expert" club became a profound honor in his classroom as students bought into the huge value of academic success:

> I was guardedly optimistic that my seventh graders would find merit in earning the title of "English Expert," which meant that they took a quiz demonstrating mastery on all of the objectives from the previous six-week unit. Success started slowly, and only two students got every answer correct on the first try. But each week brought another chance to take a mastery quiz (different questions, same unit objectives for six weeks), and incrementally, more and more students ended up getting their names on the roll of English Experts. Many would stop occasionally to check the bulletin board, almost as if they feared their name would suddenly disappear. Some even brought in friends from my other classes to show them the board and share their achievement. Those who were not yet Experts begged me to grade their quizzes before leaving the classroom that day. While the system took some planning and upkeep to implement because I was constantly signing their progress charts and writing new questions, it was worth it. Demanding 100 percent mastery communicated the value of persistence and the primacy of our academic skills. Best of all, with all of the different ways to earn status at school, I was thrilled that it was cool to be an Expert.

Another important theme in highly effective teachers' use of visual representations of progress is student empowerment. Making the pace of progress clear encourages students to take ownership of their own learning.

To encourage student ownership and accountability in the classroom, many teachers make a point of tasking students with producing the illustrations of progress—graphs, charts and stickers, or narrative reports on strengths and weaknesses. Blair Beuche, a high school Spanish teacher in Baltimore, explains that her students manage their own progress tracking sheets (a map of the fifty target achievements of her Spanish class) because she wants "to invest . . . students and empower them in this process. I wanted to make them feel like they had control of their learning, and that they are the center of the learning process. Because of the new tracking systems, students held themselves more accountable for their work and were more cognizant of their mastery. I found that students worked harder for the big goal."

Martin Winchester, a veteran teacher in the Rio Grande Valley, points out that a teacher enjoys both professional and personal benefits when students take ownership of tracking their progress and learning:

> I looked at ways to give my students more ownership over their own learning and shifted many of my tracking systems to student-led, self-directed means for students to track their own progress. This turned out to be a huge catalyst for student motivation and accountability. I also began to have students do an initial self-assessment of their compositions or projects before they turn them in to me so that I can look at what they perceive are the strengths and weaknesses of their work and I can share feedback on where I agree or disagree with their self-assessment. This has proved to be not only effective in creating more student ownership and independent learners, but has cut down on the sheer volume of grading work as well as shifted the focus to analysis as well as evaluation. My feedback is not only more targeted now but better aligned with how students perceive their own work and progress. The benefits of these strategies for me and my family were tremendous because I could continue to do something that I loved while making the time to be a husband and a father.

Finally, as several of these highly effective teachers suggest (and as we will discuss in more detail in Chapter Five), these illustrations of student progress extend beyond student focus and investment. They inspire and inform the teachers' hard work and improvement as well. Consider Anna Lutey's description of the inextricable link between showing students their progress and improving her own:

> At the beginning of the implementation of the bar graphs, my students seemed like they were thinking, "Yeah, yeah, what is Miss Lutey doing now?" In addition to the unenthusiastic greeting, our test scores were going down, which spurred a critical analysis of WHY, WHY, WHY is this happening? I started changing my instruction, pulling small groups

during school and after school, and allotting more time for rereading and discussion. Our weekly comprehension test results for reading went up from 46 percent to 83 percent. . . . When I revealed the bar graph to the class, they went *crazy*. They finally saw the results of their hard work. Now they see that they can do it if they work hard. Now I have students asking for the results and waiting to hear if they made growth.

Without fail, classrooms in which students are making dramatic academic achievement are ones where the teacher has created some form of "dashboard" for students—a concrete representation of students' academic growth that lets them see their progress. When students can see the results of their hard work, they are willing to put in more hard work, more quickly internalize the value of achievement, and begin to own their educational progress. Graphic representations of progress drive a culture of achievement in the classroom and that environment leads to greater student achievement.

## Purposefully Employing Role Models

Chrissie Coxon's third graders talk about "boundary breakers"—leaders who overcome obstacles to solve problems and benefit others. Ms. Coxon has made boundary-breaking role models a central theme of her classroom: Mohandas Gandhi, Rosa Parks, Dr. Martin Luther King Jr., Congressman John Lewis, Wangari Maathai, Majora Carter, and Newark (New Jersey) mayor Cory Booker. These leaders have played a central role in her reader's workshop, social studies, and homework reading and writing.

The strong culture of achievement in Ms. Coxon's classroom is built from students' deep relationship with such boundary breakers—whether those relationships are driven by virtual interactions with historical figures (Gandhi and Rosa Parks, for example), in-class appearances (Majora Carter, founder of Sustainable South Bronx), or class trips to meet the subjects of their studies (Congressman Lewis at the U.S. Capitol). Ms. Coxon's students feel that they genuinely know and are guided by these exceptional leaders. They reference them in their shout-outs and appreciations of each other in morning meeting and at dismissal. And Ms. Coxon and students refer to these leaders in their discussions of student behavior and integrity. It is not unusual to hear students say to each other, "That is so Gandhi of you!"

The imagined and real presence of these leaders in her classroom pays off in student learning. In her second year as a teacher, Ms. Coxon's students on average made more than two years' worth of reading growth and mastered over 91 percent of all third-grade math standards. Every student left her classroom reading at or above grade level.

Many teachers use role models in one form or another. The most successful teachers, like Ms. Coxon, infuse their classroom with role models who reinforce the same messages and values of hard work and achievement the teacher is marketing in the classroom. In our experience, role models who successfully increase student investment in working hard toward academic achievement meet three criteria:

1.  They appeal to students' self-identities in some way, perhaps sharing students' background, interests, or experiences.

2.  They promote, in their messages and stories, values related to achievement, effort, and teamwork.

3.  Their engagement with students is frequent and meaningful enough to influence student beliefs and behaviors.

Thus, teachers ensure that the role models will align with their classroom culture and student needs. These teachers look for connections between students and role models, a practice that devalues the random "poster role models" that sometimes appear, unreferenced, on the walls of less effective classrooms. These teachers also resist conflating "famous" with "role model" and instead draw students' attention to people who, by their actions and achievements, illustrate that hard work leads to success, even if it means making new connections with people students already know.

These criteria lead many teachers to use role models who grew up in or are from the community, giving an immediate sense of identity for the students. Shannon Dingle, a middle school teacher in the Rio Grande Valley, became an active member in community organizations in the area and used those connections to convince many local leaders to come to her class. Her students felt an immediate affinity with these leaders. She then had students think about, write letters to, and write about these leaders throughout the year in her classroom. Ms. Dingle recalls that these individuals had a huge impact on students' motivation:

> Whether it was a lawyer, accountant, or local business leader who came to speak with my students, there were always a few individuals who would think, "Hey, what that person does is interesting." Suddenly you'd hear kids start to talk about life after college and the jobs they would get. But the most influential person was General Ricardo Sanchez, a commanding officer in Iraq. General Sanchez grew up in the community, and I helped ensure that a significant number of my students attended a community event in which he talked about what his work in Iraq was like and how he rose to his position.
>
> I had students who attended share what they had learned about him with the students who had been unable to hear him speak firsthand. After that, whenever Paul would complain that he didn't have to work because they were poor and so it didn't matter what they did, they would not be successful, the other students would snap at him and point out that General Sanchez was poor, and now everyone knows who he is. Somehow he made all these intangible things that I talked about real to my students—because he was a real person, from *their* community who rose above poverty. And as they saw this, over and over, their buy-in really improved.

Some of the most influential role models are the easiest to reach, including not just students' family members but also peers. For older students, creative classroom management can turn peer pressure into a positive force, as students see and admire each other's success and feel obligated to work hard for the team. For younger students, involving older kids in their learning is often a powerful experience that leverages their natural desire to be older and bigger. Tricia Zucker, a Houston kindergarten teacher, invested the third-grade class in her kindergartners' goal to learn one hundred sight words. When the reading buddies came into the classroom, Ms. Zucker's kindergartners worked even harder to show off their skills. She saw her students, independently, "writing" (in whatever form they could) notes to their reading buddies to share the news that they had learned more sight words.

Highly effective teachers also realize that they themselves are the most important role model in the room. As discussed in reference to effective messages, these teachers recognize they are always onstage and that any contradiction between what they say and do will undermine their campaign to invest students in working hard to reach their ambitious goals. Angela Holland, a high school Spanish teacher in St. Louis, told us: "Students key in to *every* move their teacher makes. In many cases, a teacher's determination and persistence is what inspires students to press onward toward the mark of academic excellence and achievement."

Sometimes, teachers who share racial or socioeconomic background with their students can use those aspects of their identity to foster connections and maximize their own impact as a role model. Joseph Almeida, for example, relates the story of one student: "I tell them a story about a young boy who grows up without a father, blames himself for the absence of his father—the same situation for many of my students—then uses his misfortune as a motivator to achieve his personal best by performing well in school and participating in many activities, and gets accepted to a really prestigious university." Mr. Almeida's students are excited to learn the subject of the story is Mr. Almeida.

One of Mr. Almeida's colleagues, Leslie-Bernard Joseph, is of Haitian American descent and grew up in a single-parent household. Mr. Joseph believes that his shared experience with his students has facilitated relationships with them and strengthened his position as a role model. When students have expressed frustration or have lost focus because of difficult home situations, he draws on his own childhood struggles to suggest that those challenges are not obstacles but opportunities to show greater strength and resiliency. For Mr. Joseph, his own upbringing by a single mother who struggled to make ends meet is the basis for both his "no excuses" expectations and his deep appreciation of the obstacles his students face on their paths to academic success. His students have responded by embodying his well-modeled principle of accepting responsibility for academic growth and success.

We hear variations on this theme from many teachers of color with whom we work. Especially African American, Latino, Native American teachers, and teachers from low-income backgrounds believe they can play an important role as counselors for students who are grappling with the tensions involved in the pursuit of academic success—students who might, for example, face extra challenges in their effort or might fear that their pursuit could result in leaving their community behind and/or becoming disconnected from their peers.

Sarah Bass, a seventh-grade English and history teacher in Los Angeles, is an African American teacher of African American students. Not only do her students recognize a connection with her that she can leverage to influence their mindsets and investment in school, but she believes her experience as an African American means, to some degree, that she may have "less cultural learning to acquire and maybe more understanding of certain trends and patterns of behavior," all of which benefits her leadership in the classroom. At the same time, Ms. Bass says she can also highlight differences between her and her students to broaden their perspectives of their own identities and aspirations—differences that confront her students' assumptions about themselves. Ms. Bass has had to tackle her students' accusations she was "acting white" when she used advanced vocabulary or expressed her love of learning and to show her students by her example that "education is just as African American as anything else."

Jessica Tsabetsaye, a Native American teacher who returned to her Zuni community in New Mexico to teach, has no doubt that her ethnic and cultural connections to her students create trust that facilitates her influence on their hard work and academic progress. Maria Zambrano, who was born in Ecuador, teaches students mostly of Mexican descent in Los Angeles and reports that although her students' Mexican American heritage is different from her own, the fact that she appeared to be like them in some ways and spoke Spanish meant that she "didn't have to work as hard as some might to break down barriers." She believes this is an advantage that translates to increased learning opportunities for her students.

We hear similar insights from teachers who share a low socioeconomic background with their students, even when those teachers *do not* share their racial or ethnic identity. Rachel Buckler is a white teacher who grew up in a low-income household and teaches mostly African American students in St. Louis. She explains that "I don't know for sure how it has translated to academic achievement for my students, but being able to talk from experience about things like being on free/reduced lunch, growing up in a single-parent home, and not being able to go on the field trip that kids with more money are going on has helped with motivation and investment."

At the same time, most of these teachers warn that shared identity is not a guarantee of success as a role model or as a teacher. Fernando Rangel, a Latino high school English teacher in the Rio Grande Valley who grew up there himself, emphasizes that teachers cannot enter the classroom thinking they will be successful because of their race/ethnicity or background. Rather, he has found that for teachers who share racial or socioeconomic identity with students, "the door is a little easier to open," even if success ultimately depends on "what you do once you go through that door."

Nothing about these anecdotes suggests that teachers who do not share racial or socioeconomic identities with their students cannot be exceptional role models and have an extraordinary impact on their students' lives. On the contrary, we see that all teachers, whatever their background, are looking to use whatever connections they can, including a connection drawn from a common element of identity, to build a relationship from which they can advance the life options of their students. Emily Barton, a junior high teacher in rural Louisiana, described her experience as a teacher and a role model:

> My background and life history was very different [from] my students'. We had different racial identities—96 percent of my students were African American. I am a white. Grew up in very different cultures—my students grew up in rural Louisiana; I grew up in the New York City suburbs. Different educational histories—my parents are second-generation college students, I was a third-generation college grad. Most of my students' parents had not graduated from high school. But what I found interesting was how influential both the places of difference and sameness could be in how my students related to me.
>
> Being a role model beyond the classroom required sharing information about my life beyond my knowledge of mathematics. Seventh graders are not bashful about asking these questions or telling you what they think about you. But I was careful about boundaries—especially as I was struggling with my own confidence regarding classroom management early on. I actually wish I had shared more. They were so curious about life in a big city and wanted me to take pictures of everything when I went home for the holidays. They would seek me out to ask questions about what things looked like and how people acted in New York, often drawing from things they'd read or seen on TV. They wanted to know what I did over the weekend and were so curious to find out why. They wanted to know how many sisters and brothers I had and what we ate for the holiday meals.
>
> In retrospect, it is interesting to note that the students who shared elements of my identity, be it gender or race, were definitely quicker to try to relate to me and quicker to put me in the category of role model. My five white female students . . . wanted to understand and emulate my decisions in a different way. But over time, I think I had that effect on many. I had a group of five girls (all African American) who would come help me grade and file papers during lunch every day. Over time, I got to know them well; they'd share their fears and hopes and stories. And they got to know me. They really looked to me for advice and would refer back to stories that I'd told months before in telling a story about something they did or talking through something they were facing. It was the little things that I forgot I'd even told them—what I got my sister for her birthday or why I'd chosen not to have a TV—that would often catch me off guard and remind me the power of my example.
>
> But above all it was my relentless belief in their ability to be successful and refusal to let them get away with anything less that I think left the biggest impression. I visited those students three years later, and the stories they were recollecting and the things they were saying about the impact of having me as a teacher were all centered in shared experiences of my transparent belief in their high potential. Every piece of paper they

submitted to me had to include as part of the margin, "I can do anything if I try." I told them some stories about what had led me to believe this about my own life, and even though they came from a very different schema of life, I think the stories stuck. But the biggest challenge I ever faced and the thing that proved that statement to me more firmly than any other experience was seeing that I could lead them to get on grade level. And watching me prove that to them was probably the most influential role modeling I could do.

Whether they are using others or themselves as examples, by providing role models relevant to students' lives and by employing those role models in meaningful, and not just superficial, ways, effective teachers inspire students to continue their hard work and illustrate that this work will lead to success.

## Investing Students Through Instruction and Learning

In addition to strategies that create a welcoming environment and a culture of achievement, highly effective teachers employ instructional strategies that foster student investment and encourage hard work. Three such strategies are: establishing the relevance of academic effort and content to students' aspirations, interests, and lives; teaching at the frontier of students' ability; and empowering students with choice in and ownership over their learning.

### Establishing the Relevance of Content

When students see the relevance of what they are learning, they are more inclined to want to learn—a critical element of investment. This idea suggests that teachers should address and answer the question, "Why are we learning this?" and that the teacher's answer should involve students' interests and aspirations.

Not only does this mean that teachers should be explicit with students about what they will be learning and how it connects to students' interests, but it also leads strong teachers to bring real-world context to every stage of instruction, from introducing new ideas, to practicing new skills, to assessments. Through role playing, hypothetical scenarios, real-world experiments, and external publication of learning, highly effective teachers inspire investment by keeping the purpose of and audience for student achievement close at hand.

Many teachers create culminating public demonstrations of student learning—perhaps in the form of a book, a presentation to another class, a "museum" set up in the classroom, or a public service project that calls on newly mastered skills. These productions offer students an immediate opportunity to use (and show off) their learning. These methods take them beyond the traditional art project on the bulletin board and into the realm of writing letters to city council members, companies, or school officials; making price comparison guides of groceries for their families; developing a lesson to teach younger students; or producing a play or video that illustrates key concepts from recent lessons. Students are much more likely to invest time and care in their writing, for example, when they know someone else is going to read it. Teachers whose students "go public" with their assignments in ways that will affect other people find students to be more conscious of their presentation and, as a result, more likely to see the connections between what they do inside the school walls and beyond them.

Danielle Neves, a sixth-grade English and social studies teacher in Los Angeles, described bundling the knowledge and skills from her middle school social studies and language arts class into a motivating performance of student learning:

> I always try to provide a culminating unit activity in which students can use the skills and information they've learned. For example, the first unit we do is called, "Why Study History?" I tell students that they are the superintendent of schools and that their social studies teachers are arguing over the curriculum. Some think teaching history should be stopped, others think it must continue, and others can't decide. As the superintendent, they must decide and present their argument at a press conference. We then research and discuss arguments for and against studying history. They write their speech in the form of a five-paragraph essay because that is what they are learning in English. They work in groups to rate each speech on a rubric, and the most persuasive from each group is read before the class. Everyone dresses up for the "press conference," and we videotape the speeches.

In the words of one teacher educator, "Students need to recognize and find relevance to their own lives in what you are teaching. If students can make a connection to what they already know about in their lives and experiences, it is more likely they will be interested in what you have to say." [27]

## Teaching at the Frontier of Student Ability

When you are given a task that is much too easy or much too hard, how do you feel? How does the degree of difficulty influence your motivation to complete the task?

Like all of us, students are most likely to believe they can and want to work hard and succeed when they are working at the frontier of what is comfortable for them—the nexus of challenge and ability. Like all of us, students will be most motivated to strive for success when the work is challenging but is also ultimately doable. Like many other new teachers, Rachna Fraccaro saw that when she did not calibrate the level of challenge for students' abilities, they became frustrated (if the work was too hard) or bored (if the work was too easy). When she started differentiating instruction to be sure her students were working at the frontier of their abilities, she saw that they were much more engaged, on task, productive, and happy. For example, Ms. Fraccaro uses the Developmental Spelling Assessment to differentiate her word study and spelling instruction. After administering this assessment, she is able to ensure that her students can work comfortably with spelling patterns that are on their level.

Researchers call this level of difficulty "optimally challenging"[28] or the "zone of proximal development"[29] and posit that work at that level of difficulty maximizes motivation. When work is too easy, "while it may be accompanied by pervasive positive feedback, it will not enhance the sense of competence because the activity is already well mastered. Boredom is the likely outcome." With work that is too difficult, "pervasive negative feedback will undermine intrinsic motivation and promote feelings of incompetence, anxiety, and frustration."[30]

Researcher Jeff Howard explains why teaching material that is simultaneously challenging and yet within reach is important in reinforcing the theory of malleable intelligence and motivating students to invest effort throughout their education: "Initial objectives should be somewhat challenging (involving a stretch and some real possibility of failure), but very realistic (failure may be a possibility, but the goal is within the range of what is realistically attainable). A starting point that is realistically geared to the present capabilities of the child stimulates a belief that 'I can do this' and engenders stronger commitment of effort to the task." Howard explains that this success begets more success by helping students develop perseverance and confidence even as tasks become incrementally more challenging: "Each success generates increased confidence and satisfaction and energizes a more challenging objective for the next attempt. As goals become more challenging, they evoke greater focus; the child becomes increasingly absorbed, immersed in the detail and the work. The heightened involvement alters the experience of the task. The work becomes enjoyable, learning is accelerated, understanding is deepened.[31] Howard's point is not that teachers should build students' confidence that they are "smart," which would reinforce the theory of innate or fixed intelligence, but rather that teachers should show students using the students' own efforts that hard work will enable them to become smart and succeed at school.

Given that each student's nexus of challenge and ability is somewhat different, implementation of this strategy ultimately requires differentiating instruction and practice for students who are performing at different levels in the class. Expert Carol Ann Tomlinson teaches that instruction ideally should start where students start and grow as fast as they grow.[32] Researchers have found that students feel both challenged and supported by this building-block approach. Although we will not describe the nuts and bolts of effective differentiation here, our aim is to point out a pattern we observe in high-performing classrooms: students' investment increases when teachers carefully calibrate instruction to the frontier of students' ability.

### Empowering Students with Choice and Responsibility

The most effective teachers we work with also build student investment by infusing significant choice and responsibility into student learning. In order for students to fully embrace the importance of their goals and the significant impact of their own hard work and good choices, they need to have some control over their learning.

Rebecca Cohen explained that as a seventh-grade English/language arts, reading, and drama teacher in Baltimore, she wove together notions of choice and relevance in her teaching: "I create projects that give my students choice. During writing workshop, they have the opportunity to work alone or in groups and to write for a variety of purposes. I try to make sure that the options that I create are important. The writing that they do in my classroom is not for me. It is instead for them, for their families, and even for the community." Lauren Hawley, a fifth-grade teacher in Aurelian Springs, North Carolina, recalls that at first, she mistakenly assumed strong teaching meant maintaining control of every decision in the classroom. She quickly came to realize that student empowerment and choice increased student investment and learning:

> In my first year of teaching, I thought that in order to maintain control of my classroom, I needed to make all the decisions—instructional and behavioral. It was exhausting, and it created a power struggle between me and my students. Going into my second year, I made up my mind that, wherever possible, I would give students choices and then hold them accountable to their decisions. I started in small ways, like for math homework, I often said, "Choose ten problems to complete." This gave students ownership over the assignment, and many felt that they could choose the "easy" problems, even when all the problems were relatively similar. Later, I gave them behavioral choices, like during read-aloud: "You can choose to sit in your chair or on your desk, as long as you are being an active listener." If a student was obviously distracted while sitting on his or her desk, I simply told him or her to sit in the chair instead. The more ways I gave students choices, the more willing they were to do what I asked them to do. Giving students choices created a class culture of responsibility and let them know that I was a fair and reasonable teacher. It also encouraged them to brainstorm choices in other situations and broadened their ability to problem-solve independently.

Of course, choice does not mean permissiveness. Rather than leave all choices up to students, successful teachers set up a context in which any choice students make will be on the path to the big goals and thereby increase their sense of autonomy and responsibility. Empowering students through instructional choices means giving them several excellent, productive options, and it has the ultimate effect of increasing students' willingness to work hard toward academic achievement.

This principle is directly connected to the notion of fixed versus malleable intelligence: students need to feel greater control of their experience in order to shift to a belief that their academic success will be the result of their own hard work. A number of simple experiments have established this link. For example, in one experiment, students who were allowed to choose which three puzzles they would work on were more invested—and showed more perseverance—in completing the puzzles than were students who were told which puzzles to tackle. In fact, the students who chose their puzzles continued working on them after the set time for the experiment was over, while the others usually did not.[33] Another set of experiments went further by examining the role of choice in an instructional setting. Not surprisingly, "When subjects were told what to learn, even if it was the same material that they would have chosen to learn, their learning tended to be impaired." In the researchers' language, "choice, of course, provides subjects with the opportunity for self-determination and . . . enhances their intrinsic motivation."[34]

# Conclusion: Key Ideas and Next Questions

The Teaching As Leadership rubric (see Appendix A) describes six specific teacher actions that indicate a teacher is investing students and their influencers in working hard to achieve the big goal. Highly effective teachers:

I-1: Develop students' rational understanding that they can achieve by working hard ("I can").

I-2: Develop students' rational understanding that they will benefit from achievement ("I want").

I-3: Employ appropriate role models.

I-4: Consistently reinforce academic efforts.

I-5: Create a welcoming environment.

I-6: Respectfully mobilize students' influencers.

When students in high-performing classrooms believe they can and want to reach dramatic academic achievement, their investment manifests in concrete ways that are a joy to experience. Crystal Jones's students actually groaned in pity for a student who was called out of the classroom and would miss learning time. Stephani Estes's students demanded to re-assess their skills instead of playing a game because they were confident that their hard work was going to show in their performance. Rebecca Roundtree Harris's students developed and shared with each other meta-cognitive reading strategies to tackle unknown words. In Taylor Delhagen's classroom, every student showed up after school to continue a lesson that had been disrupted in the morning. Lauren Hawley's students spent recess identifying patterns in the playground, in their clothes, and in their lunch tray because pattern identification was the objective that morning. In Janis Ortega's classroom, a struggling student taped a little reminder onto his desk: "I have the power. I can be successful."

## Key Ideas

In every case where we see amazing results for students who are facing inordinate challenges, we see a teacher who has led students to believe they can and want to succeed at the highest levels. We see a teacher who, by involving students' families and influencers, has changed students' debilitating belief that hard work does not make them smarter. When students are invested in success, rather than the teacher having to drag the students toward success, the teacher and students are pushing each other to work hard to achieve ambitious goals.

This chapter has suggested three general approaches to investing students in working hard for ambitious academic goals:

- *Student investment requires a welcoming environment* where children feel safe, comfortable, and affirmed enough to take the risks necessary to try, fail, and learn. Highly effective teachers generate that welcoming environment by having strong relationships with their students and creating a sense of team and community among the students.

- *A strong culture of achievement emanates from classrooms where students are invested in working hard toward ambitious goals.* Teachers create a context in which academic success—for each individual and for the whole group—is highly valued. These teachers create a culture of achievement by infusing the class with key messages, clearly communicating students' academic progress, and strategically employing role models that embody values that lead to great success.

- *Student investment is built through teachers' instructional decisions.* Highly effective teachers establish their objectives' relevance to students' lives, teach at a level of rigor that stretches but does not discourage students, and empower students with choice and responsibility in their own learning.

Driving all of these strategies are teachers' high expectations for their students and teachers' heavy dependence on families and influencers to reinforce students' efforts.

---

 **teachingasleadership.org**

More guidance on how to invest students and their families and influencers is available online, including:

- Specific teacher actions that most contribute to student investment

- Additional strategies for investing students in working hard toward ambitious goals

- Factors to consider in choosing among the vast menu of methods highly effective teachers use to invest students

- Common pitfalls new teachers encounter in trying to build students' sense of "I can" and "I want"

---

## Next Questions

In our experience, highly effective teachers' use of these investment strategies is a necessary foundation for helping students overcome great odds and make dramatic academic achievement. With these principles and strategies in mind, you are ready to consider how to address these next questions in the context in which you work:

- How can I best develop investment strategies for the students in my classroom, given their age, interest, experiences, and needs?

- How can I infuse these principles and strategies of investment in my planning for student instruction and behavior?
- What biases am I bringing to my community, my students, and my students' families that I should watch for and work to resolve?
- What indicators do I want to watch for as signs of successfully investing students and their families and influencers in working hard to reach our big goals?

In a highly effective teacher's classroom, these ideas combine to create a space where learning pervades every second and every action in the day. Remember Anne Lyneis, the teacher introduced above who worked with Hannah to see that effort correlated with success? In her classroom, she has achieved a vision of student investment to which all of us can aspire:

> My students have taken ownership over their own learning and they are curious about learning and excited to learn as much as possible. My students always turn in homework. After school I always see my students reading their books off by themselves and I have received many phone calls from parents explaining that they can't get their son or daughter to put their books down at home—all they want to do is read. My students rarely miss school, and parents call saying that their son or daughter was sick but they cried and complained until they let them go to school. They know how important every day is.
>
> Invested students love school, they want to work hard and they see the value of everything that they are learning. It wasn't easy getting my students to understand the importance of education and get them to want to work hard. But now they have internalized the importance and. . . next year even when I am not their teacher they will be just as successful as they were in my classroom because an education, and working hard, is something that they want.

## "WHAT IF YOU'RE WRONG?"

 teachingasleadership.org

*An excerpt from Ms. Lora's Story, a case study in Teaching As Leadership, available online at www.teachingasleadership.org.*

"It's going to take lots and lots of hard work, Anthony."

Ms. Lora was on one knee in front of him, and he peered down into her eyes intently. She once again was playing the "prove it" card; Anthony really responded to the idea that he could prove his doubters wrong.

"You're going to have to make a decision, Anthony," she continued. "If you really want to prove it to people, I can help you. But you're not going to be able to prove it doing the regular stuff. You're going to have to make a choice to stay late and work harder than you ever have before."

This was probably the tenth time they had had this conversation. Anthony remained silent, but never took his eyes off Ms. Lora. Ms. Lora stared back at him, trying simultaneously to suppress her doubts and to will into his mind a belief that he could excel academically. She was having to choose her words very carefully since Anthony's mother was still one of those people whom they needed to prove wrong.

Anthony maintained his lock on Ms. Lora's eyes and then asked, "What if you're wrong?"

It was his first contribution to the several-month-long, otherwise-one-way conversation. It struck Ms. Lora as unbearably insightful. Anthony had come to accept the idea that it takes hard work to do well; he just wasn't sure *his* hard work would lead to success.

Ms. Lora once again felt the absurdity that he must hear in her encouragement. Why in the world would he want to get his hopes up on the half-baked promises of some new teacher when everyone else in his life, including his own mother and previous teachers, has told him he cannot succeed?

Ms. Lora was trying to mentally process that challenge when Anthony asked another question: "Do you really think I can do it?"

Ms. Lora responded quickly this time. "Anthony, I would not be here having this conversation with you if I didn't. We can do this together."

"Okay," he said flatly.

She longed to see him smile his dimpled smile, but instead his round face looked sad. He then pulled his backpack onto his shoulders and lumbered out the door to find his brother.

# 3
# Plan Purposefully

SET BIG GOALS 1

INVEST STUDENTS AND THEIR FAMILIES 2

PLAN PURPOSEFULLY 3

EXECUTE EFFECTIVELY 4

CONTINUOUSLY INCREASE EFFECTIVENESS 5

WORK RELENTLESSLY 6

**IN EVERY ENDEAVOR,** from lesson plans, to long-term plans, to classroom management plans, successful teachers start by determining the end result they want to see in their students' learning and behavior. They are clear how they will know that result has been reached. Then they plan backward from that result to their starting point, creating an efficient path to success.

> *Once I could imagine all the steps to success in my mind, my plan was ready.*

**STATE STANDARDS SAID** my sophomores needed to master key concepts related to natural selection. I started preparing to teach that standard by first imagining exactly what student mastery would look like if I was successful. At the end of this lesson, all students would be able to define natural selection in their own words, to provide an example of natural selection, and to identify the common misconceptions about it. Once I had in mind that vision of success, I created an end-of-lesson "exit ticket" requiring students to demonstrate those abilities. To sharpen my sense of our target, I wrote out sample responses demonstrating different levels of mastery.

Once I had a clear vision of student mastery and a good assessment to measure it, I began to map out the actual lesson. I considered my diagnostic data (showing students know little about natural selection) and researched common misperceptions about the topic. I mentally tested out some different instructional strategies, and I looked at some Web sites that sometimes give me ideas. When I really thought about my students' learning styles and internalization of these ideas, I realized I needed to keep students active. I realized that a discovery learning lesson might be effective.

**Kristin Reidy,** M.Ed., Arizona Teacher of the Year, 2007, Integrated Science, Marana High School; Ed.D. Candidate at University of Arizona

From these mental walk-throughs and with the huge help of another teacher's lesson plan, my plan took shape. I would divide students into three "species," each with a different "beak"—forks, knives, and spoons. I'd spread beans (representing "prey") in the grass outside. In five minutes simulating an entire generation, the predators would "eat" (by gathering) as much prey as they could, using only their "beaks." We'd then see which kinds of beaks were able to gobble up the most prey and why, and I would lead a discussion of key ideas. Then we would create a "new generation," with a new ratio of beaks based on who got food and who did not, and we would see how the population of birds shifted. I sketched eight statements about natural selection, several of which were common misperceptions that my students would be able to debunk after this experiment. I mapped out key ideas to shape the conversation about each statement.

By imagining my kids doing all this, I tried to identify trouble spots. Utensils can make a lot of noise when in the hands of tap-happy teens, so I didn't plan on distributing them until I'd given them clear directions. My intensely competitive students were going to need a brief primer on what constituted fair play and what did not. I would bring extra beans in case a lawn mower invaded our habitat between generations. Once I could imagine all the steps to success in my mind, my plan was ready.

> *You have to know what you want to accomplish and you*
> *have to see it in your head before you do it.*

**AS I METHODICALLY WASH** each finger and fingernail over the large metal sink outside the operating rooms, my mind is actually focused elsewhere. I'm thinking about what I expect to accomplish over the next several hours. The preoperative MRI shows the young woman's brain tumor to be in an accessible area. We believe we can remove the entire tumor, so our ultimate goal is the full function and health of our patient. By now I have many times traced back the incremental steps it will take to reach that aim.

In preparation, I have visualized every step of the surgery, searching my mind for ways to improve the procedure, avoid mistakes, or foresee problems. I watch and critique in my mind as we drape the patient, as I hear the scrub nurses review their checklist of materials, precounting the sponges and instruments, as I position the patient on the table and place the pins of the Mayfield headholder in the patient's skull. *What if the anesthesiologist is concerned about her blood pressure?* In my mind, I walk through that contingency. *What if we discover the tumor is bigger than we thought?* As I plan, I mentally address that contingency.

**Michelle Smith,** vascular neurosurgeon, New York

I can visualize making the incision, dissecting the scalp, drilling a bone flap in the skull, and beginning the delicate tumor resection under the surgical microscope. I have a crisp mental image of the MRI and of the veins and arteries that I may encounter on the dissection down to the tumor. I once again think through which of those can be sacrificed without repercussion and which must be preserved.

Like my surgical mentor taught me, you have to know what you want to accomplish, and you have to see it in your head before you do it. How well you deal with the unexpected contingencies has a lot to do with how well you make them expected.

I lift my hands from the sink, am draped by the nurses, and enter the operating room.

Success in any meaningful endeavor—from brain surgery in the operating room to brain development in the classroom—begins with purposeful planning. Before taking any action, strong leaders define the ultimate result they want, make clear how they will know they have succeeded, and only then choose and design strategies to that end. Mapping a path to success means imagining, with all the gritty detail possible, leading your team to that vision of success.

For Dr. Smith, these principles mean that the purpose of the operation is foremost in her mind as she prepares. The question she asks herself over and over is, "How can we most effectively and safely ensure this patient's full function and health?"—a question that evokes all of her knowledge of surgical methods, human anatomy, the patient's unique condition and medical history, her own strengths and weaknesses as a doctor, and the time and resources she has at her disposal to act toward that aim. Dr. Smith imagines herself performing the procedure, thinking through the potential unexpected changes to her assumptions and how she can plan for those contingencies. In a sense, Dr. Smith has performed each surgery virtually before she begins it.

For Ms. Reidy, these principles of purposeful planning mean that she starts by developing a clear vision of success for her students that is built on the state's learning standards. She creates an assessment that helps her clarify that vision and gives her a concrete destination to inform her plan to get there. Then she imagines herself leading her students to the objectives and all of the contextual realities that could help or hinder that process.

For Dr. Smith and Ms. Reidy, the outcomes they want determine their methods. (Dr. Smith developed those leadership skills in the classroom, before she became a surgeon, as a sixth-grade science teacher in Baltimore.)

That a brain surgeon would not have a thorough, purposeful plan is unthinkable. It would have been equally absurd if, following President Kennedy's proclamation about going to the moon, NASA scientists had simply hustled astronauts into whatever rocket was nearby, launched them in the general direction of the moon, and hoped for the best. Similarly, we cannot imagine success for a coach who before the game says only, "Let's win!" Or for a group of hikers who set out on a hike to a waterfall without a map and no idea where the waterfall is.

Insufficient planning is certainly no less problematic, and is arguably even more disturbing, in our high-stakes context of teaching students whose academic underperformance threatens to limit their opportunities in life.

# Foundations of Purposeful Planning

In our experience, teachers whose students are making the most dramatic academic progress think of purposeful planning—for any type of plan, large or small—as comprising three sequential principles. First, they develop a clear vision of success (as discussed with big goals) from which they can plan backward. Second, they ask themselves, "How will I know that my students have reached that vision?" and translate their image of success into some form of assessment. And third, after developing a vision and assessment, the strongest teachers design a plan by imagining themselves on that path to success, testing in their mind different strategies and anticipating different challenges to success.

In this chapter, we first look more closely at this three-part concept of purposeful planning. In the second section, we explore how this process of envisioning, assessing, and planning manifests in three of the most fundamental types of plans: long-term plans (for the year and for units), lesson plans, and classroom management plans.

## Developing Your Vision of Success

Like many other new teachers, Rachel Meiklejohn initially felt swamped by all she had to think about and plan for as a sixth-grade teacher on a Navajo reservation in New Mexico. But with the help of a colleague, she realized she was going about planning all wrong:

> When I began teaching, I was overwhelmed by all the subjects and students I was expected to teach. . . . I was staying up into the early hours of the morning just trying to figure out how I was going to get through the next day. There was no way I could look any farther down the road than tomorrow. Fortunately, another teacher in my town came to my rescue. As I would explain to him my plans for the next day, he would always ask, "Why are you doing that? What's the purpose?"
>
> At first this question annoyed me. I didn't have an answer or any time to waste thinking about it. I just needed to plan. But the real problem was that I was picking activities that I hoped would interest my students and that somehow through that interest, they would learn. I had some vague objectives but no solid ideas about what I wanted them to leave class knowing.
>
> Reflecting on his question finally made my problem obvious: stepping back and taking the time to figure out what I wanted students to be able to do by the end of the unit and then breaking that down by day revolutionized my planning. Not only did it make my teaching more effective (because I actually had something that I wanted students to learn), it also made my planning more effective. I knew what students needed to accomplish and was able to work backward from there to plan how I would get them to the objective.

In essence, to become an effective planner Ms. Meiklejohn had to start asking herself, "What is the purpose? Where are we headed?" She realized that to be an effective planner, she had to begin at the end, mapping back from a clear vision in her mind of what she wanted her students to know and be able to do and what she would see from them to demonstrate that knowledge and skill. With this realization, she made a giant step toward becoming a highly effective teacher. As a backward planner, she joined the ranks of all of the other teachers we have worked with whose students make dramatic academic progress

That student learning is maximized when teachers backward-plan is well advocated in the influential book *Understanding by Design* by Grant Wiggins and Jay McTighe:

> As the old adage reminds us, in the best designs form follows function. In other words, all the methods and materials we use are shaped by a clear conception of the vision of desired results. That means that we must be able to state with clarity what the student should understand and be able to do as a result of any plan and irrespective of any constraints we face.

You probably know the saying, "If you don't know exactly where you are headed, then any road will get you there." Alas, the point is a serious one in education. We are quick to say what things we like to teach, what activities we will do, and what kinds of resources we will use; but without clarifying the desired results of our teaching how will we ever know whether our designs are appropriate or arbitrary? How will we distinguish merely interesting learning from effective learning? More pointedly, how will we ever meet content standards or arrive at hard-won student understandings unless we think through what those goals imply for the learner's activities and achievements?[1]

This tenet is not only a habit of effective teachers but is a broadly recurring leadership principle found in all successful endeavors. "In some ways, leaders live their lives backward," explain Kouzes and Posner. "They see pictures in their mind's eye of what the results will look like even before they've started their project, much as an architect draws a blueprint or an engineer builds a model. Their clear imagining of the future pulls them forward."[2]

Highly effective teachers, like all other successful leaders, insist that their desired outcomes drive their choice and design of strategies. Less effective teachers, by contrast, choose strategies before they know exactly where they want to end up. Sometimes we find it easier to take the action we are familiar with, in hopes of achieving goals, instead of clearly defining the goals and asking, "What actions, among all the many options, will be most effective in reaching that aim?"

## Translating Your Vision into a Well-Designed Assessment

Think for a moment about the incentives and implications of developing an excellent assessment *before,* rather than *after* you teach your students. When a teacher teaches a lesson or a unit and then creates an assessment, students' success on the assessment is likely to reflect that students mastered what the teacher taught. When a teacher, having developed a clear vision of student success, creates an assessment *before* teaching the material, that assessment will inform the teacher's instructional planning and choices, and students' success on the assessment will instead reflect that students mastered what they were supposed to learn.

This is a consistent pattern among highly effective teachers: they put their goalposts in the ground before they create the gameplan, not after. They hold themselves and their students accountable to their vision of success, not to whatever material they happened to have covered.

Highly effective teachers realize that a well-designed and rigorous assessment becomes the beacon that guides the rest of their planning. North Carolina seventh-grade English/language arts teacher Jacqulyn Janacek recalls how much more efficient and effective she became when she designed her assessment alongside her vision instead of waiting until after teaching the unit:

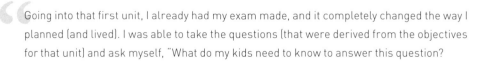

Going into that first unit, I already had my exam made, and it completely changed the way I planned (and lived). I was able to take the questions (that were derived from the objectives for that unit) and ask myself, "What do my kids need to know to answer this question?

What makes sense to teach first? What can go together?" These questions allowed me to put together a unit plan that broke down each day and how it would eventually build up to this assessment. Not only did it save me hours of time figuring out what to teach each day and how to teach it, it made sure that I was setting my students up for success on their test and it held me accountable for teaching them to that high standard.

N'Djamina Johnson, a chemistry teacher in Charlotte, North Carolina, had a similar revelation once she committed to designing the assessments for her units before taking on her daily lesson planning and instructional strategies:

When I began teaching . . . , I had a hard time making time to backward-plan. It takes time to start with a unit exam when all I wanted was to get something on paper for a lesson the next day. But day-to-day lesson planning ends up taking a lot more time than backward planning, and it is less effective in driving student achievement. When I finally took the time to create the exams before the units and the exit quizzes before the lesson plans, I started seeing true mastery. I spent less time trying to find activities to fill the period and more time purposefully selecting resources that aligned to my state standards, my unit goals, and my daily objectives. I also had a greater sense of urgency, because I knew that I needed to teach my objective well one day so that they could master the next day's objective, so they could master that unit goal, which would lead them to master all chemistry content. It was imperative to keep that daily, unit, and semester goal in mind so my students could pass the North Carolina end-of-course exam. My students ultimately passed the end-of-course exam at a rate higher than the district average, and I attribute much of that to my commitment to working with our goals in mind and with that sense of urgency I got from backward planning.

> ▶ **ASSESSING CLASSROOM MANAGEMENT AND EFFICIENCY**
>
> **WE USUALLY THINK FIRST** about academic progress (and long-term, unit, and lesson plans) when we think of assessments. But ways of measuring success are also important to classroom management and classroom procedure plans. Similarly, teachers who achieve exemplary efficiency in their classrooms are those who are using timers and charts to measure, track, and improve the time it takes for transitions, administrative tasks, starting and ending class, and other nonlearning events.

Planning gurus Grant Wiggins and Jay McTighe stress the same best practices we see in these strong teachers and articulate some of the far-reaching benefits of creating assessments before we plan how to reach them:

What would we accept as evidence that students have attained the desired understandings and proficiencies—*before* proceeding to plan teaching and learning experiences? Many teachers who have adopted this design approach report that the process of "thinking like an assessor" about evidence of learning not only helps them to clarify their goals but also results in a more sharply defined teaching and learning target so that students perform better knowing their goal.[3]

This approach may sound a lot like teaching to the test—and in some cases it is, if the test is rigorous and meaningful. The downsides of teaching to the test, and what has turned that phrase into an epithet among so many teachers, is that too many tests require low-level, rote, superficial knowledge instead of more meaningful indicators of growth like critical thinking, inquisitiveness, creativity, and problem solving. Assessing those deeper concepts is not easy, but for the highly effective teachers we have studied, such assessment is a key to dramatic student achievement.

The fundamental importance of being able to select, create, and use assessments that align with and demonstrate your vision for student success means you must become comfortable with some relatively technical aspects of assessment design. Here we highlight briefly a few of the key issues new teachers need to learn more about in working with assessments:

- *Forms of assessments.* There are many, from tests and quizzes, to daily end-of-lesson "exit slips," to performance assessments (which require students to demonstrate a task rather than answer questions), to portfolios (compiling and evaluating student work).

- *Evidence of mastery.* One objective may call for a student to be able to describe a process, while another may call for a student to be able to perform, or analyze, or merely identify a process. Often the verbs of learning goals and standards carry great influence in how an objective should be assessed.

- *Types of questions.* Does your content suggest objective or subjective forms of questions? What of the many forms of questions (open-ended or single-word answer, essay, multiple choice, performance based, and so on) match with the form of evidence you seek? Your decisions on these issues will probably be shaped by the content students are learning, the time available for the assessment, the breadth of material to be assessed, and the depth of knowledge you need to see.

- *Rigor and alignment.* Are your objectives and assessments rigorous and aligned with learning goals that students must master? Assessments that are rigorous are faithful to the full challenge of the learning standards' demands. Where the learning goals call for it, are your assessments aimed at students' meaningful understanding rather than rote, superficial knowledge?

- *Validity.* Will success on the assessment indicate that a student has truly mastered the objectives? Among other things, we must ensure that an assessment's form, language, or style does not give away answers, that we test one idea at a time, and that we are conscious of potential biases that could skew the assessment's validity as an indicator that the vision of success has been reached.

- *Reliability.* Will a particular assessment yield consistently accurate results and provide every student with the opportunity to accurately demonstrate his or her knowledge? This suggests including multiple (and varied) items to assess each learning goal, being clear about directions, and developing a standard evaluation and grading system.

- *Efficiency.* Does your assessment provide insights worth the time it takes to administer? To ensure that the answer to that question is yes, many teachers design their own assessments by prioritizing certain areas, ordering items from easier to harder to make sure students do not get stuck early, and considering how long it will take to grade the assessment.

- *Grading.* Depending on the form of the assessment, "grading" does not mean simply checking whether students' answers are right or wrong. In fact, the best methods of grading provide feedback that becomes an additional instructional tool that leads to greater student learning.

## Mapping Out a Vision-Aligned Plan by Imagining Yourself Implementing It

Once you have a vision of success and know how you will determine you have reached that vision, you can begin developing a plan to reach it. Mapping that path is an exercise in *alignment*—ensuring that every step is contributing meaningfully to getting to the destination.

For highly effective teachers, planning that path begins not on paper but in their mind. Making planning choices involves imagining oneself in the reality of the classroom, performing the actions being planned. Within that imagined virtual reality, teachers can consider the contextual factors that contribute to or inhibit success. In this way, great planners map a path to their objectives that both aligns with the ultimate result and navigates informed assumptions about the contextual reality in which they will act.

This idea can be illustrated by two hypothetical lesson plans for the same learning objective for the same classroom of fourth graders. One lesson plan faithfully fulfills a well-designed lesson plan template. Although it includes all the conventional elements of a good lesson, it was designed by a teacher who has never stepped foot in this particular classroom, never met the students, and knows nothing of the context in which the lesson is being taught. The other lesson plan was designed by a teacher who knows the students' interests, motivations, and prior experiences; has a strong command of their prior knowledge and skills; knows everything about the physical layout and resources of the room; and knows that an overeager assistant principal is likely to make a five-minute announcement on the PA system halfway through the lesson.

How are these lesson plans different? It is easy to imagine the second lesson plan will be more effective in reaching its objective of student mastery because it has been generated within a well-informed virtual reality of context and contingencies. That teacher imagines with clarity the specific issues he or she will need to navigate to reach the objective.

**LIKE DR. SMITH, STRONG** planners in all endeavors insist on considering the reality of their contexts when they make a plan. By imagining that reality as they plan, these leaders anticipate and account for problems and opportunities to more effectively reach their goal. Consider the approach of an excellent basketball coach, whose plans do not just diagram a generic play but take into consideration the size, speed, and skill of individual players on the next opposing team (and on her own team). Or imagine the secretary of commerce developing a plan for distributing innovation funding among economically depressed steel mill communities—a plan hatched not in a theoretical vacuum but from consideration of a host of political and logistical realities, including which members of Congress represent districts that would benefit, the opinions and concerns of unions, larger trends in the economy, and the way the funding will be perceived by other groups that want it. Or imagine an architect assigned to design a school who, instead of sitting down to sketch out an idea, first works to understand the educational philosophy of the school, the topography of the school site, and the time and money the district is willing to spend.[4] In each case, the planner does not plan in a vacuum but instead guides planning decisions by considering the reality in which he or she will be acting.

The neurosurgeon at the beginning of this chapter illustrated the same phenomenon. Her planning encompassed knowing her patient's history, seeing the scans of the tumor, and being familiar with all the resources and processes in the operating room. By walking through the operation in her mind, aligning her every virtual action with the results she sought, she created a more effective plan. This is, once again, a principle of leadership that cuts across all sectors. Plans that are well aligned with their aims are created from imagining their implementation.

For strong teachers, a number of factors guide the imaginative journey that is part of planning for student learning. Here are a few of the factors that teachers mentally weigh as they plan:

• *The nature and cognitive demand and rigor of the goal.* Sometimes the learning goal or objective itself suggests particular means of achieving it. Generally objectives that involve lower-level thinking skills such as knowledge and comprehension invite a teacher to direct, tell, and show new materials. Somewhat higher cognitive levels such as application or analysis might call for students to explore the concept individually or in a collaborative group before moving to a more teacher-led explanation.

• *Relative priority of the content.* The learning standards for one particular grade and subject matter may cover many more ideas and skills than can be taught in a year. Teachers must choose and prioritize those many ideas. One of the factors that informs their planning is how much time they want to give various learning goals.

• *Students' prior knowledge.* A teacher embarking on a plan needs to ask, "Where are we beginning?" Diagnosing students' prior knowledge shapes strategic choices in a number of ways. First, you may discover you need to spend more or less time than you thought on certain objectives. Second, by determining what your students know and understand, you can leverage and build from that foundation (and navigate gaps and misunderstandings) to accelerate new learning.

- *Students' development, learning styles, and motivations: Cognitive, physical, and social development.* Generally children's cognitive, physical, and social skills develop in somewhat predictable sequences. Not surprisingly, those patterns can have implications for how a student learns because they play a role in how the student perceives information, relates to others, and manages the working of his or her mind and body.

- *Learning modalities.* Although some experts suggest that the learning objective itself should trump in decisions about instructional strategies, if you know that your students have preferred learning styles—visual, auditory, tactile, or kinesthetic, for example—you may be able to choose instructional strategies more purposefully.[5] Strong teachers avoid relying too heavily on any one modality.

- *Student interests.* Students have interests related to content, the social dynamics of grouping strategies, the liveliness and pace of the instruction, and much more. All of those factors should be percolating in your mind as you choose among instructional strategies.

- *Pedagogical content knowledge* (or, *How students best learn an idea*). This body of knowledge centers on "the ways of representing and formulating the subject that make it comprehensible to others."[6] Pedagogical content knowledge includes not just a teacher's command of the idea being taught but also the teacher's understanding of effective ways to teach that content to a particular age group of students. The teachers we see with strong pedagogical content knowledge understand and foresee students' common misunderstandings about a particular subject that might inhibit their learning.[7] How, for example, might your planning for an astronomy unit be shaped by the realization that your sixth graders believe the seasons are caused by the earth's moving closer to and farther from the sun? Or how could you inform your early literacy lessons with the understanding that your kindergartners find very confusing the fact that an "s" always makes an /s/ sound while a "c" sometimes makes an /s/ sound? Or what if you are planning a life science unit or lesson for students who define life as "things that move"?[8] Highly successful teachers seek out and employ practices that are particularly effective in their subject area and for their students. Highly effective teacher Kate Tarca described how these considerations fill out the substance of her lesson plan: "Once I have the skeleton ideas for a lesson plan, I always plan the details around likely misconceptions, disturbances, and shortcomings. When planning for my third-grade math lessons, I would ask myself: At what point is Richard likely to get restless, and how can I invest his interest and engage his thinking at that point? Which counterexample to the rule is Miguel likely to discover, and how can I clarify my point with more examples? At what point are Shari and Jacob likely to master this concept, so I can be ready with more challenging problems and extending questions? If my lesson had an answer for each of these students, then it was ready for execution."

- *Culturally relevant pedagogy.* In a landmark study with native Hawaiian children in the Kamehameha Elementary Education Program in Hawaii, researchers found that aligning instructional practices with cultural styles (toward heterogeneously grouped collaboration, culturally appropriate praise, and focus on comprehension over phonics, for example) led to significant gains in reading achievement.[9] *Culturally relevant pedagogy* refers to attempts to match instructional choices with the cultural styles of students.[10] Some scholars believe that students of a particular race, ethnicity, or cultural background respond particularly well to cooperative learning models[11] or "cross-age peer teaching and role modeling."[12] More specifically, some scholars contend that African American students, for example, respond better to instructional strategies that encourage "interpersonal interaction, multiple activities, and multiple sensory modalities than in quiet classrooms in which students are supposed to pay attention to tasks more than people, print more than sound, and do only one thing at a time."[13] Similarly, some scholars contend that Hispanic students, because of unique and common elements of their cultural background, perform particularly well in mixed-ability learning groups.[14] This type of grouping should be used often, some scholars believe, because Hispanic culture places an emphasis on cooperation rather than competition when working toward the attainment of goals.[15]

The relevance of students' racial, socioeconomic, linguistic, and cultural background to a teacher's planning decisions is, however, the subject of some debate. Some teachers and scholars are skeptical of these findings, in part because they believe these methods would also well serve students outside the studied group. Some teachers and scholars find such generalizations unhelpful, and others find them offensive.[16]

While our own studies do not address these questions directly, our experience does indicate that highly effective teachers approach planning with an intention to know as much as possible about their students so as to inform their instructional choices and that the cultural background and values of each student are often part of that calculation. In our experience, the most effective teachers ask, "How does this student best learn?" on an individual basis, even if they are also pondering generalizations about their students' cultural learning styles. This approach is mirrored in a study of education-related activities of four ethnic groups in Boston (Puerto Ricans, African Americans, Chinese Americans, and Irish Americans): "Differences *within* racial or ethnic groups may be greater than differences *between* them on all of these family factors, including support for their children's education, use of extended families and community networks, and involvement in schools."[17] Thus, sometimes the greatest obstacle to culturally congruent pedagogy is the broad diversity of cultures a teacher encounters in his or her classroom.[18]

- *Time and resources available.* When you sit down to imagine yourself leading your students to success on your vision-aligned assessment, consider the available time and resources. How long is a class period? What text may or must you use? How many days of instruction are in the year? Is there a science lab? Will your students have access to paper?

These factors inform teachers' imagined instructional choices as they create a plan that is well-aligned with relevant student learning goals.

# Three Forms of Classroom Plans

With the three fundamental components of purposeful planning—envisioning, developing an assessment, and planning—in mind, we will now look at how these ideas manifest in some of the most prominent types of classroom plans:

- Long-term plans (year-long plans and unit plans)
- Lesson plans
- Classroom management plans

We also look briefly at how these principles of purposeful planning call for differentiated instruction to maximize student success.

## Long Term Plans

A year-long plan charts the grouping and sequencing of the learning goals your students will master in your class. A unit plan maps, over some fraction of the year (perhaps a month or six weeks), a purposefully grouped set of learning objectives that will be taught together. As we explore in the next section, a lesson plan then details the actions a teacher will take to ensure student mastery of one of the unit's learning objectives.

The relationship among long-term plans, unit plans, and lesson plans calls to mind an online map as you zoom in from a broad, overarching perspective (the long-term plan for the year) to a mid-altitude view of one part of the map (the unit plan), to the most granular view (the lesson plan). In a sense, this zoom-in process is a form of backward planning: from the big goal of the long-term plan to the atomized day-to-day actions of lesson plans.

Eric Scroggins, the teacher in New York who was motivated by the success of students in a wealthier community to lead his eighth graders to earn high school credit on the state's Regents Exam, describes his planning approach as an iterative process of more and more detailed maps, moving from the broadest to the most specific. Mr. Scroggins attests that this planning turned his daunting but inspiring big goal into a manageable list of tasks:

> At the beginning of the year, I mapped out the sequence of my units based on the topics covered by the Earth Science Regents Exam. Then for each unit, I would sit down with the text, New York State standards, and past exam copies and make a list of what my students needed to know (concrete knowledge) and then what they needed to be able to do with that knowledge (skills). I then translated that list into objectives using Bloom's taxonomy as a guide and mapped out those objectives onto a calendar for the five to six weeks. At the beginning of each week, I would take the week's objectives and write out detailed lesson plans for each objective, research best practices for teaching new concepts or skills online and through the Regents teacher network, and then gather the materials that I needed for that week.

> ▶ **THREE TYPES OF UNITS**

- *Goals-based units.* In this approach, units are logically organized around a set of learning goals related to each other. A middle school math teacher might, for example, plan a measurement unit to teach students the skills of measuring temperature, speed, volume, mass, and the dimensions of an object. An elementary teacher might create a unit on writing letters, focusing on the skills necessary to write friendly, informative, or persuasive letters.

- *Thematic units.* This approach integrates standards from multiple subject areas to reach goals focusing on a common theme or topic.

- *Project-based units.* These units are focused on producing an end product, such as a book, a play, a trip, or a presentation that serves as a rallying point for the students and motivates them to learn. Students must learn skills in order to complete the project, and therefore they see the utility of skills as they apply their knowledge.

Katie Hill, the special education teacher featured in Chapter One, tells the same story. After creating individualized big goals, she made year-long plans by grouping key ideas into monthly units: "I broke down my students' annual goals into much smaller skill sets and knowledge, which then I pieced back together to develop a personalized standards set for each student which would lead to eventual success through mastery of his or her annual goals."

### Vision, Assessment, and Plan

True to the leadership principles of purposeful planning, the most successful teachers we work with begin long-term planning by setting a vision for success. For academic goal setting, that vision of success involves learning standards.

Despite their occasionally frustrating generality and expansiveness, most state learning standards remain the critical launching pad for leading students to dramatic academic gains. They are, after all, a foundation for the vision of where you want your students to be academically. As one teacher, Luis Alonso, put it, "Standards are the most important tool in planning. . . . [They] give me a clear picture of what students will be expected to do in order to graduate and let me build my curriculum to bring them to that goal."

Frequently strong goal setters use two terms borrowed from Wiggins and McTighe's book *Understanding By Design* to describe their quest to internalize the mass of learning standards they will cover over the year: *essential questions* and *enduring understandings.* These are ways for the teacher and students to make sense of the landscape of learning goals for any given course. Essential questions are the fundamental questions addressed by the learning standards for a course. These are deep questions that stimulate thought, provoke inquiry, and spark more questions about the core ideas of the learning standards.[19] The questions lead to "deep and transferable understandings" rather than rote or superficial ones. In Wiggins and McTighe's terms, essential questions "go to the heart of things—the essence. What is democracy? How does this work? What does the author mean? Can we prove it? What should we do? What is its value? Honest pursuit of such questions leads not only to deeper understandings, but also to more questions."[20]

Related to and in some cases generated by those essential questions are what Wiggins and McTighe call "enduring understandings"—the most important ideas in a course. These are such large concepts that students will be able to apply them beyond this class to their future endeavors in school and life—concepts like *correlation does not ensure causality* or *an effective story sets up tensions about what will happen next.* Much like the six pillars of leadership we are using to organize the information in this book, enduring understandings are a framework to help make sense of smaller facts and details.[21]

Highly effective teachers embark on a quest for these profound, fundamental concepts in their attempt to understand and organize their learning standards—a process that informs year-long plans from a sequence of unit plans. With the standards-inspired vision of success for the year or the unit established, the second phase of consideration is the assessment. How will students demonstrate that they have met the vision? You have many choices related to the form of assessments, the form of questions, variations in available time, the test's validity and reliability, and so on. Once a vision and an assessment are set, the third element of purposeful planning, the conventional notion of planning, involves figuring out a logical sequence of ideas, allocating appropriate time for ideas, and building remediation and contingency time into the year-long or unit plan.

## The Benefits of Year-long and Unit Plans

Like all other purposeful plans, year-long and unit plans accelerate learning by offering you and your students focus and a sense of urgency and by showing you exactly what has to happen in order to reach your goals. They provide benchmarks to gauge your progress. Working with a long-term plan, you can ask yourself, "Are we where we need

▶ **SCRIPTED CURRICULUM: WORKING WITH PREMADE PLANS**

**SCHOOLS AND DISTRICTS CREATE** and purchase all kinds of assessment and curricular tools to support their teachers' effectiveness, including scripted curricula that plan out a teacher's instruction. The nature and quality of these materials vary widely. Some administrators require strict adherence to those plans, and others give teachers a great deal of freedom in using the resources.

Highly effective teachers make the most of those resources and parameters. To do so, they bring the vision-assessment-plan approach to these premade plans and ask themselves where the plan is headed, how the plan accounts for knowing that the goal is reached, and how the plan leads students to that goal.

You need to understand why the plan includes a particular learning goal sequence and consider how those plans meet the diagnosed needs of your students. What prerequisite knowledge does the plan assume, and how does that match with your students' prior knowledge? While working with these resources requires a different process from the one used to create your own plans from scratch, the same fundamental questions guide planning with a scripted program.

to be at this point in the year?" Bay Area first-grade bilingual teacher Sonja Elder emphasized this point when she told us that long-term plans make "you constantly reassess where you are and where you're headed so you can correct errors sooner rather than later. Teaching without a long-term plan is like going on a road trip without an atlas: it's bound to get you lost."

The year-long and unit-planning processes are meant to clarify and organize the knowledge and skills you will teach in ways that can save you time and energy. Over and over, our teachers report that while setting a vision, creating assessments, and mapping out a plan, they discovered relationships and interdependence among ideas they had not previously considered. Kristen Taylor, for example, a sixth-grade teacher in St. Louis, told us she knew she wanted her students to be ready for algebra when they left her classroom, and she assumed that would mean being able to solve for a variable. When she looked at the standards, however, she realized that first they would have to understand a number of prerequisite learning goals. "I realized," she says, "that if I tried to teach them how to solve for a variable before they understood algebraic patterns, they would not be able to find the pattern they needed in order to solve for the variable." Her engagement with the standards saved her perhaps weeks of lost learning time by helping her order and prioritize key ideas.

Kate Schrepfer, who teaches in the Mississippi Delta, recalled her anxieties about what and how she could teach science and reasoning skills to her high school students. Once she "made the standards her friend" by studying, prioritizing, and atomizing them, she was able to see clearly where she wanted to take her students and how that destination was going to prepare them for Biology I the next year. All the rest of her assessments and planning flowed from that begin-at-the-end vision informed by standards. She set her big goal around students' mastery of the learning standards:

> I thought logically about six overarching principles to biology, which became my units: (1) scientists ask questions and conduct experiments to learn more; (2) all living things are made up of smaller parts working together; (3) our genetic code determines everything from our looks, to our actions, to our susceptibility to diseases; (4) the diversity of our world is due to evolution; (5) there are relationships between organisms and their environment, and human actions can affect them; and (6) plants and animals are made up of body parts working together to help them function. Once I had my unit titles, I broke down the state standards into daily lesson objectives at each level of Bloom's taxonomy and ordered these into one of the six units. This way, every single day, my students and I knew that whichever objective we covered was necessary for promotion and scientific literacy.

For many teachers like Ms. Taylor and Ms. Schrepfer, the long-term planning process generates a much-needed sense of calm and control even as it increases their sense of urgency. Chris Ott recalls the first time he mapped out his year as "the single best action I ever took. . . . It gave me comfort knowing that I would be able to cover all of the material I needed to." Carrie Gonnella called creating her long-term plan "the best thing I did for myself to destress the day-to-day planning. I never had to go home and say, 'Gosh, what am I teaching tomorrow?' I never had to worry I was forgetting something incredibly important. Just looking at my calendar made me content."

## Lesson Plans

A lesson plan is a map of instructional strategies and student learning experiences that leads students to master particular objectives that connect to long-term instructional goals. Just as unit plans make up a long-term plan, lesson plans are the building blocks of a unit plan.

Highly effective teachers use many different forms and templates for lesson planning. Given the impracticality of an exhaustive tour of the many forms of lesson plans, here we will introduce the fundamental elements of lesson plans by exploring one of the most basic types of lesson plans: the five-step, direct, instruction plan. Think of this five-step lesson plan as a simplified starting point on which a teacher can elaborate and improve to ensure student learning.

The five-step lesson encapsulates a basic "I do, we do, you do" approach, involving a gradual transfer of responsibility for knowledge and skills from the teacher to the students. In terms of the students' experience, the teacher first shows or models for students what they need to know or be able to do ("I do"). Then students are given adequate time to practice together with assistance from the teacher and peers ("We do"), followed by a period in which they attempt to demonstrate mastery of the knowledge and skills on their own ("You do"). This generic model suggests that with the lesson opening, the teacher ensures students know what they are about to learn and how that relates to what they know already and where they are headed.

▶ **COMPONENTS OF A GENERIC LESSON PLAN**

| | |
|---|---|
| Beginning | Lesson opening: hook, preview, objective, connection to prior knowledge |
| Middle (the heart of the lesson) | Introduction of new material ("I do") Guided practice ("We do") Independent practice ("You do") |
| End | Lesson closing: review key ideas, check for understanding, bridge to next concepts |

As a teacher coaches students through the material by drawing on students' preexisting knowledge, the teacher presents key ideas and engages students in multiple opportunities to practice. These activities can have varying levels of support to provide greater clarity around the main concept or skill. During this time, teachers also measure student understanding of the objective through formative checks. This is the real heart of the lesson and includes introduction to new material, guided practice, and independent practice. In the lesson closing, the teacher pulls everything together to summarize what was covered, checks for understanding again, and communicates why it is relevant to the big goals. Students then leave with a clear understanding of the main concept of the lesson and how they can apply the concept to future situations.

This lesson plan model works on a direct instruction theory, through which the teacher is delivering knowledge and skills. Other lesson plan models are more student driven and built on discovery. Still others emphasize more collaborative approaches. Although strong teachers seem to choose different lesson models depending on the nature of the objective they want students to master, we offer this direct instruction model because it is an efficient and manageable approach and new teachers can easily master it. (More guidance on lesson planning is available at teachingasleadership.org.)

### Visualizing and Assessing Mastery of a Lesson Objective

Before you can create a lesson opening or begin thinking about how to deliver content, you must determine what outcomes you expect students to produce. What exactly should they know or be able to do by the end of the lesson? What evidence do you need in order to determine whether students have achieved your goal?

The vision of success for a lesson plan is student mastery of a lesson objective. In our experience, this simple idea is one of the most telling indicators of a teacher's potential to effect significant

> ▶ **APPLYING THE VISION-ASSESSMENT-PLAN APPROACH TO CLASSROOM PROCEDURES AND SYSTEMS**
>
> **YOU KNOW THAT CLICHÉD** scene in movies when a teacher is calling roll and students are droning "present," one by one, for what seems like forever? Can you imagine a worse use of valuable learning time?
>
> In some classrooms, the amount of time students are actually engaged in learning activities is shockingly low. In one study, only 40 percent of the school day was left to actual learning activities.
>
> Even in the best scenario, your time with your students is limited. Given our ambitious goals, we can't afford to waste any time, let alone 60 percent of it. The benefits of efficiency can be huge. If you managed to save just twenty-five minutes a day with effective procedures (just four or five minutes per period in some settings), that adds up to about seventy-five hours of additional instructional time over the year for your students.
>
> You will not be surprised to hear what highly effective teachers say about setting out to ensure their classrooms are run smoothly and efficiently: First, envision an efficient classroom with thoughts like these:
>
> - We should be engaged in the substance of learning within two minutes of the start of class.

academic gains with students. And because the success of a lesson starts with its objective, how you design the objectives can have far-ranging implications for students' academic growth.

Because learning standards and even the slightly more detailed versions (sometimes called learning goals) often do not provide the concrete guidance from which to design specific lessons, each learning goal must be translated into discrete, specific lesson objectives. Those lesson objectives drive lesson planning and are grouped into unit plans. Here are a few deceptively simple examples:

- Students will be able to list the vowels and make the various sounds each produces. (From kindergarten literacy instruction)
- Students will be able to solve word problems involving gravitational and elastic potential energy. (From a mathematics unit on cars in a physics class)
- Students will be able to write a paragraph with a topic sentence and supporting sentences. (From a project-based pen-pal unit in fifth grade)

Strong objectives are student-achievement-based, measurable, and rigorous. Developing objectives that meet those criteria is an art and science worthy of considerable effort, given that

- There is no reason that taking attendance or gathering homework should take away one second of learning time.
- Some of my students are going to finish their essays more quickly than others, so I need some meaningful additional independent learning experiences.

One teacher told us, "The most detailed lesson plans I ever wrote taught procedures." Although every classroom has unique procedural needs, here are some of the trouble spots for which highly effective teachers recommend a well-considered plan (we explore classroom efficiency in the next chapter):

- Taking attendance
- Getting class started
- Getting the attention of the class
- Distributing materials
- Giving instructions
- Making smooth transitions between activities
- Dealing with planned interruptions
- Managing student needs (bathroom, water, and so forth)

learning is likely to be limited when an objective is poorly designed. The following table captures best-practices related to objective design, and offers strong and weak examples of those characteristics.

| Key Insight | Examples to Aim For | Examples to Avoid |
| --- | --- | --- |
| The best way to ensure an objective is student-achievement-related is to start objectives with the phrase, "The student will be able to . . . " (sometimes represented by the acronym SWBAT). | • *The student will be able to order* fractions with different denominators.<br><br>• *The student will be able to identify and describe* the rhythm and rhyme structure for a limerick.<br><br>• *The student will be able to assess and compare* strengths of two leaders of twentieth-century America. | • The teacher will present a lesson on ordering fractions with different denominators.<br><br>• Reviewing rhythm and rhyme structure of limericks.<br><br>• Read about historical figures. |
| The verb of an objective is a good indicator of whether it is measurable. | • The student will be able to *list three ways* that bones help the body.<br><br>• The student will be able to *describe* the conditions in Europe that led to World War II. | • The student will be able to *understand* that bones help the body.<br><br>• The student will *learn* the conditions in Europe that led to World War II. |
| The objective's verb affects the rigor or cognitive level of the objective, which should align with the learning goal from which the objective is derived. | An objective that requires students to analyze primary historical data to draw insights about differences between two cultures, when that is what is required by the learning standard. | An objective that states that students will be able to "name key historical figures" from each of two cultures is not rigorous enough if the learning standard calls for students to be able to analyze primary sources and compare two different cultures. |

This notion of developing a vision—in this case, mastery of an objective—is closely related to the assessment. When the objective is rigorous, measurable, and focused on student achievement, the objective begs the question, "How will you know it has been achieved?" Heather Tow-Yick, like so many other teachers we have interviewed, recalls that her teaching improved significantly when an observing colleague asked her precisely that question: "This question revolutionized how I thought of each lesson. I realized concretely how important it is to have a tangible way of knowing I accomplished my goal for the day. Additionally, I was able to think about how every single thing I did and said in my lesson was for the purpose of driving my students to achieve the objective for the day." Ms. Tow-Yick's reflection makes a critically important point about translating your vision into an assessment. The best teachers do not first think to themselves, "What test will assess student learning?" Rather, they think, "How can my students prove they have mastered the knowledge and skills they need to learn?" The answer to that broader question tells a teacher a lot about the appropriate assessment.

Justin Yan, a sixth-grade science teacher in Charlotte, North Carolina, whose students successfully tackled eighth-grade material, described the same sort of process taking place as he planned for learning goals related to the lithosphere. When he carefully considered the relevant objectives, he came to realize, "I didn't just want my students to be able to answer fifty rigorous multiple-choice questions; rather, I wanted them to be able to articulate all the happenings of the lithosphere at a high and memorable level. They need to become earth scientists in the way they speak." For Mr. Yan, thinking carefully about what it should look like for his students to master the objective led him to change his assessment. He needed more authentic, less superficial assessments. Not surprisingly, his demanding vision of and assessment for student success significantly shaped his choices of strategies and methods.

Highly effective teacher Cheyenne Batista-São Roque applies the same rigorous "imagining" to her assessments themselves. In fact, she takes the assessments she will give her students to ensure they are rigorous, demanding, efficient, and meaningful:

> One of the most powerful experiences I had as a new teacher was to take one of my own classroom assessments. From a sixth-grade perspective, everything from the physical aspect of writing my name on the top of the paper (*gosh, why isn't there more room up here?*) to reading and interpreting the questions and answer choices (*did we ever cover THAT word in class?*) completely revolutionized my approach towards lesson planning, delivering instruction and developing test questions. I became much more conscientious about aligning these three components for my students.

## Planning a Path: Choosing Among Instructional Strategies

With good lesson objectives (vision) translated into what you want to see your students know and do (assessment), the remaining element of lesson planning is mapping your students' path to that definition of success. Planning is not a just a theoretical exercise: effective teachers practice their plans in their mind's eye as a means of identifying hidden problems and opportunities for student learning.

Recall the factors that help inform a teacher's vividly imagined planning: the rigor of the content, how students learn, students' prior knowledge, how students engage with the particular subject matter at hand, and students' background and culture, to name a few. Those factors apply to the lesson planning process just as they inform a teacher's selection of instructional methods. For example, perhaps you have come to realize that three of your students are much more engaged when they are up and moving around, so you imagine ways to get them physically involved in your lesson on metaphors. Or perhaps you have half as many copies of *Of Mice and Men* as you have students. That fact should obviously inform your lesson plan.

In addition to these general factors that inform planning, a teacher who sits down to plan a lesson is also informed by another list: the instructional strategies in his or her repertoire.

The more extensive your toolbox of instructional methods, the more purposefully you will be able to align your strategies with your objectives. The most effective teachers recognize that they must build a broad, diverse menu of instructional strategies and skills so that "imagining themselves on the path" means virtually testing out different approaches to reach the best outcomes. Here are a few of the methods that must be part of any teacher's repertoire:

- *Teacher modeling and demonstration.* This is one of the most common and basic instructional methods across the grade levels: students gain a lot from simply being shown how to do something. Kindergarten teachers model how to form letters of the alphabet. Chemistry teachers show students how to balance equations. A writing teacher models for students how to edit sentences and paragraphs. The most effective modeling and demonstrations include an element of metacognitive narration by the teacher that directs students' attention to fundamental elements of proper procedure. Modeling is also a great opportunity to illustrate common errors students should avoid.

**DURING HER FIRST YEAR** of teaching, first-grade teacher Sara Egli was seeing less-than-expected growth in her students' reading comprehension, so she consulted a mentor about the problem. Her mentor asked Ms. Egli to describe her planning process. Ms. Egli explained that she identified the relevant literacy objective, found a text that supported that objective, chose an assessment from the curriculum, and then plugged in the details. Even in the course of talking about that process, Ms. Egli had what she calls a "revelation": she was skipping careful consideration of what she wanted to see in her students that would demonstrate mastery of the objective:

> I realized I wasn't actually visualizing exactly what my students should be doing or learning. I could say it, but I wasn't truly identifying the key skills or knowledge my students should be mastering, and more specifically what that looked like for a first grader. By skipping this hugely important first step, my lessons were mediocre. I quickly understood why my students weren't making growth. My entire planning process changed from that moment.

With that insight, Ms. Egli began to think about how she would see and assess that knowledge and those skills. She began to identify the key ideas and skills that she wanted students to take from a reading comprehension lesson and sketched out what students' performance of those skills would look like. In that process, Ms. Egli was bridging from her vision of success to an assessment that would ensure the vision was reached.

> For example, first-grade students need to master the skill of making predictions before and during reading. To a fluent reader, this seems very simple. As a new teacher, I was certain I could teach this skill to all of my students without much planning or deep thought. After my first predicting lesson, I realized that I had no idea if any of my students had actually mastered the skill. I assumed at least some, if not most, of them had, but I had nothing to prove that. To correct this problem, I started over

• *Lecture.* Although "lecture" may conjure up the image of a stodgy professor droning on while students doodle or doze to escape the monotony, lecturing is sometimes an efficient way to present or review material with the entire class. Teachers might choose to lecture when, for example, they have a limited amount of time. The key to an effective lecture is that the teacher is constantly reflecting on what students are doing and thinking. Jessica Kaufman, a third-grade ESL teacher in Houston, reminds us that the effectiveness of a lecture, like any other instructional method, has much to do with how the teacher interacts and checks for understanding along the way:

> I always thought that lecturing was most useful when I was constantly assessing along the way and involving students as much as possible instead of just blabbing. You have to find ways to make sure they're with you during a lecture—something more than just "Great! They are all looking at me! They get it!" You've got to incorporate questions, encourage students to think about what you're saying, and predict where you might be headed. Stop to have students share a thought with their neighbor about what they just

at the beginning. First, I broke the objective into the essential skills and knowledge. Students must first be able to define the word *prediction* and describe the process a good reader goes through to make predictions. Second, the student must be able to actually go through that process and make their best guess about what might happen next. I now had a good base knowledge of what "students will be able to make predictions about a text" means in a first-grade classroom, but I still needed to create a vision for exactly what my students would be doing to demonstrate mastery.

**Sara Egli,** First Grade, Arizona

This was early in the year, and many of my students were not yet writing complete sentences. I decided that making illustrations and labeling to their best ability would be the most appropriate assessment. Some students were able to write sentences about their pictures, beginning with "I predict . . .," while other students simply wrote the first letter of the word that described the elements in their pictures. During this independent practice time, I was able to talk with students who needed to orally describe their pictures in order for me to ensure mastery.

This entire vision setting and planning process did not require much additional time, especially considering that poor planning had already led me to having to replan and reteach the lesson. It really only took me holding myself accountable to think, "How will a six-year-old who has never heard the word *prediction* demonstrate that he or she can actually make a prediction?" It seems simple but made drastic differences in my classroom instruction. I remember a feeling of constant confusion and uncertainty during my first month or so of teaching. Revising my planning process and creating clear visions for student mastery was a true remedy to this process. It made a bigger difference in my confidence that I was leading my students in the correct direction than any other changes I made that year. It has also helped lead me to continued success in my classroom. Visions of student mastery are invaluable to getting lessons right the first time, even in my fifth year as a teacher.

> heard, or ask students to summarize the lecture or bring up points that are confusing. There are many ways you can engage students in your lecture, but it takes some planning up front.

- *Question and discussion.* Teachers often ask questions to gain information about what students do and do not yet understand. But questions should also be asked to stimulate student thought. In this way, questioning is a fundamental and powerful instructional tool. Researcher Jere Brophy found that questions-based discourse was one of the most common and most powerful tools for introducing new material and checking for students' understanding.[22]

- *Discovery learning.* Discovery learning is geared toward higher-level objectives and is used to help students deduce general ideas, concepts, or definitions from specific examples. During discovery learning lessons, teachers often provide students with materials and guidelines for engaging those materials, encouraging students to make observations, form and test hypotheses, and infer concepts. This technique is often used, for example, in science classes, where students learn concepts through the experience of conducting a lab or experiment.

- *Centers.* Centers are specified areas in the classroom that allow students to work independently or in small groups at their own pace on particular objectives. Their usefulness in highly individualized classrooms makes them popular for special education and early elementary teachers. In order to support the individual needs of each student, centers may be permanent fixtures, such as the classroom library or reading center, or changing ones that support a current unit of study. They require a front-end investment of time to create and to familiarize students with the learning center processes. Amy Klauder, in her experience working in early childhood education and elementary classrooms, has found centers to be extraordinarily effective: "Centers allow us to create purposeful learning opportunities for our students. In my preschool, we incorporate the whole range of developmental objectives into centers—from fine motor development to language, literacy, and science. Choosing interesting themes not only helps in our planning, but keeps our students engaged. . . . I never underestimate the value of social development during centers too. Our students learn how to cooperate by negotiating who will be the customer and who will run the store in the dramatic play center."

- *Grouping strategies.* Choices about how to group students is another axis of decision making in lesson planning. Would a whole-group setting or a small-group setting most facilitate students' mastery of this particular objective? Or (more realistically) what combination of grouping arrangements will lead to the greatest student learning? A whole-class grouping is particularly efficient for presenting new information. A small group is appropriate when a teacher needs to differentiate instruction or content.

- *Cooperative learning.* Cooperative learning is a hybrid of grouping and instructional strategy. As used in highly effective classrooms, it involves more than just placing students in small groups and having them complete an activity together. Cooperative learning involves dividing up students' responsibilities, collectively completing assignments, and reporting back to the whole group, all of which is meant to mitigate the risk that not all students will benefit from the group learning. Cooperative learning requires students to be responsible not only for their own learning but also for the learning of all others in the group and, according to some experts, thereby "creates the potential for cognitive and metacognitive [thinking about how they are working and thinking] benefits by engaging students in discourse that requires them to make their task-related information-processing and problem-solving strategies explicit (and thus available for discussion and reflection)."[23] Some argue that cooperative learning facilitates interdependence, instills individual and group accountability, teaches interpersonal skills, and allows time for group cohesion and reflection.[24]

Bilingual/English as a Second Language teacher Stephen Ready notes that this method requires explicit instruction and practice: "Students have to be taught to work cooperatively. Even with my high school students, we have to practice the procedures and systems we use to work in groups. It takes a lot of work to develop smooth-running small groups in which ALL students are mastering the objectives."

Cooperative learning, however, may hide individual students' lack of learning. Jerry Hauser recalls that as a teacher in Los Angeles, he "overrelied on cooperative learning. There are some things that it's good for, but at the end of the day, each student needs to truly master the material—and too often working in groups means individual students don't get as much practice as they need if they're ultimately going to be able to do the work on their own."

## Rigor and Mastery

Alongside instructional methods, another important set of concepts informs teachers' lesson planning: rigor and mastery. These are two words that we almost inevitably hear from highly effective teachers as they talk about academic planning—and especially lesson planning. *Rigor* refers to the level and appropriateness of academic challenge presented by the content. How valuable is what students are learning to their quest for the big goal? Is it appropriately challenging so that meaningful progress is made toward the goal? *Mastery* refers to the extent to which students have command of what they are being taught. Is this lesson plan reaching its objective? What are students understanding or misunderstanding?

To gain insight into rigor, we examine whether what we are asking students to do would be a substantive step toward the achievement of a sound big goal. (If we are using with our eighth graders the same objectives some teachers are using with their fourth graders, our teaching lacks rigor.) To gain insight into mastery, we investigate what students are learning from what they're being asked to do. (If students cannot demonstrate the knowledge and skills we are teaching, we must focus on mastery.)

As you choose from among the instructional methods available to you, strive to ensure both rigor and mastery in your lesson plan. This means that you are asking yourself (in the virtual implementation of your planning), "To what extent are students learning?"

Figure 3.1 helps illustrate how rigor and mastery intersect to maximize student learning.

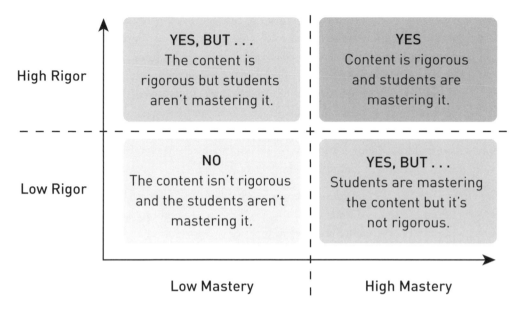

Figure 3.1  The Intersection of Rigor and Mastery

### Differentiating Instruction

Teachers who take seriously the concept of purposeful planning are inevitably drawn toward planning for unique subsets of, if not individual, learners. When we commit to ensuring that every student is mastering an objective and because we understand the reality that our students have different learning styles, motivations, strengths, and prior knowledge, we begin to think about differentiating plans to maximize every student's growth. Shannon Dingle put this idea in simple terms: "My planning always starts with looking at which skills each student needs to master to meet their goal and then looking at where they are now. Backward planning for each student between these two points—that's what differentiation is. And all it takes is clear diagnostic data and a clear view of what specific skills make up your goal."

One of the reasons highly successful teachers achieve outstanding results with their students is that they use various methods to individualize their instruction to meet the unique learning needs in their classroom. That is, they not only plan their lessons for the class, they also plan adjustments to those lessons so as to ensure every student in the room masters the objective. This practice, known generally as *differentiation*, is central to the ability to lead all students to your ambitious goals. You must consider their individual learning styles and capitalize on them.

According to differentiation guru Carol Ann Tomlinson, different students might need a differentiated assignment for three reasons: differences in students' readiness (current performance level), interest (motivation or engagement), and learning profile (development level, learning modality, cultural differences, and special needs).[25] Again, teachers who are committed to leading all students to mastery of the objectives will naturally and necessarily consider these factors in their academic planning. Meanwhile, as Tomlinson points out, teachers have a number of options for differentiated adjustments to students' engagement of key concepts. The teacher can make adjustments to product (what students are asked to produce), process (how students are taught a concept or skill), or the content itself. The key in those adjustments is to keep in mind they are being made as a means to the end of mastering the objective. That end does not change. By differentiating, the teacher is simply seeking the most effective way to get there for each student.

The degree to which highly effective teachers modify and diversify their instructional delivery or behavioral management depends on the unique needs of their students. Each student's mastery of the objective—no matter what the student's learning style—is what makes a successful lesson. More often than not, those varying learning styles and differences call for more substantive modifications than you can make on the fly during a lesson. They require purposeful planning.

Guidance on how to differentiate instruction, as well as examples of effective differentiation, are available online at teachingasleadership.org.

## The Temptation of Activity-Driven Lessons

The logic of starting the planning process by determining where you are headed seems compelling enough. And yet virtually all of the teachers we work with, including those whose students demonstrate dramatic academic growth, attest to the easy temptation to skip past end visions, learning standards, and assessment design and slip into planning that is not driven by student outcomes but is instead governed by what a teacher wants to do.

One of many testaments to the dangers of not starting with a clear vision came from Emma Doggett, an eighth-grade U.S. History teacher in the Rio Grande Valley. For one lesson, her objective was that "students will be able to compare and contrast the British and colonial armies." Her planning, however, was commandeered by her attraction to an activity that would be fun, and she lost sight of the need to drive home that objective.

She recalls creating an elaborate game of dodgeball in which one team used strategies employed by British troops and the other used techniques employed by the colonial armies during the Revolutionary War. Although the students had tons of fun, she never guided and debriefed students' understanding of what the game represented. Her experience reveals both the appeal and the shortcomings of planning from an activity-driven (instead of vision-driven) perspective:

> The British "army" was required to stand still, illustrating the strict formation of the British troops during the war and the advantage that the colonists had as they used guerrilla tactics to their advantage. After an incredibly fun day of running around outside bouncing balls off each other, I was convinced my students had mastered this objective through such a kinesthetic analogy. Four weeks later, however, as we reviewed for the exam, I asked my class to complete a Venn diagram representing the similarities and differences between the armies. I was shocked when I discovered that in almost every diagram were the words "the British soldiers could not move their arms."

The lesson Ms. Doggett learned on that particular day was much more meaningful (and accurate) than the lesson her students learned. Afterward Ms. Doggett forced herself to articulate a "big question of the day" for every lesson—a question that helped keep her eye on the purpose of the lesson, even if she was infusing fun methods into the learning. She recalls, "I then planned backward from this question to develop a lesson that drove toward understanding. When my class was objective driven, my students became engaged in the lessons because of the value of what we were learning rather than because of the props, games, and fun involved."

In the table below, we have captured some of the common activity-driven mistakes made by new teachers.

▶ **LESS EFFECTIVE ALTERNATIVES TO BACKWARD PLANNING**

| Wrong | Why | Right |
|---|---|---|
| "What can we do that the kids will enjoy?" | What you think students would find enjoyable may or may not lead to actual learning—and students may not enjoy it as much as you think if they aren't sure there's a purpose behind it. | Which of these standards, learning goals, and objectives are most important? Why? Which are less important? Why? How can I make sure that my students master all of the most important standards, learning goals, and objectives? |
| "How was I taught this objective when I was in school?" | You may be able to design more effective ways to teach key ideas than you experienced in your own classrooms. | |
| "We do as much as we can each day." | The most effective teachers we work with usually describe their efforts in terms of ambitious end goals; less effective teachers describe their efforts as doing "as much as they can" each day. | |
| "We really have to get through all of these topics by the end of the day [week or year]." | If you are driven by what is covered, you are not focusing on student learning. It is possible for you to touch on every topic in the list and end up with students who have learned nothing. | |

Activity-driven lessons can take many forms. Perhaps the teacher has a personal preference for lecture, or thinks an activity will engage the students, or saw another teacher use an instructional strategy and wants to try it out. All of those factors may be legitimate considerations, but they all must be secondary to choosing methods that most effectively reach the outcome the teacher wants for the students. As Wiggins and McTighe explain:

> Many teachers begin with and remain focused on textbooks, favored lessons, and time-honored activities—the inputs—rather than deriving those means from what is implied in the desired results—the outputs. To put it in an odd way, too many teachers focus on the teaching and not the learning. They spend most of their time thinking, first, about what they will do, what materials they will use, and what they will ask students to do rather than first considering what the learner will need in order to accomplish the learning goals.[26]

Like Ms. Doggett with her British soldiers who could not move their arms, all teachers are susceptible to the draw of activity-driven planning, whereby lessons or units are designed around some engaging activity rather than designed toward a key learning objective. As teachers, we have all found ourselves wondering, "What would be really engaging and exciting for the kids?" It is, in fact, a hugely important question: student learning can and should be engaging and exciting, but a fun activity cannot trump but must cause student learning. One of Ms. Doggett's colleagues, Seth Cohen, recalled:

> Before coming to my own realization about this concept, I remember struggling over my lesson plans for hours to devise whatever new and exciting activity we were going to be doing in class, and hoping that those activities would get at whatever objectives I needed to teach. It is not that the activities were devoid of objectives, but that the objectives were an afterthought. That time and energy could have been put to much better use had I started not with how we were going to get somewhere, but where we needed to get to in the first place. Once I began planning with the end in mind, I recognized that if I knew where I needed my students to be at the end of a lesson, week, or unit, then I could purposefully craft my lessons to reach those outcomes.

When you are planning purposefully, you are beginning at the end, starting with a vision of the knowledge, behavior, habits, skills, or actions you want students to demonstrate at some point in the future. In the words of Wiggins and McTighe, "Only by having specified the desired results can we focus on the content, methods, and activities most likely to achieve those results."[27] In a nutshell, highly effective classroom leaders do not first ask themselves, "What should I do?" but instead ask themselves, "What must students learn?"

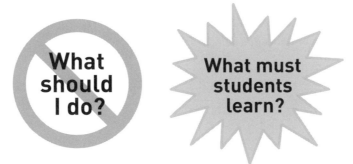

## Classroom Management Plans

Highly effective teachers treat classroom management and culture just as they do student learning: they purposefully plan for it. They bring the same vision-assessment-plan approach to student behavior and community that they bring to lesson planning and the same vision-first treatment they bring to academic achievement. They begin by envisioning the interactions they ultimately want to see among students; only then do they start to think about what strategies will lead to that destination.

Recall Taylor Delhagen who created a vision of "global citizens" in his classroom. Although he may not have had state or national standards shaping that vision, he employed the same process as if he were creating a long-term academic plan. He read and thought carefully about what success should look like and articulated for himself and his students the indicators of global citizenship—accountability to the learning community, knowledge, and rigorous thinking. He parsed these general ideas into more specific indicators (like an assessment) that brought specificity to his general vision. Having established that vision, he could map a path from his students' place on the indicators at the beginning of the year to where he wanted them to be at the end.

Annie Lewis, a teacher in Baltimore who led her second graders to dramatic progress in reading, brought these purposeful vision-assessment-plan strategies to her classroom management and culture. After her first year of teaching, she was satisfied with, but not particularly proud of, the ways that she and her students interacted with each other. She felt that her students were following the rules of her classroom, but she was not sure she was having a lasting impact on their behavior. So she spent some time imagining her ideal vision: an atmosphere and positive interactions in the classroom in which the students would demonstrate persistence, empathy, respect, integrity, and responsibility in every action. She thereby articulated for her students a crystal-clear picture of how they would interact with each other:

- *Persistence:* If we find the work hard, we don't give up. We never hear whining about difficult challenges, or phrases like "I can't do this" or "I'm stupid." We cheer and celebrate each other's hard work in the face of challenges and hear "Bring it on!" whenever we hear something will be challenging.

- *Empathy:* We think carefully about how we would feel if we were in our classmates' shoes. We do not tease, name-call, or exclude classmates. We work to make others feel good, looking for things about others that impress us so that we can share those compliments.

- *Respect:* We respect ourselves, others, and things around us. We do not put ourselves or others down, and we take care of our environment. We become self-monitors of our own behavior, resolving tensions that we create. We have pride in ourselves as the best class in school—where we all feel welcomed, are proud of each other, have good friends, and are achieving.

- *Integrity:* We are honest—no lying about anything ever, even when we know that telling the truth is hard or is going to result in consequences.

- *Responsibility:* When we make mistakes, we take responsibility for fixing the problem. We hear phrases like "How can I make this right?" between students.

While the substance of Ms. Lewis's vision is informative, we also share her "star student" system (each value is a point on a star) as evidence of a fundamental process: setting a vision as the first step in any endeavor to influence students, whether it is a plan for academic achievement, or to improve students' interactions with each other.

While the most successful teachers, like Ms. Lewis, see classroom management as affirmatively building a culture of achievement and teamwork (as described in Chapter Two), a key aspect of the path to that vision is planning a way to shape and respond to student behavior. A few basic ideas go a long way toward effective behavior planning:

- Rules should be:
  - Positive statements (tell students what to do rather than what not to do)
  - Clearly stated
  - Few in number but applicable to a broad range of situations[28]
- Consequences should be:
  - Progressive—from less severe to more severe when misbehavior is repeated
  - Based on a range of interventions (verbal warning, changing seats, detention, time-out, revocation of privileges, calling or writing home, and so on)
  - Naturally and logically flowing from the event or situation
  - Designed to maintain the dignity of the student

Successful behavior management plans also include a system for monitoring and tracking student behavior. Every student needs to know where he or she stands in that system at any given moment. And teachers need a system efficient enough to implement without disrupting learning time.

These basic elements of rules and consequences are obviously critically important to a new teacher's success. Rules and consequences are, however, just the foundation for building your ultimate vision of a welcoming culture of achievement in the classroom. More guidance about building that culture is available online at teachingasleadership.org.

## Conclusion: Key Ideas and Next Questions

The Teaching As Leadership rubric (see Appendix A) describes six specific teacher actions that indicate a teacher is purposefully planning. Highly effective teachers:

P-1: Create or obtain standards-aligned diagnostic, formative, and summative assessments

P-2: Backwards-plan the year and units to achieve the big goal

P-3: Create rigorous, objective-driven lesson plans

P-4: Differentiate your plans for individual students

P-5: Establish age-appropriate long- and short-term behavioral management plans

P-6: Design classroom procedures that provide structure to students and maximize the amount and value of instructional time

## Key Ideas

All purposeful planning involves establishing a vision of success, developing a means of knowing you have reached success, and planning a path to that vision of success. This approach is a form of backward planning—starting with one's ultimate aims and then thinking about how to get there—that characterizes strong leadership in any context, including the classroom. We also see in highly effective teachers that planning is first an exercise in imagination, as the teacher envisions leading students to success and uses that virtual implementation as an opportunity to test various strategies to find the most effective choice.

These principles of purposeful planning apply to all forms of planning, including long-term planning (year-long and unit plans), lesson plans, and classroom management plans. Keep in mind these ideas related to each of those types of plans:

### LONG-TERM PLANS (YEAR-LONG AND UNIT PLANS)

- Learning standards are the starting point for your vision of student success.

- Engaging with learning standards means discerning the essential questions and enduring understandings that will shape your long-term plans.

- Year-long plans organize unit plans, which organize lesson plans.

### LESSON PLANS

- Lesson plans map instructional strategies that ensure student mastery of objectives focused on student achievement, are measurable, and are rigorous.

- There are many forms of lesson plans, but most serve the purposes of the generic five-step lesson plan:

  ○ Opening

  ○ Introduction of new material ("I do")

  ○ Guided practice ("We do")

  ○ Independent practice ("You do")

  ○ Lesson closing

### CLASSROOM MANAGEMENT PLANS

- Strong classroom management, like strong academic achievement, is built from a vision of success.

- Rules should be positive, clear, and few, and consequevnces should be progressive, logical, and respectful of student dignity.

**teachingasleadership.org**

More guidance on how to plan purposefully for student learning, behavior, and efficiency is available online:

- Tips on engaging learning standards and goals and for designing effective objectives
- Additional descriptions and how-to guides for a number of instructional methods and group strategies
- Annotated examples of good and excellent long-term plans, unit plans, and lesson plans
- Common pitfalls new teachers encounter in trying to plan purposefully

## Next Questions

With these key ideas in mind, you are poised to pursue a number of questions as you work toward dramatic student success:

- How can I engage with learning standards to inform my vision of students' success?
- How can I design meaningful assessments that will show my students have deeply internalized the skills and knowledge I am teaching?
- How can I set a challenging but realistic pace of learning in my classroom that will put us on track to meet our big goals?
- How should I map student learning across my school calendar, taking into consideration state testing cycles and major breaks, holidays, and distractions?
- How should I adjust generic lesson plan structures for a particular objective or for a subset of students to help maximize my effectiveness?
- How can I differentiate my strategies to maximize each individual student's learning?

According to our highly effective teachers, bringing principles of purposeful planning to these fundamental questions of classroom leadership yields enormous benefits for teachers and students. Teachers not only work more efficiently and save considerable time, but their work is less stressful and more manageable when they know where they are headed and how they are going to get there. When teachers plan purposefully, students learn more.

"IT STILL TASTES GOOD."

 teachingasleadership.org

*An excerpt from Ms. Lora's Story, a case study in Teaching As Leadership, available online at www.teachingasleadership.org.*

For their part, the students shared not one iota of Ms. Lora's concern that the lesson was more activity than learning. They were huddled like surgeons over their purported peanut butter and jelly sandwiches. They chattered and squealed as they passed ingredients among the tables. Streaks of purple appeared around their mouths, and Ms. Lora giggled along with Bernardo's team as he vigorously shook his hand, trying to dislodge the note card that seemed permanently stuck to his wrist with jelly.

Ms. Lora was thrilled to see that for once, Douglas seemed to be the calm eye of the storm. He was oblivious to the circus around him as he looked back and forth from his note card of instructions to his paper plate. He seemed to have a particular affinity for "how-to" essays. He was, for example, the only student in the class who had started his instruction card with "1. Pt a plat on the dsk." Douglas's nascent ability to parse a task into its essential elements was part of what gave Ms. Lora hope that he could catch up before the state test.

Under strict instructions to do only and exactly what they had written on their card earlier that morning, most students' plateless desks were by now smeared with peanut butter and jelly. Some sandwiches looked like open-faced casseroles. Others had more peanut butter outside the slices than in them.

Somehow Elena had food on both of her elbows. Ms. Lora laughed out loud as she watched Elena put a napkin between her two elbows to try to scrub them off. Ms. Lora noticed more than one student licking their pencils. Two students, entirely unselfconsciously, were feeding each other goopy wads of bread and jelly.

"Time out!" she called for the fourth time since they began. In seconds, the whole class stood perfectly still.

"Hector, tell me one step that you would add to your instructions if we stopped and started all over."

Two dozen faces turned to examine Hector's sandwich, which consisted of one slice of bread curled around a giant glob of peanut butter. It looked more like a taco than a sandwich. Judging from the ends of his fingers, he had forgotten to include any instructions about utensils as well as a plate. If there was jelly involved, it was buried deep beneath the log of peanut butter.

As he licked his fingers, Hector too looked at his "sandwich."

**"IT STILL TASTES GOOD."** *(continued)*

"I forgot to write the second slice of bread, Miss," he said with genuine regret.

"So what would you write on your instructions?" Ms. Lora pressed.

With his oily fingers splayed out on both hands, he lifted his note card up using just one finger on each hand.

"Step 6 should be. 'Put another slice of bread on top.'"

"Excellent. That sounds like a good idea."

"It still tastes good," Hector said defensively.

"Time in!" Ms. Lora called out, and the spreading and squealing and licking and giggling recommenced immediately. She would call time out again in a few minutes. If they could get cleaned up by the bathroom break, they could rewrite their instruction cards before physical education.

Given the scripted and quasi-scripted nature of the reading and math blocks each morning, the heart of Ms. Lora's creative instruction time did not begin until 11:00 A.M. While it was broken up by carefully choreographed class trips to the restrooms, lunch, and rotating ancillaries like music, physical education, and art, she coveted the three hours of self-generated instructional time she had with her students each day. She focused much of her students' energies in that time on writing, usually annexing her social studies and science objectives into the writing process as well.

While this morning's sandwich adventure was a little bit inefficient, as she watched the students try to write corrections on their cards without getting even more peanut butter on their pencils, she privately absolved herself of being activity driven in this lesson. Sure, the kids were having fun, but they really were discovering firsthand the surprising precision necessary for a good how-to essay. And, activity driven or not, Douglas Rogers was deeply engaged. Ms. Lora basked for a moment in the fun of her job.

Ms. Lora would be able to harvest the teachable moments—and the energy—of this mess for weeks. Over the next week, Ms. Lora would be modeling the full writing process in the context of a how-to essay about going to college.

Early last year, her first year in the classroom, Ms. Lora had made a nerve-wracking strategy decision that she looked back on now as critically important. Faced with competing models for and advice about how to best teach writing to students who were lacking even the most basic writing skills, Ms. Lora decided to forgo a pure start-with-basics philosophy in favor of a teach-all-layers-at-once policy. It's not that she ignored the fundamentals of punctuation, grammar, spelling, and sentence construction, but she taught all those basics in the context of writing full essays.

*(continued on next page)*

**"IT STILL TASTES GOOD."** *(continued)*

This epiphany had come to her as she was attempting to sketch out a long-term plan for the year in the first months of her teaching. If she atomized writing into the basic components that her students were lacking and then taught each one in succession, her students might end up being able to write a sentence, but there would never be time to master the arts of brainstorming, designing, outlining, shaping, and writing a full essay. So she dove in, teaching compare-and-contrast essays in the first month, even though that meant identifying and correcting sentence fragments, teaching punctuation and capitalization rules, and correcting spelling along the way.

This peanut butter and jelly party was the first step—really just the hook—for what would be a six-week unit on how-to essays. In the course of that unit, Ms. Lora would model the complete writing process (prewriting, writing, and post-writing strategies) for no fewer than four how-to essays, and the children would write six essays themselves.

After the initial hook for each type of essay, she would begin with a whole-class reading of an excellent example of the ultimate product they were aiming for—in this case, a how-to essay. Other units would similarly start with an exemplary short story, or a compare-and-contrast essay, or a letter. Before writing their own, the class would assist Ms. Lora as she modeled the complete writing pro-cess on the overhead. Students would collectively brainstorm topics and ideas, narrow them down into key concepts, outline those concepts to fit the charac-teristics of the assigned format, draft the introduction, draft the body, draft the conclusion, and edit the zipped-together product. Ms. Lora spent extra time on the group editing process to acclimate students to the idea of editing others' work; she even had a daily exercise called "wrong writing," when she facilitated the class's editing of a slightly inferior sample she displayed on the overhead.

After having been through the entire process together (perhaps over the course of a week or so), students would accept the challenge of writing their own mas-terpiece, while Ms. Lora would again model the whole process every couple of days. They would follow the same course of action at their desks, with Ms. Lora looking over their shoulders and often listening in on their editing sessions. Ms. Lora peppered these writing cycles with stand-alone mini-lessons on the basic grammar, punctuation, and spelling problems she observed in their writing.

A collective "Ohhh!" rose up from one corner of the room, and Ms. Lora looked over to see that Hector's giant peanut butter ball had rolled off his one slice of bread as he attempted to take a bite. Judging from its tracks, the glob had slid off the corner of his desk and onto the floor where it had spread with a splat into a six-inch mound. For the first time that she could remember, Douglas was the one looking at a classmate with disapproval.

"Time out!" Ms. Lora called. Crouched down to scoop up the goop, Hector froze and looked up at Ms. Lora.

# 4

# Execute Effectively

**HIGHLY EFFECTIVE TEACHERS** take every action, large and small, because it contributes to the goal of student learning. For the sake of their students, these teachers master the elemental tasks of teaching, constantly monitoring their progress and adjusting course in light of changing realities around them.

1 SET BIG GOALS

2 INVEST STUDENTS AND THEIR FAMILIES

3 PLAN PURPOSEFULLY

4 EXECUTE EFFECTIVELY

5 CONTINUOUSLY INCREASE EFFECTIVENESS

6 WORK RELENTLESSLY

> *I know that I have to investigate whether or not my instructions were clear enough for all students to be successful.*

**BEFORE STARTING A LESSON** I regularly set the particular expectations for the level of concentration and attentiveness that I expect to see from every student. *"Y ahora, vamos a empezar en ingles*. We are going to be meeting in literature circles. I need you to sit in active listening position please." My students adjust their position and look at me for the next set of instructions. "You are going to have one minute to jot down anything you're thinking of in response to, Why did she buy the collar and leash for Winn Dixie? Then after one minute, when I ask you to, you are going to turn to your partner and exchange thoughts." I give these explicit instructions in a clear and kind, but authoritative, tone while maintaining eye contact

**Joiselle Cunningham,**
Fifth-Grade Bilingual,
New York

with my students, but I know that I have to investigate whether or not my instructions were clear enough for all students to be successful. As I ask the question, I look around the room for eye contact, raised hands, and note taking. I ask myself, "Is everyone engaged?" "Is anyone showing signs of being lost?" Once my students have begun to share their thoughts with their partners, I listen to the students' conversations, moving from group to group, inserting questions and thoughts, taking note of insights and misperceptions I will address with the group. I listen for the ideas that my students have come up with in order to adjust how I will check for understanding and address student needs before the end of the lesson. As I listen to students' reports, I affirm each student's participation and effort. I

use questions to push students to think more deeply and critically about the text. I see that Joe is having trouble identifying an event from the text that makes him believe what he believes. I write this down and later find that Elizabeth has the same problem. I have a small but growing list of who will work with me more intensively during the lesson to learn to support every assertion with meaningful evidence.

> *Quickly and quietly, the groups moved to their assigned spots.*

**Sara Cotner,**
Third Grade,
Louisiana

**I PROJECTED THE TIMER** using the overhead and pressed the start button. Sixteen pairs of eyes darted to our "Where do I go for math centers?" board. Quickly and quietly, the groups moved to their assigned spots, while the materials manager for each group went to the math shelf to collect the plastic containers of supplies that corresponded to their particular centers. Six students headed directly to the kidney-shaped table. The materials manager for their group passed out a small whiteboard and dry-erase marker for each student. As they received their pens, the students began completing the five-question review of previous objectives. I watched each student work out the review problems. I helped Miya remember the difference between odd and even. I then noticed that five of the six students missed the question about geometric shapes. I reached for my anecdotal note record for that group and wrote: "Reteach geometric shapes."

> *I realize we have a problem and so I'm thinking,*
> *'What is the most efficient way to fix this problem?'*

**GOOD TEACHERS PUT A** structure in place that anticipates addressing student confusion. They expect to be finding and dealing with students' misunderstandings. For example, say I'm teaching the skill of summarizing important details in nonfiction texts. I lead the lesson but when I start looking for signs of true understanding, I start to see problems. During guided practice, kids are having a hard time distinguishing between important and unimportant details. I see them just choosing the top or bottom sentence of the paragraph. I realize we have a problem and so I'm thinking, "What is the most efficient way to fix this problem?" It doesn't make sense to reteach because I'll probably lose engagement—I've already led twenty minutes of discussion. It doesn't make sense to individually conference with all the kids around the room because too many are having trouble. And I realize the group of students that need help isn't small

**Mariel Elguero,**
Fifth-Grade
Reading,
New Jersey

enough to pull to the back of the room during independent practice. In my classroom, I've worked with students to be able to diagnose their own mastery of an idea. We have these symbols students can use to show me whether they "need help" or "can give help." I decide to change my lesson plan so I can still reach my objective. I ask students to show me whether they need help or can give help and I pair students up to go back over the key elements of distinguishing important from unimportant details. Then I can circulate to the spots in the room where I am most needed.

Effective execution happens in the details of our everyday work. It means we follow through on our actions, big and small, so that we are not just doing what we intend to do but are actually having the effect we intend to have. For strong teachers, effective execution means ensuring that everything we do contributes to the goal of student learning.

This idea is so deceptively simple that at first it hardly seems worth noting. And yet in our observations of highly effective teachers, we sometimes see two teachers go into their classrooms with similarly strong plans and come out with different results. At the end of the lesson, unit, or year, one teacher's students have made dramatic academic progress, while the other teacher's students have not. What happens in the course of a plan's execution that leads to the variable outcomes? What are the common qualities of highly effective teachers who are able to translate their strong goals, student investment, and well-crafted plans into the outcomes that they intend?

Paradoxically, effective execution is the sum of many picky details *and* the result of a singular, deep passion and commitment to student learning. From their smallest transition procedures, to their daily lessons, to their behavior management decisions, to their year-long curricular path, highly effective teachers commit to and work toward achieving desired results. This commitment drives them to insist on doing every task well, knowing whether they are on pace to success along the way, and adjusting their plans as necessary.

Like the other approaches described in this book, effective execution is common to all successful leaders in challenging contexts. As Larry Bossidy and Ram Charan found in their exploration of effectiveness in the business world, "Execution is a systematic process of rigorously discussing hows and whats, questioning, tenaciously following through, and ensuring accountability. . . . In its most fundamental sense, execution is a systematic way of exposing reality and acting on it."[1] Teacher Rob LoPiccolo's approach to his classroom would fit seamlessly into this study of cross-sector leaders. Execution, he says, "is about knowing if it's working, responding to in-the-moment realities, and never forgetting the goal or getting distracted by unimportant things."

For the highly effective teachers whose practices served as the model for this chapter, the important things are students, their success, and their future. We see that effective execution is driven by the high stakes of our work and an intense desire to broaden opportunities for children who have been unjustly deprived of them.

Our task is to illuminate how effective teachers translate that passion into achieving outcomes. We have broken down successful teachers' methods of effective execution into discrete principles. In this chapter, we first identify and articulate the general tenets embodied by highly effective teachers and then explore some of the manifestations of those concepts in highly effective teachers' day-to-day actions.

## Key Elements of Effective Execution

In the highly productive classrooms we have studied, we see that effective execution—the results-oriented interaction with one's environment that you saw in the vignettes at the beginning of this chapter—is the sum of three related ideas. These tenets—doing well what must be done, insisting on seeing reality, and adjusting course as circumstances change—manifest in a number of teacher actions in and around the classroom.

### Doing Well What Must Be Done

In any endeavor, there are better and worse ways to do every necessary task, and strong leaders—including strong teachers—always insist on the better way. Successful doctors must master human anatomy, organic chemistry, patient relations, insurance bureaucracy, and much, much more. Successful astronauts must master physics, piloting the craft, electrical engineering, human physiology, and much, much more. Successful politicians must master public policy, public speaking, campaign finance regulations, budget processes, constituent interests, and much, much more.

Teachers must be great communicators, strong systems and people managers, and excellent planners. They must have strong content area knowledge, but also how their students most effectively engage that content. They must understand grading systems, learning disabilities, learning technology, and their community's cultural norms. From communicating difficult ideas, to comforting an upset student, to grading homework, to designing a plan to invest students in a big goal, highly effective teachers work hard to get the greatest return on every action they take. In the words of leadership expert John Gardner, this is the element of "task competency"—"knowledge a leader has of the task at hand"—and it is one of the key elements that distinguishes effective execution in the classroom.[2]

With the most successful teachers, we see two actions that lead to a high level of task competency. First, these teachers are constant learners. They are forever seeking not only new ideas but also insights into how to make what they are already doing even more effective. (The next chapter explores this tendency more fully.)

Second, these teachers practice. While a less effective teacher might accept that the early morning class gets less effective instruction because it is the first time he or she delivers the lesson, highly effective teachers work out the kinks before they get in front of students. Moreover, they practice the skills they use to serve their students.

Jessica Eastman is a sixth-grade math teacher in Oakland whose students started the year, on average, at a third-grade level but then grew by an average of 2.4 years' worth of math proficiency in a single year. Ms. Eastman got these amazing results in part by practicing and mastering the details of her daily actions:

> In college, I always noticed that when I practiced before going into any sort of interview, I did so much better. Even if they didn't ask the questions I practiced, if I had practiced out loud . . . my responses were much more clear and concise. As a teacher, I found the same to be true in my classroom. I would practice lessons out loud in my car on the way to school, and found that this made my actual lessons clearer and helped me have a sense of where I was going during the lesson. For example, I might discover that my in-car version of my lesson on probability needed to be better translated into language that an eleven-year-old could understand, and I could work out those adjustments right then and there and be ready when I actually delivered the lesson to my students.

Ms. Eastman told us that she even practiced managing student discipline, asking friends to pretend to be students so she could address their off-task behavior. Not having someone to play that role did not stop her. Sometimes, she says, "I'd stand in front of an empty classroom and practice responses to common misbehaviors. I'd imagine a student tapping a pencil over here, or a student with her head down over there, or a student talking to another student here, and I'd actually perform the response required by my behavior management system."

Maia Heyck-Merlin, as a highly effective fourth-grade teacher in Louisiana, also found that attention to detail, and the "dry-runs" it suggests, was critical to her success as a teacher and now as chief talent officer at Achievement First, a successful charter school system:

**Maia Heyck-Merlin**
Fourth Grade,
Louisiana

> In both planning and execution, details matter—whether the papers to be handed out are going to be stacked or collated, whether my kids enter the classroom past this table or that table, whether I make sure our behavior awards are passed out every single Friday without fail. Everything matters in the classroom because getting those things wrong costs three or four minutes of fumbling and precious learning time. That is why I insist on a dry run or dress rehearsal for key events—whether that is a lesson I'm teaching or a "leadership weekend" hosting dozens of candidates for principalships at Achievement First. For me, maximizing effectiveness means ensuring no wasted efforts, and that means not just creating a minute-by-minute action plan but physically walking through the process—a dress rehearsal—ahead of time so that you can smoke out potential glitches.
>
> For any endeavor, in the course of these dry runs, I force myself (and those around me) to think of five things that could go wrong and think through how to respond. I really do believe there are always five things that are going to go wrong with any plan, and so you might as well try to foresee what they will be. Of course, some of what goes wrong you will not have thought of. The way I think about it is that there are always some sets of things that you cannot anticipate, but there are also a whole heck of a lot of things you can. So if we can be as far ahead as possible on things we can anticipate, then we can better deal with what we can't. Being well planned allows you to execute better in the moment because you are constantly aware of the steps that will lead you to success. When one step gets missed, I can easily adjust course, flex the plan, anticipate a missed deadline, call an emergency meeting, or something else because I can see the big picture impact of a small step.

Ms. Eastman and Ms. Heyck-Merlin's dedication to practicing parallels a story about Winston Churchill. When Churchill's voice boomed from the bathroom where he was bathing, his valet thought something was wrong. The valet stuck his head in to check and Churchill said from the tub, "I was not speaking to you, Norman, I was addressing the House of Commons."[3] Leaders in all settings master the skills they need to be successful through constant learning and deliberate practice.

## Insisting on Seeing Reality

A second, related idea that seems to drive all strong teachers' effective execution is their insistence on knowing how they are doing as they work toward success. These teachers track how well they are performing key actions as they perform them.

Although perfect data are rarely available, a pattern among the strongest teachers is their desire to build systems that generate and constantly synthesize streams of data and information they receive in their classroom. Like other strong leaders, they know that good judgment, especially when it is required while they are in the classroom, requires "the ability to combine hard data, questionable data and intuitive guesses to arrive at a conclusion that events prove to be correct."[4]

As we observe highly effective teachers, we see them employing a variety of ways of seeing reality. These teachers are constantly monitoring students' learning and engagement, asking questions, and watching student interactions—all to ensure they know how well their plan is working. They use brief end-of-lesson assessments, student interest surveys, and objective-mastery tracking systems to get a better understanding of student progress. They employ informal and interpersonal observations to sense when a student is upset, recognize that their analogy mystified the students, or realize that attention is waning in the classroom and it is time for everyone to stand up and stretch. Successful leaders rely on an amalgam of inputs to ensure they have an accurate enough sense of their audience's engagement to make meaningful adjustments to their actions.

Many of the highly effective teachers we work with see themselves as armchair sociologists and scientists, refusing to assume anything, including—and especially—the key inference that students are mastering the lesson's objectives. They look for actionable evidence of success or trouble. What is each student doing? What is each student not doing? Why? While the urgency and intensity of your quest to put students on a different academic trajectory means that you must also work from hunches, instincts, and best guesses, whenever possible, real data (including qualitative observations) about students' learning should also inform your actions.

Sophia Pappas, for example, as a pre-K teacher in Newark, New Jersey, made observing and recording her students' actions an integral part of her teaching. By reflecting on her anecdotal notes, she could identify trends in student growth, as well as lingering gaps and misunderstandings. She began to see interactions among students that she wanted to foster and some she wanted to change. Ms. Pappas's advice is that this system of observing students must be part of an ongoing process of data collection, reflection and analysis, and planning:

> You have to have a systematic way of note taking—it cannot be sporadic or disconnected from the goals you are trying to achieve with your students. In fact, it is an important vehicle for producing gains with your students over time. Maybe that means focusing on one or a few students in a particular day, a particular set of skills in all students, or some combination of the two. We do this all the time in early childhood education to equip ourselves with the insight into each student's progress, interests, and learning styles needed to differentiate instruction, but I don't see why it's not a good idea for older students too. Being purposeful about observing students helps you plan well, and it also helps you make better in-the-moment adjustments.

Even while highly effective teachers seek more and more information to inform their decisions, they avoid the paralyzing data overload that can overwhelm otherwise successful leaders. These teachers, even while they insist on an unvarnished view of their own progress, keep moving forward based on the best judgments they can make with the time and information they have. Some of the highly effective teachers we work with seek out data and at the same time subscribe to the words of President Franklin D. Roosevelt: "But above all try something."[5]

Some teachers call this "do it, fix it, try it"—an approach that values the learning that comes from trying an action over the learning that comes from merely thinking about performing an action. Such teachers view even complex puzzles and choices with an inclination to act. Have your students' latest round of essays revealed that their writing skills are progressing much more slowly than you expected? The most successful teachers often come up with several possible instructional strategy adjustments and will immediately carry out at least one. Is a particular student acting out in ways that are disrupting his and others' learning? Effective teachers acknowledge they may be uncertain about what interventions are going to work, but they are most definitely going to start trying to intervene. Are students increasingly distracted by frequent pencil sharpening? The most effective teachers waste no time in implementing a policy that requires pencils to be sharpened before or after class. And then they move on.

As you might expect, researchers see the same duality of insistence on data and action among successful leaders in any context. Thomas Peters and Robert Waterman, for example, found that excellence in leaders and organizations is in fact predicted by a tendency to act even when there is uncertainty. Action, instead of being a sign of impetuousness, generates greater learning and in turn greater certainty the next time: "Getting on with it, especially in the face of complexity, does simply come down to trying something. Learning and progress accrue only when there is something to learn from, and the something, the stuff of learning and progress, is any completed action."[6]

## Adjusting Course as Circumstances Change

Brand-new and less accomplished teachers sometimes assume that effective implementation means faithful loyalty to their well-designed plan. Highly effective teachers, by contrast, realize that reality changes and plans sometimes have to change too.

The reasons that novice teachers sometimes respond to changes by seeking refuge in their plan are understandable. The plan offers comfortable certainty in the midst of sometimes unsettling uncertainties. They have spent so much time on the plan that they do not want to abandon it. They may not trust themselves to make on-the-fly adjustments effectively. Whatever the reason, if a teacher sticks to the plan in the midst of a changing context, students' learning is likely to suffer.

The most successful teachers and leaders are quick to make strategic adjustments when incoming data and information signal a change in the circumstances. These teachers bring wise adaptive judgment to their plans as they execute them, staying loyal not to the path in the plan but to its ultimate purpose. Strong teachers adjust course as called for by the reality around them to ensure the objective is met.

We can find evidence of this principle of leadership in any context. Imagine that you are the captain of a high-tech sailboat racing in the rough-and-tumble America's Cup regatta. You have charts and plans for sailing as quickly and efficiently as you can to the finish line. Before you ever step foot on the boat, you are studying tides, currents, weather patterns, and many other factors—all in the name of the imagined-implementation planning we discussed in Chapter Three. You start the race with a solid plan for success. But the open ocean, not unlike a classroom, has inevitable surprises. Perhaps the wind is higher or lower than you expected, or a crew member gets sick. As the captain of the ship, you are constantly comparing all of those incoming realities with your original assumptions, always being aware of the finish line, and making adjustments that will maintain your path to that end. One leadership expert calls this "adaptive capacity" and emphasizes that great leaders must be prepared to instantaneously "assess the results of their actions, correct their course, and quickly act again."[7]

Remember from Chapter Three the neurosurgeon's plan to remove her patient's brain tumor? The patient is alive today because Dr. Smith embodied the principles of purposeful planning. At the same time, the patient is alive today because Dr. Smith ultimately *deviated* from her plans. Here's the rest of the story from Dr. Smith: "With 90 percent of the tumor resected, we unexpectedly encountered a significant artery projecting through the base of the remaining mass. An injury to this artery could be devastating. Thinking again about our ultimate aim of a fully functioning and healthy patient, the attending made the call. We stopped the resection. We used radiation therapy to manage the rest of the tumor." Dr. Smith, by planning well but then adjusting course, achieved her aim of full function and health for her patient.

As in any other challenging endeavor, the context around teachers is often shifting—sometimes in a helpful way and sometimes not. As seventh-grade English/language arts teacher Jacqulyn Janecek put it, "It takes about a week of working in a school to realize that you cannot plan for everything—schedules change, there are assemblies, students forget their work, pipes burst, and fire drills and announcements interrupt instruction." Great plans foresee some of the possible challenges, but even the best plan does not foresee them all.

So a plan is critically important but is built from a virtual reality in which the contexts and challenges are assumed, not known. Like piloting a boat and performing brain surgery, effective execution in the classroom involves real-time comparison between the imagined reality when you created your plan with the actual reality when you are implementing it.[8] If you have planned well, the distance between that imagined reality and the actual reality will usually be small and manageable, but unforeseen contingencies inevitably arise. Sometimes adjustments to your plan are necessary in order to effectively and efficiently reach your objectives. In the words of Ms. Janecek, "Whether it's changing around your class schedule, holding some students during an open time, rearranging the order you were going to do something, or cutting out an interesting but not absolutely necessary example or activity . . . you have to keep working to reach your objective."

A teacher's day is made up of a string of these rapid judgments, usually triggered by changing or newly realized contexts.[9] Here are a few of the many examples we have seen:

| The context in which you are acting changes. . . | | . . .so you adjust your strategies to ensure you stay on track to meet your goal |
| --- | --- | --- |
| Your two-minute quiz just revealed that half the class failed to master the concept you were teaching. | → | You adjust your plan to enlist three of the high-performing students to lead small group practice of the concept. You trim five minutes off the review plans and use the five minutes of contingency time you had built into the plan to add ten minutes to the guided practice component of this lesson. |
| In the course of walking around the room, you realize that Brian is particularly hyper-active today, but you also notice he settles down every time you stand within a couple of desks of him. | → | You move the demonstration to a table on the side of the room next to Brian and continue your instruction uninterrupted. |
| Two students just had a confrontation in front of the rest of the class. Your early attempts to engage the room in an aca-demic discussion are falling flat. You can see many students glancing over at the two students who had the argument and sense that many other students are pretty upset. | → | To ensure long-term stability in the class-room and reestablish an environment focused on learning, you address this tension immediately. You make the difficult decision to move today's objective to tomorrow and revisit the unit plan over the next couple of weeks to fit the next schedule. You ask every-one to rearrange their desks into a circle for a class meeting. |

# What Effective Execution Looks Like in the Classroom

The most tangible signs that a teacher embodies these elements of effective execution are:

- Communicating key ideas
- Coordinating student practice
- Checking for student understanding
- Tracking progress
- Using organization and routine to maximize efficiency
- Asserting authority by consistently following through on high expectations

In our experience, teachers who translate the general principles of effective execution into these actions are likely to lead their students to dramatic academic achievement.

## Effectively Communicating Key Ideas

Strong communication with students is at the core of teachers' effective execution of their plans, whether those plans are aimed at academic progress, classroom management, or class-room efficiency.

Not only do great teachers communicate accurate information to students, they also process that content in ways that maximize student understanding. Highly effective teachers are masters of the key idea. In their planning process and when they are implementing a plan, they always have in mind a handful of the most important ideas that students must understand to master the objective. And they return over and over to those few ideas in various ways. Some teachers flag these key ideas in their lesson plans. Others map out the "take-home messages" that they want to be sure to emphasize.

Dramatically successful teachers also demonstrate strong communication by empathetic communication. These teachers define *communication* not as what is said but as what is understood—a direct manifestation of the general principle of insisting on an unvarnished view of one's impact. During a lesson, these teachers are focused on what students are hearing and understanding rather than on themselves.

This skill, in part, enables a teacher to determine whether students are learning from what the teacher is conveying, but New Haven, Connecticut, Spanish teacher Melanie Laputka suggests that empathetic communication is more than that. "If you're mostly focused on what you are doing and not focused enough on your students' reception or reaction, you're not really there," Ms. Laputka emphasizes. "Your students will pick up on that and they won't be there either." Hearing yourself in the way that your students are understanding you is a skill that builds connections with students, and these connections foster greater learning.

As successful teachers build and are aware of the in-the-moment connections with their students that signal an exchange of ideas, we see them employing the same effective communication tools as other leaders in other arenas. Notice how similar this list, drawn from analysis of videos of highly effective teachers, is to a list of characteristics of the most effective communicators you can think of in any sector. Strong communicators customarily:

- Use a positive and engaging tone
- Have expressive body language
- Employ varied and engaging vocal expressiveness
- Maintain constant eye contact with students/audience
- Purposefully repeat key ideas
- Make logical transitions
- Are enthusiastic about the subject matter (and audience understanding)
- Include elements of suspense, drama, and excitement in the exploration of new ideas
- Use accompanying visual aids and cues, such as graphic organizers, underlining, or using different colors on the board, to clarify key ideas and their relationship with one another

## Coordinating Student Practice

Highly effective teachers deftly coordinate students' interactions with the knowledge and skills being mastered. Coordinating student practice involves managing and monitoring student actions and evaluating and steering those actions to maximize learning. High school math teacher Jacob Lessem describes how critical this part of each lesson is in his classroom:

> For me, student practice is sometimes the most active part of the day, the part where I'm doing the most teaching. During guided and independent practice, I'm always circling and not just saying, "Are you doing your work?" but I'm checking each kid's work, I'm doing one-on-one tutorials, I'm doing impromptu small group work, and I'm doing impromptu differentiation. If a kid is struggling, I'll go back and quickly make up some problems, or if a kid is really getting it easily, I'll make up some extension problems. One of the real core areas where my teaching happens is during this time. It's so key to make sure I'm doing all this. To me, one of the big mindset changes that I had when I started was that I thought teaching meant standing in front of the kids and then telling them to practice it. But really, the standing in front is not the most important part at all. The most important part is when they're engaging with the material and I'm going around and circling and doing as much as I can to make sure they're getting it.

One foundational step in coordinating student practice is the clear design and communication of directions. After all, if students do not understand how or what you want them to practice, how can they practice effectively? Although it may at first seem like a relatively minor point, highly effective teachers emphasize that the ability to give clear, well-understood, and actionable directions saves hours and hours of instructional time that otherwise might be lost to false starts and reclarification. Shannon Dingle explains the importance of directions in her classroom:

> Several of my students had attention deficit hyperactivity disorder or disabilities that affect attentiveness. Before we began any activity, I had them, especially students who I knew had challenges with attention, repeat my directions back to me in their own words, and this made our time in the classroom so much more productive. I made a point to do this with assessments, because I wanted to ensure that I was getting a true assessment of what my students knew and didn't know instead of having mistakes made because they didn't understand or pay attention to the instructions.

Almost without exception, the most successful teachers treat direction giving with great care, paying close attention to detail. They wait for the entire class's attention, instruct the class not to act on the instructions until they say it is time, lay out the instructions in a few simple steps, and question students to ensure that they understand the directions. Only then do their students launch into the task at hand.

## Checking for Understanding

As a thought experiment, imagine for a moment you have the miraculous ability to read students' minds. As you are teaching, you can instantaneously see what students are thinking, understanding, and wondering. Imagine how radically that would change your effectiveness as a teacher.

In classrooms where students are making dramatic academic achievement, teachers actu-ally *have* found ways to read students' minds. These teachers have developed systems and skills that answer, in real time, the question "What are students learning?" and thus have created systems that reveal mastery of rigorous lessons.

In one amazingly productive classroom, we see a teacher looking out at a sea of white squares of whiteboard, on which each student has used a dry-erase marker to complete an equation. The teacher is able to review all of the students' work almost instantaneously and to gauge their understanding. In another classroom, we see an elementary teacher who has taught her students the alphabet in American Sign Language. She is continuously asking questions of the class, and every student is signing the first letter of the answer to each question. She is thus able to instantly gauge and react to mastery and misunderstanding. In every outstanding class-room, we see a teacher who employs effective questioning techniques to thoroughly probe, in a supportive way, students' understanding as new ideas are being presented.

Checking for understanding—as a means of providing the teacher with real-time knowl-edge of student learning—dramatically increases teachers' effectiveness and students' academic achievement. Sixth-grade math teacher Daniel Sellers learned this very quickly during his first year of teaching. He recalls that initially he sometimes "taught" an idea without trying to determine what students had taken from the lesson. He would then see problems when students attempted to use the new concept on their own. More often than not, they ended up coming to him with questions that showed they had not understood the material. So Mr. Sellers reconfig-ured his approach to check for understanding in the course of his instruction:

> This was something that I was continuously working on, always refining and improving. I started by writing in specific times throughout the introduction of new material and the guided practice parts of the lesson where I would stop and check for understanding. This kept me from "barrel-rolling" through the lesson just to get to independent practice. I also wanted to make my checks for understanding so consistent that my students knew when to expect them (after every other example, I would stop to check for understand-ing), to the point where my kids knew what was coming and could be ready to explain their answers. The second part of that, of course, is expecting my students to explain their answers clearly (so others could understand them). Eventually they got to the point where they were reteaching to each other what I had just introduced to the class.
>
> In order to ensure that I was getting a representative sample of students, I tried lots of different methods—everything from random selection of popsicle sticks with student names on them to giving extra [awards in our classroom incentives system] for students who could clearly explain an answer to using whiteboards and similar methods for instant checks.
>
> Through my instruction and checks for understanding I now know exactly which students get it, and which students need continued support as they begin to work independently.

My focus on this aspect of teaching has been rewarded each year: as I finish up with a lesson and push my students off on their own, I watch as they eagerly get down to work, independently practicing what they have just learned.

Virtually all of the highly effective teachers we work with can share stories of times when their check for understanding revealed their lesson was a complete disaster. Rachel Donaldson Dahl, an elementary school ESL teacher in Phoenix, confessed to us: "There is a moment (in my case, many moments) in all teachers' lives where we look at our students and realize, 'They have *no* idea what I am talking about.'" Worse than a disastrous lesson, however, is not even knowing you have taught one.

Teachers' means of reading students' minds take many forms—from standard probing questions to reading body language and facial expressions. Ms. Laputka, the Spanish teacher in New Haven, offered the following advice: "Get to know individual students' personalities, so that you can learn how to read their expressions, their reactions. If they're looking around the room in puzzlement, they're probably not getting it. You're looking for a mix of under-standing and a mix of investment."

As we have contrasted the approaches of highly effective and less effective teachers, we have discerned several keys to effective checking for understanding:

• *Maintain focus on the most important ideas.* Not surprisingly, the key to successful checking for understanding is not only the teacher's effective questioning and mind-reading systems; it is also the teacher's constant focus on the purpose of the lesson. Teachers frequently ask lots of questions of their students, but if those questions are not directly related to the key components of the objective at hand, they do not shed light on how students are progressing toward mastering that objective. Effective teachers primarily ask questions about the key ideas, and they do so throughout the lesson (not just in one spot). A corollary to this point (as discussed in Chapter Three on planning) is that you must first have a clear vision of what student mastery should look like. Science teacher Rob LoPiccolo made this point emphatically:

What makes up effective execution? Good questioning of your students and the ability to give them the time and space to learn, also the ability to constantly read and assess your students to get feedback on whether or not something is working—constantly, constantly, constantly checking for understanding in every way. But more than anything, you have to know your objective of your lesson, and you have to know what skill you are looking for your students to display. There are infinite ways to check for understanding, but none of them will work unless you know what answer you want back.

• *Use stronger methods than "Got it?"* If you ask students, "Do you understand?" you will not know whether your idea has been understood, no matter what the response. Students, for a whole range of reasons, may not be the best judges of their own mastery of skills. Lars Clemensen, an elementary school teacher in New Jersey, realized that checks for understanding have to be more targeted than he first thought:

> " As a first-year teacher, I would ask my students if they had any questions after a lesson. Hearing none, I assumed my students were right there with me. But it was after the first formal assessment that I realized that my students were not with me and in fact did not grasp what I was teaching at all. Simply asking my students if they understood was not the way to gauge their grasp of a concept. Rather, quick checks for understanding in the way of exit slips, quick quizzes, or sharing with a neighbor proved to me a bit more accurately where my students were at every step along the way. "

This caution about trusting students' self-reported understanding comes with a caveat. Even as highly effective teachers like Mr. Clemensen are looking for reliable ways to know whether and how much students understand, they are also attempting to build in their students the metacognitive skills necessary to recognize the extent of their own understanding. Strong teachers work to teach students to think critically about what they do and do not understand and thereby are able to put more confidence in responses they get to, "Does anyone have any questions?"

• *Strive to gauge all students' understanding.* Less effective teachers may believe they have checked for understanding when they ask one or two students (usually students who volunteer often) to explain the idea being taught. Out of necessity, strong teachers also use a small sample size to make judgments about the successful transfer of knowledge and skills, but strong teachers also ask themselves, "How certain am I that the five students I heard from are representative of the whole class's understanding?" During student practice, effective teachers monitor all students' work to get an accurate sense of how well students understand, and they are careful not to spend all of practice time with a small number of students. Effective teachers also teach their students how to evaluate each other's work and help each other

## ▶ RESPONDING TO STUDENT MISUNDERSTANDINGS

**CHECKING FOR UNDERSTANDING IS** not just an opportunity for you to learn what students don't understand; implemented well, it also becomes an instructional tool from which students can learn.

Making checks for understanding a teaching tool begins with high expectations for student responses. If a student gives an inaccurate response, strong teachers seek to uncover the misunderstandings at the root of that response. (Less effective teachers often go on to another student looking for the right answer.) Strong teachers do not accept partially correct answers from students; they tell them what parts are accurate, what parts need to be improved, and why.

We have observed that when students give wrong answers, highly effective teachers consistently:

- Question further to see where student understanding breaks down
- Support the student with leading questions to arrive at understanding
- Return to the matter soon to ensure that understanding has improved

improve their understanding of key ideas. In addition, teachers train their classroom aides and paraprofessionals so as to maximize their ability to gauge student understanding and assist with clarifications.

▶ **THE EXPERIENCE OF STUDENTS IN A CLASSROOM WHERE. . .**

| The Teacher Checks for Understanding Frequently and Effectively | The Teacher Checks for Understanding Rarely or Ineffectively |
|---|---|
| The students feel: | The students feel: |
| • The teacher cares about their mastery and learning | • The teacher's purpose is getting through the lesson, not ensuring the students understand |
| • Invited to indicate publicly when they are confused and need help | • They can't learn (because the teacher obviously assumes they will under-stand from the lesson as it was given) |
| • Liberated to make mistakes because they know the teacher is going to make sure, in the end, they get it | |
| • Valued | • Ignored |

• *Probe beneath the surface.* At every phase of the lesson, effective teachers seek to determine not just whether students understand, but also how much they understand and the reasons that they do or do not understand. In practice, this means digging deeper with follow-up questions, carefully gleaning student understanding from written work, and closely monitoring group discussions to gauge individual students' comprehension.

Pedagogical research validates these patterns we see in highly effective teachers' class-rooms. The research indicates that checking for understanding might be one of the more powerful tools at a teacher's disposal. A synthesis of more than 250 studies concluded that checking for student mastery along the way "does improve learning. The gains in achieve-ment appear to be quite considerable . . . amongst the largest ever reported for educational interventions."[10]

For tips on effective questioning techniques, see www.teachingasleadership.org.

## Tracking Progress

Another stark difference we see between two teachers who have great plans but get different results is that the more successful teachers are nearly obsessive progress trackers. Checking for understanding is about finding out what your students are learning, and tracking progress is making a record of those findings so that you can systematically adjust your approach and celebrate your progress.

Teachers who are making the greatest academic gains with their students are never sur-prised by the results. Along the way, they have meaningfully assessed students, evaluated those assessments accurately and efficiently, and promptly recorded the results in a tracking system so that the data can inform their short- and long-term planning. Jessica Eastman, the teacher who saw enormous growth in her students' math skills, explains how tracking student progress affected her teaching:

" I gave exit quizzes every day on every little piece they needed . . . , so I always knew where we were struggling and where we were doing well. Having that data means that you can adjust on the fly, helping you make informed decisions about what to reteach and when to move on. I can think of so many examples where, had I not had that concrete data, I'd have made the wrong choice. There have been times when I thought we had an amazing lesson or I was just blown away when a kid said an amazingly insightful thing that demonstrated a big leap in understanding, but the exit quiz showed that only a couple of students actually mastered the objective. And there have been times when a behavior issue made me feel that we had an exhausting, unproductive day, but the exit quiz showed me that students actually mastered the objective. "

As we discussed in Chapter Two, making student progress transparent is a powerful tool for investing students, especially students who question whether hard work correlates with success in school. Graphs and charts showing student progress are virtually always on the walls of the most productive classrooms. With younger children, these graphic representations may take on a more narrative form. In Anne LaTarte's classroom of first, second, and third graders, for example, each student has a paper hill with a picture of himself or herself attached to the slope and the objective tacked at the top. As they meet each objective that Ms. LaTarte has mapped on the path to the big goal, they "climb the hill" of understanding.

A teacher's tracking system is the data collection behind those charts, graphs, and paths up "hills." The system records student and class progress on the objectives students need to master, and it is an always present element of effective execution in the most successful classrooms.

In the strongest classrooms we have studied, a tracking system may include grading, or the numerical average of a series of summative assessment scores, but it is more than that. Tracking begins with a list of objectives that a student needs to master (which you identify as part of the process of crafting a year-long plan), and the tracking system indicates the extent to which each student has mastered those objectives over time. It allows you to observe trends in each student's understanding and misunderstanding and thus helps you plan and differentiate subsequent lessons and supplemental interventions to help ensure that all students achieve the big goal.

A quality tracking system also shows the overall picture of the class's average mastery and progress toward the big goal. This allows you to know where your class and students currently perform, as well as how far you need to travel in order to reach your goals. This knowledge will enable you to make informed, data-driven adjustments to your instruction. Although all of the planning actions described thus far are important for leading students to significant academic progress, none of them will be effective unless you consistently track student performance in a clear, organized tracking system.

As with so many of these indicators of effective execution, tracking systems can take many forms. Some teachers create a separate document for each student. Other systems break down a particular standard into its component objectives, with a place to record each student's progress. In this case, you might keep a chart with columns for each discrete skill (for example, reading two-digit numbers, representing a two-digit number with manipulatives, and so on) and a row for each student. You can make these charts in a spreadsheet, in your grade book, in your students' folders—whatever makes most sense for you. For highly effective teachers, the key question is whether the system allows them to easily and efficiently record, analyze, and respond to the data.

▶ **SAMPLE TRACKING TABLE**

| Mr. Johnston's Progress Chart Unit One: *Reading and Writing Multi-Digit Numbers* | Read Two-Digit Numbers | Read Three-Digit Numbers | Read Four-Digit Numbers | Read Five-Digit Numbers | Read Six-Digit Numbers | Read Seven-Digit Numbers | Represent a Two-Digit Number with Manipulatives | Write a Two-Digit Number in Expanded Form |
|---|---|---|---|---|---|---|---|---|
| Class average | | | | | | | | |
| Diana | | | | | | | | |
| Sylvia | | | | | | | | |
| Pasquale | | | | | | | | |
| Leticia | | | | | | | | |

Aaron Pomis, a middle school science teacher in North Carolina, used a tracking system in his classroom, reaping all the benefits of knowing the reality around him in order to ensure his effectiveness:

> I have seen the overwhelming benefits of tracking and sharing progress toward big goals. In my classroom, students are first greeted by an entire wall dedicated to tracking the percentage of students who are masters of any given objective in our content. Students see the numbers change after tests and quizzes, and we often begin lessons pointing to the tracking wall to see which objective we will be working to master next. Second, after each benchmark test, my fifth-grade students are given a full spreadsheet that transparently details and color-codes each student's level of success on each objective tested. Through mini-lessons and joint analysis, students at the middle of the year are able to diagnose the most pressing academic issues of our class, identify potential solutions, and carry out their own next steps. After reviewing our last benchmark test spreadsheet, students passionately argued for additional homework and review sheets for more practice to master global winds and analyze weather data. They formed study groups during lunch and study hall that paired the highest performers with students struggling with the material, and

students exchanged telephone numbers with others in class whose academic strengths aligned with their weaknesses. A change was seen immediately, with the number of phone calls [to me] about homework decreasing but students turning in stronger homework. Mastery scores on the next benchmark test skyrocketed.

Mr. Pomis explains his students' high scores with his use of progress trackers: "The solutions and strategies to achieve our goal were not just created by teachers, they were created by students motivated by the clear and transparent display and communication of their progress toward their goals." The power of his approach is both in the logistics and spreadsheets that organize important information and also in his purposeful use of that information to inform, inspire, and empower his students.

## Maximizing Efficiency with Organization and Routine

As a third-grade English as a Second Language teacher in Houston, Jessica Kaufman taught students who represented eight countries and five languages, who had had three different temporary teachers over the course of the previous year, and many of whom were unable to navigate day-to-day interactions in English. Yet by the end of the year, each student's reading level and writing ability had improved by at least a year and a half according to the district's assessments, and all of her students were able to be self-sufficient in English in public interactions. Ms. Kaufman's principal explained this dramatic student achievement with a simple observation: "There is never a minute wasted." This is another concrete embodiment of effective execution in superproductive classrooms.

Previously we discussed the ability of big, inspiring goals to bring a sense of urgency and intensity to learning. Leaders use those strategies to help themselves and their students realize the value of every minute they have together. At the same time, that inspirational idea has a logistical corollary. Highly effective teachers use procedures and systems to maximize the value of each minute of learning. Ms. Kaufman, like all other highly effective teachers, strives for efficiency, routine, and organization. Ms. Kaufman "sweats the small stuff," squeezing extra learning time out of her day. This aspect of effective execution is built from a hypersensitivity to wasted learning time and helps explain the stopwatches, silent hand signals, and student-managed routines common in especially productive classrooms.

When teachers turn efficient practices into habits, they create routines—set processes that students learn and perform repeatedly, without the need for time-intensive directions from the teacher. Well-designed and well-executed routines are engines of efficiency. They are comforting to students and liberating for teachers. (Reflecting the dual planning and execution nature of these routines, we listed a number of examples in the previous chapter—taking attendance, getting the attention of the class, and distributing materials, to name a few.)

Emma Simson's comments are representative of those we hear from highly effective teachers about the power of routines to increase learning time:

> ❝Establishing regular routines, especially in parts of the lesson, can create smooth transitions and effective uses of time. For example, if group work is often done in similar ways with similar jobs, students know exactly what to do and how to do it. If you change the dynamics of it every time, you have to spend a lot of time teaching that new process.❞

In the classrooms where students are making dramatic academic progress, we see routines so strong that they run virtually without any involvement from the teacher. In fact, for many highly effective teachers, the measure of a well-executed routine is that it continues in the teacher's absence.

"I have found that my students absolutely thrive on our consistent classroom schedule and routine," Jennifer Rosenbaum explained. "Knowing what will happen at each point during the day allows them to focus completely on the task at hand, without having to fret about what is coming next. Additionally, they know what they are expected to do—both academically and behaviorally—at each point in the day. Providing this type of consistency helps my students feel safe in school, which ultimately allows them to focus on learning." Yael Dvorin made the same point: "Not only could my students probably do our morning routine in their sleep, they are comforted by the fact that they know what to expect. They know what will happen even before they step into my classroom. I do not need to waste time explaining to students every day how something will be accomplished, collected, or distributed."

Like behavioral rules and consequences, procedures and routines must be explicitly taught and reinforced:

### SET CLEAR EXPECTATIONS

- Discuss the purpose behind procedures and routines.
- Have students practice systems, procedures, and routines until they demonstrate mastery.
- Be clear, confident, and convincing when you introduce expectations so that students do not tune out.

### REINFORCE EXPECTATIONS

- When students do not meet expectations, let them know, and consider having them repeat them until they do meet expectations.
- Remind students of the purpose behind rules and procedures.
- Praise students when they meet expectations.
- Be clear, confident, and convincing when you reinforce expectations.

As with a standard lesson plan and with setting behavioral expectations, student practice of routines and procedures is key. We see otherwise sane teachers mimicking the sound of the bell so their high school students can "practice" not jumping up to leave until they are dismissed. We see elementary teachers, eyes closed and listening intently, giving the signal to line up at the door and sending students back to their seats every time they hear talking. We see middle school teachers stopping the dissemination of class sets of books, taking them back up, and starting over because one book was tossed onto a desk. Kelly Harris Perin shared the following story that illustrates the importance of practicing process:

> For the first two weeks of the year, I kept wondering if all of the time we spent practicing classroom procedures was worth it. We passed out our folders, got into groups, and got ready to leave class dozens of times. But by the time we were done, every student knew what to do when she stepped in the door, when to sharpen pencils, and when it was okay to whisper to a neighbor. Having really clear rules and procedures was *liberating*—it freed me from being the policewoman and let me focus on using every minute to teach. It was so easy: everyone came in, got their folders, took homework out and placed it on the corner of the desk, and began the warm-up for the day. Meanwhile, the attendance taker figured out who was present. . . . And I got to walk around, check homework, greet each student personally, and start off every period calm and focused after the first five minutes. Worth it? Definitely.

To be clear, these highly effective teachers sweat the details not because they are obsessed with control but because they see that this attention to detail translates into student learning. When less time is spent distributing materials, helping students who have been absent access missed learning, and getting started at the beginning of class, more time is free for real learning.

## Asserting Authority

When we look at the day-to-day methods of teachers whose students make dramatic academic progress and compare them to teachers whose students do not, we see another clear distinction in how these teachers implement plans in their classrooms: more effective teachers are *in charge* in their classrooms. Highly successful teachers assert their authority, walking into the classroom with a mindset that *I am responsible for and in control of what happens in my classroom.*

This mindset is the source of the closely related, and all-important, idea that successful teachers do what they say they are going to do.

By setting clear expectations and following through on them, a teacher diminishes or even removes uncertainty, drama, and tension from the teacher-student relationship, thereby clearing the way for student learning. When academic, behavioral, and procedural expectations are consistently implemented, students do not have to worry about "what happens if . . . ," and teachers are liberated from the impossible burden of case-by-case decisions. When a teacher inconsistently enforces consequences or procedures, every tension involves a negotiation. We see increases in student resistance, misbehavior, and distractions.

The first step to effectively asserting authority in the classroom is to ensure that students understand your expectations, the reasons behind them, and the consequences of not meeting them. This demonstrates that you are comfortable as the classroom leader and have a clear vision for classroom success, and it eliminates student confusion about what you expect and why those expectations are important to their success.

Highly effective teachers devote time to teaching behavioral expectations at the beginning of the year. They may ask students to brainstorm what each rule means and provide examples of what it does and does not look like in action. Or they model what it looks like to follow each rule and then review the progression and meaning of consequences, sometimes enlisting the students' assistance by having them demonstrate the actions and consequences by role play. We often see teachers leading students to practice class rules as a means of making expectations clear. These teachers understand how much instructional time they will save in the long run, so they do not move on until students demonstrate mastery of expectations.

Tara Harrington, a Charlotte, North Carolina, teacher who eclipsed old records for student achievement in her high school biology classroom, says that a foundation for her success was being explicit about how students should comport themselves in her classroom and following through on those expectations. (To appeal to her high school students' self-identity as adults, she discussed the way they *carry themselves* instead of their *behavior*.) She described and showed them what teamwork looked like, how to organize their work, and how to act. "I learned," she says, "if you don't set expectations *really* explicitly and clearly, they'll fill in the blanks of what you didn't say with their assumptions based on expectations in their previous school experiences, which may or may not resemble what you expect. You don't want to leave it to chance."

Two of the biggest pitfalls for new teachers are failing to be explicit about expectations and then inconsistently following through on them. Many new teachers initially struggle, for example, with classroom management and student behavior. In our experience, these problems are mostly symptoms of the teacher's failure to assert authority by consistently following through with behavioral expectations. Simply stated, the root of the problem is saying one thing and doing another—the very essence of ineffective execution.

Sometimes a new teacher may ignore some unacceptable behavior out of fear of upsetting or annoying the students by enforcing rules, deciding that enforcing a rule is just "not worth it." In other situations, a teacher may enforce rules with some students and not others, perhaps on the misguided notion that an infraction is an anomaly for one student but needs correcting in another. In still other situations, a teacher's authority is subverted by an unrealistic consequence spontaneously created in the heat of frustration: "That's it! Next person who interrupts our learning is walking with me to the principal's office."

Consistently enforcing expectations means you will have to do so less often. When teachers find themselves constantly policing student behavior, they may have not set and enforced clear expectations from the beginning. This is not to suggest that rules and consequences can never be changed, but that whatever they are, it is most effective to stay true to them. (Being truly consistent in your implementation puts additional pressure on designing rules that are few and meaningful. If you find that it never seems "worth it" to implement a rule, then that rule is a mistake.) Nor does this mean ruling your classroom with an iron fist and never prioritizing among the infractions that you take on. It does mean, however, that you strive for consistency, fairness, and dignity in your interactions with students; that you be careful about what bright line rules and consequences you set; and that when one of those rules is violated, the consequence follows.

The indicators of effective communication apply to rules and consequences just as they apply to academic content. We virtually never see yelling in classrooms where students are making multiple years' worth of academic progress. Their teachers tend to be composed, caring, and firm in executing their behavior system. Such teachers have a number of effective ways to quietly address minor incidents without interrupting the flow of their lessons, and they consistently respond to violations of class rules as they have said they would. Asserting authority effectively is to approach every interaction with every student in a well-considered, predetermined way and thereby be able to handle any situation that arises.

## SET CLEAR EXPECTATIONS

- Discuss the purposes behind the rules and consequences.

- Explain, model, and practice what each rule means and the consequences of breaking the rule.

- Be clear, confident, and convincing when you introduce expectations so that students don't tune out.

- Assess students on expectations and consequences until students demonstrate a clear understanding of them.

## REINFORCE EXPECTATIONS

- When students do not meet expectations, do what you said you would do: immediately assert yourself by assigning the predetermined consequence in a way that maintains student dignity.

- Remind students of the purpose behind rules and consequences as necessary.

- Praise students when they meet expectations. This is particularly effective when a student has previously struggled to meet expectations.

- Be clear, confident, and convincing when you reinforce expectations.

These patterns, modeled in the most productive classrooms we have seen, are also suggested by some of the nation's foremost researchers and thinkers on classroom management. Lee Canter and Marlene Canter verify that the key to effective assertion of authority is to clearly and confidently make your expectations for student behavior known and to follow through with your stated consequences consistently. They call this highly effective approach assertive responsiveness: "When a teacher responds assertively, he tells students exactly what behavior is acceptable and what is unacceptable, what will happen when the student chooses to behave and what will happen when the student chooses not to behave. No questions. No room for confusion."[11]

As can happen with academic expectations, new teachers may lower behavioral expectations out of well-intentioned but ill-conceived "kindness." They find themselves thinking, "Well, David is whispering to his neighbor during silent reading time, but in general is doing such a better job today than he was yesterday. I won't say anything and hope he stops quickly," or "I shouldn't tell her to stop chewing gum because then she'll be in a bad mood." These practices undermine a teacher's authority by giving students no way to predict the results of their choices. Predictability is a key component of students' sense of safety and fairness.

At the other end of the spectrum, less-effective teachers may assume they have to be harsh and believe authority is maintained through students' fear of the teacher's reprisal. These less-effective teachers may find themselves frustrated and saying, "David, stop talking *now*. Evidently you're just not capable of keeping your mouth shut," or "Spit your gum out. You now get to write, 'I will never chew gum in class again,' five hundred times."

Charlotte Phillips, a Houston kindergarten teacher, recalls that she at first mistakenly equated asserting authority with being mean and tough:

> A huge turning point in my teaching was that epiphany I had in my first year when I realized that I could have a much more powerful effect on my students' behavioral choices when I spoke to them in a neutral tone instead of in a condemning fashion when they made poor choices. Speaking to my students this way helped them to realize that when they didn't meet a classroom expectation, it wasn't simply about breaking a rule: it was about making a choice that hurt themselves or others in the classroom. It took the focus off of me as a teacher and on them as a student, and what they could do to make better choices in the future.

Ms. Phillips's anecdote highlights two related patterns in the effective execution of behavioral management plans. First, highly effective teachers frame rules and consequences as student choices—emphasizing each student's control over his or her own behavior. Students can choose to follow the rules (thereby receiving benefits, even if intangible) or choose not to by breaking the rules and incurring the consequences. Second, highly effective teachers are, without exception, positive and respectful in their administration of consequences. Maintaining your students' (and your own) dignity by using descriptive but nonjudgmental language in discussing behavioral infractions is crucial to your long-term assertion of authority.

The most successful teachers we have observed not only respond effectively when students fail to meet expectations, they also reduce the likelihood of misbehavior by praising students when they meet expectations. Ross Jensen, a fifth-grade teacher in Newark, New Jersey, attests to this idea:

> " After a disastrous first semester, I resolved to adopt a positive paradigm for my class-room. Instead of scolding off-task students, I would praise on-task students. Instead of telling those students who were misbehaving that I was disappointed in them, I would tell those students who were behaving appropriately that I was proud of them. Instead of pointing out when students acted like kindergartners, I would point out when students acted like professionals. Instead of stopping instruction to correct student behavior, I would remind students to "self-correct." The results were dramatic and immediate. "

Thus, as a function of their effective execution, excellent teachers do not look the other way because a student may be having a hard time, and they do not chastise a student aggressively and judgmentally. These teachers simply make clear the expectations and consequence for not meeting them, provide positive reinforcement when students meet those expectations, and then uncompromisingly and methodically enforce expectations as necessary.

| When the teacher sets clear expectations and reinforces them consistently, fairly, and with respect for student dignity | When the teacher sets or reinforces expectations inconsistently, unfairly, or in a way that demeans students |
|---|---|
| The students feel:<br>• Invested in the class rules and procedures<br>• In control of the teacher's responses to their actions<br>• They can focus on learning without worrying about major distractions<br>• Safe | The students feel:<br>• Unclear about why the teacher has established certain rules or procedures<br>• That consequences are the results of the teacher's whim rather than the result of their own choices<br>• Anxious about what will go wrong in class today<br>• Persecuted |

In the words of highly effective teacher Elisha Rothschild Frumkin, "Whether it is the most difficult child or the most angelic, the consequence remains the same. It protects you and your authority in the long run."

# Conclusion: Key Ideas and Next Questions

The Teaching As Leadership rubric (see Appendix A) describes six specific teacher actions that indicate a teacher is embodying the general principle of effective execution. Highly effective teachers:

E-1: Clearly present academic content

E-2: Facilitate, manage, and coordinate student academic practice

E-3: Check for academic understanding

E-4: Communicate high expectations for behavior

E-5: Implement and practice time-saving procedures

E-6: Evaluate and keep track of students' performance

## Key Ideas

Effective execution means doing what it takes to ensure that your plans have the effect you want them to. For classroom leaders, that idea means doing well what must be done, insisting on real evidence of student learning along the way, and adjusting plans when necessary to rechart the path to your goals.

Like the other distinguishing strategies of highly effective teachers, this approach to successful implementation in the classroom is actually the same as successful implementation in many other contexts. Jerry Hauser, who was a highly effective math teacher in Los Angeles, is now the CEO of The Management Center, a training center for leaders of nonprofit organizations. He shared with us his realization that highly effective teachers' effective execution makes them exactly the kind of effective managers he tries to develop in other organizations:

My job is consulting with nonprofit organizations to make them more effective. The job would be so much easier if all the managers of these organizations had been classroom teachers. So many of the fundamental challenges they have in leading a group of people to get things done are second nature to a good teacher. Maybe the most common frustration I hear from managers involves their inability to get well-intended and hard-working staff members to produce exactly what the managers have in mind. And yet, effective delegation is actually a simple three-step cycle that I—and I suspect most teachers—learned quickly in the classroom: to get a team of people to produce quality products, clearly set expectations for what is going to happen (by giving and being sure everyone understands the instructions), stay engaged along the way to make sure the work is on track (by looking at and shaping work-product along the way), and create accountability and learning (by following through on expectations) for the quality of the product. While some managers struggle with these ideas, I bet every teacher reading this instantly knows what I'm talking about.

teachingasleadership.org

More guidance on effectively executing your plans to maximize student learning is available online, including:

- Annotated video of models of strong teaching
- Lists of indicators of various levels of proficiency on the teacher actions discussed in this chapter
- Common pitfalls new teachers experience as they strive to execute their plans effectively
- Testimonials about the benefits of various elements of effective execution

## Next Questions

With these principles of effective execution in mind, a teacher is set to dig into some challenging but rewarding puzzles of effective execution in the classroom:

- How can I improve my communication skills—my tone, my body language, my emphasis of key ideas—in ways that will maximize my students' understanding?

- What procedural moments in my classroom are worth practicing with my students? How much time and energy should I put into increasing the efficiency of our time together?

- When and how can I practice the actions that will most increase my students' learning?

- How can I infuse checking for understanding into every lesson at multiple points, and how can I stay nimble enough to react and adjust to what those checks tell me?

- How can I build systems that provide me with a constant flow of data about what is and is not working?

## "LIGHT MONITOR. FORM COLLECTOR. PLANT MANAGER."

 teachingasleadership.org

*An excerpt from Ms. Lora's Story, a case study in Teaching As Leadership, available online at www.teachingasleadership.org.*

The schoolwide classroom management program's "multimanager system" had seemed absurd when she first heard about it. Ms. Lora remembered laughing with other rookie teachers at the training workshop as the facilitator put a list of about fifty "manager" roles on the screen. Something like "line monitor" seemed reasonable, but keeping up with a "cubby supervisor," a "board eraser," and a "plant manager" seemed crazy.

Now, as her new students eagerly scanned a similar list on a similar screen, it was her initial novice skepticism that seemed absurd. In her first three years as a teacher, Ms. Lora had seen the benefits of empowering her students, especially students who frequently acted out in class. She was still amazed that despite her instincts to deprive troubling students of responsibility, classroom behavior and management seemed to get better and easier the more responsibility, along with structure, she gave the students. Ms. Lora even had students with particularly severe behavioral problems who were inclined to monitor their own behavior when they had been granted some indispensable title on the classroom management team.

Of course, "indispensable" is in the eye of the beholder, and Ms. Lora was surprised each year to see what roles were in high demand.

"Light monitor. Form collector. Plant manager," one student listed.

"Thank you, Julian," said Ms. Lora. "Elizabeth, what are your first three choices?"

"Plant manager. Line director. And homework collector," Elizabeth called out as Ms. Lora took notes.

"Wow, you guys," said Ms. Lora. "You're really stepping up for the high-responsibility roles. I appreciate that. We are going to have a well-run classroom with all this leadership. Thank you."

She looked down at the next name on her list.

"Roberto, what are your top three choices?" She spoke more deliberately and slowly to him than she had meant to. Whether he noticed or not was impossible to tell given his poker-faced countenance. Only his thick eyebrows moved as he spoke.

"Time . . . monitor." Roberto, speaking quietly but determinedly in a strong Spanish accent, was struggling to read his own list. "Weather monitor. And Line director."

Ms. Lora smiled and thanked him, noting that Roberto, for whom English was new and challenging, had selected only roles that required public speaking. A good sign, she thought.

Ms. Lora had found that even when there was an inexplicable run on some particular role (last year, it was "librarian"), every student would end up thrilled with the weight of his or her responsibility *if* Ms. Lora delivered the news of the appointment personally, via a whispered statement of confidence in the student's leadership. Ms. Lora had also learned the hard way that she needed to publish the list of managers in big letters that could be read from anywhere in the classroom. The few times she had forgotten or misidentified a child's "indispensable" role had required some immediate damage control. ("Oh, I'm so sorry. I had thought you would be so good in so many roles that I just didn't remember which leadership role you had taken" was her most effective spin.)

Ms. Lora had grown to love these process matters. She had come to believe that setting a strong foundation for efficient classroom processes was probably the most important part of this routine. It was not an exaggeration to say that everything—every transition, every collection, every handraising, every plant watering—had to be explicitly discussed and thoroughly practiced. Then it had to be practiced again. Already today, she had had all the students practice not jumping and running as she mimicked the sound of the end-of-class bell. Mostly the students were giggling and covering their ears, but her point that "the bell doesn't dismiss you, I do" seemed to have been made.

"Okay, everyone," Ms. Lora said when she had collected the last of the students' top choices for leadership roles in the classroom. "Friday you will receive your assignments for the first six weeks. We'll talk more about your specific responsibilities at that time. And each of you will get a chance to practice your job at least once before you take on full responsibility. Right now, we're going to review the process for lining up to go to the bathroom. And then we'll practice it. Who can remind me what to look for as we line up to walk out the door?"

Roberto, Ms. Lora's next time monitor, raised his thin arm, and his thick eyebrows, slowly but confidently.

# 5

# Continuously Increase Effectiveness

REFLECTING CONSTANTLY on the pace of student progress toward their goals, highly effective teachers seek to improve their practice to maximize student learning.

SET BIG GOALS 1

INVEST STUDENTS AND THEIR FAMILIES 2

PLAN PURPOSEFULLY 3

EXECUTE EFFECTIVELY 4

CONTINUOUSLY INCREASE EFFECTIVENESS 5

WORK RELENTLESSLY 6

> *My evaluation of myself as a teacher begins and ends with my kids.*

**MY EVALUATION OF** myself as a teacher begins and ends with my kids. It's easy to say, "The kids just aren't getting it." But if that's the case, then I'm not doing what I need to do as their teacher. Either they're learning something or they're not. And if they're not mastering concepts they need to master, then I need to learn how to teach them more effectively. That's what I need to improve.

**Shannon Dingle,**
Middle School
Special
Education, Texas

> *I then think of ways to change my teaching . . .*

**WHEN REFLECTING ON** my teaching, I think about a quote I once heard: "There's always room for improvement. It's the biggest room in the house." I keep this in mind when I'm driving home from school, thinking about how my day went. I also keep this in mind when I start grading a test and see that a student, who I thought understood, didn't really understand. I then think of ways to change my teaching and seek out assistance from colleagues and other resources in an effort to ensure that all of my students excel.

**Norledia Moody,**
Second Grade,
Georgia

> *We must reflect with the end in mind.*

**JUST AS WE** must plan with the end in mind, we must reflect with the end in mind. I always start with the ultimate outcome I want to see: STUDENT ACHIEVEMENT. I look at my tracking system to see how my students are doing, then try to understand the nature of the problem by thinking about what students are doing or not doing (for example, by seeing the kinds of mistakes they make in their work), then consider how my own actions are contributing to the problem, and then figure out what I need to do to get better and ultimately increase my student achievement. Then repeat about once a week.

**Justin Yan,**
Sixth-Grade
Science, North
Carolina

Strong teachers increase their effectiveness by reflecting on student performance data. They seek, in their own actions, the root causes of students' successes and failures. They devise and search for solutions and learning opportunities that align with their data-revealed needs. In our experience, highly effective teachers are usually proud of their students' progress yet simultaneously insist that they can always improve. They are often their own toughest critics.

Molly Eigen, who after proving to be a highly effective teacher became a teacher trainer and coach, encourages new teachers to realize that constant improvement is an inherent element of good teaching:

> In my current role, I often see new teachers striving for perfection. I always tell them that there is no such thing as perfection in teaching; there are only results. How much did students learn, and what could you do to help them learn more and learn faster and learn with more retention or complexity? I was a good teacher, but I was always trying to figure out new ways to teach material or engage students or maximize time because, until the students I served were outperforming kids three towns over, there was room for me to grow as an educator.

**Molly Eigen,**
Special Education
Math and Science,
Texas

Researcher Jim Collins, in his study of successful leaders in other contexts, found lots of Molly Eigens: "No matter how much you have achieved, *you will always be merely good relative to what you can become*. Greatness is an inherently dynamic process, not an end point. The moment you think of yourself as great, your slide toward mediocrity will have already begun."[1]

Teachers who lead their students to dramatic academic achievement are those who are constantly and intentionally learning. They are forever challenging their students and themselves to learn, grow, and improve, all with the aim of serving their students more effectively.

# Foundations of Continuous Improvement

*Every teacher must . . . by regarding every imperfection in the pupil's comprehension not as a defect of the pupil, but as a defect of his instruction, endeavor to develop in himself the ability of discovering new methods.*[2]

— Leo Tolstoy

In our interactions with highly effective teachers, we have seen that a handful of mindsets characterize teachers who constantly improve their effectiveness. Teachers whose students are learning more each day than the day before seem to share four key beliefs.

## Effective Teaching Is a Learnable Skill

Strong teachers insist that effective teaching is neither mysterious nor magical. It is neither a function of dynamic personality nor dramatic performance. Rather, effective teaching is the hard work of setting big goals, investing students in working hard, planning purposefully, executing effectively, improving over time, and relentlessly pursuing our students' success.

This view is a foundational premise of this book. These methods are replicable, and they can be learned. "When they are doing their best, leaders exhibit certain distinct practices, which vary little from industry to industry, profession to profession, community to community, and country to country. Good leadership is an understandable and universal process," found Kouzes and Posner.[3] And that leadership, whether in the Senate, the laboratory, the battlefield, the boardroom, or an underresourced classroom full of students on the low end of the achievement gap, "is an identifiable set of skills and abilities that are available to all of us."[4]

Some observers mistakenly see static perfection in highly effective teachers. On the contrary, these teachers' conviction that great teaching is learnable derives from their own struggles to improve. When we talk to these teachers about their effectiveness, they remind us that they are far from perfect and have many skills they want to develop. They fail, they make mistakes, they get discouraged—all of which they handle with the knowledge that they can improve going forward.

Tara Harrington, for example, a nationally honored teacher in North Carolina, recalls the complete failure of a science experiment in front of her entire class as the moment that she learned to practice every experiment before she performs it in class. Sophia Pappas, whose pre-K classroom has been the model for many new teachers, put significant energy into reaching out to families in her first year but she did not critically reflect on those practices that were more or less effective at engaging families in her classroom. She recalls, with regret, that while families expressed satisfaction with the class and her dedication to their children, she missed out on opportunities to maximize their contributions to the classroom and she did not maximize their use of important resources such as her family lending library. That realization, however, spurred her to change the way she interacted with families so that every interaction included engagement in student learning and reflected ongoing efforts to tailor her approach to the personalities, interests, and work schedules of each family member.

Highly effective teachers like Ms. Harrington and Ms. Pappas, even when presented with their outstanding student achievement results, almost never describe themselves as good, bad, strong, or weak, but rather as in the process of becoming better. "I'm getting there" is a sentiment we commonly hear. Or, "Well, I have become a much more effective planner, and that has had huge payoffs for my classroom management, but I still don't have my classroom systems and organization where they need to be."

We (and psychology experts) sometimes refer to this outlook as a growth mindset. The teachers view themselves as works in progress for whom inevitable mistakes are valuable catalysts for improvement. Educational psychologist Carol Dweck explains in her book *Mindset*:

> Whether they're aware of it or not, all people keep a running account of what's happening to them, what it means, and what they should do. . . . Mindsets frame the running account that's taking place in people's heads. They guide the whole interpretation process. . . . People with a growth mindset are constantly monitoring what's going on, but their inter-

nal monologue is not about judging themselves and others. . . . Certainly they're sensitive to positive and negative information, but they're attuned to its implications for learning and constructive action: *What can I learn from this? How can I improve?*[5]

| Situation | A Teacher with a Growth Mindset Thinks . . . |
|---|---|
| Teacher attempts to reach out to the parents of a student who has been misbehaving, but the parents respond negatively or defensively. | What have I done (or failed to do) that could be leading this child's parents to respond in this way? How are my own biases leading me to approach this student or his or her parent in ways that might be contributing to the problem? How can I repair this relationship? How could I do this better with other parents in the future? Whom can I talk to for advice on what to do differently? |
| After three straight days of teaching lessons on counting money, almost every student continues to struggle mightily to master the material. | Why have my first three attempts not worked? Do I really understand my students' misunderstandings? How can I adjust my approach so that students will get it? What advice can colleagues give me? Where can I find best practices online? What broader lesson can I learn from this that might prevent me from spending so much time getting students to master a single objective? |
| Across the board, girls are progressing faster than boys on key skills. | Am I interacting differently with boys and girls in my classroom? What biases and expectations am I bringing to my actions that may be contributing to this difference? How can I ensure gender is not a factor in learning in my classroom? |

Seeing failure, mistakes, and problems as opportunities for learning is critically important in our context because we all experience failure in this work. Every teacher in this book has experienced difficult setbacks and made painful mistakes, but they nevertheless achieve great results because they have the ability to productively conceive of difficult and unsuccessful experiences as opportunities for personal learning. Just as they want their students to take academic risks, highly effective teachers do not let fear of failure prevent them from trying new things in their classrooms. They embrace inevitable mistakes as revelations of ways to improve. Not surprisingly, other studies of leadership in other sectors of society have drawn the same conclusion: "Leaders embrace error."[6]

## "Data may not tell us the whole truth, but it certainly doesn't lie."[7]

When Secretary of Education Arne Duncan said those words, he expressed the same sentiment held by highly effective teachers we have studied. (As she implemented reforms aimed at fighting educational inequity, former Secretary of Education Margaret Spellings was fond of saying, "In God We Trust. Everyone else bring data."[8])

This idea is so fundamental to self-improvement that we must raise it again. Continuously improving our effectiveness over time cannot start with our own subjective guesses about where and how we can do better. We must work from information rather than intuition. Only when we actually know in what ways we are and are not succeeding can we identify how to improve. This is not to say that we should ignore gut instincts, because they are often signals worth investigating. But to prioritize our areas of improvement, we should strive for a clear and unfiltered view of student learning. Secretary Duncan summarizes this critical idea this way: "I am a deep believer in the power of data to drive our decisions. Data gives us the road map to reform. It tells us where we are, where we need to go, and who is most at risk."[9]

When we asked what advice he would give new teachers, Chris Ott, an Atlanta middle school science and reading teacher, emphasized knowing the realities of your effectiveness: "Be real with yourself and with your students. The stakes are too high to cloud the truth. Don't let your gut tell you one thing when an overwhelming amount of valid data are telling you otherwise." Kiel McQueen, a middle school social studies teacher in Phoenix, echoed this sentiment:

> I had a football coach in high school who used to tell me, "The film doesn't lie." We would watch it every Monday, and if you didn't play well, the film would show you that. I use that same idea in my classroom: "The numbers don't lie." And the numbers really don't lie. They don't lie about how I teach, and they don't lie about what my students know. And I think it's really cool to be able to see that. It makes my teaching so much more effective when I know what I do really well and what my students do really well.

One educator suggests that "the most disheartening and discouraging" aspect of teaching is "the fact that results are so intangible and unobservable. A carpenter at the end of the day can actually see what he has built, a doctor can observe a patient responding to treatment, but a teacher oftentimes has to go along for months with relatively few noticeable results."[10] While the wait for results could be frustrating, highly effective teachers refuse to accept that they cannot find ways to gauge student learning along the way and thereby improve their effectiveness. These teachers create systems that illustrate student learning in the same way a carpenter can see a house or a doctor can observe a patient.

Highly effective teachers approach their classroom as would a social scientist. In formal, systematized ways and informal, improvised ways, they constantly gather data that illuminate areas of progress and lack of progress. In fact, a number of studies have shown that one of the more reliable predictors of student achievement in classrooms, schools, and districts is the employment of data to understand success, progress, and failure.[11]

## We Drive Our Own Improvement

Another mindset common to teachers who are constantly improving their effectiveness is the belief that they are in charge of their own improvement. In our

> ► **EXAMPLES OF DATA THAT FUEL PURPOSEFUL REFLECTION**
>
> - Student scores on assessments
> - Student work
> - Observed student actions
> - Observation notes from classroom visitors, such as administrators, colleagues, and mentors
> - Student survey responses
> - Parent survey responses
> - Videotapes of lessons

experience, less effective teachers believe that improvement is something that happens to you over time as you teach. More effective teachers, on the contrary, believe that improvement is something that you affirmatively work toward and take from your experiences.

In light of this idea, teachers need discipline to set aside time for reflection and improvement. Over and over we hear from highly effective teachers that data analysis, reflection, and self-improvement are not do-when-you-can tasks but are built into their routine alongside planning, grading, and teaching. "I am constantly formally and informally assessing students, situations and myself, and this helps me to adjust my practice continuously," explained Vanessa Muller. "I spend a huge amount of my time reflecting on how the day, week, unit, etc., is going, has gone or will hopefully go."

These teachers, like Rachel Donaldson Dahl, remark that the best times for fruitful reflection often coincide with times when she is tired because she has just completed some difficult initiative: "Taking even just five minutes to do so is refreshing, invigorating, and often sets you on the right track and allows you to be more productive for the rest of the day."

Justin May describes a form of data-based reflection that he used in his first year teaching in New Orleans—a practice that greatly improved his effectiveness:

> I recorded audiotapes of my class, five minutes here and there, a total of about twenty minutes per day, since that was the length of my commute back home. Every day on the way home from school, I'd listen to the tape. I sometimes heard myself sounding angry and scared in my interactions with my students. I just couldn't believe I talked to my kids the way I did. "What kind of person am I?" I thought. I thought a lot about what kind of a room I'd want my own child in. The tapes were so important in leading me to change.

## No Teacher Is an Island

Another prevailing mindset of highly effective teachers—and new highly effective teachers in particular—is that they need and want help. As evidenced by the frequent reference to dependence on colleagues and mentors in this book, highly effective teachers see themselves as part of a community and determine to share the benefit of that community with their students.

The first and perhaps most obvious way that strong teachers depend on other strong teachers is in the constant sharing of ideas and resources. They realize that whatever puzzle they face in investing their students, designing effective lessons, or managing classroom paperwork effectively, they work among others who have tackled those same issues. Jenny Gwin, an eighth-grade English/language arts teacher in Philadelphia, attests to the value of seeking the perspective of her colleagues:

> Often, after a challenging situation arises in class, I later approach a fellow English teacher or my dean of students and seek their help in reflecting on it. I say, "This is what happened. What would you have done there?" They are really wise and want to help me. Even if they only have five minutes to chat, they'll often help me gain important insights.

> They're often able to share with me what they have done in similar situations in the past, and often their knowledge of the school community (of a particular student, for example) proves invaluable. I do this constantly, and it has been one of my most valuable continuous practices as a teacher. *,,*

While the teachers we talked to about sharing resources emphasized that most borrowed resources and ideas have to be adjusted for their own context, over and over we heard that no teacher should have to reinvent the wheel.

Another word of advice we hear repeatedly is to think about and borrow from colleagues' strengths. Not all teachers are masters of all methods and resources, but most teachers have an area of strength to learn from. Andrew Mandel sought out those strengths as a new teacher in the Rio Grande Valley: "Do you know what your colleagues at your school are best at? If not, you're missing out. The teacher across the hall from me was not the strongest instructional planner, but she had a way with one of my most difficult students that allowed me to realize that I was using the wrong approach with him."

LesLee Bickford, a sixth-grade math and science teacher in Philadelphia, emphasized to us that, in the spirit of driving our own effectiveness, learning from others starts with outreach. "Every time I've ever approached somebody with humility, a genuine interest to learn from them, and targeted questions, I've never been turned down," she says. "But what I also discovered is that nobody is going to knock on your door and say, 'I know you're struggling with classroom management or instructional planning; let me help.' You have to play an active role in identifying the weaknesses in your classroom and seeking out resources to improve your teaching." Ellen Davis, a first- and second-grade teacher in Salt River Reservation in Arizona, echoes this advice: "If you don't acknowledge that you could use someone else's expertise, you won't find it. There are some issues where you could spend a whole weekend looking for answers and not find them, or you could spend a half-hour with a specialist and find what you need. But you have to acknowledge that you need help and that other people may have expertise or resources that you do not have."

The benefits of that outreach are not just ideas and resources but improved skills. Strong teachers make time to observe colleagues who are proving, with their students' learning, that their methods are effective. Observing proven classroom leaders is a powerful learning opportunity.

Perhaps the most complex but fruitful form of learning from the expertise around us occurs when we are observed and offered critical feedback on our own teaching practices by successful colleagues. Another simple litmus test of highly effective teachers is that they, unlike less effective teachers, seek out critical friends who will offer fresh, objective, and constructive feedback on their teaching.

That is not to say these teachers never find being observed nerve-wracking. Many tell us they do. Understandably we all see teaching as a manifestation of ourselves, and sometimes pride and ego make exposing our weaknesses to others difficult. At the same time, strong teachers recognize the benefits of that feedback for their students' progress.

North Carolina Spanish teacher Dan Tifft described for us how nervous he used to be when he was observed by mentors and coaches. He recalls that his anxieties about what observers were thinking actually affected his teaching. But then one of his mentors told Mr. Tifft he was not actually the subject of the observation; the mentor was watching the students and just listening to what Mr. Tifft was saying. "That reminded me," Mr. Tifft explains, "that the emphasis was on the students and that anyone who was giving me honest feedback could only be helping me. I still get nervous sometimes, but I welcome observers with open arms."

Highly effective teachers seek colleagues who will give them frank and critical feedback. For Lauren Hawley, that person was her principal. While some of her fellow teachers seemed to view her teaching "through rose-colored glasses," she said, "I made it clear to my principal that I needed her to help me prioritize my weaknesses. I knew I couldn't improve in every area at the same time, but I trusted her to help me determine the crucial points where my ineffectiveness most hurt my students' progress." Ms. Hawley made an arrangement with her principal in which her principal would briefly observe Ms. Hawley at least once each day, whether in the classroom, lunchroom, or hall. Each afternoon Ms. Hawley would expect a quick critical

## ▶ EXCELLENT SCHOOL VISITS

**AT SEVERAL POINTS IN** this book, teachers mention the value of "excellent school visits"—seeing firsthand what learning is happening in an equivalent classroom in a high-performing and well-resourced school. Strong teachers often use those visits to reinvigorate their efforts and to help inform the ambitiousness of their goals and expectations. Such visits, however, are also a prime opportunity to observe and learn from excellent teachers. While missing a day of teaching with students is not a decision to take lightly, sometimes taking a day or half-day to see the best teacher in the district is worth that investment of time. A number of highly effective teachers look back on the time they spent in a particularly exceptional teacher's classroom as revelatory.

Acasia Wilson managed to bring that experience to her own fifth-grade classroom. Ms. Wilson, looking at student achievement data for her school and class in Phoenix, realized that the two lowest-performing students in her class, one reading at a kindergarten level and one at a first-grade level, were both Native American. She had heard about a retired teacher who spent a portion of her career working on reservations and had an excellent reputation as a reading teacher. Ms. Wilson invited her in for a visit. "Her visit turned our classroom upside down, and I felt a fresh wave of inspiration," Ms. Wilson recalls. "We were on our feet for two hours, telling stories and acting out scenes from literature. My students were excited about reading, especially students who had previously been disinterested. That class made me realize that I needed to do things differently."

Ms. Wilson's efforts paid off: her Native American students' pace of growth increased noticeably. By the end of the year, the two Native American students who had begun at a kindergarten and a first-grade reading level were reading at a fifth-grade and fourth-grade level, respectively.

bit of advice from the principal. "By making this a daily ritual, I quickly learned to reflect independently and in partnership with my school community . . . [and] as a result, I could solve some problems almost immediately."

In our experience, the teachers who lead their students to dramatic academic achievement wholly reject some teachers' notion that their classroom is a private and personal space, not to be violated by external critique.[12] On the contrary, they view their classroom as a living, learning laboratory of improvement where even the most excellent teacher is a learner alongside students.

## A Cycle of Reflection That Leads to Increased Effectiveness

Teachers whose students are learning the most are those who view teaching as a learnable set of skills, yearn for data-based assessments of their strengths and weaknesses, see improvement as a proactive endeavor, and view self-improvement as a collaborative process.

Similarly, we see patterns in how successful teachers implement those ideas in their day-to-day quest for increased effectiveness. These teachers start by analyzing the progress their students have and have not made toward their big goal. Then, rather than immediately jumping

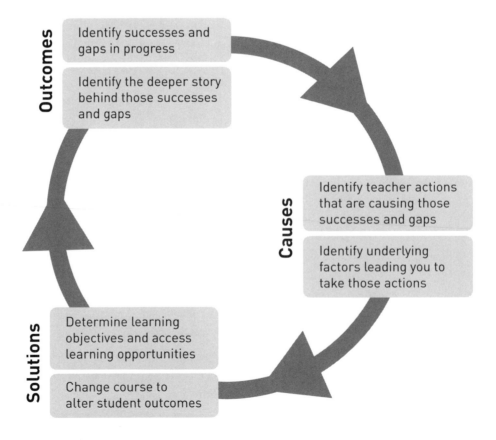

**Outcomes**
- Identify successes and gaps in progress
- Identify the deeper story behind those successes and gaps

**Causes**
- Identify teacher actions that are causing those successes and gaps
- Identify underlying factors leading you to take those actions

**Solutions**
- Determine learning objectives and access learning opportunities
- Change course to alter student outcomes

to potential solutions, they identify reasons behind those signs of encouraging or discouraging progress, a step that ensures that when they do seek out resources and help, they are targeting improvement efforts wisely.

To help share those teachers' best practices, we have described this process in the form of a reflection cycle modeled loosely on an experiential learning cycle developed by researcher David Kolb.[13] Highly effective teachers employ a cycle of reflection that first focuses on outcomes, then looks at causes, and finally develops solutions.

## Phase One: Analyzing Outcomes

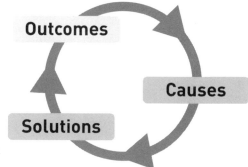

- Where is student progress on pace and not on pace to reach your ambitious academic goals?

- What student habits or actions are contributing most to that progress or lack of progress?

The reflection process always begins with what you know. What do the data tell you about where students' academic progress is on target? What do the data tell you about where student learning is lagging behind the pace necessary to reach your big goals? What do qualitative data tell you about the story behind the numerical data? In other words, the outcomes phase is about defining the right problem to solve. In our context, the key problems to solve are those related to student learning.

---

▶ **SKILLS FOR IDENTIFYING GAPS AND PROGRESS IN STUDENT LEARNING**

**TO PERFORM THIS FIRST** stage of reflection well, highly effective teachers demonstrate the ability to:

- *Discern trends.* If you have developed sound assessments, administer them frequently, and actively seek out other types of data, you can end up with quite a lot of information. Identifying trends in those data is a challenge. Are there clear patterns of mastery levels for certain types of objectives? Among certain subgroups of students? For certain types of lessons?

- *Prioritize the most critical outcome to address.* Once you have discerned patterns, another discrete skill is identifying which gaps in student learning are the most significant—that is, which ones, if effectively addressed, would move students furthest along in their progression toward the big goal? On its own, data gathering will unearth a whole series of interesting and important findings. Identifying the handful of most important areas is much more effective than trying to improve everything at once.

### Identifying Where Students Are and Are Not on Pace to Achieve the Big Goal

Perhaps your weekly benchmark data are revealing that the pace of growth in reading comprehension is not going to be enough to achieve your big goals. Or perhaps rubric scores for students' lab reports reveal that students' writing skills are low and are undermining the class goal of scoring a 4 or 5 on the Advanced Placement exam. Or perhaps your students are performing ahead of your planned pace in reading but not in writing and math. Improving your effectiveness starts with digging into the data in your tracking system and other data sources to learn where students are struggling and succeeding.

### Identifying the Deeper Story Behind Quantitative Data

While assessments of student learning will reveal areas of strength and concern, highly effective teachers think of assessment data as triggers for further investigation. Often the only way to get a true sense of the nature of that progress or lack of progress is to draw on a variety of sources of qualitative information as well: student work, your own lesson plans, videotapes of your class in action, notes from classroom observers, and responses to student and parent surveys, for example.

One school leader offers a helpful analogy for the notion that summative data have limited utility for improving effectiveness:

> Imagine a swimming coach trying to analyze the performance of his team. If he picked up the newspaper the day after the meet and read the times of his third-place swimmer, he might decide that she just has to swim faster. Yet if he had watched that swimmer at the meet, he would have noticed that she was the last one off the starting block but the fastest one in the water. At that point, his analysis would be clear: He needs to focus on getting her off the block faster.
>
> School assessment analysis is no different. Looking at state test or interim assessment results in isolation is like reading a newspaper summary of a sports event: You can only draw summative conclusions, and those conclusions might actually be inaccurate. You have to be "poolside"—or talk to those who are—to analyze effectively.[14]

Seth Cohen, who not only was a highly effective teacher himself but went on to coach and mentor many highly effective teachers in the Rio Grande Valley of Texas, reminds us, "Data come in many forms: the way students respond to questions, conversations with colleagues who've observed you, videotapes of your own teaching. Good teachers use all of this, looking for patterns in their own teaching, deciding if and how to modify their approach, and then acting on those insights."

Among the most powerful of these qualitative data sources is student work. Pedagogical experts echo what we hear from teachers: "Examining student work helps to surface and challenge many assumptions—assumptions about what students can and cannot do, about which students can do what, and about why students are or are not able to do something."[15]

Furthermore, student work products can expose which misunderstandings students may harbor. These are the "poolside" insights needed to launch meaningful reflection.

So in this first phase of reflection, successful teachers paint a clear picture of student progress by drawing on broad notions of data that provide color and depth to their understanding of that performance. They identify—with quantitative and qualitative information rather than intuition—what is and is not going well, and that knowledge is the launching point for self-improvement. In the words of some experts in using data:

> The question . . . is, "Do you really know what problem you are trying to solve?". . . Before committing to a particular course of action or investing time in developing possible solutions, it is important that you fully understand the learner-centered problem, which we define as a problem of understanding or skill that underlies students' performance on assessments. "Learner-centered problem" means that the problem is about learning, not that learners are the problem.[16]

With a vantage point on their own success and failure established, highly successful teachers can move on to reflect on how and which of their own actions are causing those outcomes.

## Phase Two: Discerning Causes

- What teacher actions are contributing to key aspects of student performance?
- What root causes or underlying factors are leading to those teacher actions?

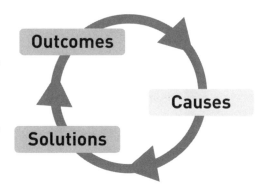

After identifying students' progress and lack of progress toward the goals, the second phase of strong teachers' reflection cycle is consideration of the teacher actions (and lack of teacher actions) that are the root causes of those outcomes. We cannot seek solutions until we understand the root causes of the problem.

### Identifying Which Action Is the Root Cause

Once you have defined the outcome you wish to improve, it is time to figure out the root cause of the current lag in progress. Highly effective teachers first seek root causes in their own actions. Because they see themselves as ultimately responsible for what happens in their classroom, they begin with the assumption that their actions and inactions are the source of student learning and lack of learning.

Notice, for example, in the following reflection from a teacher in Los Angeles, Anna Lutey, that once she recognizes a problem in student learning, she looks to her own actions for one or more explanations:

> After reviewing the data from our first-quarter language arts formal assessments, I noticed that the class scored the lowest in writing strategies and the highest in language conventions. They were specifically struggling with combining sentences. These results generated a whole series of questions. I wanted to get to the root causes of why my students performed well in one area and not so well in another. I approached the analysis of the results in two main ways. First, I wanted to check out the wording and presentation of the material in the test. Was it the wording of the questions? Did my students understand the directions? If I eliminated the test as a potential piece to the puzzle, then I started reflecting on my own practices. Did I spend enough time teaching the objective? Was my lesson effective? As a result of this deeper investigation, there were many important pieces to the puzzle that I put together. One, I spent much more time on language conventions than I did on writing strategies. I did not have an effective check for understanding to determine if my students could combine sentences. I did not plan enough time to practice over and over again. I think I might have received higher results if my check for understanding was more effective and more instructional time was allotted for the specific objective. After the test, I reviewed the results with my students' parents, sent additional resources home, and spent more time mastering the objective in class.

Ms. Lutey is thinking about how her own actions are contributing to students' progress and lack of progress and trying to identify the most fundamental—or root—cause of those outcomes. She considers a range of possible causes before digging in to try to discern the most significant root cause. This is an important trend we see among the most effective teachers: resisting the urge to quickly attribute lags in student performance to a single cause. As psychologist Ellen J. Langer explains in *Mindfulness*, "One important way in which we limit our options is to attribute all our troubles to a single cause. Such mindless attributions narrowly limit the range of solutions we might seek. . . . When we have a single-minded explanation, we typically don't pay attention to information that runs counter to it."[17] (This also reiterates the importance of grounding your thinking in data.)

Seeking the root causes involves following causation backward systematically and methodically. When performed with disciplined and careful thought, root cause analysis identifies a manageable number of influential issues and offers a road map for self-improvement. The strongest teachers we work with describe root cause analysis in the same way researchers do: "a structured questioning process that enables people to recognize and discuss the underlying beliefs and practices that result in poor quality in an organization. A root cause is a basic causal factor, which if corrected or removed will prevent recurrence of a situation."[18]

More often than not, root cause analysis is simply a process of asking why—over and over—until the primal source of the issue is discovered. Consider the puzzle of the crumbling granite at the Jefferson Memorial in Washington, D.C., a story used by one educator-author to illustrate the process of seeking root causes. Mysteriously, the granite at all the other memorials was holding up well:

*Question:* Why is the granite crumbling on the Jefferson Memorial?

*Answer:* It is hosed off more than the other memorials.

*Question:* Why is the Jefferson Memorial hosed off more than the other D.C. memorials?

*Answer:* The Jefferson Memorial has more bird dung.

*Question:* Why does the Jefferson Memorial have more bird dung than the other memorials?

*Answer:* It has more birds.

*Question:* Why does the Jefferson Memorial have more birds?

*Answer:* It has more spiders for the birds to eat.

*Question:* Why does the Jefferson Memorial have more spiders than other D.C. memorials?

*Answer:* It has more flying insects for spiders to eat.

*Question:* Why does the Jefferson Memorial have more flying insects than other D.C. memorials?

*Answer:* The lights are turned on too soon at the Jefferson Memorial, thus attracting the insects.

*Solution:* The lights were turned on later and the granite stopped crumbling.[19]

If the Park Service had acted on the first layer of explanation and stopped hosing off the granite, other problems would have arisen. If "Why?" had been asked too few times, the most efficient and effective solution would not have been found. Each of the answers is a cause of the problem, but only the final, root cause offers a locus of intervention that will solve the problem.

We see a similar pattern in excellent teachers' self-reflection. Often the most obvious and superficial explanation for a gap in student progress is not actually the root of the problem (or of the success), so solving for that superficial cause will not have the effect we want. Consider, for example, the following problem of a teacher whose students are not making significant progress and are often misbehaving. A new teacher might assume that ineffective implementation of their system of rules and consequences is the root cause, but in reality there are several possible root causes to consider. In the figure that follows, all of the first five potential causes could be contributing to the low levels of student mastery (and there may well be more). The question now becomes, which of these is most responsible for the problems in student comprehension and behavior? Are unclear or ineffectively enforced behavioral expectations leading to off-task behavior, which interferes with students' abilities to master the material and thus

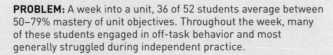

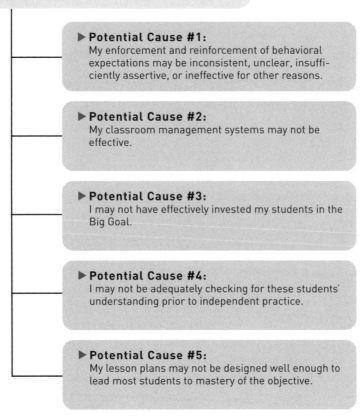

**PROBLEM:** A week into a unit, 36 of 52 students average between 50–79% mastery of unit objectives. Throughout the week, many of these students engaged in off-task behavior and most generally struggled during independent practice.

▶ **Potential Cause #1:**
My enforcement and reinforcement of behavioral expectations may be inconsistent, unclear, insufficiently assertive, or ineffective for other reasons.

▶ **Potential Cause #2:**
My classroom management systems may not be effective.

▶ **Potential Cause #3:**
I may not have effectively invested my students in the Big Goal.

▶ **Potential Cause #4:**
I may not be adequately checking for these students' understanding prior to independent practice.

▶ **Potential Cause #5:**
My lesson plans may not be designed well enough to lead most students to mastery of the objective.

lowers student investment? Or is student misunderstanding causing student frustration and subsequently off-task behavior and disinvestment in the big goal? Or perhaps students are disengaging because they do not understand *why* what they are learning is important and relevant? This requires good judgment, grounded in as much evidence as possible. This teacher may decide to delve deeper into one or more of these possible causes in a search for clearer answers. He or she may, for example, decide to further investigate the possibility that lesson plans are at the root of the problem and may ask a mentor to look through some of his or her lesson plans and discuss possible trends that could suggest specific areas for improvement. This particular investigation would be even more fruitful if the teacher could first identify more specific trends in student performance and student misbehavior.

Just as with the Jefferson Memorial example (and as so often happens in the classroom), the most obvious cause of a problem is often not the root cause. Imagine, for example, that a closer look at this teacher's data reveals that 90 percent of student misbehavior is happening during the transition from guided to independent practice. That fact might suggest that it is not the teacher's rules or classroom management system at issue but instead his or her management of student independent practice, checks for understanding during guided practice, or lesson plans. If the teacher were to change rules and consequences, the teacher might have addressed a symptom but not the underlying problem. The process of asking, "Why?" helps to uncover these central, root issues that should be the focus of a teacher's self-improvement.

Just as objective data can show a contradiction between what we think is going on in our classroom and what is in fact happening, we can also learn that we are often wrong about what is behind disappointing outcomes. Although we don't always have objective data to uncover the real causes, the key is to seek out evidence to corroborate your theories about what might be at the root of the issue. What do the data say about how the teacher's approach is pushing or holding back student progress? Do the data reveal particular strategies or methods that are more or less effective? Why are particular strategies or methods working or not working?

## ▶ SKILLS FOR IDENTIFYING ROOT CAUSES OF PROBLEMS

**LIKE IDENTIFYING OUTCOMES YOU** want to improve, identifying root causes of those outcomes requires strong critical thinking skills, including the ability to do the following:

- *Discern causal links.* The ability to accurately discern trends based on clear evidence is tremendously important. For example, after Kiel McQueen noticed from exit slips that students were averaging in the 90s on some days and in the 60s on other days, he went back to his lesson plans from those days and looked for trends. He noticed that students were performing exceptionally well after lessons in which the guided practice was more interactive (with role plays, for example). This insight represented a big step forward in his growth as a teacher.

- *Align causes to outcomes.* Another important skill is ensuring alignment between the root cause you identify and the problem that you are trying to solve. It sounds obvious, but in our experience, teachers—especially new teachers—can struggle with these connections. The ability to make these connections grows with knowledge of the core skills of teaching.

- *Prioritize the most significant cause.* Smart prioritization is important in accurately identifying root causes. In order to maximize subsequent improvements in students' performance, it is important to be able to identify which cause, if addressed, will contribute most to improved outcomes.

- *Know thyself.* Self-awareness is immensely valuable. We all have individual insecurities, discomforts, assumptions, and biases that can affect our teaching effectiveness. To accurately judge the importance of various causes of problems, our judgments must include consideration of all those internal factors.

### Identifying Why You Are Doing What You Have Identified as the Root Cause

Once you have identified how you are contributing to students' lack of progress, you reach a fork in the road. Are you ready to move on to seek solutions, or do you need to dig more into why you are contributing to students' lack of progress? Do you lack the needed knowledge or skills? Do you need to challenge a mindset that you hold? What else do you need to know, or be able to do, or believe in order to take actions that will close—rather than cause—gaps in student understanding?

Sophia Pappas, the pre-K teacher in New Jersey who kept running records of her observations as she taught, found that one of her students was not progressing and seemed resistant to participating in lessons. From her reflection on his lack of progress and her actions, she determined that she needed to increase her own knowledge and skills related to differentiating instruction. Simultaneously, she sought more information about when and how this student could best learn. From her notes and observations, she discovered that he was particularly excited when he was playing and working with blocks and responded well to silly humor— insights that helped her apply her growing differentiation skills and led to a breakthrough with the student. That insight led Ms. Pappas to implement a strategy of swooping in when her student was most excited and engaged with his blocks or silly games and subtly infusing learning into those moments. The strategy worked and the student progressed.

In one of our anonymous surveys, a teacher shared her reflections on data showing that while the reading levels of her twenty-seven Hispanic students and four white students were improving steadily, three African American students were not progressing at all. This teacher, through frank and self-critical reflection, took time to identify how her own actions were root causes of the problem:

> And when I . . . reflected on what was going on in my classroom, I hadn't reached out to their parents to the same level that I had my white students and Latino students. For many reasons, like I spoke Spanish, and so I felt more comfortable speaking with my Latino families. I felt like I would be more accepted as part of their community, just because of that language. I'm white, so I felt more comfortable talking to the white parents. And then I had this idea that—I mean, I had a bias that my African American parents were going to be more resistant to help, or harder for me to communicate with, or they would see me as a little white girl coming in to save children of color. And so, all of those things created a fear that prevented me from reaching out to those parents as I needed to, and challenging their students academically like I needed to.

By honestly examining the data-revealed reality of her classroom, and with tough self-reflection, this teacher saw the possibility that she was doubting her African American students' ability to do challenging work and perhaps doubting their parents' desire to work with her to help them achieve academically. Her recognition of that danger led her to redouble her efforts to reach out to those groups potentially affected by those biases.

## Phase Three: Identifying and Implementing Solutions

- What learning experiences will help me meet my key objectives for addressing the root causes I have identified?

- How will I change my behavior in light of the learning experiences to change student outcomes?

- How will I know that those learning experiences have successfully led to improvement? How and by when will things look different at both the causes and outcomes levels?

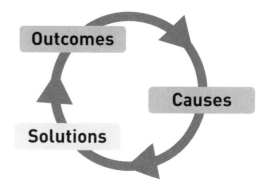

During last phase of the reflection cycle, a teacher identifies and implements solutions that address the root causes for the gaps in progress. Thus, in this solutions phase, the teacher moves from analysis to improvement, establishing the areas of growth and learning experiences needed to address the root causes and then implementing those insights in their classroom practice in order to change student outcomes.

Most teachers have many opportunities for professional development. In our experience, less successful teachers do not suffer from lack of such opportunities but rather from less than strategic selection among those options. Highly effective teachers, informed by the data-driven search for root causes we have been discussing, make smart choices about which of those resources are going to be most beneficial to their students' learning. New York special education teacher Brian Wallace explains that for him, "Getting professional development in reading instruction and implementing new classroom management techniques were effective only because I had first taken the time to identify specific problems and reflect about what I was doing or not doing that was contributing to those problems; it ensured that . . . my actions were aligned with what my students needed to move forward."

Sometimes finding solutions requires little effort beyond identifying the root causes of the problem. If, for example, your focused reflection reveals that you are inadvertently ignoring students sitting at the back of the room, several solutions become obvious. Perhaps you become more mobile in the classroom. Perhaps you change the seating chart periodically. Perhaps you institute a randomizing system for calling on students. Perhaps you rely on all three solutions.

At other times, identifying root causes of prioritized problems will raise questions for which you need additional resources. Successful teachers supplement the reflective processes with ever-expanding learning opportunities, both formal and informal. The range of resources for addressing improvement needs is wide—from university courses, to recommended books, from colleagues to the Internet. The key is choosing among those resources to improve those teaching skills in your own practice that will most help your students. As Shannon Dingle says, "I can honestly say that there wasn't a time when I couldn't find the right resource to help me once I'd decided specifically what I intended to improve."

After a teacher has identified the right resources to address the root causes of gaps in student progress, there is a final step. Highly effective teachers take the all-important last step of changing their own behavior. By adjusting course in light of the well-chosen resources, a teacher can complete the reflection cycle and change student outcomes.

# Conclusion: Key Ideas and Next Questions

The Teaching As Leadership rubric (see Appendix A) describes six specific teacher actions that form the reflection cycle common to teachers who continuously increase their effectiveness. Highly effective teachers:

C-1: Gauge progress and notable gaps

C-2: Identify student habits or actions most influencing progress and gaps

C-3: Isolate the teacher actions most contributing to key aspects of student performance

C-4: Identify the underlying factors leading to these teacher actions

C-5: Access meaningful learning experiences

C-6: After a cycle of data collection, reflection and learning, adjust course

## Key Ideas

We can learn a number of key lessons from highly effective teachers who have managed to quickly ascend steep learning curves:

- Always seek evidence of what is happening in your classroom. What are students learning and not learning? What are students doing? What patterns do you notice?

- Frequently reflect on the evidence of what is happening in your classroom, and always seek to understand why it is happening.

- Reflecting with a colleague or mentor can often help you uncover new realizations about your practices and accelerate your growth as a teacher.

- Following an outcomes-causes-solutions progression is the best way to maximize improvements in student learning.

These tenets remind us that our improved practice as teachers has a purpose. In the end, what matters is student achievement. Regardless of your approach to problem solving, reflection, and professional development, what students learn is the ultimate indicator of how successful you are. As highly effective teacher Vanessa Muller puts it, "This isn't about you—or the weight you feel. This is about children and equality and changing something much bigger than yourself. . . . The knowledge that every move I make is for something bigger than myself helps keep me going and fuels my fire to constantly improve."

teachingasleadership.org

More guidance on how to continuously increase your effectiveness is available online including:

- Additional specific indicators of strong efforts to continuously increase effectiveness
- Annotated examples of the reflective cycle in action
- Common pitfalls that often trip up new teachers as they are performing the reflective cycle
- Highly effective teachers' testimonies about the power of the reflective cycle in their classrooms

## Next Questions

With these principles of continuously increasing effectiveness in mind, new teachers are poised to pursue a number of important questions and issues as they blaze their path to dramatic student success:

- How can I get the clearest possible picture of student learning in my classroom?
- How can I seek help—in the form of critical feedback and joint problem-solving discussions—from others (mentors, colleagues, professors, administrators) to help me think through problems, causes, and solutions and help me maximize my own growth as a teacher?
- How can I identify resources and professional development opportunities that will foster my growth as a teacher?
- How can I improve my ability to accurately identify which problems, causes, and solutions are most significant?

teachingasleadership.org

*An excerpt from Ms. Lora's Story, a case study in Teaching As Leadership, available online at www.teachingasleadership.org.*

Douglas was not actually larger than his younger classmates, and, Ms. Lora's novice psychological assessments aside, the only physical hint that he was older was the disproportionate ratio of his relatively long limbs to his relatively squat body and face, a harbinger of adolescence that was otherwise reserved for a few girls in Ms. Lora's classroom. He did, however, catch one's eye as somehow different. On those unfortunately frequent days when Ms. Lora needed to remind herself of Douglas's youth, she had only to look at his hands. At the end of his long and sinewy arms were the pudgy, dimple-knuckled hands of a child.

Ms. Lora was relieved that Douglas did not immediately object to her instructions to move to a new seat, even if he did show no signs of moving to let Alfonse sit down. Douglas's projected toughness, while always shallow, was not always innocuous. As she had considered and reconsidered the seating chart, she could not help but worry about the students who ended up near Douglas. She had not, however, thought to worry about the well-being of the student who happened to have been assigned Douglas's summer school seat.

Douglas Rogers was prone to sudden storms of fury that often demanded Ms. Lora's full and immediate attention. While these incidents were difficult to manage, Ms. Lora had quickly discovered that his face was unfailingly accurate in predicting them. She had learned to watch constantly for the warning signs—a furrowed brow, clenched fists, an icy stare. One moment, Douglas might be infecting other students with his loud laugh and wide grin over a table of group work. The next, his intense eyes and furrowed brow might roll in, calling for a quick, diffusing intervention from Ms. Lora.

A frustrating variable in this cycle was the degree to which a particular method of intervention would stave off one of Douglas's angry, sometimes dangerous outbursts of anger. Those outbursts ranged from a silent but seething pout on the floor of the classroom to a tornadic whirl through a row of desks, throwing or toppling books, papers, furniture. These storms of anger sometimes resulted in physical threats to other students or teachers. Douglas's frequent home suspensions, Ms. Lora imagined, were largely responsible for his long tenure in the third grade. They certainly put Douglas further and further behind academically.

At the moment, Douglas was not moving, but by stepping between Douglas and Alfonse, Ms. Lora had established a tense stalemate. Douglas, however, seemed to be digging in. He folded his arms across his chest and turned away from Ms. Lora and Alfonse.

In search of the root causes of his behavior problems, during summer school Ms. Lora had kept a mental list of what butterfly flap seemed to have spawned each squall. Sometimes it was asking him for homework he had not completed. Rarely, it was asking him for homework he had completed. Other times it was asking him to read aloud, and other times it was waking him from his frequent naps. Sometimes Douglas himself would identify the seminal moment of a given fit of rage as when another student "looked at him."

The lack of any pattern, other than Douglas's frustration, made her sure that she had not yet figured out the real issues. She was positive that even if she could not fix those underlying catalysts, if she just knew what they were, she could design classroom interventions that would lengthen Douglas's fuse. She worked hard not to respond to his anger with her own, but her inability to figure out how to make this better filled her with frustration. As Douglas became more agitated about his seat, she recommitted herself to knowing Douglas more deeply in the hope of discovering some answers.

Ms. Lora leaned down and whispered to Douglas that she would appreciate his cooperation. Given their history together, even on his first day as a fourth grader, as he told her with a sneer and a glance that "this was my summer school seat" and he did not want to move to his assigned seat, she felt the weight of the extraordinary effort that it was going to take to help Douglas.

Douglas's seat sat empty across the room among three unsuspecting students whom Ms. Lora had identified as potentially calming influences.

"Douglas," Ms. Lora said firmly, "this was your summer school seat. But you were a third grader then. Now you are a fourth grader, and that is going to require some changes."

# 6

# Work Relentlessly

RECOGNIZING THE HIGH STAKES for their students, successful teachers assume personal responsibility for dramatic student learning, even when it means going far beyond traditional expectations. These teachers think and act creatively to navigate and overcome seemingly insurmountable obstacles, to increase the time and resources available for student learning, and to sustain their efforts over time.

1 SET BIG GOALS

2 INVEST STUDENTS AND THEIR FAMILIES

3 PLAN PURPOSEFULLY

4 EXECUTE EFFECTIVELY

5 CONTINUOUSLY INCREASE EFFECTIVENESS

6 WORK RELENTLESSLY

> *I recognize how worthwhile all of my setbacks have been in the face of getting my students to achieve.*

**Rob LoPiccolo,**
High School
Science,
Louisiana

**THE OBSTACLES THAT** inhibit our progression toward closing the achievement gap torment us all. When we pursue such important goals, we must be resolved to overcome any obstacle. When I reflect on my time in the classroom, I recognize how worthwhile all of my setbacks have been in the face of getting my students to achieve. All of them—each backbreaking, tear-jerking moment—have been worth it. Besides, none of it compares to a life without a high school diploma, without an education. That's what our students are facing. We must not rest on our successes; we must not choke on our failures. We must not get caught up in the process. We must press on. We must improve. We must do whatever is necessary to lead our students to achieve our ambitious goals for dramatic academic gains.

Mr. LoPiccolo's insistence that our role is to do whatever it takes to ensure student success pervades our conversations with teachers whose students overcome the challenges of poverty to excel academically. This relentlessness is not martyrdom; rather, it is a combination of resilience, perseverance, insight, and humility, and it drives these leaders to their goals through great difficulties.

## We Control Our Students' Success and Failure

The Introduction to this book includes our underlying premise that teachers can make a difference in the lives of students in low-income communities. We recalled the Coleman Report's discounted but still damaging assertion that 90 percent of a child's academic performance is related to his or her background and other factors outside school.[1] We argued, based on our experiences in thousands of classrooms, that despite the prevailing assumption that the achievement gap is "just the way it is," teachers have enough control over key aspects of children's lives to close the gap and change their life path.

Highly effective teachers see this idea not as a matter of policy or ideology but of personal conviction. For the successful teachers we have encountered in low-income communities—some of whom you have met in this book—the suggestion that they cannot close the achievement gap for their students is not only unacceptable but is also ludicrous. These teachers have seen their students' potential to succeed. These teachers' approach to classroom leadership embodies the belief that they are in control of and ultimately responsible for their students' success or failure.

The deeply held belief that one controls the circumstances of one's surroundings (rather than being controlled by those circumstances) is well studied and articulated by psychologists. Research indicates that some individuals tend to believe that they control their own destiny. They view their experiences as the results of their own skills and effort. Other individuals are inclined to focus on circumstances, luck, or other external factors to explain their successes or failures. Experts refer to this spectrum of perspectives as "locus of control."[2]

| External Locus of Control | Internal Locus of Control |
|---|---|
| Assumes life is controlled by external circumstances and people | Assumes responsibility and control of self and surroundings |
| Views challenges as roadblocks that limit one's influence and inhibit accomplishments | Views challenges as obstacles to be navigated and overcome on the way to goals |

The highly effective teachers from whom the ideas in this book are drawn show us that when faced with the inevitable challenges that plague the underresourced schools where the achievement gap is at its worst, teachers must respond not by giving up or making excuses but instead by asking, "How am I going to navigate these challenges for the sake of my students?" These teachers have proven the efficacy of an internal locus of control in the fight for education equity.

Tracy Epp, a highly effective teacher herself who is now the chief academic officer for the nationally recognized IDEA Public Schools[3] in the Rio Grande Valley of Texas, spends her days observing and thinking about teacher effectiveness. She says that in her experience, an internal locus of control is the distinguishing factor of strong teachers:

> Being involved in education for the last twelve years, I have had the opportunity to see a lot of teaching and a lot of different types of teachers. The main distinguishing factor between teachers whose students excel and those who don't is the mindset that as a teacher, you will view each struggle as a setback or obstacle, not a failure. The teachers who are determined to meet goals and provide their students with the best possible education simply don't make excuses. It's their M.O. They just decide that student success will happen.

Echoing Ms. Epp and our own findings in contrasting more and less successful teachers, one researcher explains:

> Accepting responsibility is an essential difference between more effective and less effective employers, teachers, principals—even parents. . . . As leaders, we must help all our teachers take responsibility for their performance in the classroom. If everyone looks in the mirror when they ask, "Who is the variable?" we will have made tremendous strides toward school improvement. This empowering approach raises the level of teacher efficacy and will eventually be passed on to students.[4]

Of course, focusing on what is in our control does not mean that we are blind to what is not. A teacher may not be able to reverse the debilitating effects of a child's asthma. A teacher may not be able to change the ways in which a student's home environment is not ideal for completing homework. A teacher may not be able to erase a child's anxieties about her family's financial pressures or a flare-up of violence in the community.

Echoing many of the teachers we have worked with, Martin Winchester told us that he has discovered in his eleven years teaching in one of America's lowest-income communities that focusing on what he can control is sufficient to change his students' academic trajectory. "One of the most valuable lessons I have learned as a teacher has been to distinguish between the things I can't change and the things I can change," Mr. Winchester says. "Hearing about the pressures and challenges my students face outside my classroom can be overwhelming and often leaves me with a sense of hopelessness. Hearing my student struggle to read aloud only reenergizes me because I know that *is* something I can change."

The teachers featured in this book demonstrate that a teacher can control enough factors in students' lives to close the achievement gap. A teacher can ensure that students realize that effort does lead to success. A teacher can ensure that classroom instruction is efficient, effective, and engaging; that time available for learning increases; that distraction from learning decreases; and that within the four walls of the classroom, students feel safe, welcomed, and encouraged to take academic risks. We have seen teachers over and over take control of factors that lead to dramatic academic achievement.

## Key Elements of Working Relentlessly

In our observations of and interactions with highly effective teachers, we see several key elements of this "whatever it takes" approach to student learning:

- Persisting through challenges and failures
- Maintaining high expectations, even when students are far behind and facing difficult challenges
- Expanding time and resources
- Expanding influence through relationships, student achievement, respect and humility, and professionalism
- Sustaining this work over time

### Persistence

Every teacher featured in this book has stories of challenges they pushed through to ensure student learning. Recall Eric Scroggins, who designed a big goal around earning high school credit for earth science. Implementing that goal was not easy:

I faced numerous obstacles in pursuing my goal of passing the Earth Science Regents Exam with my students. First, I had to gain permission from my district science coordinator to teach the curriculum. He hesitated because it was an unorthodox request and because he understandably worried that it was simply too large a leap for my students given the challenges they faced and given that I was a first-year teacher—he didn't want me setting my students and myself up for failure. Through the help of parents and ulti- mately through lobbying from my principal, I gained permission. Next, I needed to secure the resources. Regents' courses required a higher-level text and additional lab hours. I learned early on that the assistant principal was the one who ordered supplies, and I built a strong relationship with her. To support our effort, she ordered a new set of books and through persistent but nice lobbying, I eventually got enough books for every one of my students. I then wrote mini-grants for the additional prep materials I needed. Lastly, we needed more time. I received permission to use our building after school and on Saturdays and spoke to each student's parents about the necessity and expectation for attendance.

Mr. Scroggins acted on his belief that he could control the factors necessary to lead his students to success. By finding his way around the obstacles to that vision, two-thirds of Mr. Scroggins' eighth graders passed the rigorous Regents Exam (nearly double the rate at which the city's tenth graders passed the same exam), an accomplishment that opened up doors to prestigious high schools across New York City.

Sometimes, the challenges we face are more pedestrian. Jenny Gwin, an eighth-grade English/language arts teacher in Philadelphia, faced the surprisingly common challenge of not actually having her own classroom but instead pushing a cart from room to room between class periods. And yet her sense of responsibility for and control over student learning inspired her to find a way to make it work:

In the early days when I was upset with my own teaching, I found myself using not having a classroom as an excuse. But I soon realized that it's just a cart; it's not a big deal. It is not in any way an excuse for not teaching my students. I began to focus on what I could prepare so that when I walk in the room, the students have a "do now" to start learning immediately. I now walk to every classroom before school and create a shortcut on the classroom computer's PowerPoint so I don't have to waste a minute getting that set up. I have papers in stacks for a designated student to hand out right when class begins. I have put up progress-tracking posters and other materials on the walls of each room I teach in. I saw that it would do no good to dwell on the challenge. I just had to get it done.

These teachers show that having an internal locus of control boils down to persistence. Stephani Estes, a special education teacher in St. Louis, describes this approach very simply:

*Relentless* means you just don't give up. Are there days when you want to give up? Sure— that's what makes us human. But being relentless means you consciously make the decision to keep going. You won't settle for only 60 percent of your students understand- ing the concept, and you won't let your students settle for a D in your class. You go the extra mile. You never, ever, give up on a kid or a concept. You just keep going.

## Maintaining High Expectations

Another sign of highly effective teachers' internal locus of control and relentlessness is their refusal to lower expectations of their students, even in the face of harsh and difficult realities. In our experience, two situations tempt even the strongest teacher to make excuses for student underperformance, but the most effective teachers resist compromising their expectations.

### "They Are *How* Far Behind?"

Even when we have read article after article and book after book about the dire statistics of the achievement gap, the personification of those data in our students can be shocking and discouraging. Over and over we hear stories from new teachers that begin, "I just could not believe how far behind they were." You may discover that most of your fifth graders are reading on a second- or third-grade level (and the rest are just learning to read). Or you may find that your seventh-grade science students do not have the math skills necessary to perform any of the experiments called for by the curriculum and that they struggle to read your "remedial" text. Or you may be alarmed to find that your eleventh-grade English students, whom you want to help apply for college, have difficulty writing one paragraph, let alone a college entrance essay. An eighth-grade English teacher in Los Angeles, Frank Lozier described his own dismay as he discovered the reality of the achievement gap in his students' lives:

> Going into my English classroom, I was thrilled by the opportunity to bring in all the concepts that inspire me about literature—intertextuality across authors; complicated, innovative narration; race, class, and gender analysis. While I knew I had an enormous amount of work in getting my kids caught up to grade level, I spent the first weeks of September stunned by the stark reality. *Where do I start?* I thought to myself. *Spelling? Sentence structure? Vocabulary? Punctuation?* I was saddened, overwhelmed, and enraged by a system that had failed a generation of students. How could we discuss an author's choices of racial representation if my kids couldn't even independently comprehend the text? How would we produce written analyses of social injustice if they had difficulty consistently writing in complete sentences?
>
> I knew I had a choice: I could (a) keep lamenting and throw up my hands at the disturbing reality, (b) lower my expectations and remain locked into teaching only the basics rather than challenging my kids to reach higher, or (c) find a way to weave in the basics while pushing toward the highest levels of literary analysis.

Mr. Lozier, like other strong teachers, worked hard to accomplish the third option. He recalls that he had to learn to break down and prioritize the basics, draw from rigorous learning standards, and weave all of that into his insistence that students think critically about what they read and write. He resisted the pull of lowered expectations even as the magnitude of his challenge became clear.

As we have worked with highly effective teachers like Mr. Lozier, we have gathered their advice for maintaining high expectations despite students' previous low performance. Among the suggestions they offer new teachers are these:

- *Start, but don't end, with the basics.* When faced with the daunting and deflating disparity between where your students are and where you want them to be, remember the great value of focusing on the most fundamental academic skills first. This is not to say that you should water down the curriculum or dilute your goals to include only the basics; rather, no matter what your assigned grade level and subject matter, you may need to give your students an intensive, accelerated, and ongoing course in basic reading and math skills alongside your other learning standards.

- *Take literacy instruction seriously for all grades and subjects.* A closely related idea is that our students, as a general rule, lag in their literacy skills. Highly effective teachers, therefore, weave explicit literacy instruction into their content area, whatever that may be. (Training texts about teaching literacy, both for elementary and secondary students, are available online at www.teachingasleadership.org.)

- *Reap the benefits of students' intellectual capacity.* Sometimes, because our students' intellectual maturity is in fact on grade level while their skill development is not, they are ripe for massive strides forward.

- *Move faster, not more slowly.* Some teachers respond to a classroom of students who are behind by setting a slower learning pace for them. Precisely the opposite approach is needed. Your students will be behind, but they will have the capacity and potential for great growth. The principles of leadership outlined in this book allow teachers of students who are far behind to set and maintain an accelerated pace of learning in their classroom.

- *Benchmark your classroom's pace and progress against excellent classrooms.* One of the best ways to pace yourself is to keep an eye on some excellent classrooms in high-performing schools and compare your students' pace and progress with that of the students in those classrooms.

## Resisting the Soft Bigotry of Low Expectations

If the reality of our students' low academic skills is one challenge to maintaining high expectations, the reality of our students' lives is another. Sometimes our students face heavy burdens that represent very real challenges to their learning. As we come to realize those challenges, many of us struggle against allowing concern or sympathy to turn into excuses for low performance.

Even the most successful teachers we work with offer stories of their own kind-hearted reactions that degraded high expectations for their students. All of the following statements are adapted from highly effective teachers' confessed thoughts that could have or did lower their expectations of their students:

- "Camilla has to work in the evenings, so I should just let her sloppy homework slide."

- "Oscar comes to school hungry. Of course, he's going to act out during the morning meeting. I can live with that."

- "Three of my students simply did not meet the minimal standards for fifth grade this year, but they are generally well behaved and did put in some effort. I'm going to pass them on to sixth grade."

- "Visiting Michael's home was really eye-opening for me. It's just so different from my own experience. It doesn't feel right for me to come in and push Michael to focus on school when there's so much going on at home."

- "I know what a tough situation Melissa is going through. I had some of those experiences myself. I should give her a break on some of the demands of the classroom."

Because we care about our students, these are not the sorts of dilemmas that lend themselves to easy choices. How do we respond when some unjust burden of poverty is inhibiting their performance? On the one hand, it seems unfair to ignore that reality by expecting that students demonstrate their full potential, in essence asking more of our students than is asked of children in other contexts. On the other hand, compromising our expectations out of sympathy may have the same effect as assuming our students are incapable of achieving success because of their race, or socioeconomic status, or background.

The clear pattern among teachers in low-income communities whose students make the most progress is an uncompromising but caring refusal to accept any excuses for student underperformance. These teachers maintain their high expectations even as they acknowledge and show sympathy for the difficulties in students' lives. These teachers are not suggesting that effort is not important or that the burdens our students face do not matter, but they are suggesting that lowering expectations of actual outcomes, no matter what the motivation, is no favor to our students.

The most effective teachers believe that allowing sympathy or concern or pity to lower our expectations *adds* to the burdens of poverty by ensuring that students will be unable to access the life opportunities afforded students in wealthier communities. Thus, they consider enforcing high expectations to be a nonnegotiable, but incredibly difficult, element of their authority in the classroom.

Kate Sobel, an extraordinarily effective teacher and school leader, has her own reminder of the challenge and importance of asserting consistent high expectations for every student. His name was Francisco.

> *I had so much to give, but I forgot to teach. While I think I was right to support him in the ways I did, I wish I had also maintained focus on the all-important goal of teaching him to read.*

**FRANCISCO CAME INTO** my room for the first time, looked around, and grinned a wide smile. Having spent four years in the classroom, I easily looked past the too-big shoes, too-short pants, and backward T-shirt to see the excitement in this soon-to-be-a-first-grader's eyes. Francisco and his brother, Victor, spent the day putting up butcher paper, organizing the library, and unpacking boxes of fresh-tipped crayons. Francisco was off to a good start. I had big plans for the students of Room B, and Francisco was already high on my list.

I spent so much time with him that year and grew to love his toothless smile and misfit uniforms. But all of that time, I lost sight of my expectations and my primary responsibilities as a teacher. I let Francisco go through an entire year of first grade without learning to read.

I think about it all the time. It's one of those things that seemed to be part of a year flying by. I remember each incident clearly, but I can't remember when I decided to put my academic priorities aside for Francisco. There was the time when, with a tooth so rotten it made his face swell like a football, I sent him home with explicit directions to stay there until he had seen the dentist. And the afternoons when he and his brother ate peanut butter and crackers at my desk when I was content to use tutoring time to provide a much-needed snack. And all the time I spent talking to his mom about bedtime, and visits to the clinic, and getting new clothes. Somehow when Francisco walked through my doors in the morning, my mind spun through

a checklist that was different from when I greeted other students in the class. Instead of "Homework? Check. Does he know his spelling words this week? Check. Have I talked to his mom about the research project we're doing on ocean animals? Check," I jumped to sending him to the bathroom with soap and a toothbrush, checking to make sure he was wearing socks and that he brought a jacket for recess. I had so much to give, but I forgot to teach. While I think I was right to support him in the ways I did, I wish I had also maintained focus on the all-important goal of teaching him to read.

**Kate Sobel,** First Grade, California

Francisco spent a year in first grade with me, better fed and cleaner than perhaps he would have been otherwise, but because I forgot to teach Francisco, he spent two years in first grade. The year he left Room B to join a first-grade class for the second time, Francisco learned to read with his peers. Another teacher looked past the too-big shoes, too-short pants, and backward T-shirt to see his potential as a student—and he lived up to her expectations.

In our work with highly effective teachers, we have gathered practical advice from those who have wrestled with these issues. While none would say that maintaining high expectations in the face of unjust challenges in our students' lives is easy, they have shared two ways they manage that dilemma:

- *Define kindness in terms of learning rather than excuses.* Kindness takes many forms, but making excuses for poor performance cannot be one of them. If we see problems in students' lives, we do what we can to help. Meanwhile, we also must maintain a focus on learning so that the students can overcome challenges for themselves in the long run.

- *Recognize that problems outside our control do not necessarily mean there are no achievement-related solutions.* Sometimes students' living conditions are simply not in the realm of a teacher's influence. Perhaps a student is a migrant worker and has to leave in the spring to go north to work. Perhaps a student is pregnant. Perhaps a student has health issues related to environmental hazards in his neighborhood. Seeing those situations may be discouraging because the root condition or problem cannot be changed, and yet we should not allow that discouragement to hinder our view of achievement-related solutions. How can we help the student navigate those realities to attain opportunities to learn?

## Expanding Time and Resources

For teachers working with students who are years behind academically, time is perhaps their most precious resource.[5] As described in Chapter Four, great implementers get the most out of their time and resources. Relentless leaders also refuse to accept conventional limits placed on time and resources; they create and stretch time and resources for the sake of student learning.

Virtually all of the highly effective teachers we work with can identify a moment in their first year when they realize that the day is just too short; so is the year. Goal setting, investing students and families, planning and executing instructional and classroom management plans, reflecting and improving one's teaching—all of these important elements of teaching that contribute to student achievement take precious time. Leading students from their lagging starting point to your ambitious vision of success takes lots and lots of time. Faced with this reality, the teachers you have met in this book find creative ways to squeeze more learning time from the day.[6]

These teachers ensure that learning is happening before, during, and after school. When we visit a classroom where students are making exceptional academic progress, we can count on seeing students joining study sessions during lunch, getting additional help during the teacher's planning period, attending evening study sessions at school or at local restaurants, or perhaps even coming to school on weekends to work on critical learning goals. We always see teachers finding learning time in the nooks and crannies of their day. Samantha Cohen, who led her Atlanta first-grade students to mastery of Georgia's most challenging *second*-grade objectives, would, for example, "steal more time during the day" by making flash cards that reviewed math and grammar skills to use while she and her students waited in line for lunch or assemblies.

Some teachers have even collaborated with their colleagues to restructure the school day. North Carolina teachers Tammi Sutton and Caleb Dolan led the charge in their district to lengthen the school day by forty-five minutes. Jason Kamras, the 2005 National Teacher of the Year, convinced his principal to double the length of math classes—a change that led to massive increases in student math proficiency. Nicole Sherrin worked with other faculty to turn an underused schoolwide study hall into a math tutorial. Molly Eigen's notion of a "working lunch" with her high school students became a formalized institution at her school, involving several teachers and between ten and twenty students every day.

And of course, as we have seen throughout this book, highly effective teachers expand the time students are working toward learning by investing others in encouraging and achieving the students' academic goals. Maurice Rabb taught his students' families how to supplement his reading instruction, for example. Other teachers have recruited college students and other community members as volunteer tutors. Sara Egli, for example, told us:

> I always want more time. I have so many things I want to do in my classroom, and it never seems like there is time. One thing I have always wanted specifically is more time to work one-on-one with my students. It's hard to do. I decided this year that if I couldn't do it, then I would find other people who could. My first-grade team and I worked with our administration to develop an eighth-grade teacher's assistant program. Each day, one eighth-grade student comes to our classroom to work one-on-one with first-grade students. We created lesson plans, prepared materials, and provided training for these students. Now I am able to ensure that each of my students is receiving targeted instruction, even if it's not from me.

When several of Brent Maddin's high school science students were unable to stay after school for tutoring because they worked at McDonald's, Mr. Maddin set up camp there to tutor the students during their breaks. That setting was so successful that he began inviting other students, and soon he was tutoring as many as seventy-five students a week at McDonald's in the evenings.

Other resources besides time are often in short supply for teachers in low-income communities. Virtually all of the teachers we work with report they need additional materials, like books and school supplies, to maximize student learning. In the most successful classrooms, teachers find ways to obtain those resources.

First on their list of strategies is building relationships with the gatekeepers to resources. Shannon Steffes, for example, made a point to update her New Mexico school's administrative staff on her fifth-grade students' learning and progress. Ms. Steffes recalls that "when I told my principal about how our novel study on Jerry Spinelli books increased students' level of understanding of author's purpose (a highly occurring standard on our state test) from 23 percent proficient to 78 percent proficient, her first response was, 'Do you need any other books? I have some money that needs to be spent by the end of the week.'"

In addition, strong teachers look outside school channels to find more resources. This can mean applying for grants to increase technological resources in the classroom, using online donor services (like www.donorschoose.org) to buy school supplies for needy students, or creating homemade math manipulatives for your tactile learners.

Janelle Scharon, a high school chemistry teacher in Chicago, addressed her resource needs by raising funds herself:

> Writing grants and receiving funding from sponsors such as Project Aware, NASA, Jordan Fundamentals, Teaching Tolerance, and Donors Choose has alleviated the hardship of the lack of resources in my classroom. With over fifteen thousand dollars awarded in grants, students have been able to use scientific calculators, conduct traditional and current research experiments such as DNA analysis and nanofiber development, and present their work during presentations with the aid of an LCD projector. Additionally, I have been able to start and run with outside funds a chapter of the National Honor Society and initiate and coach the . . . robotics team with the aid of a NASA grant. With the support of NASA, our robotics team competed as a first-year rookie team and won a Judge's Award, and the next year, we won the regional championship and were supported by NASA and various Chicago trade unions.

Many teachers, like Leigh Kincaid, get similar results with less formal requests for resources:

> I have begged and borrowed to get the resources and materials my students need. Family, friends, and community have been kind and generous in their donations of every kind . . . books, money for our reading café, prizes, and time. . . . It didn't seem like a choice. I didn't have the materials, and my students needed them. End of question.

Ms. Kincaid's beg-and-borrow strategy serves many highly effective teachers well. We have seen teachers find resources for field trips, lab equipment, classroom libraries, and much more. Stephanie Scott started her first year as a third-grade teacher in southern Louisiana with no books in her classroom. "With mass e-mailing and a letter writing campaign, I received over seven hundred books from friends, former bosses, churches, and friends of friends who wanted to help," she reports. She also enlisted students' families to help build shelves for the growing classroom library. Ms. Scott says that "those generous donations are appreciated every day when one of my students goes to sit in the library and enjoy a book from any genre or level that they desire." While every teacher in low-income communities needs additional resources to maximize student learning, very few report that they cannot obtain some additional resources when they seek them out.

## Expanding Your Influence

In addition to increasing the time and resources available for student learning, highly effective teachers broaden their influence on problems inhibiting student learning. In essence, these teachers take an expansive view of the role of a teacher. Rather than ask themselves, "What do teachers do?" they ask, "What must be accomplished to reach our ambitious goals?"

In the words of Taylor Delhagen, "I am an educator, social worker, mentor, colleague, administrator, activist, student, and friend, all of which equate into a teacher. The amount of social responsibility is overwhelming, but also exciting. Failing to mend the achievement gap for my students is simply not an option." We hear and see demonstrated the same philosophy in virtually every classroom where students are dramatically exceeding society's expectations. A teacher does what is necessary to reach ambitious academic goals.

For Nicholas Deifel, this meant converting the school library into a science classroom so that his students could conduct experiments that would enable them to master the eighth-grade science curriculum. For Linh Luong Carpenter, this means starting her own kindergarten intervention program when the school's was cut from the budget. For Cameron Duffy, this means also teaching math because the math teacher quit. For Justin May, this means keeping nonperishable food in a mouse-proof container in his classroom for a few students who are distracted by hunger in the morning. For Shannon Dingle, this means wading through three feet of water to get to students' flooded neighborhood so that she could teach twelve children in the backyard. In all of these cases, these highly effective teachers are driven to take on unconventional roles, all in the name of ensuring student learning.

At times, removing barriers and creating pathways to student learning has less to do with the teacher's own actions and more to do with influencing the actions of others in the school or community. For example, Vanessa Muller, a New York City special education teacher, realized both the potential of her third-grade students to excel and the potential of an inclusion model (in which students would be in regular education classes with their peers while getting additional support from her) to inspire their best efforts. She worked with her school administrators to redesign student placements toward a default inclusion model (rather than an assumption that students with special needs would go into a self-contained classroom in which they would receive more structure and support but be more isolated from the regular education students in their grade). Many of the students with special needs in Ms. Muller's school thrived academically and socially in the new inclusion environment she helped design. Her own students grew more than one and a half years in reading and achieved 95 percent mastery of math standards, thereby meeting all of their Individualized Education Program goals.

Houston science lab teacher David Omenn faced a different problem when he was charged with leading labs for 660 prekindergarten through fifth-grade students each week. In this role, he found that some teachers' lack of comfort with the science materials and hands-on labs was inhibiting student learning. After building strong relationships with his colleagues, he brought the issue into his realm of influence by creating a committee of representative teachers and guiding them through training and workshops to boost their confidence and skills in teaching science. Soon Mr. Omenn had created a new challenge for himself: managing all the requests for collaboration and resources coming from teachers excited about science.

We have many similar stories of teachers expanding their influence for the sake of their students. Some teachers, for example, have been frustrated by students' "summer slide" (the loss of knowledge and skills over the summer) and have either implemented or connected their students with summer learning opportunities. Some teachers, faced with weak or nonexistent learning standards, have developed new ones that have been adopted by the school. Other teachers become advocates for their school's needs at school board meetings, work with their department chairperson to design a new sequence of courses in a particular subject, or bring some special skill, such as a command of education technology, to bear for the benefit of the school.

Whatever the form of influence you seek, three general practices—demonstrated by all of the teachers described above—should guide your actions. Teachers are able to act as agents of change on their campus only when they first earn their influence through their students' achievement, choose carefully what issues to take on, and build relationships and collaborate with their colleagues and administrators.

## Earning Influence with Student Achievement

In our experience, most teachers who successfully effect change beyond their classrooms first earn credibility inside their classrooms. Jenny Tan, who eventually became an influential force on her campus, describes this idea:

> I knew early on that the only way to be "heard" at my school was to gain respect as an educator. My first year, I worked extremely hard to get my children to master the standards and to do well on state standardized tests. During my second and third years, my hard work paid off as my colleagues and administrators listened and treated me as an equal contributor to help solve the pressing issues occurring at our school.

In fact, many teachers who become agents of change report that they were drafted into taking on key issues, once colleagues and administrators saw the results they achieved with their students. Crystal Brakke, who had worked hard to lead her students to demonstrable academic progress in her first year as a teacher, was invited in her second year to be a representative on the superintendent's advisory council, where she was able to learn about and influence some of the most challenging problems facing her North Carolina district.

Similarly, Tara Harrington, a high school biology teacher in Charlotte, found she had much more influence once she had changed the pass rate on the rigorous state end-of-course exam from 31 percent to 95 percent in her first year:

"During my first year, my administrators sometimes (and quite understandably) had some concerns regarding my teaching. The concerns subsided quickly when results from the state test were returned near the end of the year. In meeting with my principal after the state test, he mentioned my students' excellent scores and casually asked me, "What have you been doing in there?" I used this as an opportunity to share the strategies I had implemented in my classroom and some of my ideas for the upcoming year. He was immediately interested in and excited by my tracking system.

I described the purpose of my system and explained my data-driven approach to instruction, and momentum built from there. That summer, I was invited to participate in a two-week schoolwide planning conference, where my contributions helped shape our school's broader efforts around the data component of instructional design. During this summer institute, my principal presented my tracking system to my school community.

**Tara Harrington,**
High School Biology,
North Carolina

Following this initial introduction, I developed and organized training on this system for other teachers. Furthermore, I creatively planned an entire new year-long structure for my courses to maximize student learning. I built in as much flexibility as I could without compromising the ultimate purposes of this new plan, as I knew there was a possibility that I might not be permitted to follow this plan or teach in this way.

In addition, a consultant assigned to our school asked to sit down and talk with me because he was impressed with my results. I was excited for the chance to interact with him and immediately responded, "I would love to talk to you! And I also have some questions." He had so much experience in the school system, and I was able to use the conversation as an opportunity to get his feedback on my plans while also investing him in the purpose. As a result, I was able to improve my plans and gain access to more resources. He put me in touch with a contact at the state department of education, and they encouraged me to start a pilot.

To ensure the validity of the project, another teacher, a four-year veteran, was invited to use my plans and systems as part of this pilot. I was able to lead training sessions with my department to demonstrate the usefulness and purpose of transparent tracking to inform their instruction. I also highlighted the way my plans could build connections among learning objectives, account for misconceptions, and strengthen student understanding. Humbled by my colleagues' experience, I was prudent about the way in which I presented the information. I didn't present it as, "I know this is going to be the best thing for our students." I just explained my rationale, the process I went through to plan and create the components of this system, and my experience from the previous year. Specifically, I discussed my students' misconceptions, the concepts my students didn't understand, and the reasons I thought they experienced these challenges. This discussion then allowed me the chance to showcase the techniques I had developed to address those misconceptions.

I recognized that there would be certain challenges. I explained to my colleagues that I would determine why specific roadblocks arose and work to resolve the problems to help all of us next year. In addition to earning the opportunity to develop our instruction, I also found that my first-year results earned me more support from my administration in doing what I felt was best for students—whether that was instituting extra Saturday classes or using assessments that I thought were stronger than the ones I had been prescribed during my first year.

### Acting with Utmost Respect and Humility to Choose Your Causes Wisely

As they work to effect dramatic student achievement, teachers may see many ways that they could work to reduce barriers and build additional pathways to student learning. The most effective teachers do not, however, take on all of those at once. They prioritize the problems, decisions, policies, and systems that have the most impact on their students' success. They tackle only those issues they are in a position to influence because of their unique knowledge, proximity, or skills. And they do so with utmost respect and humility.

"I learned early on in my teaching career that creating change in my school was a delicate procedure," explained Richard Reddick, who taught in one of Houston's most impoverished neighborhoods. "You have to choose your battles—follow the lead and advice of experienced teachers in your school. While you might initially be frustrated with some of the administrative goals in your school, as time passes, you will find that you have a greater ability to make things happen."

Unfortunately, some teachers barrel into a new community with the mindset that they are there to fix all the problems they see. Not only is that deficit-based view of their students, families, and colleagues offensive and arrogant, but it also ignores all of the hard work already going on in the community. Imagine a new teacher who, in the first week, marches into the principal's office and demands that the policy barring field trips be changed. Imagine a new teacher who promptly tells his department chairperson how to restructure the literacy program. Or imagine a new teacher writing a letter to the editor of the community newspaper to report on a perceived misappropriation of funds in the school district. Whether or not these teachers are right on the merits of their concerns, they have probably doomed their cause with a haughty assumption that their limited perspective should inform change.

Our investigations indicate that this counterproductive approach often results from a lack of self-awareness about how one is being perceived and an inability to assume the best of the members of the school community (and the community more broadly). Such teachers have little chance of building meaningful and productive relationships with those whose help they need.

By contrast, highly effective teachers patiently earn influence by proving their leadership capabilities with extraordinary student progress in their classroom. They also respectfully and humbly develop relationships with their colleagues and administrators in order to collaborate for the sake of their students.

## Building Relationships to Collaborate with Colleagues

A message we hear frequently from highly effective teachers talking about their influence is that no teacher is an island. To maximize our influence on our students' growth, we must build and depend on relationships with those around us, including our fellow teachers, administrators, and students' families. Reading specialist Stephanie Crement discusses how important this was when she began teaching:

> I approached every interaction with the notion that I was an outsider in my new school community, and I needed to rely on the expertise of parents, fellow teachers, and other community members. I made sure that I was respectful and humble in every interaction in which I engaged. They were the experts about the community, the school, their children, and I wanted to work as a partner with them to make sure their students achieved. I believe that because of the way that I presented myself, I was well received in my community as someone who had come from the outside but was interested in achieving the same ultimate goal as my students' families, other teachers, and community members: student achievement.

The reasons for collaborating are many and obvious. We gain knowledge and skills from veteran teachers around us about our subject matter, teaching methods, and working within the system of our school, district, and community. Establishing relationships with our colleagues and administrators helps us to gain access to resources and gives us allies when we must navigate obstacles in our work. Conversely, if our colleagues do not support our efforts, our influence can be hugely diminished or negated completely.

Building productive relationships at school can be a complex endeavor. You may find an administrator's decision inexplicable. You may disagree with a school policy that others love. You may be unfamiliar and surprised by a colleague's method of teaching or discipline. You may encounter colleagues who, for any number of reasons, are hesitant to engage with you. Highly effective teachers approach the potential challenges in these relationships in several ways.

First, these teachers see that their limited experience calls for a respectful approach. They recognize that of all aspects of their personal identity, their newness may be the most glaring. Even if they have many valuable experiences and insights to contribute, they pause to reflect on the fact that there is so much they do not know. We hear from strong teachers that an authentic acknowledgment of their hope to learn is a good way to begin a relationship with veteran colleagues and administrators.

Second, highly effective teachers approach disagreements or tensions with colleagues with the aim of mutual learning and understanding rather than the aim of changing others' minds. This does not mean that you must agree with every statement and action of those around you. Sometimes you may not only disagree with others' statements and actions, but you may find them confusing or hurtful. But the most effective teachers and leaders approach disagreement in a spirit of learning.

A group of negotiation experts wrote *Difficult Conversations,* a book that shares the mindsets and tactics of individuals who work well with others, even in intense or otherwise difficult contexts. One key message in that book is that productive relationships are best developed when we each build awareness of the limits of our perspective.[7] The table here summarizes what we often are and are not aware of about ourselves. As it suggests, in any interaction, we should have a clear picture of what we mean, the challenges we are facing, how others are coming across to us, the impact that others are having on us, and their possible contributions to a problem. At the same time, we must acknowledge we may have blind spots that keep us from understand-

| I am aware of: | I am potentially blind to: |
| --- | --- |
| My own intentions | Others' intentions |
| What I am up against | What others are up against |
| How others come across to me | How I come across to others |
| Other people's impact on me | My impact on others |
| How others are contributing to problems | How I may be contributing to problems |

ing others' intentions and the challenges they are facing. Unless we listen well enough to hear and understand their reactions, we cannot really know the impact of our words on others.

Our conversation with one teacher offers a common example of these dynamics. In this case, the teacher expressed frustration with the way consequences seemed to be unevenly applied to students whom she referred to the office. It seemed to her unpredictable and unfair when one child would be sent to in-school suspension and another would be asked to write a letter of apology.

In a separate interview, we asked the principal who was making these decisions to describe some of the factors that go into disciplinary decisions that are not normally shared with teachers. We were given a whole range of factors of which the teacher was unaware. The principal, in accordance with district policy, had great leeway in determining consequences and was empowered to consider, for example, the child's previous record of misbehavior and other information that the teacher did not have. Moreover, the principal shared *his* frustration that the state and school board—in response to litigation and legislation—were constantly adding to and changing the "double issue of *War and Peace*" handbook that was supposed to govern his decisions on consequences.

Once we brought these two individuals' perspectives together, we could see the complexity in their divergent interests that became a source of misunderstanding and tension. The teacher did not see all the factors the principal was considering, and the principal did not know that his decisions affected and frustrated the teacher.

If the teacher in the example had approached her principal assuming she had all of the information she needed to know and was ready to give her principal "a piece of her mind," she would have caused even more tension, and few positive results would have been achieved.

As the book *Difficult Conversations* explains: "We can't change someone else's mind or force them to change their behavior. . . . Trying to change someone rarely results in change. On the other hand, engaging in a conversation in which mutual learning is the goal often results in change."[8]

As a representative case in point, consider the experience of Lisa Barrett who taught children with disabilities in Oakland, California. Over time she saw a pattern of insensitive comments about her students—some from students and some from teachers. Ms. Barrett recalls that "each time, my stomach turned." She decided that her best course of action was to virtually introduce her colleagues to her students and convey information about their disabilities. Rather than stew in frustration because of some insensitive comments, she set out to learn what experiences and impressions were shaping others' perspectives and to invest her colleagues in her quest to create a welcoming environment for the students. "I decided to address the issue school-wide," she says, "by presenting at a staff meeting and simply explaining why my students are in a special day class and how I would like teachers to field questions about my class."

Ms. Barrett found the simple act of outreach and education, and listening to others' reactions, was the beginning of a sea change in the way people thought about her students. "The staff was tremendously supportive, and several people approached me later to share things they had said to their class without thinking but would avoid in the future," she recalls. "Just by putting this issue in the open and trusting my colleagues' intentions, I got the support I needed."

Often this commitment to common understanding and relationship building leads teachers to engage in their broader community as well. Strong teachers realize that becoming involved in

> ▶ **PROFESSIONALISM FOR BUILDING RELATIONSHIPS**
>
> **SOME WOULD DESCRIBE EVERYTHING** we are discussing in this chapter as issues of professionalism—a focus on results, choosing causes carefully, asking others for help, and strong relationships with colleagues. In the words of Jane Henzerling, a sixth-grade English teacher in Phoenix, "Professionalism for a new teacher in a new community is listening without judgment, keeping opinions to yourself for a while, making an effort to understand others' perspectives, learning as much as you can about the community, your students, and their families, and engaging in community events on the residents' terms (not your own)."
>
> Professionalism also means respecting and following the conventions of your school and community. Behaviors that may seem to some as peripheral to your core objectives (like dressing appropriately; submitting accurate attendance records, lesson plans, and grade books in a timely manner; and arriving punctually) send strong messages to all those who are observing your behavior. These habits demonstrate that you are dependable and respect your job and your colleagues. They also help build social capital to obtain the resources and make the changes you need to best serve your students.

community activities helps cut through the newness that can leave others skeptical of their intentions. Rhiannon Carabajal, for example, made a habit of attending parent-teacher organization meetings, site-based decision-making committee meetings, and neighborhood meetings. "There was a lot I didn't do right my first year teaching," she says, "but showing up and participating in my new school and neighborhood was the perfect thing to do. I was able to meet and network with many parents and community members who were equally invested in our children."

As South Dakota teacher Krishnan Subrahmanian suggests, reaching out to help at your school or in your community can be directly related to student learning:

> If you have grand ideas to engage, motivate, and create with your students and community, first and foremost acquire the capital that is necessary to get these big projects done. Humbly asking, "What can I help other people accomplish?" will garner you the relationships and experience necessary to carry out your vision. By volunteering to help fellow staff members and administrators at concession stands, organizing a Veteran's Day program, and leading an activity that no other teacher wanted, my students were the beneficiaries because we were able to get a grant for reading incentives and prizes through the administration.

One final story, this one from Mississippi Delta fifth-grade teacher Laura Bowen, captures the essence of building relationships for productive collaboration. Ms. Bowen was partnered with a teacher whom we will call Mrs. Parker, a legendary veteran in the school. At the beginning of the year, Ms. Bowen says she was intimidated by Mrs. Parker and by the several obvious lines of difference (race, background, and experience) they would be working across. Ms. Bowen recalls that Mrs. Parker was obviously skeptical of Ms. Bowen's ability to handle and lead her students. And yet eight months later, Ms. Bowen reports:

> It is now a beautiful Sunday morning in early April. I walk into a small country church and immediately notice that I am the only white person present. However, I soon forget the color of my skin as I am welcomed with a warm embrace. The smiling woman who embraces me and introduces me as "her friend" is Mrs. Parker, a woman who has become a trusted colleague and a supportive friend. A few days later, Mrs. Parker sent a note to my classroom in which she expressed her happiness that we had worshipped together. I was also invited to return to share the church service at any time. On the return visit, I was again treated as an honored guest. These events have caused me to reflect on the evolution of my relationship with Mrs. Parker, a teacher who once looked at me with doubtful eyes. How did the expression in her eyes begin to change? When exactly was I welcomed?

> Looking back on these eight months, I now realize that there was no huge event that changed my status at Carver or with Mrs. Parker. Nothing spectacular happened to integrate me into

the group of fifth-grade teachers. There are simply a series of things that inevitably happen if you approach a new environment with respect, humility, and love. These things that happen are small building blocks that chip away at old prejudices, past threats, and deep doubts; and since all eyes are on us during our first few months, all actions and words are noticed and remembered. Thus, the cheerful hallway conversations, the long afternoons, the dedication shown to kids, the willingness to help out, and the hard work are noticed. No one will give you a medal for all of these things, but, believe me, they will notice, and they will be appreciative. And so Mrs. Parker's eyes, the eyes that were watching me the closest, took in all of these things, and she slowly began sharing herself with me. She would bring me supplies for my classroom, introduce me to family members, back me with certain difficult parents, and, most important, support me in front of the students of Carver. There has never been a time when she questioned my methods in front of others, and I am very sure that this isn't a result of her not questioning my methods. Instead, she chose to see the successes rather than the failures of my first year. Despite our disagreements over discipline (I know she thinks I baby my kids) and over the workload (reading groups aren't yet considered real work), we have managed to forge a strong relationship, one that benefits the both of us.

For my part, the relationship was necessary. In short, I needed to work with Mrs. Parker in order to be successful at Carver. However, I realize that she did not face that similar need. . . . Her spirit, character, and her strength have made my experience thus far a far more valuable one. I know that next year at Carver will be even better, in part because I will again be teaching with my friend, Mrs. Parker.

## Sustaining This Work Over Time

While the word *relentless* connotes a purpose-driven intensity, it also captures the long-term persistence demonstrated by highly effective teachers as they work for their students. The highly effective teachers we study say that working relentlessly means ensuring their efforts are sustainable over time—for the sake of their students.

Their reasoning is obvious. Burning out does not help you or your students. Being tired, impatient, or unhappy does not help you or your students. We are most happy and we best serve our students when we are energized, fulfilled, and focused—qualities we lose when we are exhausted and overworked.

Rare is the teacher who does not sometimes feel exhausted. However, in our experience, it is also rare to find highly effective teachers who are not consciously managing and limiting exhaustion by taking good care of themselves, drawing energy and support from collaboration with colleagues, and drawing energy from the inspiration inherent in leading children to increased academic achievement and opportunities in life.

Jess Bialecki, a New Orleans elementary school teacher, provides a glimpse of some of the many strategies excellent teachers use:

> I realized early on that if I wanted to be able to sustain the physically and emotionally draining lifestyle of a teacher, I was going to need to renew my energy and passion on a regular basis. I do this in a variety of ways, among them: running slideshows of ridiculously adorable pictures of my students on my computer screen during late-night planning sessions, self-enforcing a strict "no work on Friday nights" rule, volunteering for extra morning duty so that I can have non-school-related, relationship-building conversations with each of my students, indulging in my favorite TV dramas with my roommates, volunteering as the leader of a Girl Scout Daisies troop to which many of my students belong, playing on an indoor soccer team with other teachers, and enjoying the many incredible food and music festivals for which this city is well known.

### Building and Drawing on Colleagues' Support

Highly effective teachers sustain their efforts by creating a strong support network to share their burdens and challenges, at least emotionally. Your closest circle of friends, your family, your fellow teachers, counselors, custodians, and secretaries can all be important sources of support, offering a refreshingly different perspective, advice rooted in experience, and some insight into students you might be struggling with.

In addition, in the company of fellow teachers, crucial yet often tedious tasks such as grading and planning can become enjoyable and even energizing. Josh Biber describes the energy he derived from friends as an award-winning teacher in Phoenix:

> I distinctly remember one particular meeting in the fall of my second year. It was a Thursday night, and several of the fifth-grade teachers in the Phoenix Valley got together to work on how to incorporate more kinesthetic games and activities into math instruction. . . . We would get together almost monthly to collaborate, work together, do potluck, and generally have a good time. But something about this night struck me, as when 10:00 P.M. came around, there we all were, still together after three hours, more deeply engaged in the details and minutia of Coordinate Geometry Battleship than people our age should ever be. At one point, some good-natured debate over the merits of competing fraction games got pretty heated. And at that moment, in what felt like a mini-epiphany, I said to myself: "It's Thursday night at 10:00 P.M. . . . I can't be positive what all of my friends who took jobs on Wall Street are out doing right now, but I can pretty much guarantee it is as far from Math Bingo as you can get. And it turns out there is nowhere else I'd rather be, no one else I'd rather be doing it with, and without question, nothing else I would rather be working toward than this. In fact, this is exactly the kind of young adult I hoped I would turn out to be, and this is exactly the community I only dreamed I could be a part of—enthusiastically bonded together at ten o'clock on a Thursday night to improve the learning of our kids."

> There was truly never a day that went by that I didn't turn to my fellow teachers at my school, at my apartment, or in my community for the personal and professional support I needed. Next to my students, there was nothing that did more to sustain my energy than teachers around me. They are the best friends and most inspiring people I have ever known. "

## Taking Care of Yourself—For You and Your Students

In his best-selling book *Seven Habits of Highly Effective People*, Stephen Covey says that individuals who are most effective in whatever they set out to do are those who tend to their physical, mental, social/emotional, and spiritual health.[9] This idea certainly seems true for highly effective teachers.

Rachel Meiklejohn, a sixth-grade teacher in New Mexico, shared her own realization that she was going to have to step back and take care of herself if she were going to be able to support her students all year:

> My first few months as a teacher I worked hard! I felt as if I was eating, sleeping, dreaming, and breathing teaching; despite all this effort, I felt as if I was failing. My life experiences up to that point had taught me that if I just worked hard enough, I would be successful. As a teacher, however, I discovered that this strategy had its flaws. There was always one more poster I could be making, one more paper to grade, and so I drove myself to do more and more. As long as I was exerting every ounce of myself into planning and creating, I didn't feel guilty for failing to create an effective classroom because I was doing everything within my power to reach that goal. It was an eye-opening experience to realize that if I took time away from my work, not only was I happier and more balanced, and therefore better able to deal with problems that arose, but that I was able to reflect and prioritize and therefore work more efficiently. "

For some teachers, time away from work means just that. They commit to certain hours or days that are not for school-related work. For Washington, D.C., high school math teacher John London, those hours are at home each evening. "The best part about restricting my work time was that it made me more effective," he said. "The time that I did spend at school was more purposeful, and it started a cycle where I pushed myself to become more efficient."

Sixth-grade teacher Laura Powers recalls that in the middle of her first year, she was so tired she could sleep standing up even though she was working every waking hour. She decided she had to make changes, starting with taking care of herself. She joined a gym, ate healthier food, and set aside time to read books for her own pleasure instead of just for school:

> Once I took more time for my personal life, I began to see a huge impact in my classroom. My scholars started to see my increased energy, and that helped them increase their on-task behavior during all parts of my lessons. In addition, taking time for myself gave me the energy to plan better using backward design and to create well-thought-out

units for my students. By the end of my first year, all of my students met our class goal of improving their reading by 1.5 years, and a few even exceeded that goal. It was phenomenal. I owe a lot of that to the strategic planning of my days on both a professional level and a personal level. ,,

Rather than just carving out free time, other teachers commit to some particular activity, whether that is running, reading, time with friends, housework, a certain number of hours of sleep, or just getting more out of their cable subscription. This strategy requires that we know ourselves in a couple of important ways. First, the teachers who are best equipped to address their physical, mental, emotional, and spiritual health are those who recognize in themselves the early signs of discouragement, exhaustion, and resentment that signal the need to take care of themselves. Second, these teachers are self-aware enough to know what interests and activities are personally energizing and fulfilling and will therefore increase their well-being. With this combination of self-knowledge, we can diagnose and take care of our own needs in ways that are beneficial to us and our students.

Of course, everyone's indicators and relievers of stress are unique. For some, early signs of stress are headaches, foggy thought, or disorganization. A number of teachers told us they could tell they needed a break when they felt themselves becoming curt and impatient with their students. The list of examples of refreshing activities is equally varied. Kickball, trivia nights, coffee shops, journals, and blogs are all ways that teachers have said they reenergize themselves and refocus.

It is something of a paradox that ensuring you have the energy to best serve your students often means *adding* to your to-do list, not reducing it. While all of these teachers describe ways in which they work on efficiency and prioritization in their school activities, almost all of them also indicate that doing less related to school may not be the best way to address stress, discouragement, and exhaustion. Instead, they suggest thinking about what other priorities you should have in your life and fulfilling those. This may help limit schoolwork time or make it more efficient.

A recent study verifies that managing energy, not time, is the key to increased productivity.[10] In that research, various groups of hard-charging executives were trained in energy-increasing practices and instructed to use those methods instead of working longer hours to get more done. "The core problem with working longer hours is that time is a finite resource. Energy is a different story," the study finds. People who pay attention to their physical, mental, emotional, and spiritual energy are more productive in fewer hours than people who do not.[11]

Thus, a counterintuitive idea—that if you do more, you can do more—pervades our conversations with highly effective teachers. The key is to know when you are headed for trouble and turn to the activities that fulfill your needs. As Sara Monti, a special education and English as a Second Language teacher in southern Louisiana, reminds us, the issue really is that simple:

> If you need to sleep, sleep. If you need some downtime, take it. If you find yourself taking more and more time to do simple things, stop. Reevaluate. Whatever you are doing, it's not working. "Working relentlessly" means that you take ownership of the difficult process that is teaching to close the achievement gap, and a part of that is understanding that your hard work is measured in results, not hours on the clock.

## Becoming Comfortable with Your Relationship to Your Students and Community

Few endeavors are as exhausting as trying to be someone you are not. And when we are unsure or uncomfortable with our own identity among our colleagues and community, those dynamics can be distracting and draining. Highly effective teachers recognize that their ability to be effective with their students over the long haul requires reflecting on who they are as teachers, as members of the school community, and as individuals.

First-grade teacher Susan Asiyanbi, an African American woman teaching African American students, recalls expecting their shared racial and socioeconomic experiences would allow her to assimilate easily into the school and community culture. She found she needed to think about who she was from her students' perspective to fully embrace her new role:

> I had students and colleagues questioning why I was teaching in their neighborhood. I tried to explain my similar circumstance to what they were experiencing; yet they were hesitant to believe me. They mentioned how the language I spoke was proper, my style of dress was different, and how each and every day I drove in my car to another neighborhood that I called home. This was very disappointing to me, but it made me realize how important it was for me to recognize the privilege I was bringing to the classroom. Although I was a minority, I had gone to college and had amassed certain experiences that were not common to my students or their families. My perspective had completely changed. I was the same as my students in terms of skin color, but our experiences were different based on the academic freedom I had the opportunity to explore. I had to approach the situation differently. I had to approach my school community more humbly, acknowledging my privilege while expressing (through my actions) my purpose for teaching: giving my students the same opportunities I was lucky enough to receive so that they too have choices and a voice for their own life experiences.

By thinking about and understanding who she is, independent of and in relationship to her students, Ms. Asiyanbi established a sustainable mental and emotional foundation for the hard work it would take to achieve student success. Another exceptional teacher, Justin May, was similarly reflective about his own identity and relationship to his students and community, a process that was necessary for him to fully commit himself to his students' needs and growth. Mr. May, a white teacher of predominantly African American students, began his career in one of New Orleans's most impoverished neighborhoods:

" The first step to being a successful teacher in a high-poverty community is being okay with yourself. You have to be comfortable in your environment, and that can be challenging when you're a young teacher working in a setting that's entirely different from what you've experienced before in terms of people's race, culture, and background. You have to be comfortable with your differences. Kids are incredibly perceptive. They're watching you in every situation like a hawk—watching you walk down the hall, interact with colleagues, everything you do. If you're not comfortable, they see right through it.

I got comfortable by talking to a lot of colleagues, just sitting in their classrooms and talking to them. I observed other teachers as much as I could. I walked students home in the projects when I needed to connect with their families. I read about how New Orleans came about and how my students' housing projects came about. I reflected constantly.

Over time, I gradually became comfortable being a privileged white guy from Alaska teaching in an impoverished, predominantly black community in New Orleans. As I developed an understanding of the context I was in, my righteous indignation continued, but it abated, and something more powerful emerged: a love for my students and my situation. If you don't first do all of this, you can't operate in any rational way with your students. I learned that without this type of reconciliation, I was prone to working through my personal and professional insecurities in the classroom, and you're not likely to accomplish much if you do that. "

### Harnessing Inspiration and Outrage

"Remember why you are here" is another mantra of highly effective teachers who sustain their intense efforts over time. These teachers are inspired and energized by their students and consciously tap into those sources of energy to sustain their efforts.

Ellen Davis, who taught second grade on the Salt River Reservation in Arizona and whose students started the year reading on kindergarten and first-grade levels but ended the year reading on a third-grade level, is a master of these self-motivational techniques. By loving her students, she drew energy from their needs and success: "I'm so excited to see some of my students who were grumbling at the beginning of last year about how much they hated school come up to me and tell me about what they just learned in math or what they're reading," she says. "For me it might come out as, 'Give me a hug, you're doing long division!' . . . The key for me is that I'm invested in my students, I'm invested in my school, and I'm invested in how they do."

A close corollary to drawing energy from our students' potential is the energizing outrage over how educational inequity affects students' lives. Ryan Hill, a sixth-grade teacher in New York, found that it was the students who were most behind who "keep [him] working late at night and get [him] up early in the morning." For Janis Ortega, whose third graders were recent immigrants, the challenges her students' families faced to come to this country was a great motivator.

Ms. Davis, the teacher from the Salt River Reservation in Arizona, described for us ways in which she consciously stokes her outrage so as to maintain her focus and energy on the long road to academic achievement. First, she makes an effort to know the relevant statistics about her students. When she learned that two out of three of the students in her district typically would not graduate from high school in four years, she was ready to redouble her efforts. "I hear so much from parents who want really great things for their kids and wish that they had had more opportunities," she says, "and I know that it's my job to help make that happen."

To drive home the outrageousness of those statistics, Ms. Davis, like many other highly effective teachers, also makes "excellent school visits," to see what students in higher-income neighborhoods in well-resourced schools are achieving. She uses those beacons of achievement to guide and invigorate her expectations for her students. "What struck me the most was that my kids could do what [the children in the excellent school] were doing," she says, "and they shouldn't have to be able to pay twenty thousand dollars a year to get that opportunity. I really know that my kids can do everything, and if I have to work hard to ensure that they get the same opportunities as students in a high-income area, I will make it happen."

# Conclusion: Key Ideas and Next Questions

The Teaching As Leadership rubric (see Appendix A) describes three specific teacher actions that indicate a teacher is working relentlessly. Highly effective teachers:

> W-1: Persist in the face of considerable challenges
>
> W-2: Pursue and secure additional instructional time and resources
>
> W-3: Sustain the intense energy necessary to reach the ambitious big goals

## Key Ideas

In our studies of teachers whose students have and have not made exceptional academic progress, we have seen many less effective teachers working extremely hard. They are working long hours, pouring energy into their classroom and students, and yet they do not have dramatic results.

Working relentlessly is not the same as working hard; rather, it is a particular kind of working hard. As indicated in this chapter, working relentlessly is working hard in the ways that ensure you achieve your goal. In the following table, we have captured some of the insights we have received from highly effective teachers about how they distinguish working relentlessly from working hard:

| Highly Effective Teachers | Less Effective Teachers |
| --- | --- |
| Do what it takes to reach students' goals | Indiscriminately do everything they can think of that *might* contribute to reaching students' goals |
| Find hard work satisfying and fulfilling because efforts are so tied to results | Find hard work exhausting and disheartening because they cannot see their impact |
| Prioritize and choose the challenges they take on | Try to tackle everything at once |
| Judge the value of their effort by its impact on student progress | Judge the value of their effort by the number of hours they work |
| Sustain their effort for the long haul by staying healthy (mentally, emotionally, physically, spiritually) | Sacrifice their life outside school to the point that it becomes counterproductive for students |
| Recognize that their impact is greater when they collaborate with others | Misinterpret "taking responsibility" as "must do this alone" |
| Are not deterred by obstacles to achieving academic gains | Lose heart when they encounter obstacles |

If there is one idea you take away from this chapter, let it be that you control your and your students' success. That core tenet is the well from which all of the elements of working relentlessly spring. Teachers who understand their power to determine students' success or failure will go on to:

- Work through, around, and past obstacles
- Maintain high expectations, even in the face of students' significant needs and burdens
- Expand the time and resources available for student learning
- Expand their influence in order to decrease burdens and increase opportunities for student learning
- Sustain their efforts over time

 teachingasleadership.org

More guidance on working relentlessly is also available online, including:

- Additional indicators of working relentlessly
- Annotated examples of effective efforts in the face of challenges
- Pitfalls that often trip up new teachers as they attempt to work relentlessly
- Highly effective teachers' testimonies about the power of big goals in their classrooms

## Next Questions

With these foundational mindsets and actions, a teacher is ready to consider a range of questions whose answers will benefit their students, including these:

- Of the challenges facing us, which ones are most significantly holding students back from achieving the big goal?
- Which challenges are most within my control?
- What time and resource constraints are most holding us back, and how can I address them?
- What energizes me?
- How can I collaborate with my colleagues to increase the benefits for students?
- Do I have an adequate support system to sustain my efforts?

At its core, the notion of working relentlessly is not a list of things you do, but a mindset you bring to everything you do. Working relentlessly involves an unshakable conviction that you are in control of and responsible for your students' success or failure. Teachers who approach their classroom leadership with that resolve act as great leaders would in any challenging context, demonstrating "ferocious resolve, an almost stoic determination to do whatever needs to be done."[12]

## "YOU ARE GOING TO BE TOTALLY HANDSOME IN THEM."

 teachingasleadership.org

*An excerpt from Ms. Lora's Story, a case study in Teaching As Leadership, available online at www.teachingasleadership.org.*

"I already talked to her. She knows you're coming."

Ms. Lora wasn't sure whether the embarrassment of accepting the generous donation from his church or wearing the generous donation on his face was the affront to his pride, but Anthony was reluctant to meet with the nurse about his new glasses.

Ms. Lora leaned down over his desk, close to Anthony's ear, and said quietly, "Anthony, you're going to be amazed. These glasses are going to help you learn faster. Your bar graphs are going to jump up. I can't believe we didn't figure this out earlier."

Ms. Lora had always noticed Anthony leaned way over his paper to read and write, but in the last month or so, she had noticed him squinting at the PowerPoint slides and at the chalkboard more and more. When the nurse reported to her how badly Anthony needed glasses, she was temporarily furious at the principal and Mrs. Franklin for keeping Anthony locked away in the third-grade Success For All group. Ms. Lora would have noticed earlier if Anthony had been in her group.

After that initial reaction, Ms. Lora quickly shifted that blame to herself. She should have noticed Anthony needed glasses.

"And," Ms. Lora added in a hushed whisper, "you are going to be totally handsome in them." She waited a moment and then asked, "Anthony, do you want to take Cliff with you?"

Anthony nodded and slid out of his chair. Cliff, who had been sitting in the next desk unapologetically listening to their conversation, stood up too. Without speaking, the two boys walked out of the room.

# CONCLUSION

**EDUCATION CAN AND SHOULD BE** a great equalizer, a means of upward mobility for all children regardless of race, socioeconomic status, and geography. And yet the most accurate predictors of student achievement and opportunity in our society are often where a child is born, the color of a child's skin, or the yearly income of a child's family. Our system of education undermines, suppresses, and denies the potential of millions of children living in poverty.

This educational inequity is an affront to our most cherished ideals of equality and freedom. There is little equality in preparing our upper-middle-class and white children for higher education and occupational choices while instead providing children of color in low-income communities weak basic skills, vocational education, and a shot at a GED. There is little freedom for children in low-income communities who are graduating from high school without the prerequisites—not to mention the knowledge and skills—to even apply for college and who have only the narrowest spectrum of choice about their careers. Living up to our ideal as a land of opportunity means we all have a level playing field, regardless of our race, socioeconomic status, and background.

Because it erodes our ideals, the achievement gap is a threat to national security that rivals even the most dangerous and frightening threats from abroad. Our health and longevity as a democratic society are weakened when generations of children are pushed through and out of our education system without even the most basic ability to read, write, do math, and think critically. America has the largest prison population in the world,[1] at once a symptom of educational inequity and a warning of where it will lead us.

One recent study determined that the achievement gap between low-income students and their higher-income peers costs the country approximately $500 billion each year.[2] The United States currently ranks near the bottom of industrialized nations in international benchmarks, particularly in math and science. This international achievement gap costs the country as much as $2 trillion dollars each year. These achievement gaps create the "economic equivalent of a permanent national recession."[3]

The achievement gap's costs—to our human capital, national security, economic potential, and most cherished ideals—make it our nation's most pressing problem and greatest injustice.

Even as they recognize these dire realities, the highly effective teachers who every day are fighting the injustice of the achievement gap—the very individuals who are closest to this problem—insist that we can fix it. You have met in this book a small sampling of the thousands of teachers who believe, and prove, that the achievement gap is merely a temporary injustice. As simple as it sounds, these teachers believe that educational equity will be reached because they know the potential of their students to succeed.

For these teachers, educational equity is certainly about living up to our ideals and strengthening our democracy, but it is even more centrally about a first grader who started the year struggling with letter sounds and ended the year reading books by herself. It is about a classroom of sixth graders who started the year writing sentence fragments about how old they will be when they drop out of school and ended the year writing paragraphs about their determination to work hard enough to attend college. It is about high school juniors who start the year never having heard of the ACT or the SAT and end the year having convinced their principal to create a college admissions exam prep class to study word roots, deductive reasoning, and test-taking skills so that they can compete with students who are paying to take those courses. For these teachers, the quest for educational equity is most centrally about real children facing heavy burdens who are making extraordinary progress. Highly effective teachers and their hard-working students have shown us that ending educational inequity is possible.

These teachers' success forces us to ask ourselves some important questions. When we see students excelling in classrooms across the country in high-poverty schools, how can we accept the prevailing view that these students' successes are nothing more than heart-warming exceptions to the inviolable reality of the achievement gap? When we can point to more and more examples of high-performing classrooms of students of color living in low-income communities, how can we accept that only half of students in low-income communities graduate from high school on time,[4] that those who do will graduate with eighth-grade skills,[5] and that only one in ten students from low-income communities graduates from college?[6]

When we see teachers leading their students to dramatic academic progress, how can we learn from and emulate their actions to accelerate students' learning and broaden students' opportunity?

Today, thanks to the hard work of thousands of teachers within and outside Teach For America leading their students to extraordinary achievement despite extraordinary challenges, we have answers to these questions. We do not have to accept that the achievement gap is just the way it is. We do not have to accept that children of color and children from low-income communities lag behind students in other communities. We do not have to tolerate a system that allows geography to predict children's life prospects. We do not have to wonder what it takes for our children to succeed.

Highly effective teachers are charting a path to success—a path to the life-altering academic achievement for our students that will end educational inequity for our society. Like successful leaders in any difficult context, these teachers are setting an audacious vision of their students' achievement and are investing, with all manner of creative strategies, students—and students' families—in working extraordinarily hard to reach that vision. They are planning their course through challenges large and small by asking where they and their students want to end up, how they will know they have made it, and how they will most efficiently get there. And even as their students reap the benefits of those purposeful plans, these highly effective teachers are maximizing student learning by making informed adjustments to their plans in response to changing realities. These teachers are reflecting constantly on their students' progress and their own actions to seek out ways to increase their effectiveness. Inspired by the high stakes of their hard work, these highly effective teachers bring to all their efforts a relentless persistence, a determination to do whatever it takes to navigate and overcome seemingly insurmountable challenges to fulfill their students' potential.

Like the teachers you met in this book, you can employ these principles to accelerate your students' learning beyond what many people—including, perhaps, your students themselves—believe is possible. Like the teachers you met in this book, you can become an agent of change in the quest for educational equity. Like the teachers you met in this book, you can prove in your classroom with your students that the achievement gap can and will end.

Of course, knowing what success requires makes our task clearer but no easier. As you have seen in these pages, attaining dramatic academic success for students who are facing all the burdens of poverty is hard work—work that inevitably involves setbacks and failures along the way. And yet the rewards for that hard work could not be greater, for us or for our students.

Your hard work can overcome the dire statistics that predict your students' failure. Your leadership can inspire dramatic academic achievement by your students. With the path to success clearer than ever before and with the stakes for our students higher than ever before, you have the opportunity to close the achievement gap and change the course of your students' lives.

# AFTERWORD

# TEACHING AS LEADERSHIP AND THE MOVEMENT FOR EDUCATIONAL EQUITY

**WHETHER YOU ARE PART OF** Teach For America or not, if you are endeavoring to ensure that students in low-income communities achieve at high levels, your work is at the core of the most important movement in our nation today: the movement to ensure that one day, all of our children, regardless of where they are born, have the opportunity to attain an excellent education.

The problem of educational inequity is exceedingly complex. It begins outside the walls of our schoolhouses, because while children in low-income communities have the same potential as their high-income peers, they face many extra challenges. For example, because they grow up in poverty, they may not have adequate health care or nutrition, access to high-quality preschool programs, and adequate housing. Moreover, because children in low-income communities are disproportionately children of color, they are more likely to encounter the effects of societal low expectations and discrimination.

We have not given our schools and districts the extra capacity necessary to help students overcome these extra challenges. They need additional teachers and leaders who deeply believe that low-income children and children of color can achieve at high levels. Among other things, they need more hours in the school day so that students who start out behind catch up, and they need more high-quality enrichment opportunities like those that exist in higher-income areas.

The socioeconomic inequities and the lack of capacity in our schools persist because our prevailing ideology has not led to the necessary policies and investments. Among other things, we are hampered by societal beliefs that schools cannot make a significant difference in the face of socioeconomic disparities, that children in low-income communities cannot meet high expectations, and that it is not efficacious to invest in mitigating the challenges of poverty that make it hard for students to focus on school.

For children growing up in this vortex of challenges, the best hope is to encounter enough teachers who are willing to go beyond traditional expectations to compensate for the weaknesses of the system, meet their needs, and ensure they have the opportunities they deserve. At the same time, to ultimately address this problem in a sustainable and comprehensive way will require more than increasing the supply of extraordinary teachers. It will require stepping back and getting at the root causes of the problem. We need to take some of the pressures off schools by improving economies in urban and rural areas, improving the quality of health and social services, and increasing access to high-quality early education, among other things. And as long as socioeconomic disparities persist, we need to build extra capacity into schools in underresourced areas so that they can meet their students' extra needs.

As we at Teach For America consider what it will take to effect such systemic, far-reaching changes, we have come to believe that our best hope is to reach the point where leaders at every level of our education system, at every level of policy, and across all our professional sectors believe deeply that educational inequity is a solvable problem, feel a sense of personal responsibility for solving it, and possess a grounded understanding of the problem and its solutions in all their complexity. These are the perspectives that come from teaching successfully in low-income communities. We will solve educational inequity once we reach the point where our schools, policies, and investments are shaped by people who have this experience and the convictions and insights that come from leading children to fulfill their potential.

Alongside many others who are working toward the same ends, Teach For America is working to build the movement to eliminate educational inequity by enlisting our nation's most promising future leaders in the effort. By recruiting and developing outstanding, diverse recent college graduates of all academic disciplines and career interests to commit two years to teach in urban and rural public schools, we provide one more critical source of teachers who have the potential to have a significant impact on their students' academic and life trajectories. In the process, we increase the visible examples of student success, thus influencing the prevailing ideology by demonstrating that children in low-income communities and children of color can achieve at high levels. Simultaneously we build a growing force of alumni who work as lifelong leaders in the classroom, in education more broadly, and across all sectors to minimize the extra challenges facing children growing up in low-income communities, build the capacity of schools and school systems, and change the prevailing ideology through their examples and their advocacy.

As we have considered how to build a truly effective movement, we know that the central priority must be to reach the point where many more teachers are effecting the kind of academic progress that can change life trajectories. This is what is important for children growing up today, and it is also foundational for a movement that aims ultimately to address the root causes of the problem so that committed teachers can ensure the success of their students without going to the superhuman ends it can sometimes take to ensure student success in today's system.

# Sharing Teach For America's Work While Pioneering New Frontiers

While we have much more to learn about excellent teaching in our context and are eager to continue to evolve our program for training and developing teachers, every day we are asked by other teachers, school district administrators, and teacher educators to share our knowledge base with the broader community of educators who are working so hard to close the achievement gap. With full acknowledgment that this is a work in progress, this book is an effort to respond to that request.

In the coming months and years, we intend to advance our knowledge base in a number of ways. First, we will refine how we measure success. Our significant gains measurement system (see Appendix D) has helped us to support goal setting and learning at the classroom and organization-wide levels. However, given that we are working in so many different school systems and across every grade level and subject area, and given our lack of control over local standards and assessments, measuring student achievement effectively across our system remains a huge challenge. As this book goes to press, we are in the latter stages of designing an approach to student achievement measurement that is more closely tailored to our teachers' local contexts and should give teachers better tools for understanding and meeting their students' needs while giving our organization a clearer view of our teachers' impact on student learning.

Second, we continue to test the validity of the Teaching As Leadership framework and rubric as a predictor of student academic achievement. While our own marriage of student achievement data and Teaching As Leadership rubric data indicates that better teacher performance on the rubric correlates to greater gains from students, we aspire to a much more comprehensive understanding of the particular teacher actions, and combinations of teacher actions, that most influence student learning. To that end, we are embarking on two studies that we expect may validate and challenge aspects of our Teaching As Leadership model. In partnership with the Gates Foundation and researcher Thomas Kane, we are collecting evidence for a large number of teachers that will allow outside raters to assess teachers on the Teaching As Leadership rubric (and on a small number of other well-regarded rubrics). We are evaluating and contrasting the predictive power of all of these teacher performance rubrics as a way to learn about what makes an effective teacher. Also, with consultation from Jim Collins, author of best-selling business books including *Good to Great*, we are undertaking an intensive matched-pair comparison study of corps members. We will follow a large number of pairs of teachers matched on important placement variables, including school, subject, and grade level. Where we have two teachers who have had the same training and support but are achieving different results, we are taking a broad, all-encompassing look at the similarities and differences in those two teachers' mindsets, actions, and knowledge.

Third, we are continuing to learn more about the role of diversity competencies in the success of highly effective teachers of children of color in low-income communities, as well as about how to build those skills in new teachers more effectively. As indicated in this book, we have been exploring with interviews, surveys, and observations how teachers work across lines of difference for the benefit of their students. Given the complexities of these dynamics, we expect we will continue to rely heavily on the research and insight of scholars working on issues of race and class in the classroom, and we also hope to contribute our own experiences to these conversations.

Fourth, many highly effective teachers are focused not only on building students' academic knowledge and skills but also on developing the character traits in their students that are important to leading successful, fulfilling lives—traits like confidence, resilience, perseverance, and a love of learning. Like our teachers, our organization is exploring whether there are ways to define and measure those important ideas, and we are looking forward to benefiting from others' ongoing research in this realm.

## Equity Within Reach

As Teach For America reaches the end of two decades in this work, I am more optimistic than ever before about the possibility of making meaningful progress against the problem of educational inequity.

My senior year in college, the year that I dreamed up the idea for Teach For America, the movie *Stand and Deliver* made Jaime Escalante a national hero for his work in coaching students in South Central Los Angeles to pass the Advanced Placement calculus exam. His leadership was extraordinary and his results inspiring. At the same time, national interest in his story also stemmed from our collective surprise that a teacher could get kids in a high-poverty community to excel at that level. This idea was, after all, so stunning that Hollywood made a movie about that teacher, the movie became a hit, and the Educational Testing Service questioned the test results that created the drama in the movie in the first place. Today we know that Escalante's example, while worthy of great acclaim, is not so stunning. Today we know that even first- and second-year teachers are proving that students in low-income communities excel on an absolute scale when given the opportunities they deserve.

Just as visible examples of dramatically successful teachers in urban and rural areas were rare twenty years ago, we could have counted on one hand the number of schools in high-poverty communities that were putting whole buildings full of children on track to graduating from college at the same rate as children in high-income communities. Yet today, thanks largely to the pioneering efforts of educators who had a dramatic impact on their students while teaching in traditional urban and rural public schools, dozens of communities have schools that are putting hundreds of low-income students at a time on the path to graduating from college at the same rate as students in high-income communities, and many have growing numbers of such schools.

In the two decades we have been at this, sadly the national data have not yet shown significant progress in moving the needle against the problem we are addressing. And yet the question has changed. Today we no longer ask, "Can we do this?" but rather, "Can we do this at scale?" Can we ensure that not just a few classrooms and schools full of kids, but all of our children in urban and rural areas, have the opportunities they deserve?

Every day I gain more conviction that the answer is yes. In recent years, we have seen real evidence of the possibility of systemwide change. In certain communities across the country—large cities like New Orleans, New York City, and Washington, D.C., and rural communities such as the Mississippi Delta and the Rio Grande Valley—we are starting to see significant progress based on system-level data. We are seeing that enough committed leadership at the school, district, school board, and community levels can come together to produce significant, measurable results for thousands of students at a time. Wherever we see such progress, we see leaders at the core of the effort whose experience teaching successfully in low-income communities has given them the beliefs, skills, and knowledge necessary to do the right thing for children.

We know today that our vision of all children in this nation having an excellent education can be more than an idealistic notion. What we have seen over the past two decades is that educational inequity becomes solvable in the hands of committed leaders who assume responsibility for student success and will do whatever it takes to achieve it. That reality brings us back once again to this effort to understand deeply how the most successful teachers in low-income communities are achieving that success and to help incoming teachers climb up those challenging learning curves more quickly. This pursuit is critical for the futures of students growing up today, and it will also fuel the success of the long-term movement to effect fundamental change.

To those readers who are teachers and future teachers, I wish you the very best, for the sake of the students you will reach and the lessons you will learn, and also for the lessons we can all learn from you over time. Your success, and the innovations you pioneer, can help build an unstoppable movement to ensure educational opportunity for all.

WENDY KOPP
CEO and Founder of Teach For America

# APPENDIX A

# TEACHING AS LEADERSHIP RUBRIC

**EACH CHAPTER OF THIS BOOK** describes a leadership principle that distinguishes highly effective teachers in low-income communities. We call the framework created by these six general strategies Teaching As Leadership.

The comprehensive Teaching As Leadership rubric in this appendix (and available online) expands on these six general strategies, drilling down to a more granular level. The rubric lists specific teacher actions associated with each leadership principle. Each principle is represented by as many as six specific teacher actions, the same teacher actions highlighted at the end of each chapter of this book. Those teacher actions are organized as follows:

| Set big goals | B-1: Develop standards-aligned, measurable, ambitious, and feasible goals that will dramatically increase students' opportunities in life. |
|---|---|
| Invest students and others | I-1: Develop students' rational understanding that they can achieve by working hard ("I can") through evidence of students' own progress, statistics, explicit discussions of malleable intelligence, creative marketing, leveraging the big goals, etc. |
| | I-2: Develop students' rational understanding that they will benefit from achievement ("I want") through connections between class achievement and their lives and aspirations, statistics, creative marketing, leveraging the big goals, etc. |
| | I-3: Employ appropriate role models so that students identify with people who work hard toward achievement ("I can") and value academic achievement ("I want"). |
| | I-4: Consistently reinforce academic efforts toward the big goals (e.g., through praise and public recognition of success, extrinsic rewards and competition, cooperation, student-teacher relationships, etc.) even while increasing long-term investment in hard work and the big goals. |
| | I-5: Create a welcoming environment through rational persuasion, role models, and constant reinforcement and marketing to instill values (e.g., respect, tolerance, kindness, collaboration) so that students feel comfortable and supported enough to take the risks of striving for the big goals. |
| | I-6: Respectfully mobilize students' influencers (e.g., family, peers, coach, pastor, etc.) using techniques such as direct explanation, role models, modeling, constant reinforcement and marketing, etc., so that they actively invest students in working hard toward the big goals. |

| | |
|---|---|
| **Plan purposefully** | P-1: Create or obtain standards-aligned diagnostic, formative, and summative assessments (with tracking and grading systems) to determine where students are against big goals. |
| | P-2: Backwards-plan by breaking down longer-term goals into bundles of objectives and mapping them across the school year (in a long-term plan and unit plans). |
| | P-3: Create rigorous, objective-driven lesson plans so that students who complete class activities successfully will have mastered the objectives and made progress toward the big goals. |
| | P-4: Differentiate plans for individual students based on their unique learning profiles (including ongoing performance data) so that all students are engaged and challenged. |
| | P-5: Establish age-appropriate long- and short-term behavioral management plans (rules and consequences) so that, if students comply, the amount and value of instructional time is maximized. |
| | P-6: Design classroom procedures (for transitions, collecting and handing out papers, taking roll, etc.) that provide structure to students and maximize the amount and value of instructional time. |
| **Execute effectively** | E-1: Clearly present academic content (in differentiated ways, if necessary) so that students comprehend key information and ideas. |
| | E-2: Facilitate, manage, and coordinate student academic practice (in differentiated ways, if necessary) so that all students are participating and have the opportunity to gain mastery of the objectives. |
| | E-3: Check for academic understanding frequently by questioning, listening, and/or observing, and provide feedback (that affirms right answers and corrects wrong answers), in order to ensure student learning. |
| | E-4: Communicate high expectations for behavior by teaching, practicing, and reinforcing rules and consequences so that students are focused on working hard. |
| | E-5: Implement and practice time-saving procedures (for transitions, dissemination and collection of supplies or homework, etc.) to maximize time spent on learning. |
| | E-6: Evaluate and keep track of students' performance on assessments so that the teacher and students are aware of students' progress on academic, behavioral, and investment goals. |
| **Continuously increase effectiveness** | C-1: Gauge progress and notable gap(s) between student achievement and big goals by examining assessment data. |
| | C-2: Identify student habits or actions most influencing progress and gaps between student achievement and big goals. |
| | C-3: Isolate the teacher actions most contributing to key aspects of student performance by gathering data (e.g., using the TAL rubric) and reflecting on teacher performance. |
| | C-4: Identify the underlying factors (e.g., knowledge, skill, mindset) causing teacher actions. |
| | C-5: Access meaningful learning experiences that direct and inform teacher improvement. |
| | C-6: After a cycle of data collection, reflection, and learning, adjust course (of big goals, investment strategies, planning, execution, and/or relentlessness), as necessary, to maximize effectiveness. |

| Work relentlessly | W-1: Persist in the face of considerable challenges, focusing effort on the ultimate goal and targeting those challenges one can impact to increase student achievement. |
|---|---|
| | W-2: Pursue and secure additional instructional time and resources in order to increase opportunities for student learning. |
| | W-3: Sustain the intense energy necessary to reach the ambitious big goals through a variety of strategies. |

In addition to describing these specific teacher actions with which teachers embody the Teaching As Leadership principles, the rubric describes concrete indicators for five levels of proficiency on each of the twenty-eight teacher actions.[1] These proficiencies (found in the different columns of the rubric) aim to capture the difference between learning how to "follow the rules" of a given behavior or action and adjusting or transferring those rules to fit one's circumstances. The general themes you will see in the five columns of the rubric are as follows:

| Prenovice | Novice | Beginning Proficiency | Advanced Proficiency | Exemplary |
|---|---|---|---|---|
| No attempt of the action, though an attempt is warranted | An unsuccessful attempt of the teacher action | Technically performing the action | Internalizing the purpose of the action and, as a result, adjusting the action to the situation | Innovating as necessary to realize the full potential of the action in unique contexts |

The Teaching As Leadership rubric is meant to offer an objective and absolute measure of teacher performance, without regard to the teacher's level of experience. It is built with asset-based language; that is, each rubric cell specifies what skills should be present, as opposed to what skills might be missing from the teacher's performance. In this way, the rubric seeks to celebrate even the early progress that all teachers experience as they evolve and grow.

The ultimate goal of the rubric is to help teachers, working on their own or with a supportive mentor, to progress to increasingly higher proficiency levels that we believe correlate with greater student achievement.

Every aspect of the Teaching As Leadership framework, including the rubric, is continuing to evolve with Teach For America's increasing understanding of what it takes for teachers to succeed for our students.

This rubric is also the intellectual architecture for—and is available through—the online resources at this book's companion Web site: www.teachingasleadership.org.

# Teaching As Leadership Comprehensive Rubric

- Set big goals
- Invest students, families, and other influencers in working hard to achieve big goals
- Plan purposefully
- Execute effectively
- Continuously increase effectiveness
- Work relentlessly

## Set Big Goals

The classroom has a justifiably ambitious academic destination toward which all efforts can clearly point.

| Teacher Action | Prenovice | Novice | Beginning Proficiency | Advanced Proficiency | Exemplary |
|---|---|---|---|---|---|
| **B-1**<br><br>**Develop standards-aligned, measurable, ambitious, and feasible goals that will dramatically increase students' opportunities in life.** | Shows a lack of attempt or action | *In action . . .*<br>Demonstrates **attempt** to set or adopt big goals according to the criteria<br><br>*In reflection . . . .*<br>Accurately explains the main ideas behind big goals, including relationship to standards, measurability, and criteria for ambitiousness and feasibility<br><br>Describes in a compelling way why it is important to set big goals, particularly according to the criteria | • Adopts a broad, generic goal that aspires to be ambitious and feasible for the entire class and achieves that balance for at least half of the teacher's students<br><br>• Describes how the goal is aligned to key standards and identifies a **basic tool of measuring achievement of the goal** | • Designs a goal that is both ambitious and feasible for most students, based on reasoning informed by multiple sources, including diagnostic results for mastery goals<br><br>• Describes how the goal is aligned to all key standards; explains **broadly** what students should know, understand, or be able to do in order to achieve the goal; and cites the **necessary** assessment tools (e.g., achievement tests, performance-based assessments, etc.) that will be **most meaningful to students' lives** when measuring the different facets of the goal | • Designs feasible, highly ambitious goals that require intense work from each and every student, based on reasoning informed by multiple sources, including diagnostic results for mastery goals<br><br>• Describes how the goal is aligned to all key standards, explains the **specific** and **prioritized** knowledge and skills that each student will need to master in order to reach the goal—including pre-requisites and cites a **specific set** of balanced measurement tools to measure different facets of the goal that will be **most meaningful to students' lives** |

## Invest Students, Families, and Other Influencers in Working Hard to Achieve Big Goals

Students build confidence and eagerness that leads them to work hard toward short- and long-term goals.

| Teacher Action | Prenovice | Novice | Beginning Proficiency | Advanced Proficiency | Exemplary |
|---|---|---|---|---|---|
| **I-1** <br><br> **Develop students' rational understanding that they can achieve by working hard ("I can")** through evidence of students' own progress, statistics, explicit discussions of malleable intelligence, creative marketing, leveraging the big goals, etc. | Shows a lack of attempt or action | *In action . . .* <br> Demonstrates **attempt** to develop students' rational understanding that they can achieve by working hard <br><br> *In reflection . . .* <br> Accurately explains strategies for developing students' rational understanding that they can achieve by working hard <br><br> Describes in a compelling way why it is important to develop students' belief that they can achieve by working hard | • Effectively uses the same **teacher-centered** strategies in all situations to convey **generic** messages that students can achieve by working hard <br><br> • Conveys messages and implements strategies **occasionally** and **in isolation** | • Effectively uses **student-centered** strategies (based on an understanding of students and depending on the situation) to reach a **range** of students to convey that students can achieve by working hard <br><br> • **Regularly** conveys messages and employs a series of **integrated** classroom strategies | • Effectively **considers individual students** and situations when choosing strategies and messages that convey that students can achieve by working hard <br><br> • **Monitors individual students'** "I can" investment levels, effectively conveys messages and employs strategies **as often as necessary,** enables students to **empower one another,** and initiates effective efforts to **shape the larger school context** |

| SET Big Goals | INVEST Students and Others | PLAN Purposefully | EXECUTE Effectively | CONTINUOUSLY INCREASE Effectiveness | WORK Relentlessly |
| --- | --- | --- | --- | --- | --- |
| **Teacher Action** | **Prenovice** | **Novice** | **Beginning Proficiency** | **Advanced Proficiency** | **Exemplary** |
| **I-2**<br><br>**Develop students' rational understanding that they will benefit from achievement ("I want") through connections between class achievement and their lives and aspirations, creative marketing, statistics, leveraging the big goals, etc.** | Shows a lack of attempt or action | *In action . . . .*<br>Demonstrates **attempt** to develop students' rational understanding that they will benefit from achievement<br><br>*In reflection . . . .*<br>Accurately explains key strategies for developing students' rational understanding that they will benefit from achievement<br><br>Describes in a compelling way why it is important to develop students' belief that they will benefit from achievement | • Effectively uses the same **teacher-centered** strategies in all situations to convey **generic** messages that students benefit from academic achievement<br><br>• Implements strategies in **isolation** and does so **occasionally** | • Effectively uses **student-centered** strategies (based on an understanding of students and depending on the situation) to reach a **range** of students to convey that students benefit from academic achievement<br><br>• Employs a series of **integrated** classroom strategies **regularly** | • Effectively **considers individual students** and situations when choosing strategies and messages that convey that students benefit from academic achievement<br><br>• **Monitors individual students'** "I want" investment levels, effectively conveys messages and employs strategies **as often as necessary**, enables students to **empower one another**, and initiates effective efforts to **shape the larger school context** |

| Teacher Action | INVEST Students and Others | | PLAN Purposefully | EXECUTE Effectively | CONTINUOUSLY INCREASE Effectiveness | WORK Relentlessly |
| --- | --- | --- | --- | --- | --- | --- |
| | Prenovice | Novice | Beginning Proficiency | Advanced Proficiency | Exemplary |  |

| Teacher Action | Prenovice | Novice | Beginning Proficiency | Advanced Proficiency | Exemplary |
| --- | --- | --- | --- | --- | --- |
| **I-3**<br><br>**Employ appropriate role models so that students identify with people who work hard toward achievement ("I can") and value academic achievement ("I want").** | Shows a lack of attempt or action | *In action . . .*<br>Demonstrates **attempt** to employ role models<br><br>*In reflection . . .*<br>Accurately explains how to select and use role models to convey messages of persistence or academic success<br><br>Describes in a compelling way why it is important to employ such role models | • Ensures that role models convey messages of persistence **or** academic success<br><br>• Enables students to learn role models' stories through **occasional** exposure<br><br>• Uses reasonably appropriate and relevant role models with whom **at least some** students can **identify** | • Ensures that role models convey messages of persistence **and** academic success<br><br>• Enables students to gain **frequent** and **meaningful** exposure to role models<br><br>• Ensures **almost all** students have appropriate role models with whom they **identify,** based on an understanding of student subgroups | • Ensures that role models convey messages of **extraordinary** persistence **and** academic success<br><br>• Generates opportunities for students to **work directly** with role models<br><br>• Monitors individual students and ensures **all** have effective role models with whom they **deeply identify** |

| SET<br>Big Goals | INVEST<br>Students and Others | PLAN<br>Purposefully | EXECUTE<br>Effectively | CONTINUOUSLY INCREASE<br>Effectiveness | WORK<br>Relentlessly |
|---|---|---|---|---|---|
| **Teacher Action** | Prenovice | Novice | Beginning Proficiency | Advanced Proficiency | Exemplary |
| **I-4**<br><br>Consistently reinforce academic efforts toward the big goals (e.g., through praise and public recognition of success, extrinsic rewards and competition, cooperation, student-teacher relationships, etc.) even while increasing long-term investment in hard work and the big goals. | Shows a lack of attempt or action | *In action . . . .*<br>Demonstrates **attempt** to reinforce efforts toward the big goals<br><br>*In reflection . . . .*<br>Accurately explains key strategies for consistently reinforcing efforts toward the big goals<br><br>Describes in a compelling way why it is important to consistently reinforce efforts toward the big goals | • Chooses a **small set of** sound reinforcements for **all** situations<br><br>• Reinforcement system recognizes **basic** academic effort (e.g., class participation, homework completion, etc.) and mastery of a well-defined, **absolute** bar<br><br>• Consistently provides reinforcement at **regular** intervals and **sometimes** conveys the meaning of the reinforcements as a celebration of progress toward the goals | • Chooses a **variety** of appealing reinforcements to reach a range of students, based on an understanding of students and **depending** on the situation<br><br>• Reinforcement system recognizes significant academic effort (e.g., studying hard and making incremental gains) and mastery of a well-defined, **absolute** bar<br><br>• Provides reinforcements appropriately and flexibly so they are delivered only at **purposeful** intervals and **almost always** conveys the meaning of the reinforcements as a celebration of progress toward the goals to maximize impact and lead to **intrinsic motivation** | • Chooses reinforcements based on the needs of **individual** students and situations<br><br>• Reinforcement system recognizes effort in **proportion** to students' individual accomplishments<br><br>• Provides reinforcements appropriately and flexibly so they are only delivered as **often as necessary** to supplement students' intrinsic motivation, **always** conveys the meaning of the reinforcements as a celebration of progress toward the goals, and teaches students how to **reinforce their own performance** |

| SET<br>Big Goals | INVEST<br>Students and Others | | PLAN<br>Purposefully | EXECUTE<br>Effectively | CONTINUOUSLY INCREASE<br>Effectiveness | WORK<br>Relentlessly |
|---|---|---|---|---|---|---|
| **Teacher Action** | **Prenovice** | **Novice** | **Beginning Proficiency** | **Advanced Proficiency** | **Exemplary** |

| **I-5**<br><br>Create a welcoming environment through rational persuasion, role models, and constant reinforcement and marketing to instill values (e.g., respect, tolerance, kindness, collaboration) so that students feel comfortable and supported enough to take the risks of striving for the big goals. | Shows a lack of attempt or action | *In action . . .*<br>Demonstrates **attempt** to create a welcoming environment<br><br>*In reflection . . .*<br>Accurately explains key strategies for creating a welcoming environment<br><br>Describes in a compelling way why it is important to create a welcoming environment | • Effectively chooses a range of **generic** messages to support a welcoming environment (e.g., respect, tolerance, kindness, and collaboration)<br><br><br>• **Adequately** sets basic expectations for a welcoming environment as necessary and consistently and **effectively responds** to breaches, using them as opportunities to convey messages that support the welcoming environment | • Effectively chooses messages **applicable to student subgroups** within the classroom (e.g., respect and appreciation for students' diverse academic levels, skills, learning styles, special needs, language barriers, races, classes, ethnicities, sexual orientations, and backgrounds, etc.)<br><br>• **Effectively** sets expectations for a welcoming environment as necessary, **anticipates and prevents most** breaches by proactively using a variety of methods (e.g., explicit lessons, classroom jobs, community building) that will support a welcoming environment and effectively responds to breaches when they occur | • Effectively chooses messages **applicable to student subgroups** within the classroom and beyond and ensures that each student is affirmed and supported for the **unique individual** s/he is<br><br><br>• **Compellingly** sets expectations for a welcoming environment as necessary and **effectively empowers students** to become leaders in sustaining a respectful, collaborative environment for all by teaching them to affirm and support their classmates and to resolve all conflicts in peaceful and enduring ways |

| | INVEST Students and Others | | PLAN Purposefully | CONTINUOUSLY INCREASE Effectiveness | WORK Relentlessly |
|---|---|---|---|---|---|
| SET Big Goals | | | EXECUTE Effectively | | |
| Teacher Action | Prenovice | Novice | Beginning Proficiency | Advanced Proficiency | Exemplary |
| **I-6**<br><br>Respectfully mobilize students' influencers (e.g., family, peers, coach, pastor, etc.) using techniques such as direct explanation, role models, modeling, constant reinforcement and marketing, etc., so that they actively invest students in working hard toward the big goals. | Shows a lack of attempt or action | *In action . . . .* Demonstrates **attempt** to respectfully mobilize students' influencers<br><br>*In reflection . . . .* Accurately explains key strategies for respectfully mobilizing students' influencers<br><br>Describes in a compelling way why it is important to mobilize students' influencers | • Uses a **single,** formal method to interact with every student's **family** | • Uses **multiple** methods and occasions to mobilize students' **key influencers** (e.g., parents, guardians, other relatives, coaches, pastors, etc.) | • Based on an understanding of individual students and their key influencers, **customizes** interactions in order to mobilize each student's **key influencers** to invest students in working hard toward the big goals |
| | | | • **Provides** basic information and respectfully **requests help** when students are **not working hard** | • **Shares** knowledge and skills on how the influencers and the teacher can **accelerate students'** progress | • Ensures that students' **influencers are equipped** to invest and advocate for students **beyond this school year,** in addition to sharing knowledge and skills on how the influencers and the teacher can **work together to accelerate** the students' progress |
| | | | • **Shares** positive news of student performance on an **absolute** scale | • **Shares** positive news of student performance on a **relative** scale | • **Shows** influencers how **to monitor** students' performance and **recognize** progress |
| | | | • Successfully **informs** students' families of basic information | • Successfully **involves** students' key influencers | • Successfully **invests** students' key influencers |

| SET
Big Goals | INVEST
Students and Others | PLAN
Purposefully | EXECUTE
Effectively | CONTINUOUSLY INCREASE
Effectiveness | WORK
Relentlessly |

## Plan Purposefully

Instructional plans, behavioral expectations, and procedures lead students to master objectives and advance efficiently toward the big goal.

| Teacher Action | Prenovice | Novice | Beginning Proficiency | Advanced Proficiency | Exemplary |
|---|---|---|---|---|---|
| **P-1**<br><br>**Create or obtain standards-aligned diagnostic, formative and summative assessments (with tracking and grading systems) to determine where students are against big goals.** | Shows a lack of attempt or action | *In action . . .*<br>Demonstrates **attempt** to create or obtain standards-aligned diagnostic, formative OR summative assessments (with tracking and grading systems) to determine where students are against big goals<br><br>*In reflection . . .*<br>Accurately explains the criteria to consider when creating or obtaining diagnostics and assessments, as well as how they are used to determine student progress toward big goals<br>Explains in a compelling way why it is important to utilize diagnostics and assessments that meet the criteria for effectiveness | • Creates or obtains diagnostics that assess students' **readiness,** as well as formative (including lesson assessments) and summative assessments that measure each learning goal taught. Assessments contain no questions unrelated to the learning goals taught<br><br>• **Uses** items (e.g., questions, rubric rows) aligned to the objectives being tested<br><br>• Ensures assessment reveals **true mastery** of the intended objective<br><br>• Grading systems provide an **accurate** picture of student performance against goals to guide future planning, and the teacher can accurately articulate a vision of student mastery<br><br>• Creates or obtains tracking system that **records** student performance on assessments | • Creates or obtains diagnostics that assess the **extent of readiness of most students,** as well as formative assessments (including lesson assessments) that, when appropriate, scaffold questions to discern **extent** of mastery of each learning goal taught and summative assessments that measure mastery of each learning goal taught. Assessments do not contain any items unrelated to the learning goals taught<br><br>• Uses **multiple items** aligned to the same objective, in summative and, if appropriate, formative assessments (while also balancing the need for **efficiency**)<br><br>• Ensures each item reveals **true mastery** (while balancing the need for **efficiency**)<br><br>• Grading systems efficiently provide **detailed, increasingly reliable** picture of student performance against goals to guide future planning, and the teacher can accurately articulate what **explicit degrees** of student mastery look like on items<br><br>• Creates or obtains tracking system that **calculates and reports individual and class** progress toward big goals | • Creates or obtains diagnostics that provide **detailed information** about the **extent of readiness of each student,** formative assessments (as well as lesson assessments) that, when appropriate, scaffold questions to discern the extent of mastery of each learning goal taught, and summative assessments that measure mastery of each learning goal taught, including components requiring **higher-order thinking.** Assessments contain no questions unrelated to the learning goals taught<br><br>• Uses **multiple items** in **multiple modes,** aligned to the same objective, in summative, and if appropriate, formative assessments (while balancing the need for **efficiency**)<br><br>• Uses authentic assessments, when appropriate, to reveal true mastery (while balancing the need for **efficiency**)<br><br>• Grading systems are **consistent** and **extremely efficient,** provide a **detailed, increasingly reliable** picture of student performance against goals to guide future planning, and the teacher can accurately articulate what **explicit degrees** of student mastery look like on individual items<br><br>• Develops tracking system that **reports individual and class** progress toward big goals and highlights where **individual students** need improvement on **particular objectives** |

| SET<br>Big Goals | INVEST<br>Students and Others | | PLAN<br>Purposefully | EXECUTE<br>Effectively | CONTINUOUSLY INCREASE<br>Effectiveness | WORK<br>Relentlessly |
|---|---|---|---|---|---|---|
| **Teacher Action** | Prenovice | Novice | Beginning Proficiency | Advanced Proficiency | Exemplary | |
| **P-2**<br><br>Backward-plan by breaking down longer-term goals into bundles of objectives and mapping them across the school year (in a long-term plan and unit plans). | Shows a lack of attempt or action | *In action . . .*<br>Demonstrates **attempt** to backward-plan by breaking down longer-term goals into bundles of objectives and mapping them across the school year (in a long-term plan and/or unit plans)<br><br>*In reflection . . .*<br>Accurately explains the process of back-ward planning<br><br>Explains in a compelling way why it is impor-tant to back-ward-plan at the unit and long-term levels | • Uses standards-aligned learning goals to plan a **logical** unit with an assessment and **clear, student-measurable, student-centered objectives** leading to achievement of the unit goals<br><br>• Schedules objectives from the unit plan on a calendar **in the midst** of teaching the unit and/or allocates time **inappropriately**<br><br>• Uses an **appropriate** external source of data to create plan (e.g., adopts school district policies) | • **Logically** groups standards-aligned learning goals into a unit (coupled with an assessment) identifying daily **clear, measurable, student-centered, and rigorous objectives**, and creates a long-term plan (coupled with an end-of-year assess-ment) built on **grouped and sequenced** learning goals that lead to achievement of the big goal<br><br>• Schedules units from the long-term plan and objec-tives from the unit plan on a calendar **ahead of time** and allocates time **appropriately** based on the content to be taught<br><br>• Effectively **tailors** plan to class after engaging deeply with **multiple sources,** including diagnostic data (and others such as excellent school practices, veteran teacher consultation, etc.) | • **Logically** groups and clearly orga-nizes relevant standards-aligned learning goals into units (coupled with assessments) that **build upon one another conceptually** and that identify **clear, measurable, student-centered, and rigorous objectives** to be taught in each unit, creating a long-term plan that leads to achievement of unit goals and year-long academic goals<br><br>• Schedules units from the long-tem plan and objectives from the unit plan on a calendar **ahead of time,** allocates time **appropriately** based on the content to be taught, and plans for **contingencies, remedia-tion, and enrichment**<br><br>• Effectively **tailors** plan to class after engaging deeply with **multiple sources,** including diagnostic data, to create plan, and leads efforts to align plans at the **school level** (e.g., vertical teams, across subjects) | |

| | | | PLAN<br>Purposefully | EXECUTE<br>Effectively | CONTINUOUSLY INCREASE<br>Effectiveness | WORK<br>Relentlessly |
| SET<br>Big Goals | INVEST<br>Students and Others | | | | | |
| Teacher Action | Prenovice | Novice | Beginning Proficiency | Advanced Proficiency | Exemplary |
| **P-3**<br><br>**Create rigorous, objective-driven lesson plans so that students who complete class activities successfully will have mastered the objectives and made progress toward the big goals.** | Shows a lack of attempt or action | *In action . . .*<br>Demonstrates **attempt** to create rigorous, objective-driven lesson plans<br><br>*In reflection . . .*<br>Accurately explains how to align lessons to objectives and strategies for fulfilling the steps of the lesson cycle<br><br>Explains in a compelling way why it is important to align lessons to both the objectives and the lesson cycle | • Key points are **accurately** and **appropriately** derived from the objective. Components of the lesson **generally align** to the objective, to the key points, and to the way that students will be asked to demonstrate mastery | • Key points are **accurately** and **appropriately** derived from the objective. **All components** of the lesson **align** to the objective, to the key points, and to the way that students will be asked to demonstrate mastery | • Key points are **accurately** and **appropriately** derived from the objective. **All components** of the lesson **align** to the objective, to the key points, and to the way that students will be asked to demonstrate mastery, while purposefully and efficiently **building upon one another** |
| | | | • Designs activities that **technically align with the steps** of the lesson cycle | • Designs activities that **align** with and **accomplish the purpose** behind the steps of the lesson cycle | • Designs **innovative, student-centered** activities that **align with the principles** of effective lesson planning (e.g., activates prior knowledge, articulates key ideas, anticipates misunderstandings, infuses scaffolded student practice, assesses understanding) and **effectively and efficiently** lead to student mastery |
| | | | • Designs lessons that can be completed **in time available** | • Designs lessons so that **timing supports learning** | • Designs lessons so the lessons' pacing is feasible and **supports students in mastering** the objectives but also allows for **real-time adjustment** |

| SET<br>Big Goals | INVEST<br>Students and Others | | PLAN<br>Purposefully | EXECUTE<br>Effectively | CONTINUOUSLY INCREASE<br>Effectiveness | WORK<br>Relentlessly |
|---|---|---|---|---|---|---|
| **Teacher Action** | **Prenovice** | **Novice** | **Beginning Proficiency** | **Advanced Proficiency** | **Exemplary** | |

| **Teacher Action** | **Prenovice** | **Novice** | **Beginning Proficiency** | **Advanced Proficiency** | **Exemplary** |
|---|---|---|---|---|---|
| **P-4**<br><br>Differentiate plans for individual students based on their unique learning profiles (including ongoing performance data) so that all students are engaged and challenged. | Shows a lack of attempt or action | *In action . . .*<br>Demonstrates **attempt** to design differentiated plans<br><br>*In reflection . . .*<br>Accurately explains the main ideas behind differentiating plans based on student diagnostic data and/or goals of the individualized education plans (IEPs), if applicable<br><br>Explains in a compelling way why it is important to differentiate plans | • Designs content, processes, and products applicable to a **general group** of students, while complying with official accommodations and modifications, if applicable<br><br>• Crafts plans based on student **diagnostic data and/or goals of the IEPs**, if applicable<br><br>• Designs efficient plans so that the teacher can offer support to **individual students** when the whole class is working | • **Regularly** designs content, processes, and products applicable to **subgroups** of students with different needs and interests<br><br>• Crafts plans based on **multiple** sources of data (including ongoing assessments) **and goals of the IEPs**, if applicable<br><br>• Designs efficient plans and **accountability** systems to initiate various forms of **structured differentiation** (e.g., teacher rotating among established student groupings) | • Designs content, processes, and products customized for **individual students**<br><br>• Uses **multiple** sources of data to inform plans, while consistently pushing for students to **transcend past performance**<br><br>• Designs efficient plans and **accountability** systems to initiate **flexible differentiation** (e.g., students in varied groups, students working independently) |

| SET<br>Big Goals | INVEST<br>Students and Others | | PLAN<br>Purposefully | EXECUTE<br>Effectively | CONTINUOUSLY INCREASE<br>Effectiveness | WORK<br>Relentlessly |
| --- | --- | --- | --- | --- | --- | --- |
| **Teacher Action** | **Prenovice** | **Novice** | **Beginning Proficiency** | **Advanced Proficiency** | **Exemplary** | |

| **P-5**<br><br>Establish age-appropriate long- and short-term behavioral management plans (rules and consequences) so that if students comply, the amount and value of instructional time is maximized. | Shows a lack of attempt or action | *In action . . .*<br>Demonstrates **attempt** to create rules and consequences and a plan to introduce them to students<br><br>*In reflection . . .*<br>Accurately explains the criteria for, and examples of, effective rules and consequences<br><br>Explains in a compelling way why it is important to create age-appropriate rules and consequences | • Crafts rules that are **technically clear** and **positively** stated | • Crafts **student-friendly** rules, (i.e., **clear** to all students once rules have been introduced,) that are **positively** stated, and **manageable** in number | • Crafts such **clear, student-friendly** rules that all students can explain classroom expectations **in their own words** once rules have been introduced and all students can **apply them to novel situations** |
| | | | • Crafts rules that address a **core set** of needs in the classroom | • Crafts rules that address **most foreseeable** needs in the classroom | • Crafts rules that **easily apply to any situation,** as well as effective **specialized** rules based on an understanding of individual students |
| | | | • Crafts consequences that are **reasonable and logical** | • Crafts consequences that are **reasonable, logical, and likely to deter most** students from misbehavior | • Crafts consequences that are **reasonable, logical, and customized to deter individual** students from misbehavior |
| | | | • Designs **initial plan** that **clearly introduces** rules and consequences to students | • Designs **initial plan** that **requires all students to demonstrate** their comprehension of the rules and consequences | • Designs **ongoing plans** to teach and invest students in the rules and consequences |

| SET<br>Big Goals | INVEST<br>Students and Others | | PLAN<br>Purposefully | EXECUTE<br>Effectively | CONTINUOUSLY INCREASE<br>Effectiveness | WORK<br>Relentlessly |
|---|---|---|---|---|---|---|
| Teacher Action | Prenovice | Novice | Beginning Proficiency | Advanced Proficiency | Exemplary | |
| **P-6**<br><br>Design classroom procedures (for transitions, collecting and handing out papers, taking roll, etc.) that provide structure to students and maximize the amount and value of instructional time. | Shows a lack of attempt or action | *In action . . .*<br>Demonstrates **attempt** to design classroom procedures and to introduce them to students<br><br>*In reflection . . .*<br>Accurately explains the occasions for and strategies to introduce classroom procedures<br><br>Explains in a compelling way why it is important to design classroom procedures | • **Plans** procedures that address a **core set** of inefficiencies in the classroom<br><br>• Designs procedures that enable the class to **run more smoothly**<br><br>• Designs **initial plan** that **clearly introduces** procedures to students | • **Develops** procedures that address **most foreseeable** inefficiencies in the classroom<br><br>• Designs procedures that create **additional instructional time**<br><br>• Designs **initial plan** that **requires all students to demonstrate** their comprehension of the procedures | • **Innovates** procedures with the class to address **all possible** inefficiencies<br><br>• Designs procedures that create **additional instructional time** and **conserve the teacher's energy** for instructional responsibilities<br><br>• Designs **ongoing plans** that **teach** students the procedures and **invest** them in the purpose | |

## Execute Effectively

Students glean the maximum benefit from instructional plans, behavioral expectations, and procedures.

| Teacher Action | Prenovice | Novice | Beginning Proficiency | Advanced Proficiency | Exemplary |
|---|---|---|---|---|---|
| **E-1**<br><br>**Clearly present academic content** (in differentiated ways, if necessary) so **that students comprehend key information and ideas.** | Shows a lack of attempt or action | *In action . . .*<br>Demonstrates **attempt** to present academic content clearly<br><br>*In reflection . . .*<br>Accurately explains key techniques for presenting academic content<br><br>Explains in a compelling way the importance of each strategy | • Explanations are **coherent, cohesive, and correct** | • Explanations are **coherent, cohesive, and correct** with a focus on **key ideas** | • Explanations are **coherent, cohesive, and correct** and are conveyed in a **focused, meaningful, and memorable** way that illuminates **key ideas** |
|  |  |  | • Maintains **adequate** tone, pace, volume, poise, and body language well enough to capture the attention and interest of **more than half** of the students in a classroom | • Maintains **effective** tone, pace, volume, poise, and body language well enough to command the attention and interest of **almost all** of the students in a classroom | • Maintains **persuasive and compelling** tone, pace, volume, poise, and body language well enough to captivate **all** students in a classroom |
|  |  |  | • Follows content and pacing of lesson plans **faithfully, regardless of circumstances** | • Follows lesson plans **faithfully, while flexibly making adjustments** based on in-the-moment circumstances, as necessary | • Seizes opportunities to **purposefully transform** lesson plans, as necessary, in order to move further toward goals |

| SET Big Goals | INVEST Students and Others | | PLAN Purposefully | EXECUTE Effectively | CONTINUOUSLY INCREASE Effectiveness | WORK Relentlessly |
|---|---|---|---|---|---|---|
| Teacher Action | Prenovice | Novice | Beginning Proficiency | | Advanced Proficiency | Exemplary |
| **E-2**<br><br>Facilitate, manage, and coordinate student academic practice (in differentiated ways, if necessary) so that all students are participating and have the opportunity to gain mastery of the objectives. | Shows a lack of attempt or action | *In action . . . .* Demonstrates **attempt** to facilitate, manage, and coordinate student practice<br><br>*In reflection . . . .* Accurately explains key strategies for facilitating, managing, and coordinating student practice<br><br>Explains in a compelling way the importance of each strategy | • Clearly communicates **basic** instructions<br><br>• **Monitors** student performance to ensure students are **practicing**<br><br>• Follows content and pacing of lesson plans **faithfully, regardless of circumstances** | | • Clearly communicates instructions, with an emphasis on **key points and rationale**<br><br>• **Monitors** student performance and **engages** with students to offer clarification and **extend student understanding**<br><br>• Follows lesson plans **faithfully**, while **flexibly making adjustments** based on in-the-moment circumstances, as necessary | • Communicates instructions in a clear, **focused, expressive** way that illuminates **key points and rationale**<br><br>• **Facilitates** in ways that encourage students to **self-monitor, cooperate and support** one another<br><br>• Seizes opportunities to **purposefully transform** lesson plans, as necessary, in order to move further toward goals |

| Teacher Action | Prenovice | Novice | Beginning Proficiency | Advanced Proficiency | Exemplary |
|---|---|---|---|---|---|
| **E-3**<br><br>**Check for academic understanding frequently by questioning, listening, and/or observing, and provide feedback (that affirms right answers and corrects wrong answers), in order to ensure student learning.** | Shows a lack of attempt or action | *In action . . .*<br>Demonstrates **attempt** to check for understanding<br><br>*In reflection . . .*<br>Accurately explains the advantages and disadvantages of a variety of strategies for checking for understanding<br><br>Explains in a compelling way the importance of checking for understanding | • Directs questions to a **random variety** of students and can identify individual responses<br><br>• Crafts questions that would reliably discern **whether** students understand<br><br>• Asks questions about the most important ideas **occasionally**<br><br>• Upholds high expectations for successful responses and tells students **whether** they have met the standard | • Directs questions to a **representative subset** of students and can identify individual responses<br><br>• Crafts questions that would reliably discern the **extent** of student understanding (e.g., scaffolded questioning)<br><br>• Asks questions about the most important ideas **throughout** the lesson<br><br>• Upholds high expectations for successful responses and tells students **why** they have or have not met the standard | • Directs questions to **all** students and can identify individual responses<br><br>• Crafts questions that would reliably discern the **extent and root** of a student's misunderstanding<br><br>• Asks questions about the most important ideas at **key moments** throughout the lesson<br><br>• Upholds high expectations and teaches students **how to evaluate and articulate** the success of their responses |

Top-level column group headers:

| SET | INVEST | PLAN | EXECUTE | CONTINUOUSLY INCREASE | WORK |
|---|---|---|---|---|---|
| Big Goals | Students and Others | Purposefully | Effectively | Effectiveness | Relentlessly |

| Teacher Action | Prenovice | Novice | Beginning Proficiency | Advanced Proficiency | Exemplary |
|---|---|---|---|---|---|
| **E-4**<br><br>**Communicates high expectations for behavior by teaching, practicing, and reinforcing rules and consequences so that students are focused on working hard.** | Shows a lack of attempt or action | *In action . . .*<br>Demonstrates **attempt** to communicate instructions and directions and to respond to misbehaviors clearly and assertively<br><br>*In reflection . . .*<br>Accurately explains key strategies for communicating instructions and directions and for responding to misbehaviors clearly and assertively<br><br>Explains in a compelling way the importance of each strategy | • Communicates expectations clearly and assertively, as necessary, **sometimes** avoiding in-depth discussions of expectations because they are reasonably established<br><br>• Effectively uses the **same** techniques to respond justly and similarly to comparable misbehaviors while maintaining students' dignity<br><br>• **Often** reacts to violations of classroom rules immediately, clearly, and assertively in the moment<br><br>• Misbehavior **sometimes** occurs and **often** ceases in the short term with teacher's intervention | • Communicates expectations, **and often the purpose** behind them, clearly, assertively, and confidently, as necessary, **usually** avoiding in-depth discussions of expectations because they are well established<br><br>• Effectively chooses from a **range** of techniques to respond justly and purposefully to misbehaviors while maintaining students' dignity<br><br>• **Consistently** reacts immediately, clearly, and assertively in the moment<br><br>• Misbehavior **rarely** prevents the lesson from moving forward and **consistently** ceases in the short and long term with teacher's intervention | • Communicates expectations **and the purpose** behind them clearly, assertively, and compellingly, as necessary, **almost always** avoiding discussions of expectations entirely because students have thoroughly internalized them<br><br>• Effectively and appropriately discerns and **addresses individual causes** of misbehavior while maintaining students' dignity<br><br>• **Always** effectively considers **individual** students and situations when reacting in the moment<br><br>• **Students resolve and/or prevent** misbehavior by independently problem solving and making good choices |

**Table header (spanning columns):**

| SET Big Goals | INVEST Students and Others | PLAN Purposefully | EXECUTE Effectively | CONTINUOUSLY INCREASE Effectiveness | WORK Relentlessly |
|---|---|---|---|---|---|

| | Prenovice | Novice | Beginning Proficiency | Advanced Proficiency | Exemplary |
|---|---|---|---|---|---|
| **SET** Big Goals → **INVEST** Students and Others → **PLAN** Purposefully → **EXECUTE** Effectively → **CONTINUOUSLY INCREASE** Effectiveness → **WORK** Relentlessly | | | | | |
| **Teacher Action** | | | | | |
| **E-5**  Implement and practice time-saving procedures (for transitions, dissemination and collection of supplies or homework, etc.) to maximize time spent on learning. | Shows a lack of attempt or action | *In action . . .* Demonstrates **attempt** to explain procedures clearly and to reinforce them over time  *In reflection . . .* Accurately explains key strategies for explaining procedures clearly and reinforcing them over time  Explains in a compelling way the importance of each strategy | • Explains procedures clearly when needed, **sometimes** avoiding in-depth directions because **more than half** the students know and follow established procedures | • Explains procedures clearly when needed, and **often the purpose** behind them, with an **emphasis on key steps**, **usually** avoiding in-depth directions entirely because **almost all** students know and follow firmly established procedures | • Communicates procedures when necessary, **and the purpose** behind them, in a focused, memorable way that **illuminates key steps** and their relation to student achievement, **almost always** avoiding directions entirely because **all** students know and follow thoroughly established procedures |
| | | | • Effectively reinforces procedures **when they break down** | • Effectively reinforces procedures when they break down but **anticipates and prevents** most procedural breakdowns by proactively reinforcing procedures and **regularly connects** them to the purpose of maximizing instructional time | • **Proactively** reinforces procedures, ensures students can articulate their purpose, and **empowers students** to critique, monitor, and create procedures |
| | | | • **Most** procedures run **adequately with** teacher's facilitation and/or intervention | • All procedures run **smoothly and urgently with** teacher's facilitation | • All procedures run **smoothly and urgently without** the teacher's facilitation |

| | SET Big Goals | INVEST Students and Others | | PLAN Purposefully | EXECUTE Effectively | CONTINUOUSLY INCREASE Effectiveness | WORK Relentlessly |
|---|---|---|---|---|---|---|---|
| **Teacher Action** | | **Prenovice** | **Novice** | **Beginning Proficiency** | | **Advanced Proficiency** | **Exemplary** |
| **E-6** Evaluate and keep track of students' performance on assessments so that the teacher and students are aware of students' progress on academic, behavioral, and investment goals. | | Shows a lack of attempt or action | *In action...* Demonstrates **attempt** to administer diagnostic, formative, OR summative assessments, to grade accurately and to track student performance periodically  *In reflection...* Accurately explains key strategies for administering diagnostic, formative, OR summative assessments  Accurately explains process for grading and tracking student performance  Explains in a compelling way the importance of each strategy and process | • **Periodically** administers diagnostic and summative assessments to determine student **performance**  • Grades accurately and efficiently so that students are **aware** of their performance  • Tracks student performance **periodically** | | • **Regularly** administers diagnostic, formative, and summative assessments to determine student **progress**  • Accurately and efficiently grades in a way that helps students **understand** their performance and where they are **in relation to the big goals**  • Tracks student performance **regularly** so that data can inform short- and long-term planning and differentiation | • Administers assessments as **often as necessary** for students to **work to mastery**  • Accurately and efficiently grades in ways that help **individual** students **learn** their strengths and weaknesses, **improve** their performance, and see where they are **in relation to the big goals**  • Tracks student performance **immediately** so that data can drive short- and long-term planning and differentiation |

## Continuously Increase Effectiveness

Student performance improves over time through deliberate data-driven reflection, analysis, and meaningful changes to teacher performance.

| Teacher Action | Prenovice | Novice | Beginning Proficiency | Advanced Proficiency | Exemplary |
|---|---|---|---|---|---|
| **C-1**<br><br>**Gauge progress and notable gap(s) between student achievement and big goals by examining assessment data.** | Shows a lack of attempt or action | *In action . . .* Demonstrates **attempt** to gauge progress and notable gaps between student achievement and big goals<br><br>*In reflection . . .* Accurately describes a process for gauging progress and identifying gaps between student achievement and big goals<br><br>Explains in a compelling way the importance of gauging progress and identifying gaps in this way | • Accurately **notes** general student progress and gaps between student achievement and big goals<br><br>• Performs action **when asked** to do so | • Accurately **notes** progress and gaps for established student **subgroups** (e.g., "low," "middle," and "high" groups and/or class periods) against goals and **prioritizes** gaps by weighing urgency and feasibility of addressing them<br><br>• Performs action on regular occasions **beyond staff-initiated,** formal interactions | • Accurately **notes** progress and gaps of established student **subgroups,** as well as in **trends across the entire roster,** and **prioritizes** gaps by weighing urgency and feasibility of addressing them<br><br>• Performs action **continuously** |

| SET Big Goals | INVEST Students and Others | PLAN Purposefully | EXECUTE Effectively | CONTINUOUSLY INCREASE Effectiveness | WORK Relentlessly |
|---|---|---|---|---|---|
| **Teacher Action** | Prenovice | Novice | Beginning Proficiency | Advanced Proficiency | Exemplary |
| **C-2** Identify student habits or actions most influencing progress and gaps between student achievement and big goals. | Shows a lack of attempt or action | *In action . . .* Demonstrates **attempt** to identify the student habits most influencing progress and gaps between student achievement and big goals<br><br>*In reflection . . .* Accurately describes a process for identifying the student habits or actions most influencing progress and gaps between student achievement and big goals<br><br>Explains in a compelling way the importance of identifying these student habits or actions | • Considers (based on **observation data**) **several** student actions that align with identified progress and gaps in student achievement | • Considers (based on data from **more than one source**) a **wide range** of student actions that align with key progress and gaps in student achievement | • Considers (based on data from **multiple, authentic sources**) the **full range** of student actions that align with key progress and gaps in student achievement |
| | | | • Performs action **when asked** to do so | • Performs action on regular occasions **beyond staff-initiated**, formal interaction | • Performs action **continuously** |
| | | | • Accurately **identifies** (using data and/or student work) particular student habits or actions that **would logically contribute** to student results | • Accurately **prioritizes** (using data and/or student work) a certain student habit or action that **has contributed** to student results by examining notable instances of student behavior and/or understanding and by **weighing** the feasibility and urgency of improving or capitalizing on the habit or action | • Accurately **prioritizes** (using data and/or student work) a specific, **well-documented** student habit or action that **explains** student results by looking for a causal relationship between confirmed instances of student behavior and understanding, **weighing** the feasibility and urgency of improving or capitalizing on the habit or action, and **confirming theories** against data |

| Teacher Action | Prenovice | Novice | Beginning Proficiency | Advanced Proficiency | Exemplary |
|---|---|---|---|---|---|
| **C-3**<br><br>Isolate the teacher actions most contributing to key aspects of student performance by gathering data (e.g., using the TAL rubric) and reflecting on teacher performance. | Shows a lack of attempt or action | *In action . . .* Demonstrates **attempt** to identify a teacher action that could logically contribute to trends in student performance<br><br>*In reflection . . . .* Accurately describes a process for considering teacher actions that could contribute to trends in student performance<br><br>Explains in a compelling way the importance of considering teacher actions in this way | • Considers (based on **observation** data) **several** teacher actions that could explain identified student habits or actions<br><br>• Performs action **when asked** to do so<br><br>• Identifies a teacher action that **would logically contribute to notable** trends in student performance | • Considers (based on data from **more than one source**) a **wide range** of teacher actions that could explain key student habits or actions<br><br>• Performs action on regular occasions **beyond staff-initiated,** formal interactions<br><br>• Determines a **key** teacher action that **contributes** to **notable** trends in student performance by using the TAL rubric and by **prioritizing** teacher actions based on the feasibility and importance of improving or capitalizing on them | • Considers (based on data from **multiple, authentic sources**) the **full range** of teacher actions that could explain key student habits or actions<br><br>• Performs action **continuously**<br><br>• Efficiently determines **the key** teacher actions that **explain definitive** trends in student performance by using the TAL rubric, **prioritizing** teacher actions based on the feasibility and importance of improving or capitalizing on them and **confirming the theory** by examining all of the relevant aspects of student performance |

| Teacher Action | SET Big Goals | INVEST Students and Others | | PLAN Purposefully / EXECUTE Effectively | CONTINUOUSLY INCREASE Effectiveness | WORK Relentlessly |
|---|---|---|---|---|---|---|
| | | Prenovice | Novice | Beginning Proficiency | Advanced Proficiency | Exemplary |
| **C-4** Identify the underlying factors (e.g., knowledge, skill, mindset) causing teacher actions. | | Shows a lack of attempt or action | *In action . . .* Demonstrates **attempt** to identify potential root causes that are logically aligned to identified teacher actions <br><br> *In reflection . . .* Accurately describes a process for identifying potential root causes that could explain identified aspects of teacher actions <br><br> Explains in a compelling way the importance of identifying root causes in this way | • Considers **causes** that could explain identified aspects of teacher actions | • Considers a **range of causes** that could explain key aspects of teacher actions | • Considers the **full range of causes** that could explain key aspects of teacher actions |
| | | | | • Performs action **when asked** to do so | • Performs action on regular occasions **beyond staff-initiated,** formal interactions | • Performs action **continuously** |
| | | | | • Identifies **potential** root causes that **are logically aligned** to identified teacher actions | • Determines **a** root cause that **contributes** to an identified teacher action by listing potential underlying factors, using data, reflecting honestly, and **prioritizing** based on solid evidence | • Determines **the** root cause that **explains** an identified teacher action by using data, nuanced observation, and honest reflection; by **prioritizing** based on strong evidence; and by **confirming the theory** by examining all of the relevant teacher actions |

| SET Big Goals | INVEST Students and Others | | PLAN Purposefully | EXECUTE Effectively | CONTINUOUSLY INCREASE Effectiveness | WORK Relentlessly |
|---|---|---|---|---|---|---|
| **Teacher Action** | **Prenovice** | **Novice** | **Beginning Proficiency** | **Advanced Proficiency** | **Exemplary** |

| **C-5**<br><br>Access meaningful learning experiences that direct and inform teacher improvement. | Shows a lack of attempt or action | *In action. . .*<br>Demonstrates **attempt** to engage in learning experiences aligned with the root cause<br><br>*In reflection. . .*<br>Accurately describes a process for determining and accessing a resource or learning experience aligned with a root cause<br><br>Explains in a compelling way the importance of engaging in learning experiences aligned with a root cause | • Pursues resources or learning experiences that **technically align** with the underlying factor<br><br>• Performs action **when asked** to do so<br><br>• **Completes** a learning experience that **improves** the teacher's knowledge, skill, or mindset to some degree | • Pursues **credible and meaningful** resources and learning experiences that **align** with the underlying factor<br><br>• Performs action on regular occasions **beyond staff-initiated,** formal interactions<br><br>• **Maximizes** a productive learning experience and **masters** the pursued knowledge, skill, or mindset | • Pursues and/or creates **varied and valuable** resources and learning experiences (by consulting veteran teachers, reading articles, attending workshops, etc.) that are **efficient, targeted, and customized to align** with the underlying factor<br><br>• Performs action **continuously**<br><br>• **Masters** the knowledge, skill, or mindset sought and **extends opportunities** to expand learning into other domains and needs |

| | SET Big Goals | INVEST Students and Others | PLAN Purposefully | EXECUTE Effectively | CONTINUOUSLY INCREASE Effectiveness | WORK Relentlessly |
|---|---|---|---|---|---|---|
| **Teacher Action** | Prenovice | Novice | Beginning Proficiency | Advanced Proficiency | Exemplary |
| **C-6**<br><br>After a cycle of data collection, reflection, and learning, adjust course (of big goals, investment strategies, planning, execution and/ or relentlessness) as necessary to maximize effectiveness. | Shows a lack of attempt or action | *In action. . .*<br>Demonstrates **attempt** to create and implement an action plan<br><br>*In reflection. . .*<br>Accurately describes a process for choosing strategies that align with identified problems and causes in the classroom and creating an action plan in order to implement those strategies<br><br>Explains in a compelling way the importance of adjusting course after cycle of collecting data, reflecting, and learning | • Chooses strategies that **align with** identified problems and their causes in the classroom<br><br>• Performs action **when asked** to do so<br><br>• Creates action plan that is **technically feasible** to implement<br><br>• **Implements** the plan | • Chooses strategies that would **solve** the key problems and root causes in the classroom and that build upon the teacher's and the classroom's **strengths**<br><br>• Performs action on regular occasions **beyond staff-initiated,** formal interactions<br><br>• Creates action plan that is **personally feasible** to implement **independently**<br><br>• **Implements** the plan with fundamental **commitment and follow-through** | • Chooses multiple strategies that would **transform** student performance and that build upon the teacher's and the classroom's **strengths**<br><br>• Performs action **continuously**<br><br>• Consistently gauges what is both **personally ambitious and feasible** to implement **independently**<br><br>• **Pursues contingencies** if initial solution is ineffective and/or **broadens impact** of the classroom change by sharing it with others |

## Work Relentlessly

Time, energy, and resources are maximized to reach the goal.

| Teacher Action | Prenovice | Novice | Beginning Proficiency | Advanced Proficiency | Exemplary |
|---|---|---|---|---|---|
| **W-1**<br><br>Persist in the face of considerable challenges, focusing effort on the ultimate goal and targeting those challenges one can impact to increase student achievement. | Shows a lack of attempt or action | *In action . . .*<br>Demonstrates **attempt** to implement strategies of persistence<br><br>*In reflection . . .*<br>Describes personal strategies for persisting in the face of considerable challenges<br><br>Explains in a compelling way why such strategies are important | • Generally **avoids making excuses** about challenges<br><br>• **Maintains** effort when faced with challenges (i.e., does not give up) | • Consistently **targets** for resolution those challenges that will **most move students closer** to the goals<br><br>• **Increases** effort when faced with challenges | • **Widens circle of what is in his or her control to target** challenges that hold students back from meeting classroom goals<br><br>• **Prioritizes** investment of time and effort to focus on the most pressing challenges and works **purposefully and efficiently** toward their resolution |

| Teacher Action | SET Big Goals | INVEST Students and Others | PLAN Purposefully | EXECUTE Effectively | CONTINUOUSLY INCREASE Effectiveness | WORK Relentlessly |
|---|---|---|---|---|---|---|
| | | Prenovice | Novice | Beginning Proficiency | Advanced Proficiency | Exemplary |
| **W-2** Pursue and secure additional instructional time and resources in order to increase opportunities for student learning. | | Shows a lack of attempt or action | *In action . . .* Demonstrates **attempt** to implement strategies to pursue additional instructional time and/or resources *In reflection . . .* Describes strategies for identifying additional instructional time and/or resources Describes key techniques for swaying constituents Explains in a compelling way why such strategies and techniques are important | • **Identifies** time and/or resource constraints that impact student achievement | • **Isolates key** time and resource constraints that **significantly** impact student achievement | • **Targets** the **most feasibly addressed** time and/or resource constraints that **most urgently and substantially** impact class performance |
| | | | | • Considers and pursues a **workable solution** to address time and/or resource needs | • Considers and pursues **purposefully selected substantial solutions** to address time and/or resource needs | • Pursues **bold, far-reaching solutions** to address time and/or resource needs |
| | | | | • Effectively uses a **few** persuasive techniques to **sway** those who control time and resources, when necessary | • Employs a **variety of appropriate** persuasive techniques (e.g., logic, appeal to values, exchanging) to **gain support** of those who control time and resources, when necessary | • **Builds purposeful, lasting alliances** through compelling persuasive techniques most appealing to those who control time and resources, in order to **gain widespread approval**, when necessary |
| | | | | • Implements the time and/or resources acquired such that they have a **temporary** impact on student achievement | • Integrates the time and/or resources acquired into the classroom such that they have a **sustained** impact on student achievement | • Ensures that the time and/or resources acquired have a **sustained** impact **beyond the teacher's classroom, students, and tenure** at the school |

| | SET Big Goals | INVEST Students and Others | PLAN Purposefully | EXECUTE Effectively | CONTINUOUSLY INCREASE Effectiveness | WORK Relentlessly |
|---|---|---|---|---|---|---|
| **Teacher Action** | **Prenovice** | **Novice** | **Beginning Proficiency** | **Advanced Proficiency** | **Exemplary** |
| **W-3**<br><br>Sustain the intense energy necessary to reach the ambitious big goals through a variety of strategies (e.g., (a) building meaningful personal relationships with students, (b) reminding themselves of the high stakes involved in their work, and (c) taking care of themselves to ensure an ability to take care of their students, etc.). | Shows a lack of attempt or action | *In action . . .*<br>Demonstrates **attempt** to implement strategies to sustain intense energy<br><br>*In reflection . . .*<br>Describes personal strategies for productively addressing low energy and motivation<br><br>Explains in a compelling way why such strategies are important | • **Constructively indicates** when she or he is losing energy and motivation<br><br>• **Addresses low** energy and motivation by productively implementing a **limited** number of strategies | • **Anticipates** when she or he may lose energy and motivation<br><br>• Proactively takes steps to **sustain** energy and motivation through a **combination** of strategies | • **Consistently maintains the right balance** for the individual to avoid losing energy required to reach goals<br><br>• Leads the effort to create **a culture that sustains** the collective energy and motivation through a **combination** of strategies |

# APPENDIX B

# ABOUT TEACH FOR AMERICA

**TEACH FOR AMERICA** is the national corps of top recent college graduates who commit to teach for two years in urban and rural public schools and become life-long leaders in the effort to expand educational opportunity. Our mission is to build the movement to eliminate educational inequity by enlisting the nation's most promising future leaders in the effort. We currently have over seven thousand first- and second-year Teach For America corps members teaching in about three dozen regions across the United States, as well as about twenty thousand alumni who are continuing to work from inside and outside the field of education to address the root causes of the problem.

## Our Teachers' Impact

The impact of Teach For America corps members on student achievement is at least as great as that of other new teachers and often exceeds that of experienced and certified teachers in the same schools. Corps members' positive impact spans subject areas and grade levels, from prekindergarten through high school. The most rigorous study to date found that students of corps members attained greater gains in math and equivalent gains in reading compared with students of other teachers, including veteran and certified teachers. For

> ### ▶ THE PROBLEM OF EDUCATIONAL INEQUITY
>
> **IN AMERICA TODAY, EDUCATIONAL** disparities limit the life prospects of the 13 million children growing up in poverty. On average, fourth graders in low-income communities are already three grade levels behind their peers in high-income communities. Half of these students won't graduate from high school. Those who do graduate will read and do math, on average, at the level of eighth graders in high-income communities.

this experimental study, researchers used random assignment of students to teachers at the elementary school level in multiple regions.[1] A team of researchers found similar results based on a review of several years' worth of student achievement data for grades 3 through 8 in New York City. The group concluded that Teach For America corps members are more effective than their traditionally certified counterparts in terms of impact on student achievement in math and just as effective in reading/language arts.[2] A study of Teach For America corps members teaching at the high school level in North Carolina found that they were, on average, more effective than non–Teach For America teachers in all subject areas, especially in math and science. That was true even when Teach For America corps members were compared with experienced, fully certified teachers.[3]

## Alumni Leadership

While only one in ten corps members say they were interested in the teaching profession before joining Teach For America, nearly two-thirds of our alumni remain in the field of education, where they are having a significant impact. They are running many of the most successful schools in low-income communities, winning the highest teacher accolades, and pioneering innovative reform efforts. In regions where Teach For America has been placing corps members for fifteen years or more (such as Oakland, California; New Orleans; and Washington, D.C.), alumni within the education system and across all sectors, forming a critical mass, are taking dramatic steps to provide opportunities for all students.

As of 2009, more than 380 alumni lead schools across the country, and more than 20 have founded and continue to lead some of the country's most innovative nonprofits. In addition, a growing number of Teach For America alumni are pursuing careers in public service, including more than 500 who work in government, politics, or advocacy, and over 25 who serve as elected officials. Teach For America alumni include the founders of the highly successful KIPP Network, YES College Prep schools, and IDEA Public Schools. The chancellor of the Washington, D.C., public schools and key leaders in a number of urban and rural districts are Teach For America alumni. Teach For America's alumni also include elected school board officials in locations such as Los Angeles, Houston, and North Plainfield, New Jersey.

To learn more about Teach For America, visit www.teachforamerica.org.

# APPENDIX C

# OUR APPROACH TO TEACHER DEVELOPMENT

## Recruiting and Selecting Teachers

Teach For America recruits on more than 350 college campuses, seeking seniors and recent graduates from all academic majors and backgrounds who have demonstrated outstanding achievement, perseverance, leadership, and a commitment to expanding opportunities for children in low-income areas. We recruit individuals who have the skills and commitment to make an impact on the academic prospects of students growing up in low-income communities and to exert long-term leadership in the effort to eliminate educational inequity.

Through two decades of research and with the support of many people in the broader academic community, Teach For America has developed a set of selection criteria based on qualities found to be predictive of corps member success:

- A record of past achievement: achieving ambitious, measurable results in academics, leadership, or work

- Perseverance in the face of challenges

- Strong critical thinking skills: making accurate connections between cause and effect and generating relevant solutions to problems

- The ability to influence and motivate others

- Organizational ability: planning well, meeting deadlines, and working efficiently

- An understanding of Teach For America's vision and the desire to work relentlessly in pursuit of it

- Respect for students and families in low-income communities

> ▶ **APPLICATION NUMBERS**
>
> **APPROXIMATELY 35,000 INDIVIDUALS** applied to Teach For America's 2009 corps. At more than 130 colleges and universities, over 5 percent of the senior class applied; at Ivy League schools, 11 percent of all seniors applied, including nearly 20 percent of African American and Hispanic seniors.
>
> Admission to Teach For America is highly selective, with 15 percent of applicants earning acceptance to the 2009 corps. Teach For America is the number one employer of graduating seniors at more than 20 schools, including Georgetown University, Spelman College, and the University of North Carolina at Chapel Hill.

The selection process includes a review of candidates' online application, telephone interviews, and day-long in-person final interviews that allow candidates to demonstrate their strengths in a five-minute sample teaching lesson, group discussions, problem-solving activities, and one-on-one conversations with selectors. At each of the several stages of the recruitment and selection processes, we select individuals who demonstrate the strongest potential to be successful. Finally, we work to matriculate every candidate we accept, coordinating a complex campaign of multiple interactions with accepted applicants. Approximately 80 percent of our offers are accepted.

In 2009, this process resulted in a corps of four thousand teachers with an impressive record of achievements:

- Average grade point average: 3.6

- Average SAT: 1344 (of those who reported it)

- Percentage with leadership experience in college: 89 percent

Eighty-five percent of the new corps was made up of college seniors, and the remaining 15 percent were mid-career professionals or graduate students.

Each of these four thousand teachers brings a unique set of career aspirations, academic majors, and personal backgrounds. The 2009 corps represents more than five hundred colleges and universities in all states and the District of Columbia. Their academic majors span a wide spectrum: 34 percent from the social sciences, 12 percent from language and literature, and 12 percent from math, science, and engineering.

We make a particular effort to recruit members who share the racial or socioeconomic background of the students we serve, and our corps is more diverse than the campuses where we recruit. Among the 2009 corps, 30 percent are people of color, including 10 percent African American and 7 percent Latino, and 25 percent are Pell Grant recipients. By comparison, at all four-year colleges and universities in the United States, African Americans make up 9 percent of the graduates and Latinos make up 7 percent. Of the graduates at the top 450 schools in the country, 5.2 percent are African American and 6.2 percent are Latino.[1]

## Philosophy of Teacher Development

Over twenty years, our methods for preparing corps members to be successful teachers in low-income urban and rural areas have evolved dramatically. With the Teaching As Leadership framework as its intellectual centerpiece, the program consists of intensive preservice training before corps members teach full time and includes regular support and professional development throughout the school year from experienced mentors and coaches.

This model of teacher preparation, support, and development rests on the premise that there are five key drivers of new teacher learning and performance. (See Figure C.1.)

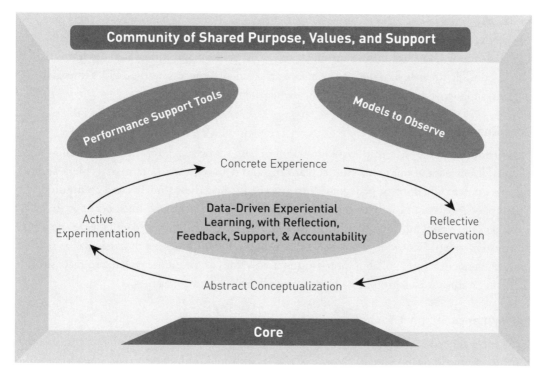

Figure C.1  Key Drivers of Teacher Learning and Performance

*Note:* The embedded cycle of experiential adult learning
(represented by the arrows) is drawn from the work of David A. Kolb.

## Experiential Learning

At the center of this model is experiential learning—what teachers learn firsthand from their classroom experiences and the progress their students make. To maximize the value of that experience, it must be:

- *Data driven.* Teachers must have clear goals for student learning and must use data to identify progress and gaps in student learning on the path to those goals. Data help teachers know whether their efforts are working and also fuel their curiosity and intrinsic drive to continue increasing their effectiveness.

- *Infused with feedback and reflection.* Teachers need to reflect on their student learning data, instructional practices, and emotional experiences. This model leads teachers to analyze the relationship between their actions and student outcomes, a process that helps them understand what led to their actions, what new or different actions they can try next time, and what learning experiences will assist them in knowing how to take those actions. This cyclical reflective process, grounded in student results, serves the dual purposes of fueling ongoing learning and solving real problems.[2]

- *Implemented in a spirit of accountability with support.* From the beginning of their preservice teaching experience, our teachers are responsible for student learning in their classrooms. Our staff, during summer preservice training and in regional programs, is responsible for ensuring their corps members' students' success, and provides intensive and supportive management of these new teachers.

### Core Knowledge

Experiential learning must rest on a foundation of core knowledge. Teachers must build foundational knowledge about instructional planning and delivery, classroom management and culture, content and content pedagogy, learning theory, and their students and community. That knowledge must be delivered in concrete and applicable ways and must occur at times in a teacher's development when they are most relevant and needed. We also emphasize the need for teachers to build knowledge of their own strengths and weaknesses, in particular as related to their interactions and collaboration—often across lines of differences related to race, socioeconomic status, or background—with students, families, and colleagues.

### Performance Support Tools

New teachers need access to effective resources, ranging from student assessments and lesson plans to sample letters to parents. New teachers learn from building on strong resources in addition to creating their own resources.

### Role Models

New teachers need opportunities to observe and learn from both strong and developing teachers. These role models help them envision effective teaching and build confidence that they are on a developmental path that will lead them to effective teaching. Models and observations are most effective when paired with guided commentary to help new teachers recognize how they are executing key actions.

### Shared Purpose, Values, and Support

The benefits of these elements are magnified when new teachers are part of a welcoming and supportive environment of colleagues with shared purpose, values, and support. Like their students, when teachers feel comfortable with and connected to each other, they are able to take risks, ask for help, admit mistakes, experiment, learn from colleagues, and sustain themselves both physically and emotionally.

## Preservice Training System

Incorporating these principles of teacher learning and performance, Teach For America has developed a comprehensive preservice and in-service program model for preparing, supporting, and developing teachers.

Before they begin their first year of teaching, all new teachers must complete a rigorous pre-service training program (the "institute"), which begins in mid-April and lasts until the school year begins in the late summer or early fall. It includes independent work, supervised clinical practice, seminars and workshops, and online learning.

## Independent Work

Shortly after they are accepted into Teach For America, corps members receive assignments that include reading a set of curriculum texts developed by Teach For America, conducting classroom observations of experienced teachers, and completing reflection assignments. These assignments require thirty to forty hours to complete. The goals of the assigned work are to help corps members become familiar with the Teaching As Leadership framework, develop an understanding of their roles and responsibilities as highly effective teachers, and identify and adopt the mindsets of exemplary teachers. A subset of corps members engages in additional content-area learning.

## Regional Induction

Corps members spend up to a week, prior to attending the institute, in the region where they will be teaching in the fall. During that time, they become familiar with school- and district-specific policies, programs, and curricula. They also prepare to get the most out of their institute experience and begin meeting state teacher credentialing requirements.

## Training Institute

The institute, which takes place during the summer before corps members start teaching full time, builds on what they have learned through their independent work to ensure that they become highly effective beginning teachers. While the institute lasts for five weeks, each day is scheduled for fourteen hours of activity so corps members gain a total of approximately nine to ten weeks of training. The institutes, held on university campuses, are run by Teach For America institute staff. Corps members are not enrolled in university-based programs at these universities but do typically enroll in university-based programs in the regions where they teach.

### ▶ LOCATIONS OF INSTITUTES

**AMONG THE LOCATIONS THAT** our teachers attend preservice training institutes are:

- Atlanta, Georgia (Georgia Institute of Technology)
- Chicago, Illinois (Illinois Institute of Technology)
- Houston, Texas (University of Houston)
- Los Angeles, California (Loyola Marymount University)
- Mississippi Delta in Cleveland, Mississippi (Delta State University)
- New York, New York (St. John's University)
- Philadelphia, Pennsylvania (Temple University)
- Phoenix, Arizona (Arizona State University)

The institute is focused on teaching corps members the daily skills they will need, regardless of the subject area or grade level they teach:

- Lesson planning according to the principles of backward design
- Delivery of content
- Facilitating group practice
- Checking for understanding
- Investing students
- Classroom management
- Crafting daily assessments
- Assessing student performance
- Tracking student progress and adjusting course to ensure student mastery
- Engaging with students, families, and colleagues and administrators across lines of difference

The institute has two main components: summer school teaching and curriculum sessions. Corps members teach in summer school classrooms similar to those in which they will teach in the fall. Each corps member teaches as part of a three- or four-person collaborative that is supervised and mentored by both a veteran teacher from the school and Teach For America staff members. Teachers rotate in and out of the role of lead teacher, a system that allows corps members to attend training sessions and also provides lower student-teacher ratios during daily academic intervention sessions with students beyond the daily classroom lessons. Corps members receive regular feedback about their teaching, engage in reflection and conversations about refining their practice, and identify solutions to improve their methods to ensure that students meet summer school goals. They also observe one another's teaching and sometimes evaluate videos of themselves teaching.

Every day while at the institute, corps members attend training sessions where they gain the foundational knowledge needed to become highly effective beginning teachers. These sessions are led by veteran teachers, including specialists in literacy instruction chosen for their proven record of leading students to dramatic academic progress. Our training curriculum (as well as the textbooks we have developed that corps members are required to read before the institute) is broken down into the following core subjects:

- Teaching As Leadership
- Instructional Planning and Delivery
- Classroom Management and Culture
- Elementary and Secondary Literacy
- Diversity, Community, and Achievement
- Learning Theory

At the institute, we aim to meet the needs of our summer school students as we meet the needs of our new teachers. We provide corps members with a set of performance support tools, the Student Achievement Toolkit, which helps them take what they have learned and apply it immediately in their summer school classrooms. The toolkit typically includes ambitious and feasible academic goals for the students, a unit plan, diagnostic and final assessments, and tools to track student performance. The toolkit's design facilitates students' academic progress in line with the particular learning requirements and curricula of the district's summer school program. The content is aligned with the district-mandated assessments students must pass at the end of the summer.

This table provides an overview of the daily structure of our summer training institutes:

| Morning/Early Afternoons | |
| --- | --- |
| **Classroom teaching** | A key component of the summer institute is a well-structured and well-supported teaching experience. |
| | Corps members prepare in small groups called collaboratives to teach in district summer school programs, under the supervision of veteran educators from the hosting school campus and Teach For America's instructional staff. |
| | Corps members work with this team to set objectives for summer school students, diagnose student needs, track student progress, and create effective lesson plans. |
| | Each corps member has a block of time every day when he or she is the lead teacher of the classroom. |
| **Sessions/ reflection and rehearsal** | Corps members attend curriculum sessions based on the skills associated with the Teaching As Leadership framework. Also, they reflect on their teaching with their corps member advisor and rehearse new skills in group sessions with their colleagues. |
| **Afternoons/Evenings** | |
| **Individual feedback** | Corps members receive individual feedback and coaching from their advisors. |
| **Lesson planning clinics and seminars** | Corps members participate in lesson planning clinics and attend seminars to learn content- and grade-level-specific pedagogy. |
| **Planning and preparation for teaching** | Corps members spend the evenings planning and rehearsing lessons for their summer school classroom. They have access to tools that will assist them in acquiring the key skills they will need as teachers, such as long-term planning, unit planning, lesson planning, classroom management, student and parent investment, student diagnosis, and data tracking. These tools also allow corps members to make use of best practices that have evolved over many years and with the input of many experts. The support tools include the following:<br><br>• Sample plans that match district curricula<br><br>• Models that corps members can imitate and adjust as needed<br><br>• Content-rich and well-structured templates |

### Transition to the Regional Program

Once corps members return to their regions from the institute, they participate in a series of meetings, workshops, and training sessions with their regional program teams and complete online course work. The goal of the program in the weeks before and after teaching begins is to help corps members build a strong foundation for the work they will do throughout the school year. While the institute focuses on daily teaching skills that can be generally applied in any classroom, the program during this phase focuses on year- and unit-level foundations specific to corps members' teaching environment (for example, grade level, subject, school, or district).

During this period, regional program teams work with corps members to ensure they are prepared to provide sound instruction to their students early in the school year. To that end, we help corps members set goals for their students, determine how to measure progress toward those goals, and develop their first units. To gain these skills and knowledge, corps members are required to complete an average of twenty-five hours of online course work during this time. We also work with corps members to ensure they know how to use the in-person and online resources offered. As part of this process, all corps members have access to a Student Achievement Toolkit, similar to the one they received during the institute. It is a collection of documents and resources tailored to the grade level, subject, and region in which corps members teach. Each toolkit is designed to help corps members create data-driven, achievement-focused classrooms. It includes model course goals, long-term instructional plans, and first-unit assessments and plans for each grade and subject area. It also includes diagnostic tests, ongoing assessments, and student achievement tracking tools.

Also during this period, regional program teams help corps members establish strong relationships within their schools and districts, as well as with Teach For America staff members called program directors (typically they are former successful teachers who work with new corps members throughout the school year). We believe that these relationships are key to teachers' success in the classroom. Based on the corps members' completion of the online course work and one-on-one conversations with their program directors, the regional program teams determine what combination of support and professional development each teacher will receive during the school year by working with groups of other teachers or individually with a program director.

## Ongoing Support System for Teachers in the Classroom

Because all new teachers, especially those working in low-income communities, face intense and numerous challenges in their schools and classrooms, we invest significant time and resources in providing ongoing support for corps members throughout their two-year commitment. There are four main components to this support and professional development model.

### Observation and Coaching

Many schools and districts provide corps members with mentors—veteran teachers with years of experience and a wealth of knowledge. These relationships are extremely valuable for corps members as they take on the steep learning curve all teachers experience in their first year.

In addition, each corps member is paired with a Teach For America program director, who provides feedback and support based on student data from and observations of the corps member's class. Throughout the year, corps members and program directors engage in one-on-one co-investigation conversations, during which they reflect on student data to identify and find causes of and solutions to problems or gaps in student achievement. This coaching approach builds new teachers' ability to independently evaluate student outcomes, identify causes of any problems, and seek solutions.

Program directors who monitor student learning in classrooms adjust their support according to corps members' needs. Teach For America holds program directors accountable for the performance of their corps members' students and tracks progress toward student achievement goals throughout the year.

## Online Resources and Community

We have developed TFANet, an online support network. Within TFANet, the Teaching and Learning Center is a place where corps members and alumni have access to information, tools, and resources designed to boost their effectiveness as teachers and where corps members can exchange ideas and questions with one another. It has four components:

- *Resource Exchange.* Corps members and alumni have access to a searchable and browsable database of tens of thousands of instructional resources (lesson plans, classroom rules,

### ▶ BUILDING CONTENT-SPECIFIC PEDAGOGICAL KNOWLEDGE

**THE TEACHING AS LEADERSHIP** framework is a general pedagogical model meant to support teachers in all grades and subjects. We also recognize the value of content-specific pedagogy. As changes in the education landscape have improved our ability to predict corps members' teaching assignments in their schools, we have been able to infuse more pedagogical content knowledge in training and support systems.

For example, we have invested in expanding the tools and resources for new teachers to reflect content-specific instructional strategies. We are working to supply corps members with high-quality diagnostic, summative, and formative assessments specific to their placement areas, and we also want to develop and use online vehicles, such as the Resource Exchange, to increase corps members' access to premade long-term plans, unit plans and lesson plans specific to their content areas. We are developing training and ongoing support by creating online communities and advice forums customized to particular placement areas and equipping program directors with greater knowledge about supporting corps members facing challenges specific to content areas. There is a growing library of videos showing role models and virtual classroom visits specific to content areas. And we are planning to enhance our self-directed online instructional offerings, including subject-specific e-learning courses, workshops, and curriculum texts.

photos, links, and so on), some of which have user reviews and ratings. In addition, these resources are vetted by staff members with expertise in specific content areas; they highlight resources on their blogs on the Web site. Corps members and alumni can also share their knowledge with one another by uploading their own resources.

- *Advice and community support.* Corps members and program directors can ask questions and receive answers and advice. For example, columnists answer questions from corps members (such as, "How do I incorporate writing when we don't have enough classroom time?"), providing specific recommendations or steps that teachers can take, and bloggers provide resource recommendations on specific content areas based on the most popular search terms in the Resource Exchange section.

- *Video resources and models.* Corps members can watch narrated, annotated videos of classroom observations of effective teachers at work. These videos illustrate particular aspects of excellent teacher practice in specific content areas and allow corps members to see how these practices are executed in a real classroom.

- *Self-directed online learning.* Corps members have access to courses, workshops, and our curriculum texts that we are continuing to develop. One such resource available is the Teaching As Leadership Online Navigator (TALON), a multimedia guide to the Teaching As Leadership framework that features video models, testimonials, and advice for each of the specific teacher actions within the Teaching As Leadership framework at varying levels of teacher proficiency, as well as detailed how-to guides, common pitfalls, and useful strategies. Corps members access these resources independently and in consultation with their program directors, whose coaching directs them to pursue self-directed learning online.

## Regional Learning Sessions

In most regions, teachers meet regularly in content- and grade-level specific learning teams led by experienced teachers to discuss ongoing challenges, share best practices, and work together on professional development. Activities might include creating and exchanging lesson plans and other instructional materials, modeling exemplary lessons, examining student work, and collaborating to track student progress. These meetings provide a prime venue for in-person professional collaboration and support among corps members.

## Certification and Master's Programs Through University Partnerships

Corps members in most regions participate in university-based teacher certification or master's degree programs designed to ensure they meet all state certification requirements. These programs supplement the training and support that Teach For America provides, helping corps members acquire additional skills and support to lead their students toward significant academic achievement.

> ▶ **SUPPORTING ALUMNI**

**WITH LEADERS IN EDUCATION,** politics, policy, and many other sectors, Teach For America's network of over twenty thousand corps members and alumni is a growing force for social change. Drawing inspiration and ideas from one another, they are tackling some of the most challenging issues affecting children in low-income communities across the country, bringing us closer to realizing our shared vision of educational equity and excellence.

Teach For America works to foster a dynamic network among alumni and to inspire and support their ongoing commitment to students and communities. We help them pursue career and civic choices that maximize and sustain their impact on the achievement gap individually and collectively. We do so by providing engaging opportunities and customized tools, resources, and information to help them regularly reflect on their career and civic choices and pursue those choices purposefully. We also offer ways to help them meaningfully connect with each other and Teach For America, and we provide forums to help advance their thinking on issues of educational reform.

- *Teaching and Learning Center:* The approximately two-thirds of our alumni who remain in education after their two-year commitment can draw on Teach For America's teacher support resources through TFANet.org.
- *Career and Leadership Center:* Alumni have access to resources such as career coaching, alumni mentors, résumé drives, career Webinars, and a robust job board.
- *Regional alumni affairs team:* Staff members meet one-on-one with alumni, host events, and develop strategic partnerships to support alumni career and civic goals and to connect alumni with one another.
- *Special initiatives:* Initiatives in school and teacher leadership, political leadership, social entrepreneurship, and policy and advocacy leadership help alumni build skills, readiness, and networks to accelerate their impact in these fields.
- *Graduate school and employer partnerships:* Hundreds of graduate school partners and employers offer special benefits to Teach For America corps members and alumni, such as two-year deferrals, scholarships, internships, and career mentoring.

# APPENDIX D

# HOW WE LEARN FROM OUR TEACHERS

**TEACH FOR AMERICA'S** size and reach gives it a unique vantage point on educational inequity in America. Since its inception in 1990, Teach For America has recruited, selected, trained, and supported over twenty thousand teachers in urban and rural low-income communities across the country. Currently hundreds of Teach For America program staff, many of whom were highly effective teachers themselves, have responsibility for training and supporting corps members.[1] These teachers and staff also work with an extensive network of veteran teachers in summer and regional school placements, as well as the faculty of university partners in the several dozen regions where we place and support teachers.

Among these many thousands of teachers and staff members, Teach For America has facilitated an ongoing conversation about what is and is not working in our teachers' classrooms. For twenty years, we have employed a mixture of qualitative and quantitative inquiries into teachers' actions and mindsets, the training and support structures that most improve teachers' effectiveness, and the challenges to student learning in our teachers' classrooms. In pursuit of best practices among the most effective teachers, in the past decade we have put considerable energy into evaluating student learning in our teachers' classrooms so that we can consider connections between teachers' effectiveness and their mindsets, knowledge, and actions.

## Defining, Measuring, and Tracking Student Learning

We define the effectiveness of corps members by the extent to which they increase students' academic achievement. In our first decade, we relied on surveys of principals to assess teachers' effectiveness. Although that system did help generally delineate strong from weak teachers, its inherent subjectivity limited the data's usefulness for evaluating what distinguishes effective teachers and what elements of our program are most improving teachers' effectiveness.

As more and more districts and states implemented standardized assessments in the 1990s, Teach For America sought to harvest the student achievement data coming from those assessments to provide a clearer view of teacher effectiveness. In our dozens of regions, we needed a system that allowed us to interpret and aggregate results across a patchwork of assessments and contexts, since corps members teach different grades and subjects in different schools and districts using different curricula and varied assessments. To that end, we worked to evaluate and ensure the rigor of the district-, state-, or teacher-created assessments our teachers were using to measure student learning, and we developed methods of translating the many forms of student data into a universally comparable measurement.

To help us and our teachers set goals that align with our mission of closing the achievement gap, since 2002 we have evaluated teachers' student achievement data through this system and put teachers into one of several performance categories: significant gains, solid gains, or limited gains. We charge corps members with the aim of achieving the most ambitious of these categories, "significant gains," with their students, given the fact that the students we serve are often years behind their peers in higher-income areas. The following table offers an overview of how those categories of performance are defined for three different axes of student learning: student academic growth, student mastery of rigorous content standards, and closing the gap with performers in well-served schools:

| | Significant Gains | Solid Gains | Limited Gains |
|---|---|---|---|
| **Academic growth** | 1.5 or more years | 1.0 to 1.4 years | Less than 1 year |
| **Mastery of standards** | 80 percent of standards mastered | 70 to 79 percent of standards mastered | Less than 70 percent of standards mastered |
| **Distance to performers in well-served schools** | 20 percent (secondary grades) or 24 percent (elementary grades) of gap closed | 10 percent of gap closed | Less than 10 percent of gap closed |

This significant-gains system of measuring and tracking teacher effectiveness has served us well but is far from perfect. Given the wide range of grades, subjects, and geographies in which corps members teach and the difficulty of obtaining timely access to state and district data, the assessments and assessment data used by corps members still vary widely in quality and rigor. Furthermore, while the system of benchmarks for significant gains provides corps members with ambitious student learning goals that are explicitly grounded in our quest for educational equity, these goals are still not fully calibrated to context. (They might be, for example, more or less ambitious depending on the subject and grade being taught, the assessment being used, and the starting point of the students.)

We are improving our student achievement measurement system in two ways. First, we are investing resources and working to get higher-quality assessments and assessment data in the hands of corps members. Second, we are analyzing student learning data to produce more calibrated goals that are tied to the achievement of high-performing teachers in each context.

We believe this improved student achievement measurement system will provide a more precise view of teacher effectiveness, accelerating our work to determine what teacher actions and mindsets most correlate with students' success.

## Investigating Our Teachers' Practices

Given the high stakes for our students, we invest considerable time and energy learning about our teachers' actions and those actions' influence on student learning. Our methods of investigating teachers' practices are varied and iterative—an approach we describe as an ongoing conversation rather than as a discrete study. The content of this book is a snapshot of that ongoing conversation and an articulation of what we have learned so far.

Among the most productive methods of investigation we use to inform this conversation are:

• *Teacher observations and debriefs.* Program directors observe, coach, and support first- and second-year teachers. These staff members come together regularly in their regions and periodically nationally to share insights and patterns of teacher practices and needs. In some cases, observations are videotaped. Many other staff members, in various capacities, also observe and share impressions of teachers.

• *Co-investigative reflection sessions.* Several times a year, teachers have an extended conversation with staff members in which the teacher brings to the table evidence of student learning and, using the cycle of reflection described in Chapter Five, identifies root causes of gaps in student learning in order to improve his or her effectiveness. In some cases, we videotape those conversations. Those conversations are a rich source of insight on teachers' actions and mindsets. We track data from these conversations to inform teacher performance and development needs.

• *Yearly recognition of highly effective teachers.* Each year, regional staff nominate for awards teachers who are achieving particularly dramatic progress with their students and exemplify the practices we are finding most effective. These teachers are recognized in their regions and nationally with the Sue Lehmann Award for Teaching Excellence. We analyze and discuss the documentary and video evidence of these teachers' practices, classrooms, and students, a process that provides valuable insight into the practices of highly effective teachers.

• *Rubric norming on teacher video and documents.* As we continue to improve our Teaching As Leadership framework and rubric, we have normed ourselves on the rubric by collectively analyzing video clips or teacher documents and using discrepancies in rubric scoring to catalyze conversations about how to define and articulate levels of proficiency on key teacher actions.

• *Online resources.* Our teachers (as corps members and as alumni of our program) are members of an online community in which they can share, search, and rate resources; discuss their challenges, needs, and advice; and access training and support materials. Teachers can watch annotated videos of their colleagues performing various teacher actions at all levels of proficiency. How teachers are interacting with those online resources is another source of insight into teachers' needs, strengths, and actions.

• *Teacher surveys.* Several times a year, we survey our teachers to learn what resources and structures they are finding most and least helpful to their work. We analyze those data on dozens of variables (teachers' effectiveness, resources accessed, school placement, grade level, region, gender, race, experience, effectiveness, and so on), seeking out patterns.

• *Teacher surveys and interviews on discrete issues.* As we see patterns in these sources of information to explore, we launch discrete initiatives on particular issues, such as how teachers use learning standards in the process of designing big goals, or how teachers who share racial or socioeconomic identity with their students approach the resulting opportunities and challenges, or what methods the most effective teachers are using to assert their authority with students at the beginning of the school year. These initiatives often involve a combination of the methods described above, in particular teacher surveys, observations, and interviews.

The analysis of these incoming streams of information involves dozens of national and regional program staff and is informed by external research and external researchers. We partner and consult with a number of top experts in the field, some of whom have served on our research advisory board and others who are serving as advisors for specific research efforts.

## Using Student Data and Teacher Data to Explore Best Practices

When we can see what the teachers making significant gains are doing differently from those making solid and limited gains, we gain insight into how to move more teachers into the category of significant gains.

By bringing together data showing student learning and other data showing teacher actions, we shed light on a number of important questions. What resources are the most effective teachers using and not using? What resources did teachers who moved out of the limited-gains category most rely on? How do the lesson plans of teachers making significant gains differ from those whose students are making solid gains? What patterns are there in the ways teachers in these three categories of student achievement describe their relationship with their students? How do the teachers whose students are achieving enormous growth make instructional choices? When we examine these teachers' application files, what indicators seem to predict this teacher's making significant gains with students and what of our selection criteria are not correlated with measures of student learning?

As we investigate and debate these questions based on the data, each new hypothesis catalyzes new questions and more studies. In the last few years, for example, through data analysis, document review, and focus groups, we have looked closely at how teachers design and set goals that most influence student learning. We have gathered and studied the most effective teachers' systems for monitoring, publishing, and celebrating students' progress. We have evaluated countless year-long and unit plans, lesson plans, and classroom management plans, distilling the common qualities of those belonging to teachers whose students are most successful. Through extensive interviews with teachers of all backgrounds, experiences, and identities, we have looked at how more and less effective teachers address challenges related to race, class, language, and power dynamics that arise in our work. We have met with some of the growing number of teachers in our network who have achieved strong results with their students for five and sometimes ten or fifteen years, learning how these teachers make their success sustainable.

These iterative and on-going investigations are the primary sources of Teaching As Leadership.

# TEACHER BIOGRAPHIES

**THE IDEAS IN *TEACHING AS LEADERSHIP*** are distilled from the experiences of teachers whose students in low-income communities are making dramatic academic progress (as described in the Introduction and Appendix D). The teachers whose names appear in this book are a sampling of those highly effective teachers.

In some cases, these teachers' words and insights have been pulled directly from the raw data of our investigations—from surveys, or videotape, or their own writing in nomination forms for teaching awards. In some cases, their words have been offered in response to targeted inquiries about some particular aspect of their teaching practice. Some of these teachers are still in the classroom, and others are not, and some of them have been or currently are Teach For America staff members. In all cases, they have had a significant impact on the lives of their students.

We are offering additional information about these teachers here because:

- We want to bring to life the levels of student achievement we are seeing in these classrooms.

- We want to celebrate and acknowledge these teachers' accomplishments.

- To have listed each teacher's student progress in the text itself would have been cumbersome.

**Almeida, Joseph.** On average, Mr. Almeida's fifth-grade students in New York City began the year reading two years below grade level. By the end of the year, they had improved their reading levels by an average of two years. Every single one of his students—including all thirteen of his students with Individualized Education Programs, eleven of whom had not passed the state test the previous year—passed the fifth-grade state math test by scoring a 3 (proficiency) or a 4 (advanced proficiency), and over 40 percent of them (a school record) passed with advanced proficiency. He had similarly dramatic results in social studies. In addition, Mr. Almeida founded and organized the annual end-of-year awards ceremony and talent show at his school. He currently teaches sixth-grade math at KIPP Infinity Charter School, one of the top-performing public schools in New York City.

**Alonso, Luis.** As a ninth-grade physical science teacher in New Orleans, Mr. Alonso helped lead over 90 percent of his students to pass the district science exam (as contrasted with 58 percent passing in the district). He also brought his technological savvy to his school and students, teaching the school's first computer programming classes, maintaining computer labs, and teaching colleagues to use technology in their classrooms. Today he is employed by Google, where he works with the people behind Google for Educators, a resource for teachers, and he helps with outreach programs that target schools in low-income neighborhoods.

**Asiyanbi, Susan.** As a fourth-grade math and science teacher in Newark, New Jersey, Ms. Asiyanbi led her students to over 80-percent mastery of grade-level standards. She subsequently held a variety of positions at Teach For America, where she directed key elements of the teacher preparation program. Ms. Asiyanbi subsequently earned her M.B.A. from the Kellogg School of Management at Northwestern University and is currently a senior leader consultant for Sears Holding.

**Barrett, Lisa.** The elementary students (first through fifth grade) with special needs whom Ms. Barrett taught in Oakland, California, improved an average of 2.2 grade levels in reading and 1.7 grade levels in math, based on assessments such as the Weschler Individual Achievement Test and Brigance. As a result of her work with students, a number of them were reclassified from "mentally retarded" to "specific learning disability," and at least two of them exited the special day class setting and were able to successfully attend general education classes for most of the school day. Ms. Barrett served on both the leadership team and the faculty counsel at her school, and she was twice nominated for the Symantec Recognition for Innovative Teaching award. She has also recruited, selected, trained, and placed exceptional teachers in special education classrooms across Oakland for the New Teacher Project. She continues to work closely with the Oakland Unified School District on issues related to teacher quality and also works with four Phoenix, Arizona, school districts to recruit, select, and train teachers for high-need area classrooms.

**Barton, Emily.** Ms. Barton's seventh-grade math students in Opelousas, Louisiana, entered her class doing math on an early-fifth-grade level. By the end of the year, they had improved 2.7 grade levels and were on grade level in math according to district and state assessments. Ms. Barton later spearheaded and led Teach For America's Connecticut region, and she currently serves as the executive director of Teach For America's Washington, D.C., region.

**Bass, Sarah.** As an English and history teacher at Frederick Douglass Academy Middle School in Los Angeles, Ms. Bass led approximately 82 percent of her students to scores of "proficient" or higher on 80 percent of state standards (as demonstrated by regular assessment and California's Standardized Testing and Reporting). She has been awarded an Abele Teaching Fellowship and has been named Seventh Grade Teacher of the Year at Frederick Douglass Academy. Ms. Bass is currently pursuing an M.F.A. in creative writing at the University of West Indies as a Fulbright scholar, and her long-term goal is to found a K-12 academy of science and the arts for African American boys.

**Batista-São Roque, Cheyenne.** As a sixth- and eighth-grade English/language arts teacher in New York City, Ms. Batista-São Roque led all of her students to passing scores on the state exam. She subsequently managed state department of education clients as a program manager for education assessment reporting at the Grow Network/McGraw-Hill, and is currently a fourth-grade teacher at the American School of Campinas in São Paulo, Brazil.

**Beuche, Blair.** Ms. Beuche's high school Spanish students in Baltimore, Maryland, entered her class with no background knowledge of the language. By the end of the year, her Spanish I and II students mastered all objectives with an 84 percent mastery average as measured by a rigorous teacher-compiled final exam based on the state standards. Her students were able to write a 750-word essay and hold a conversation in Spanish for five minutes by the end of Spanish II. Ms. Beuche subsequently worked as a mentor and coach to Teach For America corps members in eastern North Carolina and is currently dean of students of a K-8 school in Michigan.

**Bialecki, Jess.** When New Orleans, Louisiana, first-year teacher Ms. Bialecki assessed her first-grade students at the beginning of the year, she found that they were entering her class reading, on average, at an early kindergarten level, with only one student reading at grade level. They averaged below the thirtieth percentile in the school district on the Dynamic Indicators of Basic Early Literacy Skills assessment. By the end of the year, they had achieved an average of 1.44 years growth in reading and scored at almost the seventy-fifth percentile in the district on the DIBELS assessment. Furthermore, they exceeded their class fluency goal of an average of forty words per minute, and sixteen of her twenty-one students were at or above grade level in math by the end of the year.

**Biber, Josh.** The year before Mr. Biber arrived at Laveen Elementary School in Phoenix, Arizona, only 22 percent of the school's fifth graders scored "met" or "exceeding" on the state math test, and only 27 percent scored "met" or "exceeding" on the state reading test. Each year he was in the classroom, his students averaged two years of reading growth and more than 80 percent mastery of math content. In his second year of teaching, when he served as grade-level chair, 70 percent of the school's fifth graders scored "met" or "exceeding" on reading and 71 percent scored "met" or "exceeding" in math—the highest scores in the district that year, and the highest that his school had ever achieved. Mr. Biber is currently the executive director of Teach For America's Greater Boston region.

**Bickford, LesLee.** On average, Ms. Bickford's sixth-grade math students in Philadelphia entered her class performing on a third-grade level in math. Many struggled to do double-digit addition and subtraction, and five of them were unable to add single digits, a first-grade skill. By the end of each of her years of teaching, Ms. Bickford's students averaged almost 90 percent proficiency of sixth-grade math standards, meaning that on average, they grew three years over the course of the school year. Most of her science students had never before taken science classes. By the end of the year, they averaged 84 percent proficiency of sixth-grade science standards. Ms. Bickford currently works to help Teach For America recruit more outstanding teachers across the country.

**Bookbinder, Pamela.** During her first year teaching New York City sophomores, Ms. Bookbinder increased the school pass rate on the Global History Regents Exam by more than 55 percentage points. During her second year, when she taught the same students as juniors, more than 90 percent of them passed the U.S. History Regents Exam. After she looped with them for a third year to twelfth-grade government, 100 percent of her students received credit for the course, and over 95 percent of them applied and were accepted to college. Ms. Bookbinder currently recruits teachers for Achievement First.

**Bowen, Laura.** As a fifth-grade teacher at Carver Upper Elementary School in Indianola, Mississippi, Ms. Bowen consistently led her students to more than 1.5 years of growth in reading (as measured by the Developmental Reading Assessment), and she was named Teacher of the Year for both Carver Upper Elementary School and the entire Indianola School District. She subsequently taught fifth grade at KIPP DC: KEY Academy, where she was honored with the Board of Directors' Award. After serving as vice principal at KEY Academy, Ms. Bowen received a KIPP Fisher Fellowship in spring 2006 and subsequently opened KIPP DC: LEAP Academy, an early childhood/elementary school serving predominantly low-income African American students. She is now entering her third year as principal of LEAP, with an enrollment of 280 prekindergarten and kindergarten students. In 2008–2009, in a seven-month period, LEAP's prekindergarten students made sixteen months of vocabulary growth, nine months of math growth, and ten months of early literacy growth, and the kindergartners moved on to first-grade reading and doing math above grade level.

**Brakke, Crystal.** Of Ms. Brakke's seventy-two eighth-grade language arts students in rural North Carolina, only 35 percent entered her class reading on grade level. Since the high school graduation rate in the county was around 40 percent, she became obsessed with getting her kids ready for high school so they could have a better chance of graduating and have broader career options. At the end of the year, over 80 percent of her students were reading on grade level. Ms. Brakke has subsequently worked in a variety of capacities at Teach For America, where she currently contributes to teacher preparation efforts.

**Buckler, Rachel.** As a developmental reading instructor at a middle school in St. Louis, Missouri, Ms. Buckler led her 67 students to an average of 2.25 years reading growth as assessed by the SRI. The next year, her 112 English/language arts students attained an average of 1.75 years of growth in reading on the Developmental Reading Assessment and an average of 81 percent mastery of prioritized Missouri state standards. Ms. Buckler was nominated for the Pettus Award (a St. Louis Public Schools Teacher Honor Program), named Middle School Team Leader, and served on the District Textbook Adoption Committee and the School Improvement Committee. She currently teaches seventh and eighth grade, at Bronzeville Lighthouse Charter School in Chicago, a public school serving low-income, primarily African American students.

**Carabajal, Rhiannon.** Ms. Carabajal's success with her government and economics students led to her being named Teacher of the Year at Jefferson Davis High School in Houston. Ms. Carabajal (now Ms. Killian) returned to the classroom, teaching seventh-grade arts and humanities at Yes Prep East End Campus in Houston, where 98 percent of the seventh graders (taught by her and three colleagues) passed the 2009 state writing exam, 60 percent of them earning "commended" performance, almost triple the statewide "commended" percentage for students classified as economically disadvantaged. In addition, 92 percent of her school's seventh graders passed the state reading assessment, matching the statewide pass rate for students classified as nondisadvantaged.

**Carpenter, Linh Luong.** When Ms. Carpenter's kindergarten students first entered her classroom at DJ Meyer Elementary in San Jose, many of them lacked prerequisite skills. Fewer than half of them could recognize their first name written out. On average, they could identify only eight letters of the alphabet and seven numbers. By the end of the year, all students knew all letters and sounds of the alphabet. As a class average, students could read 74 sight words (30 words is the California State Standard), count to 95 (to 100 is an end-of-first-grade standard), and write numbers from 1 to 100 in order (an end-of-first-grade standard). All students met the California Standard of writing one sentence with correct capitalization, spacing, and punctuation, with 85 percent of students able to write a structured five-sentence paragraph. Ms. Carpenter currently works as a mentor and coach for Teach For America teachers in Los Angeles.

**Clemensen, Lars.** Mr. Clemensen taught seventh- and eighth-grade English at Public School 11 in the Paterson, New Jersey, Public School District. At the beginning of the school year, roughly one-third of his students scored "proficient" on the Grade Eight Proficiency Assessment in Language Arts, New Jersey's benchmark for students. By March, at the time of the test, more than two-thirds of his students had advanced in grade level and proficiency for New Jersey's state language arts standards. Mr. Clemensen received the Teacher of the Year award for Public School 11, an honor chosen by the school's administration, faculty, and parent-teacher organization. Mr. Clemensen subsequently served as executive director of Teach For America's New Jersey region for two years, before moving to Long Island to assume the role of founding principal of Hampton Bays Middle School, the first green school in New York State. He has served as its school leader during the planning phases and since its opening in 2008.

**Cohen, Rebecca.** Ms. Cohen has taught English/language arts in low-income communities in Baltimore, Maryland; New York City; and Weslaco, Texas. When she taught at Dr. Armando Cuellar Middle School in Texas, 93 percent of her students passed state reading and writing assessments (compared to 85 percent statewide), with 35 percent attaining "commended" performance (compared to 29 percent statewide). Ms. Cohen has been named Weslaco Independent School District Teacher of the Year and Dr. Armando Cuellar Middle School Teacher of the Year. She currently works on curriculum and professional development for Achievement First.

**Cohen, Samantha.** Ms. Cohen's first-grade students in Atlanta, averaged more than two years of reading growth on a battery of core assessments for fluency and comprehension, with many students improving from preprimer levels to second- and third-grade reading levels. In math, they mastered, on average, more than 85 percent of the first- *and* second-grade Georgia math standards, effectively leaving her classroom a year above grade level. Ms. Cohen currently serves as the senior managing director of programs for Teach For America's Atlanta region, working to increase the effectiveness of Teach For America teachers in the area.

**Cohen, Seth.** Mr. Cohen's fifth-grade students in Donna, Texas, entered his classroom averaging more than two years below grade level in reading skills. While in his classroom, they advanced, on average, 1.5 grade levels in reading. In addition, they demonstrated mastery of more than 80 percent of the fifth-grade math objectives. Mr. Cohen subsequently joined the Teach For America's Rio Grande Valley staff, working for four years in various capacities relating to training and supporting Teach For America corps members. He is currently an Equal Justice Works fellow with the Health Justice Program at New York Lawyers for the Public Interest. His project seeks to stem the tide of health care disinvestment and improve health outcomes in Central and East Brooklyn by providing direct transactional and civil legal services and leveraging community advocacy strategies.

**Cotner, Sara.** Ms. Cotner began her career as a third-grade teacher in south Louisiana, where she was named Wal-Mart State Teacher of the Year. She subsequently taught sixth-grade reading and writing at KIPP Academy Middle School in Houston, where 99 percent of her students passed the state test and more than half of them scored "commended." She has also worked as an independent education consultant and as an adjunct faculty member at Teacher U at Hunters College in New York. Ms. Cotner currently teaches first, second, and third grades at a public Montessori school in Houston and is in the process of starting a nation-wide network of Montessori charter schools for economically disadvantaged families.

**Coxon, Chrissie.** Ms. Coxon's third-grade students in the South Bronx, New York, achieved an average of 2.07 years of reading growth. While they had entered, on average, slightly below grade level, all of them ended the year at or above grade level, with over half of the class reading at a fifth- or sixth-grade level. In math, the class averaged 91.4 percent mastery of all third-grade state math standards. Ms. Coxon currently teaches kindergarten science as a founding lead teacher at SPARK Academy in Newark, New Jersey.

**Crement, Stephanie.** Ms. Crement began her career teaching seventh- and eighth-grade language arts in East Palo Alto, where her students entered her classroom reading an average of two to three years below grade level. By the end of the year, according to the Gates-MacGinitie Silent Reading Test, her students had improved their reading levels by 1.5 to 2 grade levels, and all of her seventh-grade students were able to write a five-paragraph essay as expected by the California seventh-grade writing proficiency test. Ms. Crement sub-sequently worked as a literacy coordinator for a K–3 school, and then worked as a mentor and coach to Teach For America teachers in Philadelphia. For the past four years Ms. Crement has been working as a literacy specialist in Boston Public Schools, working directly with students and helping to support teachers with literacy instruction.

**Cuesta, Felicia.** Having scored below the fifteenth percentile on the state exam the previous year, the students in Ms. Cuesta's remedial seventh-grade English class at George Washington Carver Middle School in Los Angeles entered her class with low academic confidence, frustration and disengagement with school, and low reading comprehension skills. When they left her classroom, fifty-one of her fifty-nine students had scored at or above the mastery level on the state grade-level assessment, and two-thirds of them scored high enough on the district's reading fluency test to leave the remedial program for a mainstream English class. Ms. Cuesta currently leads efforts to continuously increase the effectiveness and stewardship of Teach For America corps members in Los Angeles.

**Cueto-Potts, Monique.** As a third-grade bilingual teacher in New York City, Ms. Cueto-Potts led her students to average growth of 2.0 grade levels in math and 1.5 grade levels in reading each year. She then taught English/language arts at KIPP Academy Lynn in Massachusetts, where she served as the fifth-grade chairperson, created and developed a differentiated curriculum, and led her students from the forty-eighth percentile to the seventy-fifth percentile in language and from the thirty-seventh percentile to the sixty-second percentile in reading on the Stanford-10. Ms. Cueto-Potts is currently the coordinator of recruitment and admissions for the Institute for Recruitment of Teachers, an organization working to reduce the critical underrepresentation of minority groups on the faculties of schools and colleges, as well as to address the attendant educational consequences of these disparities.

**Cunningham, Joiselle.** When they entered her bilingual classroom in Community School 92 in New York City, Ms. Cunningham's fourth-grade students were reading, on average, on a mid-first-grade level. They could not identify New York on a map. They were far behind in math and science. They already had a reputation for misbehavior. And some had learning disabilities. After two years with Ms. Cunningham, they had improved by an average of almost four grade levels in reading in English (and approximately two grade levels in Spanish), and 100 percent of them scored at or above grade level on the New York State fifth-grade social studies exam (well above the New York City pass rate of 55 percent). This was the first bilingual class in the school's history to outperform its monolingual counterparts on the test. Furthermore, the students achieved 90 percent mastery of fifth-grade science standards and 85 percent mastery of fifth-grade—and of many *sixth*-grade—math standards.

**Dahl, Rachel Donaldson.** Ms. Dahl began her education career at Clarendon Elementary School in Phoenix, Arizona, where the majority of her fifth-grade English language learners entered her classroom not speaking any English but left having grown an average of 2.1 grade levels in English reading ability. She later moved to Los Angeles to help start the Gabriella Charter School, whose unique dance-themed standards-based curriculum was designed for students in the underresourced MacArthur Park neighborhood. Ms. Dahl currently serves as the instructional leader at Namaste Charter School on the southwest side of Chicago. Namaste's mission of "educating children from the inside out" addresses students' health and wellness needs in order to foster higher academic achievement.

**Davis, Ellen.** Ms. Davis began her career teaching first and second grades on the Salt River Reservation in Arizona, where only one-third of students earn high school diplomas in four years. Her first-grade students began the school year without knowledge of letter sounds (a skill usually acquired in kindergarten) and left her reading class reading early-second-grade texts, an average growth of 2.5 grade levels. Her second-grade students began the year with mid-first-grade mathematics mastery and left her classroom performing on an early-third-grade level, demonstrating an average 1.5 years of growth. Ms. Davis subsequently taught pre-K at KIPP SHINE Prep in Houston, where her students came into her classroom with 14 percent letter/sound knowledge and left with an average of 92 percent mastery, reading on a mid-kindergarten level. She was named a KIPP Miles Family Fellow, serving as the dean of curriculum and Instruction at SHINE, and she is now a Fisher Fellow with KIPP Chicago-Gary, preparing to open KIPP Ascend Charter Elementary School in Chicago in fall 2010.

**Deifel, Nicholas.** Mr. Deifel's eighth-grade science students in Baltimore began the year far behind, because they previously had only a series of permanent substitute teachers. As an additional challenge, Mr. Deifel was assigned to use the library as his classroom. Although the library was not set up as a classroom (let alone as a lab classroom), Mr. Deifel found creative solutions and led his students to high achievement on assessments based on the eighth-grade state science standards. Furthermore, he designed labs, projects, and science fair participation that developed an appreciation for the scientific method and its application in his students and he saw these experiences change the way they approached problems. Mr. Deifel is currently working on a Ph.D. in Chemistry at the George Washington University, after which he intends to teach in a university setting.

**Delhagen, Taylor.** Mr. Delhagen teaches tenth-grade global studies at the School for Democracy and Leadership in Crown Heights, Brooklyn. This course is designed to be taught over a two-year span, culminating in the Global Regents Exam, which students must pass in order to graduate from high school in New York State. Mr. Delhagen's students had only one year to learn these two years of material. Despite that challenge, 51 of the 57 students passed the exam on their first attempt (far exceeding the New York City pass rate of 41 percent). While teaching, Mr. Delhagen has supported first-year Teach For America corps members as an adjunct instructor at Fordham University. He currently teaches global studies at a new Achievement First High School in Crown Heights.

**Dingle, Shannon.** As a middle school special education resource writing teacher at Ringgold Middle School in Rio Grande City, Texas, Ms. Dingle designed and implemented a differentiated writing curriculum for seventy middle school students with varying disabilities, mainly learning disabilities, emotional disturbances, and mental retardation. All of the students she taught for at least one year averaged between 1.5 to 2.5 years of growth in literacy (reading and writing), and the students she taught for two consecutive years each made at least three years of growth in literacy. Every student also mastered 100 percent of their Individualized Education Program goals. During her first two years of teaching, fourteen students from resource classes moved into mainstreamed general education classes. Ms. Dingle is the recipient of one of the 2004 Innovation Grants from the National Education Association's Foundation for the Improvement of Education. She currently designs professional development resources for special education corps members for Teach For America.

**Doggett, Emma.** Based on their race and socioeconomic status, Ms. Doggett's eighth-grade U.S. history students in Roma, Texas, were projected to perform 25 percent below the state average on the end-of-year state test. In fact, they not only exceeded the state average but performed equal to white students, the highest-performing subgroup of students in Texas. Following her time in the classroom, Ms. Doggett spent four years (three as executive director) working on the regional staff of Teach For America in the Rio Grande Valley. She is currently pursuing an M.B.A. at Harvard Business School, with the goal of returning to educational leadership.

**Dolan, Caleb.** After teaching middle school English and reading in Gaston, North Carolina, for four years, Mr. Dolan (along with colleague Tammi Sutton) cofounded KIPP Gaston College Prep in 2001, a school serving primarily African American students living in the poor, rural area around Gaston. Gaston College Prep has grown from a school of 80 fifth graders to a fifth- through twelfth-grade campus with 660 students. All 48 members of its first graduating class began college (with over $2 million in scholarships) in fall 2009. Mr. Dolan has been named a Fisher Fellow and Wal-Mart Teacher of the Year.

**Duffy, Cameron.** Ms. Duffy began her career as a middle school French teacher at Sedgefield Middle School in Charlotte, North Carolina. When she learned that some of her eighth-grade students did not have a math teacher, she volunteered to teach that class in addition to her French classes. She found the math students were, on average, on a sixth-grade level. In order to graduate from middle school and go on to ninth grade, they needed to pass the Math End of Grade test (EOG) with a score of 3 or 4. Her students were scoring 1s and 2s at the beginning of the year but by the end of the year, nineteen of her twenty math students passed the EOG with a 3 or 4, and all of them were on at least an eighth-grade level. In addition, all of her French classes mastered more than 80 percent of their objectives. Ms. Duffy currently is a recruiter for Teach For America staff positions.

**Dvorin, Yael.** Ms. Dvorin teaches third grade at W. J. Bryan Elementary School in North Miami, Florida. Her third-grade class exceeded their big goal of averaging 1.5 years of reading growth, improving by 1.6 years of reading growth as a class, and the four retainees in her class passed the state exam to be promoted to the next grade level.

**Eastman, Jessica.** On average, Ms. Eastman's sixth-grade students in Oakland, California, began the year on a third-grade level in mathematics. By the end of the year, students had improved an average of 2.4 grade levels, and five students had grown five years in their math development. Ms. Eastman was honored as the Alameda/Contra Costa Math Teacher of the Year, and in her fourth year, she became her school's operations and development manager, overseeing fundraising events for the school and managing operations for various projects with students and teachers. Ms. Eastman also helped start a community organization, Great Oakland Public Schools, and she currently manages professional development opportunities for Teach For America corps members in the Bay Area.

**Eckler, Gillette.** Ms. Eckler began her teaching career at Granville T. Woods Public School 335 in New York City as a fourth- and, later, fifth-grade general education teacher. Her students began fourth-grade reading significantly below grade level. By the end of fourth grade, they had grown 2.25 years in reading (as measured by Fountas and Pinnell assessments) and had 90.08 percent mastery in math. She then taught the same students in fifth grade, and after that year, they had grown another 2.24 years in reading, for a total of 4.49 years of growth in two years of school. In math, they achieved 87.66 percent mastery of state standards to surpass their class goal for the second year in a row. Many of these students were admitted to some of the most selective middle schools in New York City. Ms. Eckler currently teaches fifth-grade English/language arts, coaches teachers, and serves as head of the English/language arts department at Achievement First Crown Heights Middle School in Brooklyn, New York.

**Egli, Sara.** Ms. Egli teaches first grade at Maurice C. Cash Elementary School in Phoenix, Arizona, where her students consistently make tremendous academic gains. In 2008–2009, Ms. Egli taught in Arizona's English language development program, where all of her students spoke a primary language other than

English. In August, two of her students were reading on grade level. By the following May, twenty-one of them, or 84 percent, were reading at or above grade level. Ms. Egli was named a finalist for 2009 Arizona Teacher of the Year, and she continues to teach at Cash Elementary while earning her master's degree in educational administration and supervision from Arizona State University.

**Eigen, Molly.** Ms. Eigen taught special education math and science at McAllen High School in the Rio Grande Valley in Texas. All of her students were labeled with a disability severe enough that they were assigned to her self-contained special education classroom. She nevertheless insisted on creating a final assessment that covered the general education standards for biology, physical science, and health, and over 90 percent of her students achieved at least a 70 percent on that assessment. While at McAllen High, Ms. Eigen received Region One Service Learning Grants and McAllen Junior League Creative Teacher Grants and was named a finalist for Teacher of the Year. She held a variety of positions with Teach For America, where she worked to strengthen the training and support provided to corps members. Ms. Eigen is currently the director of teacher coaching and professional development for the Mastery Charter School Network in Philadelphia.

**Elder, Sonja.** Ms. Elder taught bilingual first grade at Nystrom Elementary in Richmond, California. She had approximately seventeen students each year, ranging dramatically in English proficiency and academically from just below grade level to preschool level (two years behind). Her students' average improvement in English reading, Spanish reading, and math was 1.5 grade levels, with every student advancing at least one grade level and some making up to 3.5 years of progress. Their average writing progress (in Spanish) was 1.3 grade levels. Ms. Elder subsequently earned degrees in law and public policy from Duke University. She now works as a law clerk to David Tatel of the U.S. Court of Appeals for the D.C. Circuit in Washington, D.C.

**Elguero, Mariel.** Ms. Elguero began her career as an eighth-grade English/language arts teacher in Newark, New Jersey. Her students started the year at least two years behind in reading and ended the year on or just below grade level. Ms. Elguero subsequently became a founding fifth-grade reading teacher at Rise Academy, a KIPP charter school in Newark, where her students have consistently made impressive academic progress. In her fourth year of teaching, her fifth-grade team's students came in reading in the mid-third-grade level (3.7) and started sixth-grade reading on average at an 5.5-grade level, almost closing the achievement gap in a single year.

**Ellsworth, Diana.** Seventy-eight percent of Ms. Ellsworth's first-grade students in Atlanta began the year labeled "significantly below grade level," but by the end of the year, 100 percent of them met or exceeded state standards for reading and language arts and 95 percent did so for math. Ms. Ellsworth later taught fifth-grade language arts at KIPP WAYS Academy, where 98.5 percent of her students passed the Georgia Fifth Grade Writing Test (compared to 92 percent in Atlanta Public Schools and 93.8 percent in the state of Georgia), 93 percent "met or exceeded the standard" on the Georgia Criterion Reference Competency Test (compared to 79 percent in Atlanta Public Schools), and 86 percent scored in one of the top two levels of the state writing test (compared to 61.5 percent in Atlanta Public Schools and 66 percent statewide). Ms. Ellsworth subsequently served as executive director of Teach For America's Atlanta region, and she currently works for McKinsey & Company as part of its growing education practice.

**Epp, Tracy.** When Ms. Epp began her career teaching eighth-grade social studies at Cueller Middle School in Weslaco, Texas, the school had recently been rated by the state as academically unacceptable. Her school reorganized into teacher teams, meaning the same five teachers taught the same group of students. Her team was considered the "low" group, and some people expected little from them. However, Ms. Epp's team's students outperformed every other team in the school, including the "pre-AP" team at the end of the year. On the state social studies exam, 90 percent of Ms. Epp's students passed, and the passing rate was over 90 percent in math, science, and reading as well. Ms. Epp is currently the chief academic officer for IDEA Public Schools, an open-enrollment charter district that serves over five thousand students in ten schools across the Rio Grande Valley. As of 2009, IDEA College Prep has graduated three classes: 100 percent of its graduates matriculated into college and all remain enrolled.

**Estes, Stephani.** When Ms. Estes began teaching self-contained special education at Cleveland NJROTC High School in St. Louis, Missouri, the students in her class had never been taught using the same curriculum as their general education peers. By the end of the year, they had achieved, on average, 79.75 percent mastery of all course objectives and all but two had met their aggressive Individualized Education Program goals. Ms. Estes currently works at Starcom Worldwide, where she is the national strategy supervisor for Disney Parks. She teaches Saturday School at KIPP: LEAD in Gary, Indiana.

**Feinberg, Michael.** Mr. Feinberg is cofounder of the KIPP (Knowledge Is Power Program) Foundation and the superintendent of KIPP Houston, which includes eight middle schools, six primary schools, and a high school. To date, over 90 percent of the KIPPsters who have graduated from the KIPP Houston middle schools have gone on to college. Mr. Feinberg began his career teaching fifth grade in Houston, before cofounding KIPP with Dave Levin in 1994 and establishing KIPP Academy Houston a year later. In 2000, he cofounded the KIPP Foundation to help take KIPP to scale. Today, KIPP is a network of eighty-two high-performing public schools around the nation serving twenty-one thousand children. In 2004, Mr. Feinberg was named an Ashoka Fellow, awarded to leading social entrepreneurs with innovative solutions and the potential to change patterns across society. In 2005, Mr. Feinberg led the effort to start a public K–8 school in Houston for Hurricane Katrina evacuees from New Orleans. The school, NOW College Prep (New Orleans West), opened in ten days. In 2006, Mr. Feinberg and Mr. Levin were awarded the Thomas B. Fordham Prize for Excellence in Education, and the National Jefferson Award for Greatest Public Service by a Private Citizen. In 2008, Mr. Feinberg and Mr. Levin were named to the list of "America's Best Leaders" by *U.S. News & World Report* and received the Presidential Citizens Medal in the Oval Office of the White House.

**Fierst, Karen.** Ms. Fierst began her career teaching special education in the South Bronx, New York City. Each of the twelve students in her fourth-grade special education class met all of their Individualized Education Program (IEP) objectives in just four months, and they far exceeded them after she revised their IEP goals to make them significantly more rigorous. This led her principal to use Ms. Fierst's IEPs as models for other teachers. Ms. Fierst subsequently worked at a private school for students with learning disabilities, and she has made two trips to Nairobi, Kenya, to live in an orphanage, work at its school, and provide professional development for teachers. Ms. Fierst is currently a member of a learning research team at a private school in the Bronx, working with students, providing professional development for teachers, and seeking ways to incorporate research-based practice into the school culture.

**Fraccaro, Rachna.** At the beginning of the school year, more than half of Ms. Fraccaro's second-grade students at Morrell Park Elementary School in Baltimore, Maryland, were below grade level in reading and math. By the end of the year, they improved their reading skills by an average of 1.75 grade levels and their math skills by an average of 1.5 grade levels. Ms. Fraccaro is now a third-grade teacher in the Arlington, Virginia, public school system.

**Frumkin, Elisha Rothschild.** Ms. Frumkin's sixth-grade language arts and math students at Sherwood Githens Middle School in Durham, North Carolina, began the year at least 1.5 grade levels behind in reading and at least one grade behind in math. By the end of the year, each student had gained ground, some advancing as much as 2.5 grade levels in reading and 1.5 grade levels in math. After serving as youth director at Beth Israel Congregation in Owings Mills, Maryland, and as assistant principal at Temple Rodef Shalom in Falls Church, Virginia, Ms. Frumkin joined the staff at Congregation Beth El in Bethesda, Maryland, where she is the assistant education director and family education director.

**Gonnella, Carrie.** Only 7 percent of the students in Ms. Gonnella's seventh-grade math class in East Palo Alto, California, had passed the sixth-grade Standardized Testing and Reporting (STAR) math test the previous year—a statistic that ranked them among the lowest-performing groups in the entire state. At the end of that year, 71 percent of them passed the seventh-grade STAR math exam, more than doubling the district rate (31 percent) and far exceeding the state rate (41 percent). Ms. Gonnella currently teaches in Durham, North Carolina.

**Griffith, Kwame.** Mr. Griffith's fourth-grade students in Houston, all of them African American and almost all of them living in poverty by one or more government definitions, entered his classroom multiple grade levels behind in both reading and math—some as many as four years behind. For the two and a half years prior, they had been taught by a series of substitutes. Two years later, after Mr. Griffith had looped with his students to fifth grade, his students were reading on grade level and doing math more than a half-year above grade level. Mr. Griffith has subsequently held a variety of positions on the staff of Teach For America and currently serves as executive director of Teach For America's Atlanta region.

**Gwin, Jenny.** Ms. Gwin's eighth-grade language arts students at Young Scholars Charter School in Philadelphia entered her class with little formal skill in essay writing. By the end of the year, 91 percent of her students scored proficient or advanced on the Pennsylvania System of School Assessment (PSSA) State Writing Exam, far exceeding the overall state pass rate (69%) and more than doubling the pass rate in the school district of Philadelphia (41%). Ms. Gwin currently teaches eighth grade at KIPP Philadelphia Charter School.

**Hancox, Jessica.** When Ms. Hancox began teaching third grade at Clark Street Elementary in North Carolina, it was one of the lowest-performing schools in the county. After being in her class, every single one of Ms. Hancox's students passed the rigorous state End of Grade Reading Test and 87 percent passed the End of Grade Math Test, well above the state pass rates of 85 percent in reading and 72 percent in math, and far exceeding her school's average of 74 percent and 43 percent, respectively. Ms. Hancox currently works as a mentor and coach to Teach For America elementary school teachers in North Carolina.

**Hanson, Alexis.** Ms. Hanson began her career teaching eighth-grade physical science and seventh- and eighth-grade English as a Second Language Science at Virgil Middle School in Los Angeles, where her students achieved 80 percent mastery of state standards. Ms. Hanson currently teaches biology and anatomy and physiology at Animo Pat Brown Charter High School, where almost every student qualifies for free or reduced lunch and half currently have English as a Second Language designations and where her students have outperformed state averages on the California Standards Test (CST) in biology. In 2008–2009, 56 percent of her students scored "proficient" or higher (26 percent "advanced") and only 14 percent "below basic" (3 percent "far below basic"), well above district averages of 24 percent "proficient" or higher (9 percent "advanced") and 42 percent "below basic" (22 percent "far below basic").

**Harrington, Tara.** The year before Ms. Harrington began teaching there, her Charlotte, North Carolina, high school had performed last on the state-mandated end-of-course (EOC) assessment in biology. Two years before, only 17 percent of the school's students had passed the test. In the previous year, 31 percent had passed, and not a single student had earned a 4, the highest possible score. Ms. Harrington found that, on average, her tenth-grade students were reading on a sixth-grade level, they were reading graphs with only 20 percent accuracy, and they were, on average, interpreting, conducting, and calculating measurements on a middle school level with 30 percent proficiency. She also learned that the state's formula of predictive data suggested that only 10 percent of her students were expected to pass. Ms. Harrington improved the pass rates on the EOC from 31 percent to 93 percent, the highest pass rate in the district. The following year, her students did even better, passing at 95 percent.

**Harris, Rebecca Roundtree.** Ms. Harris has been teaching in California's Compton Unified School District since 2001. She currently teaches at Laurel Street Elementary School, where 94 percent of her fifth-grade students scored either "proficient" or "advanced" on the state assessments for both language arts and math in 2008–2009.

**Harris Perin, Kelly.** As a social studies teacher at Rosa Fort Middle School in Tunica, Mississippi, Ms. Harris Perin taught eighth graders who entered her room with low reading and writing levels and a total lack of research experience. By the end of the year, each of Ms. Harris Perin's students completed a capstone project including independent research, a term paper, and an oral presentation, demonstrating skills and knowledge well beyond where they started the year. Ms. Harris Perin currently works on the recruitment staff of Teach For America.

**Hauser, Jerry.** Mr. Hauser began his career as a high school math teacher in Compton, California, where he advanced his students from a basic math track to precollege curriculum. He subsequently worked as an associate at McKinsey & Company before serving as the chief operating officer at Teach For America and CEO of the Advocacy Institute. Mr. Hauser is currently CEO of the Management Center, where he continues to pursue his dual passions for promoting social change and creating high-performing organizations.

**Hawley, Lauren.** Ms. Hawley's fifth-grade students in Aurelian Springs, North Carolina, began the year reading, on average, on a mid-third-grade level, with only two of her fourteen students reading on grade level. By the end of the year, the students improved an average reading level of 1.5 years, and nine of them were reading at or above grade level. In math, her students began the year having mastered only 38 percent of core fourth-grade skills, yet in her class, they succeeded in mastering 83 percent of rigorous fifth-grade skills. Ms. Hawley currently works for Live It Learn It, an educational nonprofit that provides experiential learning opportunities for fourth-, fifth-, and sixth-grade students in Title I Public Schools in Washington, D.C.

**Henzerling, Jane.** In her first year of teaching, Ms. Henzerling's bilingual students entered fifth grade at Greenfield Elementary in Phoenix, Arizona, with a wide range of skill levels in English: some were monolingual Spanish speakers, some spoke Spanish and English but were not literate in either language, others spoke both languages but read and wrote only one of them. After being in her class for two years (she moved with them to sixth grade), all of Ms. Henzerling's students had reached at least the proficient level (as defined by the state) in reading, writing, and speaking English, and more than 25 percent of them had reached advanced levels on the Language Assessment Scales. Following a few more years of teaching, Ms. Henzerling served as executive director of Teach For America in Miami-Dade, where her work was recognized with multiple awards, including the Miami Today Gold Medal Award, Greater Miami Chamber of Commerce NOVO Award for Non-Profit Innovation, South Florida Business Journal Heavy Hitter in Education, Bank of America Neighborhood Builder, and the Florida Marlins Heart of the Community Award. In 2009, Ms. Henzerling was granted a fellowship from Building Excellent Schools to found and lead a K–8 college preparatory charter school in San Francisco's Mission District, which will open in 2011.

**Heyck-Merlin, Maia.** Over half of Ms. Heyck-Merlin's fourth-grade students at Delmont Elementary School in Baton Rouge, Louisiana, entered her English/language arts (ELA) classroom below grade level. By tracking her students' reading levels using Fountas and Pinnell, Soar to Success, and the Developmental Reading Assessment, and then individualizing instruction, Ms. Heyck-Merlin led her students to tremendous gains, with 90 percent of them passing the ELA Fourth Grade Louisiana Educational Assessment Program (LEAP) exam. Impressed by the students' achievement, her principal asked her to teach writing to the entire fourth grade the next year. She subsequently served as executive director of Teach For America in south Louisiana and directed summer training institutes for Teach Baton Rouge and Teach For America. Ms. Heyck-Merlin was named Teacher of the Year at Delmont Elementary and was selected for Top 40 under 40 Baton Rouge and the Fulbright Memorial Fund Teacher Exchange. She currently is the chief talent officer for Achievement First, a network of college preparatory public charter schools in Brooklyn and Connecticut.

**Hill, Katie.** The students in Ms. Hill's middle school special education class in North Carolina had cognitive disabilities, with IQs in the thirties to forties. When she first met them, they were, on average, reading below a first-grade level, and some were unfamiliar with all the letters. Most were not able to give personal information such as their parent or guardian's name, their phone number, their address, or their lunch identification number. Two weeks into school, only one student was familiar enough with the school community to identify any teachers other than Ms. Hill and her teaching assistant, and few were able to navigate the building to reach the cafeteria, the gym, the restrooms, or the main office. Some people saw her students as unable to learn basic academic and functional skills and incapable of ever living independently. By the end of the year, however, her students had made, on average, 1.6 years of reading growth and approximately three years of growth in math. They also mastered 83 percent of the grade-level standards they were aiming for as a class. Ms. Hill teaches middle school special education at Joy Charter School in Durham, North Carolina.

**Hill, Ryan.** At Intermediate School 164 in Washington Heights in New York City, the nine sixth-grade classes were ranked by reading scores. Mr. Hill asked his principal for the lowest-ranked class. By the end of the year, those students had risen to be the second-highest-scoring class in the school. Mr. Hill subsequently became the founding principal of TEAM Academy Charter School, a KIPP school in Newark, New Jersey. Since then, TEAM has grown from one school to three, serving over a thousand students (with plans for twenty-five hundred in the next five years), and he has become the executive director of the New Jersey region for KIPP. TEAM schools have routinely far exceeded the academic results of the Newark district, and 100 percent of their alumni have gone to college preparatory high schools. Mr. Hill has received the Bank of America Local Heroes Award and been named by the *New Jersey Star-Ledger* as one of "11 New Jerseyans to Watch."

**Holland, Angela.** Although many of the students in Ms. Holland's Spanish classes at Sumner High School in St. Louis, Missouri, began the year lagging behind in their Spanish skills, over 93 percent of her students mastered the state Spanish standards for their respective courses. As a law student at Vanderbilt University, she established the Juvenile Division of Vanderbilt's Street Law Program at Pearl-Cohn High School in Nashville, Tennessee, as part of a national initiative designed to provide citizens with information about the law to assist them in their daily lives. Ms. Holland is currently an associate with the law firm Reed Smith, LLP in Washington, D.C.

**Janecek, Jacqulyn.** As sixth graders, 68 percent of Ms. Janecek's seventh-grade English/language arts students at Eaton Johnson Middle School in Henderson, North Carolina, had passed the state reading comprehension end-of-grade exam. Although this was above the state average, Ms. Janecek felt that it needed to be (and could be) much higher. She introduced a reading challenge at the beginning of the year, and each class raced to see how many books they could read before they took the state exam. Her sixty-one students finished the year having read a group total of 1,342 books; 97 percent of them passed their end-of-grade exam, and they gained an average of five points on their exam (about double the typical annual growth). Ms. Janecek continues to teach seventh-grade English/language arts at Eaton Johnson.

**Jensen, Ross.** As a fifth-grade language arts and social studies teacher at Luis Munoz Marin Middle School in Newark, New Jersey, Mr. Jensen led his students to an average of two grade levels of growth in reading (as judged by the McLeod Assessment of Reading Comprehension). Furthermore, they outperformed their school average by 65 percent on the Language Arts Literacy section of the New Jersey Assessment of Skills and Knowledge (NJASK). Mr. Jensen currently contributes to Teach For America's efforts to provide support and learning experiences to its teachers.

**Johnson, N'Djamina.** The year before Ms. Johnson began teaching chemistry at E. E. Waddell High School in Charlotte, North Carolina, only 39.3 percent of the school's chemistry students had passed the state end-of-course chemistry exam, about half the state pass rate of 77.1 percent. Her students walked into her class dreading chemistry, yet Ms. Johnson's efforts led to continuously increasing pass rates each year she taught, with 82 percent of her students passing the exam in spring 2009, one of the highest pass rates in the district. Ms. Johnson currently attends the University of North Carolina-Chapel Hill School of Medicine.

**Jones, Crystal.** On average, Ms. Jones's first-grade students in Atlanta, Georgia, began the year as non-readers; very few knew even basic sight words. But whereas only two of her students were reading on a kindergarten level at the beginning of the year, 90 percent were reading at or above a third-grade level by the end of the year and the remaining 10 percent were reading on at least a mid-second-grade level. In math, her students improved by an average of 2.5 grade levels, and 90 percent of them were at or above grade level in math by the end of the year. Ms. Jones is currently executive director of Teach For America in Jacksonville, Florida.

**Joseph, Leslie-Bernard.** As a fifth-grade English/language arts teacher at Public School 70 in the Bronx, New York City, Mr. Joseph consistently led his students to great academic gains. One year, only one of his fifty students entered his class reading on grade level; by the end of the year, thirty-one students were reading at or above grade level. In another year, 20 percent of his students came in having been socially promoted despite failing the New York State English Language Arts exam in fourth grade. After a year in his class, every one of the students passed the fifth-grade English/language arts exam—the first time some of them had ever passed a state reading exam. Mr. Joseph is a 2009 CUP Fellow in public policy for the Council of Urban Professionals and is the founding dean of Students at Coney Island Prep, the first charter school in South Brooklyn and the first charter school to be located in public housing.

**Kamras, Jason.** Mr. Kamras, a math teacher at John Philip Sousa Middle School in Washington, D.C., was named National Teacher of the Year in 2005. Mr. Kamras successfully lobbied his principal to double the time allotted for math instruction and redesigned the math curriculum to emphasize the increasing use of technology in order to meet all learning styles and put instruction into a real-world context. At the start of the first year of the double math program, 80 percent of his students were "below basic" on the Stanford 9 from the spring before they came to him. That percentage fell to 40 percent after one year of the program. Mr. Kamras currently serves as the director of human capital strategy for teachers in the District of Columbia Public Schools. In this role, he leads the district's efforts to ensure a highly effective teacher for every classroom.

**Kane, Tyson.** As middle schoolers, only 5 percent of Mr. Kane's high school biology and bilingual biology students at Locke High School in Los Angeles had performed "proficient" or higher on the California state test for middle school life sciences. At the end of the year, Mr. Kane's students exhibited strong growth, with 32 percent of his students scoring "proficient" or higher on the state biology exam, above the district pass rate of 23 percent and far exceeding his school's overall pass rate of just 6 percent. Mr. Kane is currently the principal at Chicago Bulls College Prep, a campus of the Noble Network of Charter Schools in Chicago, which is in its inaugural year.

**Kaufman, Jessica.** Because Ms. Kaufman's third-grade class was the English as a Second Language section in a primarily Spanish-bilingual school (Piney Point Elementary in Houston, Texas), her class was a mix of speakers of languages other than Spanish, Spanish speakers who were transitioning out of bilingual classes, and students who had been retained in a previous grade or had emotional difficulties. Using methodologies typically designed for gifted students, she helped her students develop critical thinking skills and autonomy as they engaged the academic standards. All of Ms. Kaufman's students scored at grade level on the state test, with several of them testing well beyond their grade level in math and reading. Some even tested as gifted in some areas.

**Kerr, Arianne.** Ms. Kerr's eighth-grade English as a Second Language (ESL) students in Memphis, Tennessee, started the year reading far below grade level and writing at a level 1 proficiency on the state-mandated rubric, a score that reflects an inability to respond to the prompt with relevant subject matter, poor to no sentence construction, and a total lack of organization and creativity. Nine months later, they had improved an average of nearly three grade levels in reading, and every student had a score of "proficient" in the end-of-the-year state-mandated writing test. In addition, as their American history teacher, she led her students to 83 percent mastery of the general education American history standards. Furthermore, Ms. Kerr served on a districtwide ESL curriculum development team and served as ESL coordinator for the largest ESL program in the district. She is currently a youth education and career development specialist for at-risk children at Arizona Women's Education and Employment in Phoenix.

**Kincaid, Leigh.** The year that Ms. Kincaid arrived at her school in Atlanta, only 32 percent of fourth-grade students were meeting grade-level reading expectations and only 41 percent were demonstrating grade-level proficiency in math as measured by the Georgia State Criterion Referenced Competency Exam. Ms. Kincaid led her fourth graders to significant improvement, with 83 percent meeting or exceeding grade-level proficiency in reading, 82 percent doing so in math, 82 percent in English/language arts, 88 percent in science, and 88 percent in social studies. Ms. Kincaid subsequently worked with a public education NGO in Haryana, India, as an American India Foundation Fellow before joining the staff of Teach For America, where she has worked to support, develop, and increase the effectiveness of Teach For America's teachers in Hawaii.

**Klauder, Amy.** Ms. Klauder began her career as a first-grade teacher at Dr. Marjorie H. Dunbar Elementary School in the Bronx, New York City. After teaching for four years in New York City and receiving her master's degree from Bank Street College of Education, Ms. Klauder moved to Chicago, where she was an assistant director/education director at a National Association for the Education of Young Children–accredited preschool. Ms. Klauder is currently a reading coordinator at Chicago International Charter School Loomis Primary Academy in Chicago.

**Kronemeyer, Emily.** Ms. Kronemeyer's fifth- and sixth-grade English as a Second Language students at Cesar E. Chavez Community School in Phoenix, Arizona, typically entered her classroom reading at a low-second-grade level, and by the end of the year the class average was at least a fourth-grade level based on Qualitative Reading Inventory reading assessments. Each year, her students achieved the school's highest scores on the Arizona's Instrument for Measuring Standards exams in their grade. Ms. Kronemeyer was named Teacher of the Month and received the High Student Expectations Award at the Chavez Community School. She currently is director of high school placement for KIPP Charlotte, North Carolina. In this role, she ensures that the school's eighth-grade students are prepared to be successful in excellent high schools so that all will be able to attend college on graduation.

**Kulkarni, Anjali.** Ms. Kulkarni teaches first-, second-, and third-grade special education in the Bronx, New York City. At the beginning of her first year of teaching, 90 percent of her second graders were unable to read, and those who could read were reading at a prekindergarten or kindergarten level. After two years in Ms. Kulkarni's class, her students' reading levels improved by over three grade levels (several of them are now reading at a fourth-grade level) and 100 percent of them passed the third-grade state mathematics test.

**Laputka, Melanie.** Ms. Laputka teaches high school Spanish at Cross CT Scholars in New Haven, Connecticut. Her students have consistently achieved over 1.5 levels' growth in the Interagency Language Roundtable rubric, averaged 90 percent on a listening assessment, over 87 percent in reading achievement, and over 72 percent in reading proficiency. Ms. Laputka has also served as a data team leader and has coached basketball at the school, and she has assisted with training and support of Teach For America foreign language teachers.

**LaTarte, Anne.** The first-, second-, and third-grade students in Ms. LaTarte's special education classroom at Public School 128 in Washington Heights in New York City improved their reading by approximately 2.5 grade levels based on the Early Childhood Learning Assessment System and achieved nearly 80 percent mastery of all of their math Individualized Education Program goals on rigorous, standards-aligned assessments. Furthermore, her students published ten rigorous writing assignments over the course of a year (including a play that they wrote, directed, and performed), and several of them were moved to collaboratively taught or mainstreamed settings after their time in her classroom. Ms. LaTarte currently works in the Division of Accountability and Achievement Resources at the New York City Department of Education through the Broad Residency Program.

**Lessem, Jacob.** Mr. Lessem began his career teaching a variety of math and science classes at Zuni High School in New Mexico, where his Basic Math 1 students had an average growth of approximately two grade levels each year on a grade-level placement assessment. In addition, he started the school's first robotics team, and many of his physics students and robotics students have gone on to have success in college science and math classes. Mr. Lessem subsequently moved to Chicago to be part of the founding staff at Rauner College Prep, a school serving a high-needs population of students on Chicago's Near West Side, where his math students consistently outperform district averages and his robotics team has garnered numerous awards.

**Levin, Dave.** Mr. Levin began his career teaching fifth grade in Houston. He is cofounder of the KIPP (Knowledge Is Power Program) Foundation and the superintendent of KIPP New York City, which includes four middle schools, an elementary school, a high school, and KIPP to College, a comprehensive advocacy and support program for all alumni of those schools (currently 650) in high school, college, and beyond. In 1994, he cofounded KIPP with Mike Feinberg and established KIPP Academy Houston a year later. In 2000, he cofounded the KIPP Foundation to help take KIPP to scale. Today KIPP is a network of eighty-two high-performing public schools around the nation serving twenty-one thousand children. In 2004, Mr. Levin was named an Ashoka Fellow, awarded to leading social entrepreneurs with innovative solutions and the potential to change patterns across society. In 2006, Mr. Levin and Mr. Feinberg were awarded the Thomas B. Fordham Prize for Excellence in Education and the National Jefferson Award for Greatest Public Service by a Private Citizen. In 2008, Mr. Levin and Mr. Feinberg were named to the list of "America's Best Leaders" by *U.S. News & World Report* and received the Presidential Citizens Medal in the Oval Office of the White House.

**Lewis, Annie.** Ms. Lewis led her second-grade students in Baltimore to improvements of between 1.5 and 2.5 years in reading levels and led the majority of her students to mastery of 100 percent of grade-level math standards, as measured by Baltimore City Public Schools benchmark tests. Ms. Lewis subsequently joined the staff of Teach For America, where she has made significant contributions. Among other things, she is the author of the most recent edition of Teach For America's *Elementary Literacy* text, which has been described by G. Reid Lyon, the former chief of the Child Development and Behavior Branch within the National Institute of Child Health and Human Development (NICHD) at the National Institutes of Health (NIH), as "a superb document that leaves nothing to chance. It clearly explains the whys, whats, and hows of reading development, reading difficulties, and reading instruction. It is current and comprehensive and one of the best reviews I have seen." Ms. Lewis has led (and continues to lead) the overhaul of virtually every aspect of the organization's preservice training model, resulting in substantial improvements.

**Lohela, Kevin.** The majority of Mr. Lohela's third-grade students at Public School 196 in New York City entered his room below grade level—some dramatically so—and class mastery of even basic math skills was below 40 percent. When the third-grade bilingual class was broken up in November, two months before the state English/language arts exam, Mr. Lohela walked into class to find several new students who spoke limited English. From one-on-one tutoring before school, to working lunches, small group instruction, and after-school instruction, a profound sense of urgency permeated each day. By the end of the year, all nineteen of Mr. Lohela's students, including the ones from the bilingual class, either met or exceeded the state standards for third grade in both math and English language arts as determined by the end-of-year state exams. Mr. Lohela is currently the academic dean at Achievement First Crown Heights Charter School in Brooklyn, where 100 percent of third and fourth graders scored at or above grade level in math and 91 percent of third graders and 98 percent of fourth graders achieved the same in reading on the state assessments, well above district averages.

**London, John.** Mr. London teaches high school math in Washington, D.C. His ninth-grade Algebra I class made an average of 1.5 years worth of academic growth in mathematics according to the Performance Series computer adaptive test.

**LoPiccolo, Rob.** Mr. LoPiccolo spent seven years as a ninth-grade physical science teacher at Opelousas Senior High School in Opelousas, Louisiana, and then at Glen Oaks High School in Baton Rouge, where he was named Teacher of the Year and earned National Board certification. Over the years, he has assisted with the training and support of teachers for Teach For America, Teach Baton Rouge, and the New Teacher Project. He has served as director of curriculum and International Baccalaureate programs for IDEA Public Schools in the Rio Grande Valley in Texas, and he is currently executive director of the Collaborative, a non-profit that does innovative curriculum work for IDEA and Uplift Education in Dallas.

**Love, Mekia.** Ms. Love began her career teaching fifth-grade reading, writing, and science in Indianola, Mississippi. The majority of her students entered her class more than two grade levels behind in reading, and they had scored, on average, at the twenty-sixth percentile on the reading portion of their Stanford 10 test. By the end of a single year, they had improved to the fifty-sixth percentile. Ms. Love later taught fifth-grade reading at KIPP DC: KEY Academy, where she won a Department of Education American Star of Teaching Award and a Kinder Excellence in Teaching Award. She currently serves as vice principal of KEY Academy.

**Lozier, Frank.** Mr. Lozier began his career as an eighth-grade English teacher at Whaley Middle School in Compton Unified School District. In his first year as English department head, the department increased the number of students "proficient" or "advanced" on the California Standards Test (CST) by 143 percent. After four years at Whaley, Mr. Lozier moved to New York City to teach in the Bronx and to earn his master's degree and administrative credential from Columbia University. He subsequently joined Teach For America to contribute to their efforts to train and support teachers. Mr. Lozier has since returned to Compton Unified as the vice principal at Vanguard Learning Center. He is also in the doctoral program at UCLA.

**Lutey, Anna.** At the beginning of the school year, only a handful of Ms. Lutey's fourth-grade students at Camino Nuevo Charter School in Los Angeles had scored at grade level or above in math on the California Standardized Test. By the end of the year, twenty-four of her twenty-seven students had done so. Ms. Lutey currently works as an operational consultant and supervisor.

**Lyneis, Anne.** As a second-grade teacher in Jackson, Louisiana, Ms. Lyneis taught a group of students who began the year reading, on average, 1.5 years below grade level. After a year in her class, 83 percent of the students left second grade on or above grade level. In 2007–2008, Ms. Lyneis was named Teacher of the Year at Jackson Elementary School and in the East Feliciana Parish School District. She currently teaches third grade at KIPP SHINE in Houston, Texas.

**Maddin, Brent.** Mr. Maddin began his career teaching biology, chemistry, physics, and physical science at a high school in rural Louisiana, where he received his National Board Certification. He later moved to the Rio Grande Valley to help found IDEA College Prep, a public charter school whose subsequent success led it to be ranked by *U.S. News & World Report* as the nineteenth best high school in the entire nation. Over the years, Mr. Maddin has actively mentored and trained new teachers for Teach For America and The New Teacher Project. He has co-written a national chemistry curriculum for The New Teacher Project and co-created the K–12 science curriculum map for the IDEA Public Schools. Mr. Maddin is currently director of teaching and learning for Teacher U in New York City, where he is helping to design a new teacher training program in partnership with Achievement First, KIPP, Uncommon Schools, and Hunter College. He is also pursuing a doctorate in education policy, leadership, and instructional practice at the Harvard Graduate School of Education.

**Mandel, Andrew.** By the end of 2001–2002, most of Mr. Mandel's seventh graders at Myra Green Middle School in the Rio Grande Valley became "English Experts," signifying they had scored 100 percent on teacher-created assessments that tested grade-level expectations. They also wrote pieces representing one or two columns of rubric growth in writing. In addition, each year Mr. Mandel's students created and published a book through Learn and Serve grants from the Texas Education Agency: one on the history of their town, Raymondville, and a second on Islam and multicultural tolerance and respect after September 11. The proceeds from their book sales funded the purchase of novels for their school library, and they were recognized in the Southern Poverty Law Center's magazine for their work. Mr. Mandel has subsequently served in a variety of roles at Teach For America, where he currently seeks to bring together teachers and innovative multimedia professional development resources.

**Marshall, Kristy.** As a first-grade English as a Second Language teacher at Sullivan Elementary School in Phoenix, Arizona, Ms. Marshall used dynamic differentiated instruction to lead her students to significant academic growth—in fact, five of her students were able to transition to mainstream language arts instruction after a year in her classroom. Her principal regularly brought guests from the district and state to visit her classroom as a model of dynamic, differentiated language arts instruction. Ms. Marshall subsequently moved to Atlanta, where she recruited teachers for Teach For America and gave motivational speeches at high schools across the state of Georgia before joining the staff of New Balance, for whom she currently works as an independent sales representative.

**May, Justin.** Mr. May began his teaching career in one of the most impoverished neighborhoods in New Orleans, where most of his first-grade students began the school year well below grade level. Some of them had never been to kindergarten. Many of them were reading on the lowest possible level on the Developmental Reading Assessment. By the end of the year, twenty-one of Mr. May's twenty-four students were reading above the "ready for second grade" level, and a handful were reading above a "ready for third grade" level. Mr. May has subsequently served as executive director of Teach For America in New Mexico, completed graduate work in special education at Bank Street College of Education, and taught in the South Bronx, New York City. He currently teaches second grade in Lincoln, Vermont.

**McQueen, Kiel.** Mr. McQueen teaches middle school social studies at Sierra Vista Elementary in Phoenix, Arizona. In 2008–2009, the students in his four social studies classes were able to master a year and half of curriculum in one year and averaged 82.2 percent mastery of prioritized social studies standards.

**Meiklejohn, Rachel.** As a sixth-grade teacher at Navajo Middle School in New Mexico, Ms. Meiklejohn led her students to approximately two grade levels of growth in reading, as measured by the STAR/Accelerated Reader assessment. She has subsequently coached and mentored Teach For America teachers in New Mexico, taught essay writing in the Transitional Studies Department at the University of New Mexico, and taught seventh- and eighth-grade literature at Amistad Academy, an Achievement First Charter School, in New Haven, Connecticut, where only 4 percent of her seventh graders began the year reading on grade level and 77 percent ended the year doing so. Ms. Meiklejohn currently serves as academic dean of Amistad's upper school.

**Minkel, Justin.** Mr. Minkel began his teaching career as a fourth-grade teacher in West Harlem, New York City, and later returned to his hometown of Fayetteville, Arkansas, where he teaches second and third grades at Jones Elementary, a school where 93 percent of the students receive free and reduced-price lunch and 85 percent are English language learners. He began teaching second grade with eighteen students reading below grade level according to the Developmental Reading Assessment (DRA), but after completing a two-year loop with the class from second to third grade, seventeen of those eighteen students were reading on grade level, while the remaining student improved from a Level A (emergent reader) to a DRA level of 24, almost on grade level. In addition, 100 percent of his students scored "proficient" or "advanced" on the state exam. Mr. Minkel is a recipient of the Milken Educator Award and was named 2007 Arkansas Teacher of the Year. He now teaches half-time through a job-share, while taking care of his eighteen-month-old daughter two days a week, working as a consultant with a proposed charter school, and revising a fantasy novel for readers in the middle grades.

**Monti, Sara.** As a sixth- and seventh-grade special education inclusion math teacher at Park Forest Middle School in south Louisiana, Ms. Monti led her students to mastery of carefully prioritized standards aligned to the rigorous end-of-year eighth-grade state test. She subsequently taught English as a Second Language at the same school, and she currently teaches in Ecuador.

**Moody, Norledia.** Once a student of Teach For America teachers, Ms. Moody began her own teaching career by joining Teach For America. Ms. Moody's second-grade students in Atlanta began the year reading, on average, at an early first-grade level, roughly one year behind. By the end of the year, they were reading at a late third-grade level, almost a full year *ahead*. In between her initial tenure at Frank L. Stanton Elementary and her subsequent return to that school, Ms. Moody headed Teach For America's recruitment efforts at Historically Black Colleges and Universities, almost doubling the number of Teach For America applicants from HBCUs during her two-year tenure.

**Moonves, Alaina.** The students in Ms. Moonves's first-grade special education class came to her with unique social and emotional needs. Already, many people (including the students themselves) had given up on their chances of being successful in school. Yet Ms. Moonves refused to accept low expectations, and by the end of her first year with her students, they had been transformed from nonreaders to proud readers, had mastered 85 percent of first-grade math standards, and had exceeded their behavioral and emotional goals. By the end of her second year with them, they had improved their average reading level by more than two additional years, and had mastered 87 percent of second-grade math standards. Ms. Moonves is currently attending New York University School of Law. She has interned at Partnership For Children's Rights (a non-profit special-education law firm) and hopes to work in the field of special education law in the future.

**Morgan Dixon, Tanya.** Mrs. Morgan Dixon began her career in education as a history teacher at South Atlanta (Georgia) High School before transitioning to Link Community School in Newark, New Jersey, where she served as dean of students, director of the summer academy, and a history teacher, leading 100 percent of her history students to perform at or above grade level. During the summers, she worked at the United Nations in the Office of Children and Armed Conflict, where she researched and reported on schools and reintegration programs in conflict regions and served on delegations to both Guatemala and Cuba. After her time at Link, she served as the executive director of REACH Prep, a nonprofit organization that provides African American and Latino children access to a consortium of twenty-three top independent schools in Connecticut and New York. She also directed the opening of six new public schools in New York City for St. Hope and the Urban Assembly. Mrs. Morgan Dixon is the founder of GirlTrek, a public health nonprofit and concurrently serves as the director of strategic initiatives at Achievement First.

**Muller, Vanessa.** At the beginning of the year, Ms. Muller's third-grade special education students in the Bronx were between one and three years behind in reading and math skills and convinced that they were failures. By the end of the year, their reading levels had improved by an average of 1.83 grade levels, and 82 percent of her students passed the New York State English/Language Arts Regents Exam, with 38 percent of them meeting or exceeding grade-level standards. Furthermore, 92 percent of them passed the New York State Math Exam, with 71 percent meeting or exceeding grade-level standards. Due in part to the success of her students, Ms. Muller's school moved to a more inclusion-based special education model, a transition that she oversaw as the school's data manager and collaborative team teaching coach, and that helped remove her school from the New York State "schools in need of improvement" list. Ms. Muller has been awarded a fellowship to attend Bank Street's Leadership for Educational Change program, and she currently works at Harlem Success Academy as a leadership resident, in preparation for opening her own Harlem Success Academy.

**Nagaraj, A. J.** As a member of the 2006 Hawaii charter corps, Mr. Nagaraj taught tenth- and eleventh-grade social studies in the rural community of Wai'anae, Hawaii. Although he primarily focused on modern Hawaiian history and U.S. history, he also taught classes in career planning and U.S. government. While teaching in Hawaii, he coached a team of students in the University of Hawaii Business and Marketing Plan competition and in writing a curriculum for a statewide SAT prep nonprofit. Mr. Nagaraj is on the admissions staff of Teach For America.

**Neves, Danielle.** Ms. Neves taught sixth-grade English and social studies to students of all levels at Markham Middle School in Los Angeles. On average, students in her intervention reading class entered her classroom reading at an early first-grade level and left having raised their reading level by 2.5 years. Students in her honors class were already scoring "proficient" and "advanced" on standardized tests, so Ms. Neves challenged them with upper-grade literature, and they consistently analyzed the literature at high levels and completed multipage responses to literature essays. She subsequently joined New Leaders for New Schools and moved to Oakland, where she founded Sankofa Academy and served as principal for five years. Ms. Neves is currently the principal of Woodridge Elementary and Middle School in Washington, D.C.

**Omenn, David.** The year before Mr. Omenn came to Clemente Martinez Elementary in Houston, Texas, just 34 percent of the school's fifth graders had passed the Science TAKS (Texas Assessment of Knowledge and Skills). On the beginning-of-year diagnostic, his fifth-grade science lab students performed on average on a second-grade level, many of them not knowing any of our solar system's planets or how to use basic tools like a thermometer. By the end of his first year, 66 percent of Mr. Omenn's fifth graders passed the TAKS and they had, on average, progressed by an average of 1.75 grade levels. The next year, despite again beginning at a second-grade level, his students grew an average of 2.5 years in science and 80 percent of them passed the state test. Mr. Omenn currently manages aspects of Teach For America's recruitment efforts.

**Ortega, Janis.** Ms. Ortega's fourth-grade bilingual students began the school year in Los Angeles reading well below grade level. They left her classroom having improved their reading levels by an average of over a year and a half and attained the highest bilingual class score in seven years on the math state exam in her school, with 93 percent of them scoring "proficient" or higher. Ms. Ortega has subsequently led the finance committee for a statewide infrastructure bond to benefit affordable housing and consulted for a downtown Los Angeles charter school, providing curriculum training to their after-school tutors and writing grants to secure funding for additional resources. Ms. Ortega currently works on the development staff of Teach For America.

**Ott, Chris.** Coming out of sixth grade, only five of Mr. Ott's one hundred science and reading students at John F. Kennedy Middle School in Atlanta had passed the Georgia Criterion Referenced Competency Test (CRCT). Complicating matters, midway through the academic year, the time allotted each week for science was cut in half schoolwide. Nonetheless, Mr. Ott's students mastered an average of 79 percent of grade-level science content, and leaving his eighth-grade classroom after two years, they greatly exceeded the state average on the CRCT during the first year physical science was tested. Furthermore, 100 percent of his students met or exceeded standards on the state test in reading, meaning that leaving eighth grade, each of them was reading at or above grade level. Mr. Ott currently manages aspects of the preservice training that Teach For America provides to its corps members.

**Pappas, Sophia.** As a prekindergarten teacher at Madison Elementary School in Newark, New Jersey, Ms. Pappas consistently led her students to remarkable academic progress. Many students entered her class unable to identify any letters or letter sounds or to read print from left to right, but nearly all of them left her class on grade level and over half were above grade level. Her classroom was identified as a model classroom for other teachers in her district, and Teach For America has used her classroom as the model for training its early childhood corps members. She has interned with the New Jersey Department of Education's Early Childhood Education Division and published *Good Morning, Children: My First Years in Early Childhood Education* (2009), a memoir about her teaching experiences based on a blog she wrote about her classroom for Pre-K Now in 2009. Ms. Pappas is currently pursuing a master's degree in public policy at the Harvard Kennedy School of Government. She plans to continue pursuing her lifelong goal of ensuring that all children receive the educational opportunities they deserve.

**Phillips, Charlotte.** The majority of Ms. Phillips's kindergarten students at Woodrow Wilson Elementary School in Houston, Texas, were at a preprimer reading level on entering her class. Their alphabetical and phonological awareness was minimal, and most did not know how to write or read their name. By the time her students left her class in May, 90 percent of them were reading at a beginning-of-first-grade-level or above. Ms. Phillips has subsequently served in a variety of capacities at Teach For America, where she currently works to strengthen the alumni network.

**Pierce, Katie.** The students in Ms. Pierce's sixth-grade bilingual program in New York City started the year demonstrating an average of 64 percent mastery of state writing standards (whether they wrote in Spanish or English) and 41 percent mastery of social studies standards. By the end of the year, the students in both of her classes demonstrated an average of 91 percent mastery of rigorous grade-level writing standards and 82.5 percent mastery of social studies standards. With the help of her coteacher, who taught reading, the students in their two classes made an average of three years of reading growth in English, and for the first time in the history of the school, no seventh-grade transitional bilingual class was needed, because all of the students were ready to complete seventh grade in an English as a Second Language or mainstream English environment. Ms. Pierce is currently pursuing a doctor of physical therapy degree at Northern Arizona University in Flagstaff, with an interest in working primarily with children in underserved communities.

**Pomis, Aaron.** Mr. Pomis has taught middle school science in two school districts in North Carolina. He has been teaching at KIPP Charlotte since its inception in 2007, serving students in Charlotte's lowest-income communities. In 2007–2008, only 41 percent of North Carolina fifth graders—and only 18 percent of the state's African American fifth graders—scored "proficient" on the state science test. Under Mr. Pomis's leadership, 73 percent of his fifth-grade students (all but one of whom were African American) achieved proficiency. Mr. Pomis has also served as a mentor and coach for Teach For America corps members in Charlotte and as the chairman of the board of directors for the Community Charter School, an arts-integrated K–5 charter school in Charlotte.

**Powers, Laura.** As a sixth-grade special education English/language arts and social studies teacher (and later as a reading teacher with the Success for All program) at Middle School 50 in Brooklyn, New York City, Ms. Powers ensured that every one of her students was able to achieve at least one and half years of growth in reading comprehension and fluency, with many improving even more dramatically. In addition, 100 percent of her students achieved 80 percent mastery in sixth-grade social studies standards, and all of her students achieved the goals in their Individualized Education Programs. Ms. Powers currently teaches special education at Prospect Hill Academy Charter School in Boston.

**Probasco, Christine.** As a third-grade teacher at Thoreau Elementary School on the Navajo Nation, Ms. Probasco led 86 percent of her homeroom students to at least 1.5 grade levels of growth in reading and led her reading students to an average growth of 0.75 grade levels per quarter. In addition, 92 percent of her students mastered 80 percent of New Mexico grade-level math standards. Ms. Probasco served as grade-level chair, cochair of the reading committee, and cosponsor of Thoreau High School's College Success Program. She is currently working toward a Ph.D. in language, literacy, and sociocultural studies, with a long-term goal of improving and shaping teacher education programs to better prepare teachers to make significant gains in their classroom.

**Rabb, Maurice.** When his students entered Mr. Rabb's kindergarten class in Los Angeles, none of them could read, the majority of them did not know the alphabet, and several could not speak English. By the end of each year, more than 85 percent of Mr. Rabb's students were reading at or above grade level, including all of the students who came into his class with no English-language ability. Mr. Rabb later taught English in Japan. After attending law school, he returned to Japan, where he currently works in the corporate department for a U.S. law firm.

**Rangel, Fernando.** Mr. Rangel's tenth-grade English students in the Rio Grande Valley in Texas entered his class with weak writing and reading skills. A number of them told him that they had only read a single book in their entire academic career, and many had never written beyond a paragraph in a number of their classes. By the end of the year, student scores on the state exam increased by 9 percent over the previous year, and many of his students received a score of 3 or higher on the essay portion of the state exam after previously scoring only 1 or 2. Mr. Rangel continues to teach tenth-grade English in the district, where he has helped develop the tenth-grade curriculum, helped design a creative writing program, and trained trainers for the Abydos International writing program.

**Ready, Stephen.** Mr. Ready has been a teacher for seventeen years since he began teaching English as a Second Language (ESL) and English at Donna High School in Donna, Texas. Over the years, he has taught ESL, Leadership, gifted and talented English, honors English, and world history in public high schools (all Title I schools), and adult ESL at a university and in two prison settings. He is now a bilingual resource teacher and English Learners Department chair at Menlo-Atherton High School in Atherton, California, in charge of the program for the approximately four hundred English learners at the school.

**Reddick, Richard J.** Dr. Reddick began his career as a fourth-grade teacher at E. O. Smith Educational Center in Houston, Texas. While there, he served on the superintendent's Advisory Committee on Alternative Certification Programs for the Houston Independent School District. He subsequently worked in student affairs at MIT, Cal Poly-San Luis Obispo, and Emory University, and he is currently an assistant professor of higher education at the University of Texas at Austin. His research looks at how students of color from high-poverty, high-minority–populated high schools access higher education in central Texas, and he has coauthored and coedited books on the black family, historically black colleges, and the impact of *Brown* v. *Board of Education* on multiracial equity in American education.

**Reidy, Kristin.** Ms. Reidy began her teaching career as a biology teacher at Glen Oaks High School in Baton Rouge, Louisiana. She subsequently returned to her alma mater, Marana High School, in Tucson, Arizona, where her tremendous success as a ninth-grade science teacher led the Arizona Educational Foundation to name her the 2007 Arizona Teacher of the Year. Ms. Reidy is currently an associate principal at Marana Middle School and pursuing a doctorate in educational leadership at the University of Arizona.

**Rhee, Michelle.** Ms. Rhee's students at Harlem Park Community School in Baltimore, Maryland, began the year scoring at the thirteenth percentile on nationally recognized standardized tests. By the end of her second year with the same students, 90 percent were scoring at the nineteenth percentile. Ms. Rhee subsequently founded The New Teacher Project (TNTP), a national nonprofit that partners with educational entities to increase the number of outstanding individuals who become public school teachers. Under her leadership as CEO and president, TNTP worked with more than two hundred school districts in twenty-three states and recruited, prepared, or certified approximately twenty-three thousand new teachers. Ms. Rhee is currently chancellor of the District of Columbia Public Schools system.

**Rittenhouse, Talla.** Ms. Rittenhouse taught math at Strawberry Mansion High School in Philadelphia, where her students consistently outperformed district averages on districtwide benchmark exams. At the beginning of the year, less than 30 percent of her eleventh-grade Algebra II students could demonstrate mastery of ninth-grade Algebra I standards, and many could not add or subtract fractions or positive and negative numbers. Ms. Rittenhouse currently works to help recruit staff members for Teach For America.

**Rosenbaum, Jennifer.** Many of Ms. Rosenbaum's prekindergarten three-year-old students in Washington, D.C., came to school without any knowledge of letters or numbers and with limited reading comprehension, math, and social-emotional skills. By the end of the year, they grew an average of two levels (approximately equivalent to two years) on prioritized skills from the Creative Curriculum Developmental Continuum and far exceeded the pre-K four-year-old literacy and math standards for Washington, D.C. Five of her fifteen students had learned how to read. Ms. Rosenbaum currently serves as a mentor and coach for first- and second-year Teach For America early childhood teachers.

**Ruelas, Veronica.** In 2008, Ms. Ruelas was named a Golden Apple Teacher of Distinction in Illinois. In her nine years of teaching, she has taught a wide range of courses: elementary and middle school physical education, second- and fifth-grade self-contained/inclusion, and sixth-, seventh-, and eighth-grade math, science, and language arts—and she has taught tap, jazz, and ballet to preschool through eighth-grade students. In her current role as a middle school math teacher at the Academy of St. Benedict the African in Chicago, Ms. Ruelas has led 85 percent of her students to an average or above-average score on the end-of-year state math test and helped ensure that 100 percent of the school's students had a high school placement by February of their eighth-grade year.

**Ruszkowski, Christopher.** Mr. Ruszkowski's seventh- and eighth-grade social studies students in Miami, Florida, typically began the year with around 15 percent mastery of the standards. By the end of each year, each of his classes consistently averaged above 80 percent content mastery. Mr. Ruszkowski later served as site manager for Miami Teaching Fellows for The New Teacher Project (in conjunction with Miami-Dade County Public Schools) and as site manager for Louisiana Teaching Fellows (in conjunction with the Recovery School District). Mr. Ruszkowski has been named a finalist for the Rhodes Scholarship and produced the documentary *Students of Katrina: Paths to Classrooms After the Storm.* He is pursuing a master's degree in educational leadership at Stanford University.

**Schankula, Rachel.** As a fifth-grade teacher at Carver Elementary School in Indianola, Mississippi, Ms. Schankula led her students to an average of 1.5 grade levels' growth in reading on the STAR reading assessment. She has subsequently held a variety of positions with Teach For America, where she has led the evolution of the organization's program staff development model since 2005. She was instrumental in the development of the coinvestigation model of problem solving, as well as the frameworks and trainings around various staff positions designed to help Teach For America teachers maximize their effectiveness. Ms. Schankula continues to lead the evolution of the organization's teacher support and development model.

**Scharon, Janelle.** As a chemistry and robotics teacher at ACE Technical Charter High School in Chicago, Ms. Scharon led her students to 84 percent mastery of rigorous grade-level standards. She is currently a program director for the New Teacher Center in Chicago.

**Schrepfer, Kate.** Ms. Schrepfer began her career teaching tenth-grade biology as well as ninth-grade science skills and reasoning in Leland, Mississippi. At the beginning of her first year of teaching, a number of her science skills and reasoning students did not know that plants were living things, but by the end of that year, they were creating simulations of the bioengineering of plant genes, and over 80 percent of her students mastered over 80 percent of the state standards. Ms. Schrepfer subsequently taught seventh-grade science at View Park Preparatory Accelerated Charter Middle School in Los Angeles before moving to Washington, D.C., to teach physics and biology at Maya Angelou Public Charter School, where her students improved their scores on the Maya Angelou Quarterly Interim Benchmark Exam by an average of 30 percentage points. Ms. Schrepfer is currently a professional development specialist for District of Columbia Public Schools.

**Scott, Stephanie.** Ms. Scott began her career as a third-grade teacher in south Louisiana, where she led her students to gains of over 1.5 years in reading level. She subsequently joined the staff of the first KIPP early childhood and elementary school in Houston as the instructional coach for new teachers and was a founding member of the first- and second-grade teams. Ms. Scott was recently chosen for KIPP's Fisher Fellowship and will be the principal of an elementary school opening in New York City in August 2010.

**Scroggins, Eric.** As an eighth-grade science teacher in New York City, Mr. Scroggins led his students to tremendous success on the tenth-grade New York State Earth Science Regents Exam. Two-thirds of them passed the exam (thus earning high school credit), approximately double the pass rate of New York City tenth graders. Mr. Scroggins has subsequently held positions with Teach For America, including executive director of the St. Louis and Bay Area regions. He currently oversees key aspects of Teach For America's growth nationwide.

**Sellers, Daniel.** When Mr. Sellers began teaching sixth-grade mathematics in Warren County, North Carolina, only 40 percent of the sixth graders at his school had passed the state math exam the previous year, well below the state pass rate of 62 percent. At the end of his first year of teaching, 72 percent of his students had passed the standardized test. The following year, 97 percent passed, and their scale scores were higher on average than students from upper- and middle-income schools in North Carolina, essentially closing the achievement gap between his students and their peers in wealthier communities. Mr. Sellers is currently the executive director of Teach For America in the Twin Cities.

**Sherrin, Nicole.** As a seventh- and eighth-grade math teacher at the Alfred F. Garcia Elementary School in Phoenix, Ms. Sherrin raised the school's eighth-grade mathematics achievement from lowest in the district to highest in a single year. In addition, she created and directed a mathematics enrichment program and a math tutorial program, which motivated and prepared twenty-four of twenty-seven participating pupils to enter honors algebra in high school, and she designed, fundraised, and implemented a dropout prevention program for former students. Ms. Sherrin later taught at a KIPP school in the South Bronx, helped launch Britain's Teach First program, worked as assistant principal in Washington, D.C., and is currently a middle school assistant principal in Madison, New Jersey.

**Simon, Melissa.** Ms. Simon's sixth-grade students at George Washington Carver Middle School in Los Angeles began the year reading, on average, at a fourth-grade level. By the end of the year, they had improved their reading levels by an average of 2.2 years; every student improved by at least 1.5 years, and many gained 4 to 5 years of reading growth in just 1 year. Furthermore, six of Ms. Simon's Intermediate English as a Second Language (ESL) students were able to skip Advanced ESL and mainstream into regular English classes, an extremely rare occurrence. Ms. Simon is the recipient of the City of Los Angeles Inspirational Teaching Award and the George Washington Carver Middle School Outstanding Instruction Award. She currently recruits corps members for Teach For America.

**Simson, Emma.** The year before Ms. Simson began teaching social studies at Bladensburg High School in Prince George's County, Maryland, the school's pass rate on the state Government High School Assessment, required for graduation, was 52 percent. The next year, 91 percent of Ms. Simson's students passed. She is currently pursuing a master's degree in evidence-based social interventions at Oxford University.

**Smith, Michelle.** As a middle school science teacher at "full-inclusion" Canton Middle School in Baltimore, Dr. Smith had students of all grade levels and tracks in the same classroom at the same time. To address the needs of all of her students, she successfully developed rigorous hands-on multidisciplinary lessons geared to a variety of learning styles and levels. Later, as a medical student at the University of Pennsylvania, she led a medical student interest group that trained fellow medical students to teach lessons on AIDS in low-income public school classrooms. Dr. Smith is in her sixth year of a seven-year residency program in neurological surgery at Weill-Cornell Medical Center in New York City.

**Smith, Preston.** Mr. Smith began his career as a first-grade teacher at Clyde Arbuckle Elementary School in San Jose, California, where he was named Teacher of the Year. After three years at Arbuckle, Mr. Smith collaborated with neighborhood families to found and lead LUCHA Elementary School, a small school focused on high academic achievement and parental involvement. (LUCHA stands for Learning in an Urban Community for High Achievement.) After three years of operation, LUCHA received an Annual Performance Index score of 881, making it the highest-ranked elementary school in the district, and was the seventh-best low-income elementary school in California. Mr. Smith subsequently cofounded and served as principal of Rocketship One Public School, which he and his cofounder have recently expanded into a multiple-school organization called Rocketship Education.

**Sobel, Kate.** Ms. Sobel's first-grade students at Mayo Elementary School in Compton, California, outperformed the school's other first graders. She also served as grade-level chair, lead teacher, literacy coach, and Family Literacy Program director, working alongside parents to advocate for their children's rights in the district. Ms. Sobel currently serves as principal of the Harvard K–8 Campus of Camino Nuevo Community Charter Academy in Los Angeles, which scored an 828 and ranks ten out of ten (ten being the highest) on the state Academic Performance Index when compared to California schools with similar demographics.

**Steffes, Shannon.** On average, Ms. Steffes's fifth-grade students at Rocky View Elementary in New Mexico entered her class three grade levels below expected performance. Under her leadership, they improved by an average of 2.2 reading levels and 1.8 years in math. Ms. Steffes has received a New Mexico Regional Quality Center Award of Excellence and a Phi Delta Kappa Honor Society Scholarship, and her classroom was selected as a Gallup McKinley County Schools Demonstration Classroom. Ms. Steffes currently serves as the coordinator of the Regional Quality Center, a state-based organization that emphasizes setting classroom goals, the use of data in the classroom, student investment, action planning, and teacher and student reflection.

**Storm, Melissa.** Dr. Storm began her career teaching students with emotional and behavioral disabilities in St. John's Parish, Louisiana. Her students consistently improved their social/emotional skills and mastered, on average, 90 percent of their ambitious Individualized Education Program goals related to behavior by the end of the year, while improving both their reading and math levels by an average of one grade level. Dr. Storm subsequently spent five years teaching special education in public schools in Colorado and Virginia. Since earning her Ph.D. in educational psychology at the University of Virginia, Dr. Storm has worked at the American Institutes for Research in Washington, D.C., where she is a senior research analyst and works on state and federally funded projects, supporting initiatives for students with disabilities, and working on policy requests in special education.

**Subrahmanian, Krishnan.** Mr. Subrahmanian's special education students at Todd County High School on the Rosebud Indian Reservation in Mission, South Dakota, improved their reading levels by an average of two years, made three grade levels worth of gains in math, and attained 80 percent mastery of state science standards. Mr. Subrahmanian also founded the Todd County High School Oral Interpretation Team and led them to an Outstanding Team Award (awarded to top eight teams in the state) at the South Dakota State Speech Tournament. He is the recipient of a Gates Cambridge Scholarship and a Todd County High School Teacher of the Year Award, and he directed the Todd County One-Act Play competition, which advanced to the State festival and garnered two Outstanding Actor Awards. After receiving his master's degree in education on a Gates Cambridge Scholarship, he worked as a border state director and then a regional director for the Obama campaign. Mr. Subrahmanian is currently a medical student at Stanford University, researching the best ways to prevent the alarmingly high rates of cancer that occur on reservations in the Northern Plains.

**Sutton, Tammi.** Ms. Sutton began her career teaching seventh-grade language arts and social studies at Gaston Middle School in Gaston, North Carolina, where she increased pass rates on the state end-of-grade tests from 43 percent to 100 percent in writing and from 48 percent to 93 percent in reading. Ms. Sutton then cofounded (with Caleb Dolan) KIPP Gaston College Preparatory in 2001, which has consistently ranked among the top ten schools in the state in sixth-, seventh-, and eighth-grade reading and math. In 2005, Ms. Sutton founded KIPP Pride High School for its first class of ninth graders. Every student in Pride High's first graduating class (the class of 2009) was admitted to at least two colleges and they collectively received over $2 million in scholarships. Ms. Sutton has been named Sallie Mae New Teacher of the Year, Gaston Middle School Teacher of the Year, Northampton County Teacher of the Year Runner Up, and a recipient of the Kinder Excellence in Teaching Award.

**Tan, Jenny.** Ms. Tan began her career teaching second, third, and fifth grades at Washington Accelerated Elementary School in Los Angeles. In her final year there, she taught math and science to both fifth-grade classes at her school while her partner teacher taught reading. Of the fifty students, forty-six passed the math California Standards Test, almost double the state pass rate that year. Ms. Tan is currently the elementary principal at Andre Agassi College Preparatory Academy in the heart of Las Vegas's most at-risk neighborhood, where students have consistently scored above the district averages for all grade levels and subject areas. The elementary, middle, and high school components of Agassi have all been designated "high achieving" by the state of Nevada, a designation received by fewer than 8 percent of Nevada schools.

**Tarca, Kate.** Ms. Tarca began her career teaching third grade in Atlanta, where she led her students to two years' growth in reading and 84 percent mastery of third-grade math standards. She subsequently taught fifth-grade reading and writing at KIPP DC: WILL Academy. Ms. Tarca is currently a literacy coach for Randolph Public Schools in Massachusetts.

**Taylor, Kristen.** Ms. Taylor's sixth-grade students at Jefferson Elementary in St. Louis began the year with very low reading fluency. By the end of the year, they had improved their reading levels by an average of 1.78 years. While only four of Ms. Taylor's eighteen students were reading on grade level at the beginning of the year, fourteen were reading at or above grade level at the end of the year. In addition to teaching sixth grade, Ms. Taylor has written the districtwide fifth- and sixth-grade math curriculum for the Normandy School District. She is pursuing a Ph.D. in curriculum and policy at the University of Missouri at St. Louis.

**Thomas, Eric.** When the school leadership at Mr. Thomas's Baltimore high school decided to divide the school into "academies," he convinced them to let him create an academically rigorous Journalism Institute in which he would work closely with the same group of students from their sophomore year until graduation. He developed six rigorous semester-long journalism classes, resurrected the school paper (which had been defunct for twenty years), and required students to make college visits and enroll in summer programs at local colleges. At a school where only half of the students earn their high school diplomas and only a quarter attend four-year colleges, 100 percent of the students in Mr. Thomas's three-year Journalism Institute were accepted to at least four four-year colleges, and 100 percent attended the four-year college of their choice. Mr. Thomas is currently the principal of Rauner College Prep, a campus of Noble Street Charter School in Chicago, whose students outperformed students at other nonselective Chicago high schools by more than three points on the ACT in 2008–2009.

**Tifft, Dan.** When Mr. Tifft began teaching high school Spanish at Hillside High School in North Carolina, most of his students were either first-time foreign language learners or were repeating the class after having had three or more Spanish teachers in the previous year. By the end of their time in his classroom, nearly all of Mr. Tifft's students met the state standards for Spanish I and II. Mr. Tifft is currently the tenth-grade English teacher and English department chair at Saint John's School in San Juan, Puerto Rico, where he has created a new school newspaper and founded a HAM radio club.

**Tow-Yick, Heather.** Fewer than half of Ms. Tow-Yick's English/language arts (ELA) students in South Bronx (New York City) entered the eighth grade at the seventh-grade entry level for reading. When they left her classroom, all but one had scored "proficient" or above on the eighth-grade ELA exam. Ms. Tow-Yick subsequently worked as a strategy consultant at the Bridgespan Group, where she developed the domestic strategy for an international educational media company, projected revenues and expenses for a school leadership nonprofit, and conducted organizational analysis for a national high school network of academies. She also served as special assistant to Chancellor Joel Klein at the New York City Department of Education. Ms. Tow-Yick currently works to attract, engage, retain, and develop top-performing staff members at Teach For America.

**Tsabetsaye, Jessica.** Ms. Tsabetsaye's tenth- and eleventh-grade physical science students in Zuni Pueblo demonstrated over 80 percent mastery of the New Mexico standards. Ms. Tsabetsaye is currently in a master's of science physician assistant program at the University of St. Francis in Joliet, Illinois. She plans to return to her community of Zuni Pueblo to provide health care services and education and continue working with local school districts.

**Wadhwani, Nisha.** At the beginning of the year, most of Ms. Wadhwani's seventh-grade science students in Los Angeles were multiple years behind grade level in math—only 4 percent of her students could use a ruler to accurately measure inches and centimeters. A third of her students were reading at a third-grade level or lower. By the end of the year, they had averaged over 80 percent mastery of content standards, and most of the students were reporting that science was now their favorite subject. Ms. Wadhwani continues to teach seventh-grade science in Los Angeles.

**Wahler, Erin.** Ms. Wahler's fifth-grade students in Zuni, New Mexico, began the year averaging a late-third-grade reading level. By the end of the year, they had improved their reading levels by 1.5 years on the Assessment of Reading Comprehension. In addition, they increased their fluency by an average of 25 words per minute, finishing at an average of 130 words per minute, above the fifth-grade benchmark score of 124 words per minute. Her students' gains increased each additional year she taught in Zuni. In fall 2009, after four years in Zuni, Ms. Wahler joined the staff of Atlas Preparatory School in Colorado Springs.

**Wakefield, Victor.** Mr. Wakefield's fifth-, sixth-, and-seventh grade English language arts students at West Gary Lighthouse Charter School in Indiana improved their reading levels by an average of 2.3 years (as measured by the Northwest Evaluation Association [NWEA] Reading Assessment). Both his sixth graders and seventh graders ended the year with an average score above the expected grade-level equivalent score, with the sixth-grade mean score moving from the twenty-seventh percentile to the fifty-first percentile against the national norm. Mr. Wakefield currently recruits outstanding recent college graduates for Teach For America.

**Wallace, Brian.** The students in Mr. Wallace's special education class at Middle School 3 in New York City had a classwide average of 1.71 years of reading growth and 81 percent mastery of New York State math standards. They also showed more improvement in their New York State English/language arts exam scores than any other special education class in the entire school. In addition, three of his twelve students were moved into less restrictive special education environments because of the progress they made in his class. Mr. Wallace currently works as a mentor and coach to Teach For America corps members who teach special education in New York City and tutors formerly incarcerated students who are now in an alternative high school program.

**Wilson, Acasia.** Ms. Wilson's fifth-grade students in Phoenix, Arizona, averaged 1.5 years of growth, and the majority of them left her classroom reading at or above grade level. In one year, the two students who began the year furthest behind (reading at a kindergarten and a first-grade level) were the ones who displayed the most growth, ending the year reading at a fifth- and a fourth-grade level, respectively. Ms. Wilson later participated on the development team of Teach For America in Phoenix, where she worked to dramatically increase the size of the corps of Teach For America teachers serving low-income students. She then served as a volunteer in a small community in the Himalayas in India, where she assisted with curriculum development and teacher training. Ms. Wilson currently works for an educational nonprofit in Los Angeles, serving low-income youth seeking careers in the skilled trades and engineering, and she is a fellow in the Leadership Los Angeles program.

**Winchester, Martin.** As chief schools officer for IDEA Public Schools in Donna, Texas, Mr. Winchester supervises the recruitment, training, and evaluation of all elementary and secondary principals for a system of schools that consistently outperform the state averages in all areas while serving a predominantly low-income, Latino student population. In 2009, the district won the H.E.B. Excellence in Education Award for the best small district in the state. IDEA College Prep, where Mr. Winchester taught for many years, was ranked as the nineteenth best high school in the nation by *U.S. News & World Report*, and 100 percent of its alumni are currently attending four-year colleges. In his eleven years in the classroom, Mr. Winchester has twice been named a school system's Teacher of the Year. He earned National Board Certification in 2004 and has worked during the summer in training and support of new teachers. Mr. Winchester was a finalist for the $100,000 Kinder Excellence in Teaching Award and was presented with the first and only AmeriCorps alumnus award for continued service by President Bill Clinton in January 2001.

**Winfield, Jane.** Ms. Winfield teaches global history in New York City. Her students all came to her class after experiencing significant past failures. Some had been expelled from previous schools. Some had been to prison. Some had been chronically truant at previous schools. Those who had previously taken the New York

Global History Regents Exam had generally scored between 25 and 35 (out of 100), far below the minimum score required for graduation (65). She had one semester to prepare her students for this exam, which is typically taught over a two-year span. On average, her students' score has increased to 70 to 75 each semester, with over 90 percent of her students who take the exam earning passing scores.

**Yan, Justin.** Since the primary focus in elementary school had been reading and math, Mr. Yan's sixth-grade science students in Charlotte, North Carolina, entered his class with limited prerequisite knowledge; in fact, fewer than half of them could interpret fourth-grade-level science texts. By the end of each year of teaching, his students had attained over an average of 80 percent of sixth-grade science content standards. In addition, all of them participated in a schoolwide science fair that Mr. Yan organized, and one of the winning students subsequently took third place in the districtwide fair. Mr. Yan was recognized as Outstanding First Year Teacher of the Year at his school. He currently recruits outstanding recent college graduates to Teach For America.

**Zambrano, Maria.** As a sixth-grade early-intermediate English as a Second Language teacher at Nimitz Middle School in Los Angeles, Ms. Zambrano was assigned a group of students who had failed the course the previous semester. Over half of these students had learning disabilities or severe behavior problems. English as a Second Language promotion in Los Angeles Unified is based on students' test scores from the scripted curriculum's (High Point) assessments. The average unit test scores at the beginning of the year hovered around 38 percent. Ms. Zambrano's average High Point unit test scores rose to 83 percent by the end of the spring semester. At the end of the year, twenty-nine students moved forward to the next English as a Second Language level.

**Zucker, Tricia.** Dr. Zucker began her career as a kindergarten teacher at E. D. White Elementary in Houston, Texas, where approximately 90 percent of her students learned one hundred sight words and she was named the Houston Independent School District's Intern of the Year. She subsequently taught kindergarten in a low-income, rural setting in Virginia. She completed her reading specialist certification and then a Ph.D. in reading education at the University of Virginia, where she received a Doctoral Research in Education Science Award from the Center for Advanced Study of Teaching and Learning. Dr. Zucker is currently a postdoctoral research fellow at the University of Texas Health Science Center at Houston in the Children's Learning Institute, where her research focuses on approaches for ensuring the school readiness of children at risk for academic difficulties due to the effects of poverty.

# NOTES

## Introduction

1. See the Maryland online education report card for schools in Baltimore City at http://www.mdreport card.org.

2. National Center for Education Statistics. *National Assessment of Educational Progress (NAEP)*, 1998, 2000, 2002, 2003, 2005 and 2007 Reading Assessments.

3. See the Texas online education report card at http://ritter.tea.state.tx.us.

4. "Diplomas Count 2007: Ready for What?" *Education Week,* 2007.

5. See the Texas online education report card at http://ritter.tea.state.tx.us.

6. Foote, D. "Lessons from Locke." *Newsweek*, Aug. 11, 2008, writing about her book *Relentless Pursuit: A Year in the Trenches with Teach For America*. New York: Knopf, 2008.

7. National Center for Education Statistics. *National Assessment of Educational Progress (NAEP)*, 2005 Reading Assessments.

8. For a discussion of the history of the report, see Viadero, D. "Race Report's Influence Felt 40 Years Later: Legacy of Coleman's Study Was New View of Equity." *Education Week*, June 21, 2006.

9. Marzano, R. J., Pickering, D. J., and Pollock, J. E. *Classroom Instruction That Works: Research-Based Strategies for Increasing Student Achievement*. Alexandria, Va.: ASCD, 2004, p. 2. The full 1966 Coleman Report—*Equality of Educational Opportunity*—is available online at Education Information Resource Center http://eric.ed.gov.

10. Blankstein, A. M. *Failure Is Not an Option: Six Principles That Guide Student Achievement in High-Performing Schools*. Thousand Oaks, Calif.: Corwin Press, 2004, p. 8.

11. Smith, A. "Equity Within Reach: Insights from the Front Lines of America's Achievement Gap." 2005. http://www.teachforamerica.org/research/report_member_views.htm/.

12. See Boyd, D., and others. *How Changes in Entry Requirements Alter the Teacher Workforce and Affect Student Achievement*. Teacher Pathways Project, 2005, pp. 15–16.

13. Ibid.

14. See, for example, Ready, T., Edley, C., Jr., and Snow, C. E. (eds.). *Achieving High Educational Standards for All: Conference Summary*. Washington, D.C.: National Research Council, 2002.

15. Marzano, R. J. *What Works in Schools: Translating Research into Action.* Alexandria, Va.: ASCD, 2003, p. 7.

16. Sanders, W. C., and Rivers, J. C. *Cumulative and Residual Effects of Teachers on Future Student Academic Achievement.* Knoxville: University of Tennessee Value-Added Research and Assessment Center, 1996.

17. Kane, T., Gordon, R., and Staiger, D. "Identifying Effective Teachers Using Performance on the Job." Washington, D.C.: Brookings Institution, 2004, p. 8.

18. Peske, H., and Haycock, K. *Teaching Inequality: How Poor and Minority Students Are Short-Changed on Teacher Quality: A Report and Recommendations by the Education Trust.* Washington, D.C.: Education Trust, 2006, p. 11.

19. For inspiring examples of this alignment, see Ladson-Billings, G. *The Dreamkeepers: Successful Teachers of African American Children.* San Francisco: Jossey-Bass, 2009.

## Chapter One

1. Kouzes, J., and Posner, B. *The Leadership Challenge.* (4th ed.) San Francisco: Jossey-Bass, 2007, p. 105.

2. Kotter, J. P. *Leading Change.* Boston: Harvard Business School Press, 1996, p. 7.

3. Collins, J., and Porras, J. I. *Built to Last: Successful Habits of Visionary Companies.* New York: HarperCollins, 1997, pp. 92–93.

4. Ibid., p. 93.

5. Academy of Achievement. "Getting America Online: Steve Case Interview. " July 2007. http://www.achievement.org/autodoc/page/cas1int-5.

6. Research on the impact of big goals on student learning echoes precisely what we see and hear from highly effective teachers who are leading their students to dramatic academic achievement. "Effective goals are both specific and measurable," Alan Blankstein finds. "They clearly identify the evidence that must be monitored to assess progress. They also set a time frame for completion. For example, 'We will increase our students' average state test score by 20% this academic year' is a good, specific goal. 'We will help all kids become lifelong learners,' on the other hand, is too vague to be useful." Blankstein, A. M. *Failure Is Not an Option: Six Principles That Guide Student Achievement in High-Performing Schools.* Thousand Oaks, Calif.: Corwin Press, 2004, p. 90.

7. Texas State Legislature. *Part II: Texas Education Agency Chapter 111 Subchapter C. High School.* Texas Administration Code 19. Austin: Office of the Secretary of State of Texas, 1996, p. 8.

8. California State Board of Education. *English-Language Arts Content Standards for California Public Schools: Kindergarten Through Grade Twelve.* Sacramento: California Department of Education Press, 1997, p. 12.

9. South Dakota Board of Education. *South Dakota Social Studies Standards 6–8.* Pierre: South Dakota Department of Education, 2006.

10. Collins, J. *Good to Great and the Social Sectors: A Monograph to Accompany Good to Great.* New York: HarperCollins, 2005, pp. 7–8.

11. Ibid.

12. Bennis, W. *On Becoming a Leader.* New York: Basic Books, 2003, p. 192.

13. Rosenthal, R., and Jacobson, L. *Pygmalion in the Classroom: Teacher Expectation and Pupil's Intellectual Development.* New York: Holt, 1968.

14. Marzano, R. J. *The Art and Science of Teaching: A Comprehensive Framework for Effective Instruction.* Alexandria, Va.: ASCD, 2007, p. 163. Marzano notes that "the effect of teacher expectations on student achievement might be one of the most well-researched aspects of classroom instruction."

15. Ibid., p. 162.

16. Tatum, B. D. *Why Are All the Black Kids Sitting Together in the Cafeteria?* New York: Basic Books, 2003.

17. Ibid., p. 6.

18. Thompson, G. *Through Ebony Eyes: What Teachers Need to Know But Are Afraid to Ask About African American Students.* San Francisco: Jossey-Bass, 2004, p. 189.

19. Entman, R. *Young Men of Color in the Media: Images and Impacts.* Washington, D.C.: Health Policy Institute, 2006.

20. Entman, R. *Race and the Media: A Decade of Research.* Chicago: Human Relationships Task Force, Human Relations Foundation of Chicago, 2000.

21. Rose, L., and Gallup, A. "37th Annual Phi Delta Kappa/Gallup Poll of the Public's Attitude Towards the Public Schools." *Phi Delta Kappan*, 2005, *87*(1), 41–57.

22. The other top responses were teacher quality and principal/administrator quality.

23. Smith, A. "Equity Within Reach: Insights from the Front Lines of America's Achievement Gap." 2005. http://www.teachforamerica.org/research/report_member_views.htm.

24. Entman, *Young Men of Color in the Media*, p. 15.

25. Bender, S. W. *Greasers and Gringos: Latinos, Law, and the American Imagination.* New York: New York University Press, 2003.

26. Harris, R. J. *A Cognitive Psychology of Mass Communication.* New York: Routledge, 2009, p. 75.

27. Kinnick, K., White, C., and Washington, K. "Racial Representation of Computer Users in Prime-Time Advertising." *Race, Gender and Class in the Media*, 8(4), 96.

28. Barth, P. "A Common Core Curriculum for the New Century: Aiming High for Other People's Children." *Thinking K-16,* 2003, *7*(1), 13.

29. See Patterson, E. B. "Poverty, Income Inequality, and Community Crime Rates." *Criminology,* 2006, *29*(4), 755–776.

30. See the Children's Defense Fund Web site: http://www.childrensdefense.org/child-research-data-publications/child-poverty.html.

31. Barlow, M. H. "Race and the Problem of Crime in *Time* and *Newsweek* Cover Stories, 1946–1995." *Social Justice*, 1998, *25,* 149–182.

32. Nieto, S. *Affirming Diversity: The Sociopolitical Context of Multicultural Education.* New York: Longman, 1996, pp. 41–42.

33. Collins and Porras, *Built to Last,* p. 94.

34. Kouzes and Posner, *The Leadership Challenge.*

35. Ibid., p. 117.

36. Ibid., p. 134.

37. New York State Education Department. *Mathematics Core Curriculum: MST Standard 3: Prekindergarten–Grade 12.* Albany: New York State Education Department, 2005, p. 47.

## Chapter Two

1. In researchers' terms, this is the expectancy × value model. The model of motivation holds that the effort that people are willing to expend on a task is the product of (1) the degree to which they expect to be able to perform the task successfully if they apply themselves (and thus the degree to which they expect to get whatever rewards that successful task performance will bring), and (2) the degree to which they value those rewards, as well as the opportunity to engage in the processes involved in performing the task itself. From Brophy, J. *Motivating Students to Learn.* (2nd ed.) Mahwah, N.J.: Erlbaum, 2004, p. 18. This notion of expectancy value is originally attributed to American psychologist John Atkinson. See also Stipek, D. *Motivation to Learn: Integrating Theory and Practice.* (4th ed.) Boston: Allyn & Bacon, 2001, p. 144.

2. Stipek, *Motivation to Learn*, p. 12.

3. Texeira, M. T., and Christian, P. M. "And Still They Rise: Practical Advice for Increasing African American Enrollments in Higher Education." *Educational Horizons*, Spring 2002 *8*(3), pp. 117–118.

4. Steele, C. "A Threat in the Air: How Stereotypes Shape Intellectual Identity and Performance." *American Psychologist*, 1997, *52,* 613–629.

5. Aronson, J., Cohen, G., and McColskey, W. "Reducing Stereotype Threat in Classrooms: A Review of Social-Psychological Intervention Studies on Improving the Achievement of Black Students." Washington, D.C.: Regional Educational Laboratory Southeast, July 2009.

6. Bempechat, J. "The Role of Parent Involvement in Children's Academic Achievement." *School Community Journal*, 1992, *2*(2), 31–41.

7. Ibid.

8. Dweck, C. *Self-Theories: Their Role in Motivation, Personality, and Development.* Philadelphia: Psychology Press, 2000, p. 3.

9. Ibid., pp. 2–4.

10. Ibid., p. 9.

11. Marzano, R. J. *What Works in Schools: Translating Research into Action.* Alexandria, Va.: ASCD, 2003, p. 151.

12. Covington, M. V. *Making the Grade: A Self-Worth Perspective on Motivation and School Reform.* Cambridge: Cambridge University Press, 1992, p. 16.

13. Blankstein, A. M. *Failure Is Not an Option: Six Principles that Guide Student Achievement in High-Performing Schools.* Thousand Oaks, Calif.: Corwin Press, 2004, p. 167.

14. See Smith, A. "Equity Within Reach: Insights from the Front Lines of America's Achievement Gap." 2005. http://www.teachforamerica.org/research/report_member_views.htm.

15 Gonzalez, N., Moll, L. C., and Amanti, C. *Funds of Knowledge: Theorizing Practices in Households, Communities, and Classrooms.* Mahwah, N.J.: Erlbaum, 2005.

16. Bempechat, J. "Learning from Poor and Minority Students Who Succeed in School." *Harvard Education Letter,* 1999, *15*(3), 34.

17. Lareau, A. *Home Advantage: Social Class and Parental Intervention in Elementary Education.* Lanham, Md.: Rowan and Littlefield, 2000.

18. Ibid., p. 9.

19. Marzano, *What Works in School,* pp. 47–48, 49.

20. Pianta, R. C., and others. "Opportunities to Learn in America's Elementary Classrooms." *Science,* 2007, *315,* 1795–1796.

21. Buckingham, M., and Coffman, C. *First, Break All the Rules: What the World's Greatest Managers Do Differently.* New York: Simon & Schuster, 1999, p. 103.

22. McCombs, B. L., and Whisler, J. *The Learner-Centered Classroom and School.* San Francisco: Jossey-Bass, 1997.

23. Bryk, A. S., and Schneider, B. *Trust in Schools: A Core Resource for Improvement.* New York: Russell Sage Foundation, 2002, p. 31.

24. "Educators as Applied Developmentalists: An Interview with Michael J. Nakkula and Eric Toshalis." *Harvard Education Letter,* Jan.–Feb. 2007. http://www.edletter.org/insights/nakkula.shtml. See Nakkula, M. J., and Toshalis, E. *Understanding Youth: Adolescent Development for Educators.* Cambridge, Mass.: Harvard University Press, 2006.

25. Kouzes, J., and Posner, B. *The Leadership Challenge.* (4th ed.) San Francisco: Jossey-Bass, 2007, p. 16.

26. Marzano, R. J. *The Art and Science of Teaching: A Comprehensive Framework for Effective Instruction.* Alexandria, Va.: ASCD, 2007, p. 26.

27. Theobald, M. *Increasing Student Motivation: Strategies for Middle and High School Teachers.* Thousand Oaks, Calif.: Corwin Press, 2006, pp. 6–7.

28. Deci, E. L., and Ryan, R. M. *Intrinsic Motivation and Self-Determination in Human Behavior.* New York: Plenum Press, 1985, p. 318.

29. Vygotsky, L. S. *Mind and Society: The Development of Higher Psychological Processes.* Cambridge, Mass.: Harvard University Press, 1978.

30. Ryan, R. M., Connell, J. P., and Deci, E. L. "A Motivational Analysis of Self-Determination and Self-Regulation in Education." In C. Ames and R. Ames (eds.), *Research on Motivation in Education.* Vol. 2: *Classroom Milieu.* Orlando, Fla.: Academic Press, 1984, pp. 17–18.

31. Howard, J. "The Third Movement: Developing Black Children for the 21st Century." In B. Titwell (ed.), *The State of Black America.* Washington, D.C.: The National Urban League, 1993, pp. 14–15.

32. See Tomlinson, C. A. *The Differentiated Classroom: Responding to the Needs of All Learners.* Alexandria, Va.: ASCD, 1999, p. 2.

33. Ryan, Connell, and Deci, "A Motivational Analysis of Self-Determination and Self-Regulation in Education," pp. 17–18.

34. Perlmutter, L. C., and Monty, R. A. "The Importance of Perceived Control: Fact or Fantasy?" *American Scientist,* 1977, *65*(6), 759–765.

## Chapter Three

1. Wiggins, G., and McTighe, J. *Understanding by Design.* (Exp. 2nd ed.) Upper Saddle River, N.J.: Prentice Hall, 2005, p. 14.

2. Kouzes, J., and Posner, B. *The Leadership Challenge.* (4th ed.) San Francisco: Jossey-Bass, 2007, p. 17.

3. Wiggins and McTighe, *Understanding by Design,* pp. 8–9.

4. See, for example, Schön, D. A. *The Reflective Practitioner: How Professionals Think in Action.* New York: Basic Books, 2007, pp. 81–88.

5. See, for example, Hawk, T. F., and Shah, A. J. "Using Learning Style Instruments to Enhance Student Learning." *Decision Sciences Journal of Innovative Education,* 2007, *5*(1), 1–19.

6. Shulman, L. "Those Who Understand: Knowledge Growth in Teaching." *Educational Researcher,* 1986, *15*(2), 9.

7. For examples of math-based research on content pedagogy, see Ball, D. L., Thames, J. J., and Phelps, G. "Content Knowledge for Teaching: What Makes It Special?" *Journal of Teacher Education,* *59*(5), 389–407. Hill, H., Ball, D. L., and Schilling, S. "Unpacking 'Pedagogical Content Knowledge': Conceptualizing and Measuring Teachers' Topic-Specific Knowledge of Students." *Journal for Research in Mathematics Education,* 2008, *39*, 372–400. Pam Grossman is researching content pedagogy in English/language arts contexts. Grossman, P. L., and Loeb, S. "Looking Across Measures: Implications for Policy and Research on Instructional Quality." Paper presented at the American Educational Research Association Annual Meeting, San Diego, Calif., Apr. 2009.

8. Ormrod, J. *Educational Psychology: Developing Learners.* (4th ed.) Upper Saddle River, N.J.: Prentice Hall, 2002.

9. Vogt, L. A., Jordan, C., and Tharp, R. G. "Explaining School Failure, Producing School Success: Two Cases." *Anthropology and Education Quarterly,* 1987, *18*(4), 276–286.

10. Gay, G. *Culturally Responsive Teaching: Theory, Research, and Practice.* New York: Teachers College Press, 2000.

11. Gay, G. "A Synthesis of Scholarship in Multicultural Education." Oak Park, Ill.: North Central Regional Educational Library, 1994, p. 18.

12. Smith, G. P. *Common Sense About Uncommon Knowledge: The Knowledge Bases for Diversity.* Washington, D.C.: American Association of Colleges for Teacher Education, 1998, p. 66.

13. Sleeter, C., and Grant, C. *Making Choices for Multicultural Education: Five Approaches to Race, Class, and Gender.* (6th ed.) Hoboken, N.J.: Wiley, 2009, p. 67.

14. Trueba, E. T., and Bartolome, L. "The Education of Latino Students: Is School Reform Enough?" *ERIC Digest*, 1997, *123,* 1–10.

15. Griggs, S., and Dunn, R. "Hispanic-American Students and Learning Style." *ERIC Digest*, 1996, *5,* 1–6.

16. Frisby, C. L. "One Giant Step Backward: Myths of Black Cultural Learning Styles." *School Psychology Review*, 1993, *22,* 535–557.

17. Hidalgo, N. M., and others. "Research on Families, Schools and Communities: A Multicultural Perspective." In J. A. Banks and C. Banks (eds.), *Handbook of Research on Multicultural Education.* New York: Macmillan, 2001, p. 514.

18. Nieto, S. *Affirming Diversity: The Sociopolitical Context of Multicultural Education.* New York: Longman, 1996, p. 148.

19. Wiggins and McTighe, *Understanding by Design,* p. 106.

20. Ibid., p. 107.

21. Ibid.

22. Brophy, J. "Generic Aspects of Effective Teaching." In M. C. Wang and H. J. Walburg (eds.), *Tomorrow's Teachers.* Richmond, Calif.: McCutchan, 2001.

23. Ibid., p. 32.

24. Adapted from Johnson, D. W., Johnson, R. T., and Johnson-Holubec, E. J. *Cooperation in the Classroom.* (6th ed.) Edina, Minn.: Interaction Book Co., 1993. Stahl, R. J. "The Essential Elements of Cooperative Learning in the Classroom." *ERIC Digest*, 1994, *3,* 1–4.

25. Tomlinson, C. A. *The Differentiated Classroom: Responding to the Needs of All Learners.* Alexandria, Va.: ASCD, 1999.

26. Wiggins and McTighe, *Understanding by Design,* p. 15.

27. Ibid.

28. Although we have drawn these best practices from highly effective teachers' classrooms, many of those teachers have been strongly influenced by some of the excellent resources available about classroom management. For example: Canter, L., and Canter, M. *Assertive Discipline: Positive Behavior Management for Today's Classroom.* Santa Monica, Calif.: Canter and Associates, 2001; Wong, H. *First Days of School.* Mountain View, Calif.: Harry K. Wong Publications, 2004; and Chip Wood's *Responsive Classroom* Series. Turner Falls, Mass.: Northeast Foundation for Children.

## Chapter Four

1. Bossidy, L., and Charan, R. *Execution: The Discipline of Getting Things Done.* New York: Crown, 2002, p. 22.

2. Gardner, J. W. *On Leadership.* New York: Free Press, 1990, p. 50.

3. Ibid., p. 51.

4. Ibid., p. 49.

5. Peters, T. J., and Waterman, R. H. *In Search of Excellence: Lessons from America's Best-Run Companies.* New York: HarperCollins, 1982, p. 119.

6. Ibid., p. 134.

7. Bennis, W. *On Becoming a Leader.* New York: Basic Books, 2003, p. xxiii.

8. See Schön, D. A. *The Reflective Practitioner: How Professionals Think in Action.* New York: Basic Books, 1984.

9. See Lampert, M. *Teaching Problems and the Problems of Teaching.* New Haven, Conn.: Yale University Press, 2003.

10. Marzano, R. J. *The Art and Science of Teaching: A Comprehensive Framework for Effective Instruction.* Alexandria, Va.: ASCD, 2007, p. 13.

11. Canter, L., and Canter, M. *Assertive Discipline: Positive Behavior Management for Today's Classroom.* Santa Monica, Calif.: Canter & Associates, 1992, p. 27.


## Chapter Five

1. Collins, J. *Good to Great and the Social Sectors: A Monograph to Accompany Good to Great.* New York: HarperCollins, 2005, p. 9.

2. Tolstoy, L. "On Teaching the Rudiments." In L. Wiener (ed.), *Tolstoy on Education.* Chicago: University of Chicago Press, 1967.

3. Kouzes, J., and Posner, B. *The Leadership Challenge.* (4th ed.) San Francisco: Jossey-Bass, 2007, p. xiii.

4. Ibid., p. 23.

5. Dweck, C. *Mindset: The New Psychology of Success.* New York: Random House, 2006, p. 209.

6. Duncan, Arne. Speech to Fourth Annual IES Research Conference. June 8, 2009.

7. Bennis, W. *On Becoming a Leader.* New York: Basic Books, 2003, p. 188.

8. See Spelling, Margaret. Speech on School Choice. April 5, 2006. There is some dispute about the original source of the line. Some suggest it was W. Edwards Deming, the management and effectiveness guru who dramatically influenced manufacturing during World War II with his methods of statistical quality control.

9. Duncan, Arne. Speech to Fourth Annual IES Research Conference. June 8, 2009.

10. From a letter published in Kane, P. R. (ed.). *The First Year of Teaching: Real World Stories from America's Teachers.* New York: Walker and Co., 1991, p. 104.

11. Luce, T., and Thompson, L. *Do What Works: How Proven Practices Can Improve America's Public Schools.* Dallas, Tex.: Ascent Education Press, 2005, p. 35.

12. These highly effective teachers' thoughtful acceptance of critical feedback, so important to maximizing one's effectiveness, is counter to the unfortunate culture of privacy and noninterference in education, which serves to inhibit improvement by shutting out fresh, critical eyes. Schmoker, M. *Results Now: How We Can Achieve Unprecedented Improvements in Teaching and Learning.* Alexandria, Va.: ACSD, 2006, p. 14. Richard Elmore, for example, one of the nation's leading thinkers on the effects of federal, state, and local education policy on schools and classrooms, bemoans "injunctions to respect the autonomy of teaching and the mystery of its fundamental practices—hence the inviolability of individual teachers' choices about what to teach and how." Elmore, R. F. *Building a New Structure for School Leadership.* Washington, D.C.: Albert Shanker Institute, 2000, p. 7.

13. The Kolb cycle suggests that learning best occurs through concrete experience, abstract conceptualization, reflective observation, and active experimentation. Kolb, D. A. *Experiential Learning: Experience as the Source of Learning and Development.* Upper Saddle River, N.J.: Prentice Hall, 1983.

14. Bambrick-Santoyo, P. "Data in the Driver's Seat." *Educational Leadership,* 2007–2008, *65*(4), p. 44.

15. Boudet, K. P., City, E., and Murnane, R. (eds). *Data Wise: A Step-by-Step Guide to Using Assessment Results to Improve Teaching and Learning.* Cambridge, Mass.: Harvard Education Press, 2005, p. 88.

16. Ibid., p. 81.

17. Langer, E. J. *Mindfulness.* New York: De Capo Press, 1989, p. 51.

18. Dew, J. *The Seven Deadly Sins of Quality Management.* Milwaukee, Wis.: American Society for Quality, 2003, p. 60.

19. Jenkins, L. *Permission to Forget: And Nine Other Root Causes of America's Frustration with Education.* Milwaukee, Wis.: ASQ Quality Press, 2005, p. xiii.

## Chapter Six

1. Marzano, R. J. *What Works in Schools: Translating Research into Action.* Alexandria, Va.: ASCD, 2003, p. 7.

2. Researcher John Rotter first described this phenomenon in 1954. Rotter, J. B. *Social Learning and Clinical Psychology.* Upper Saddle River, N.J.: Prentice Hall, 1954. Today it is a well-accepted theory of human psychology. See Maltby, J., Day, L., and Macaskill, A. *Personality, Individual Differences and Intelligence.* Upper Saddle River, N.J.: Pearson Prentice Hall, 2007.

3. By helping to populate IDEA College Prep Academy with such teachers, Ms. Epp has helped make it the nineteenth-ranked high school in the United States, according to *U.S. News & World Report,* a

ranking system that gives no consideration to the fact that the school serves students from some of the lowest-income neighborhoods in America. "Best High Schools: Gold Medal List." *US News & World Report,* Dec. 4, 2008.

4. Whitaker, T. *What Great Principals Do Differently: Fifteen Things That Matter Most.* Larchmont, N.Y.: Eye on Education, 2003, p. 19.

5. And that is before you consider the fact that most district, state, and commercial curricula require more hours to implement than exist in the school year. Marzano, R. J., and Kendall, J. S. *Awash in a Sea of Standards.* Aurora, Colo.: Mid-Continent Research for Education and Learning, 1998.

6. A number of researchers point out that not only is increased time, but more effective use of time, is important to student learning. See Silva, E. *On the Clock: Rethinking the Way Schools Use Time.* Washington, D.C.: Education Sector, 2007. A national task force on public education comprising cross-sector leaders put the use of instructional time at the top of their list of recommendations. Brown, C. G., Rocha, E., and Sharkley, A. *Getting Smarter, Becoming Fairer: A Progressive Education Agenda for a Stronger Nation.* Washington, D.C.: National Task Force on Public Education, 2005.

7. Stone, D., Patton, B., Heen, S., and Fisher, R. *Difficult Conversations: How to Discuss What Matters Most.* New York: Penguin, 2003.

8. Ibid., pp. 137–138.

9. Covey, S. R. *The Seven Habits of Highly Effective People: Powerful Lessons in Personal Change.* New York: Free Press, 2004.

10. Schwartz, T., and McCarthy, C. "Manage Your Energy, Not Your Time." *Harvard Business Review,* Oct. 2007, pp. 63–73.

11. Ibid., p. 65.

12. Collins, J. *Good to Great.* New York: HarperBusiness, 2001, p. 30.

## Conclusion

1. Warren, J., et al. *One in 100: Behind Bars in America.* Washington, D.C.: Pew Center on the States, 2008.

2. *The Economic Impact of the Achievement Gap in America's Schools.* McKinsey & Co: Social Sector Office. Apr. 2009, p. 5.

3. Ibid. p. 5.

4. "Diplomas Count 2007: Ready for What?" *Education Week,* 2007, *26*(40).

5. National Center for Education Statistics. *National Assessment of Educational Progress (NAEP),* 2005 Reading Assessments.

6. Mortenson, T. "Family Income and Higher Education Opportunity, 1970–2003." *Postsecondary Education Opportunity,* 156, June 2005.

## Appendix A

1. The five levels of proficiency are loosely informed by the work of Robert Kegan's theory of stages of maturity and how adults think about skills. See Kegan, R. *In over Our Heads: The Mental Demands of Modern Life*. Cambridge, Mass.: Harvard University Press, 1994.

## Appendix B

1. Decker, P. T., Mayer, D. P., and Glazerman, S. *The Effects of Teach For America on Students.* Princeton, N.J.: Mathematica Policy Research, 2004.

2. Kane, T. J., Rockoff, J. E., and Staiger, D. O. "What Does Certification Tell Us About Teacher Effectiveness? Evidence from New York City." *National Bureau of Economic Research,* 12155, 2006.

3. Xu, Z., Hannaway, J., and Taylor, C. *Making a Difference? The Effects of Teach For America in High School.* Washington, D.C.: Urban Institute/CALDER, 2008–2009.

## Appendix C

1. These numbers were calculated from *U.S. News & World Report*'s list of "more selective" and "most selective" colleges (http://colleges.usnews.rankingsandreviews.com/best-colleges) and from data showing the number of bachelor's degrees granted to students of various ethnic groups by those colleges available at the Integrated Postsecondary Education Data System Web site at the National Center of Education Statistics. (http://nces.edu.gov/IPEDS).

2. The cyclical reflective process is adapted from David A. Kolb at Case Western Reserve University. See Kolb, D. A. *Experiential Learning: Experience as the Source of Learning and Development.* Upper Saddle River, N.J.: Prentice Hall, 1983.

## Appendix D

1. In 2010, Teach For America will have over six hundred staff members training teachers at its summer institutes and over three hundred staff members working to develop and support teachers in their regional classrooms.

# ABOUT THE AUTHOR

**STEVEN FARR** leads Teach For America's efforts to discern what distinguishes teachers whose students in low-income communities achieve dramatic academic growth. Those findings inform the organization's teacher selection, training, and support. Farr also works to build the organization's knowledge by learning from and sharing with other organizations working toward educational equity.

Since 2001, Farr has overseen various elements of Teach For America's teacher training and support efforts, as well as studies of the best practices of highly effective teachers. He managed the research and development of a number of Teach For America's training texts, including *Instructional Planning and Delivery, Classroom Management and Culture, Learning Theory,* and

**Steven Farr**

*Diversity, Community, and Achievement.* He has contributed to the development of the Teaching As Leadership framework and rubric, as well as some of Teach For America's online resources built around those ideas.

Farr's work in education began in 1993 when he joined Teach For America as a corps member in the Rio Grande Valley after graduating from the University of Texas's Plan II Honors program. For two years, he taught high school English and English as a Second Language in Donna, Texas, at Donna High School, where he was nominated for Teacher of the Year by his colleagues. He then attended Yale Law School, focusing on issues related to education. He coauthored "The Edgewood Drama: An Epic Quest for Education Equity" for the *Yale Law and Policy Review,* an overview of the policies and politics affecting school finance in Texas in the wake of the U.S. Supreme Court's 1973 decision that education is not a fundamental right. While attending Yale, Farr taught English as a Second Language at Quinnipiac College and represented children in special education matters through the school's legal clinic.

After law school, Farr served as a law clerk for the Honorable William Wayne Justice in Austin, Texas. Farr then taught and litigated civil rights and disabilities issues at the Georgetown University Law Center's Institute for Public Representation until 2001, when he joined the staff of Teach For America as vice president of training and support.

Farr currently serves as Teach For America's Chief Knowledge Officer.

# ACKNOWLEDGMENTS

**ABOVE ALL, I WANT TO EXPRESS** our appreciation to the primary sources of the ideas in this book: the teachers and students who have contributed to our learning with their insights, efforts, and success.

I also would like to offer this insufficient recognition to the many people whose names should also be on the spine of this book—colleagues at Teach For America who have identified, debated, critiqued, and tested the patterns we have been seeing in our teachers' classrooms. Special thanks go to Wendy Kopp, Matt Kramer, Annie Lewis, Andrew Mandel, Aylon Samouha, Rachel Schankula, and Jeff Wetzler who, among others, have contributed mightily to both our findings and how we communicate them. I also thank all of the extraordinary teacher coaches on staff whose observations, videos, surveys, and insights have driven and challenged our evolving hypotheses about what it takes to ensure our students' success. Thank you to the Michael & Susan Dell Foundation for supporting our work to hone and share these ideas.

Many others have contributed to the development and production of this book, all of whom deserve more recognition than they have received. I especially thank Darcy Thompson, whose partnership and support I appreciate immensely. Thanks also go to Katie Bowen, Cynthia Cho, Tracy-Elizabeth Clay, Jamie Cumby, Nicole Baker Fulgham, Melissa Golden, Heather Harding, Kevin Huffman, Rebecca Kockler, Urvi Patel, Alice Ricks, Kristina Riego, Josh Wetterhahn, Rebecca Young, Monique Zurita, and all of the other colleagues at Teach For America who added this project to their full plates. I appreciate immensely Margaret Cate, Sara Cotner, Rebecca Dameron, Mayme Hostetter, Brent Maddin, Liz Marcel, Ellen McElhinny, Elisabeth Parker, Heather Peske, and others outside Teach For America's staff whose efforts helped shape this book. Thank you to the 2009 corps members who read and critiqued drafty drafts of this text and improved it immensely with their insights and critiques: Rachelle Copeland, Ruchi Gupta, Cait Hylan, Tianna McCullough, Ashley Morris, Patrick Tanis, and Alexis Vitanza.

I am grateful to the whole army of people who have contributed to the online resources that accompany this book, including, to name a few, LaNiesha Cobb, Seth Cohen, Elizabeth Cole, Carolyn Demefack, Erin Easterling, Doug Friedlander, Gaby Grekin, Casey Parks, Sheela Prasad, Philip Schweiger, Matt Snyder, Alisa Szatrowski, our friends at GMMB, and especially to all the teachers who have made their struggles and successes learning experiences for others. Special thanks go to Aurora Lora for sitting through interminable interviews, introducing us to her students and school, and sharing even the most emotionally trying memories of her experience. We appreciate her willingness to let us learn from her success, failure, and growth.

I also thank the highly effective teachers in my family: my mother, Anna; my father, Jerry; and my sister, Joanna. I know firsthand how lucky their students are. And last but most, I thank my wife, Hannah, and our children, Ella and Jeremiah, for their patience and support through the years of distracted conversations, obsessive scribbling, and creeping mess—and for all the book-related inconveniences as well.

Steven Farr
Chief Knowledge Officer
Teach For America

# INDEX